Hollywood Unions

Hollywood Unions

· ·

EDITED BY KATE FORTMUELLER AND LUCI MARZOLA

Rutgers University Press

New Brunswick, Camden, and Newark, New Jersey

London and Oxford

Rutgers University Press is a department of Rutgers, The State University of New Jersey, one of the leading public research universities in the nation. By publishing worldwide, it furthers the University's mission of dedication to excellence in teaching, scholarship, research, and clinical care.

Library of Congress Cataloging-in-Publication Data

Names: Fortmueller, Kate, author. | Marzola, Luci, author.
Title: Hollywood unions / Kate Fortmueller and Luci Marzola, editors.
Description: New Brunswick : Rutgers University Press, 2024. | Includes
    bibliographical references and index.
Identifiers: LCCN 2024011187 | ISBN 9781978830585 (paperback) |
    ISBN 9781978830592 (hardcover) | ISBN 9781978830608 (epub) |
    ISBN 9781978830622 (pdf)
Subjects: LCSH: Motion picture industry—Employees—Labor unions—
    United States—History. | Television broadcasting—Employees—Labor
    unions—United States—History. | Motion picture industry—California—
    Los Angeles—History. | Labor unions—California—Los Angeles.
Classification: LCC PN1993.5.U6 F6755 2024 | DDC 384.806579493—dc23/eng/20240522
LC record available at https://lccn.loc.gov/2024011187

A British Cataloging-in-Publication record for this book is available from the British Library.
This collection copyright © 2025 by Rutgers, The State University of New Jersey
Individual chapters copyright © 2025 in the names of their authors

References to internet websites (URLs) were accurate at the time of writing. Neither the author nor Rutgers University Press is responsible for URLs that may have expired or changed since the manuscript was prepared.

♾ The paper used in this publication meets the requirements of the American National Standard for Information Sciences—Permanence of Paper for Printed Library Materials, ANSI Z39.48-1992.

rutgersuniversitypress.org

Contents

Current Hollywood IATSE Locals (as of 2023)

Local 33   Stagehand Technicians (theater local with jurisdiction in Los Angeles)*

Local 44   Affiliated Property Craftspersons

Local 80   Motion Picture Grips, Crafts Service, Marine, First Aid Employees, and Warehouse Workers

Local 600   International Cinematographers Guild (includes publicists)

Local 695   Production Sound Technicians, Television Engineers, Video Assist Technicians and Studio Projectionists

Local 700   Motion Picture Editors Guild

Local 705   Motion Picture Costumers

Local 706   Make-Up Artists & Hairstylists Guild

Local 728   Studio Electrical Lighting Technicians

Local 729   Motion Picture Set Painters & Sign-Writers

Local 800   Art Directors Guild

Local 839   The Animation Guild

*Los Angeles locals not fully covered in this collection.

Local 871   Script Supervisors/Continuity, Coordinators, Accountants &
             Allied Production Specialists Guild

Local 884   Studio Teachers*

Local 892   Costume Designers Guild

Acronyms

ADG	Art Directors Guild
AEA	Actors Equity Association (also Equity)
AFL	American Federation of Labor (later AFL-CIO)
AFL-CIO	American Federation of Labor-Congress of Industrial Organizations
AFM	American Federation of Musicians
AFRA	American Federation of Radio Artists (later AFTRA)
AFTRA	American Federation of Television and Radio Artists (later SAG-AFTRA)
AMPAS	Academy of Motion Picture Arts and Sciences (also the Academy)
AMPP	Association of Motion Picture Producers (later AMPTP)
AMPTP	Alliance of Motion Picture and Television Producers (Association of Motion Picture and Television Producers prior to 1982)
ASC	American Society of Cinematographers
CADU	Commercial Artists and Designers Union
CDG	Costume Designers Guild
CIO	Congress of Industrial Organizations (later AFL-CIO)
CSA	Casting Society of America
CSU	Conference of Studio Unions
DGA	Directors Guild of America
EEOC	Equal Employment Opportunity Commission

FMPC	Federated Motion Picture Crafts
HUAC	House Un-American Activities Committee
IATSE	International Alliance of Theatrical Stage Employees (also the IA)
IBEW	International Brotherhood of Electrical Workers
IWW	International Workers of the World
LADA	League of Art Directors and Associates
LiUNA	Laborers International Union of North America
M&M	Merchants and Manufacturers Association
MASE	Mutual Alliance of Studio Employees
MBA	Minimum Basic Agreement
MPA	Motion Picture Association
MPAA	Motion Picture Association of America (later MPA)
MPEG	Motion Picture Editors Guild
MPCU	Motion Picture Costumers Union
MPPA	Motion Picture Producers Association (later AMPP)
MPPDA	Motion Picture Producers and Distributors of America (later MPAA)
MPSC	Motion Picture Screen Cartoonists
NABET	National Association of Broadcast Employees and Technicians
NIRA	National Industrial Recovery Act
NLRA	National Labor Relations Act
NLRB	National Labor Relations Board
NRA	National Recovery Administration
SAG	Screen Actors Guild (later SAG-AFTRA)
SAG-AFTRA	Screen Actors Guild–American Federation of Television and Radio Artists
SBA	Studio Basic Agreement (later MBA)
SDG	Screen Directors Guild (later DGA)
SEG	Screen Extras Guild
SUE	Studio Utility Employees
SWG	Screen Writers Guild (later WGA)
TAG	The Animation Guild
UBC	United Brotherhood of Carpenters
USTG	United Studio Technicians Guild
WGA	Writers Guild of America

Hollywood Unions

Introduction

• •

Unions in Hollywood

KATE FORTMUELLER AND

LUCI MARZOLA

Hollywood is a union town—but it is not really a town, and there is not just one union. Any given project made in Hollywood—whether on the backlots, on soundstages, or in far-flung corners of the world—involves members of more than a dozen unions. Actors who are members of the Screen Actors Guild–American Federation of Television and Radio Artists (SAG-AFTRA) are driven to set by Teamster drivers to work on sets constructed by members of the United Brotherhood of Carpenters and Joiners (UBC) and wired by electricians from the International Brotherhood of Electrical Workers (IBEW). They have memorized words by members of the Writers Guild of America (WGA) and are given blocking by members of the Directors Guild of America (DGA) after being called to set by DGA assistant directors. All of this is before they have interacted with members of the most dominant union in Hollywood—the International Alliance of Theatrical Stage Employees (IATSE or the IA). The sets were designed by members of Local 800 and painted by Local 729, with props arranged by Local 44. The actors are dressed by Local 705 in the designs of Local 892, and they are made up to look just right by the members of Local 706. There would be nothing to see without the camera crew from Local 600, nor would the crew have anything to work with without the grips of Local 80 or the lighting technicians of 728. No one could make sense of the action on set if the script supervisors of Local 871 were not keeping track and the members of

1

Local 700 were not arranging it in their edit suites. And we cannot forget about the cartoonists of Local 839 (though sometimes even the industry does) who were busy at work scripting, drawing, and coloring your favorite animated series in a building across the lot and at their apartments in West Hollywood (which, by the way, is a totally different city).

In no other industry do so many different crafts and different unions come into contact—let alone collaborate—with each other. No one of these crafts could make a motion picture or a TV show without at least some of the others. The biggest movie star is dependent on union makeup artists, the most respected director on their script supervisor, the revered cinematographer on their grips. Beyond hollow calls for solidarity, the union workers of Hollywood are entirely dependent on each other to make their work happen.

This interdependence was brought into stark relief during the COVID-19 pandemic, when the role of each person on set had to be considered when imagining how to return to production safely. This book started as an idea in that spring of 2020 when media production had been entirely shut down due to the pandemic and the unions of Hollywood were negotiating protocols for the safe return to work for the industry's hundreds of thousands of workers. A year into this project, thirteen of the fourteen IATSE Hollywood locals covered in this book came as close to a collective strike as they ever had in one hundred years of bargaining with the major movie studios. Two years into the project, the WGA did go on strike with unprecedented shows of solidarity from IATSE, the Teamsters, and SAG-AFTRA, whose members soon joined them on the picket lines. And as this volume goes to print, the IATSE locals are once again negotiating with the producers. All this is to say that the history of Hollywood's unions is still happening and will continue as this volume ages. Telling this history may seem a Sisyphean task, yet the ongoing importance of these labor organizations conveys that these stories need to be told. Some of them have been told before, but more of them have not.

Hollywood Unions tells the stories of the unions and guilds that have organized the labor unique to the motion picture and television industry in the United States—the DGA, the WGA, SAG-AFTRA, and the Hollywood-based locals of IATSE. These unions represent a wide swath of the workers who make media—from directors and stars to editors and scenic artists—yet they, and by extension this volume, do not even represent all the unionized workforce in Hollywood. To do that, we would have to tell the stories of the Teamsters, the IBEW, and a myriad of other large national and small local unions whose members work at studios and filming locations throughout Southern California, as well as in other production centers around the country. With an eye toward manageability, we have left out the many important unions that represent film and television workers exclusively outside of Los Angeles. These locals often have quite different histories than the Hollywood unions discussed here, which have represented film and television work in the major studios and have histories going back at least to the 1950s, if not much earlier. Likewise, we have focused this volume on unions that do the work that is unique to film and television production in Hollywood.

We have chosen to title this volume *Hollywood Unions* due to both the geographic and the metonymic meaning of the name. Hollywood is a place—a suburb west of downtown Los Angeles in the 1910s, now in the center of the sprawling metropolis. It is a place where many early movie studios and the service firms catering to them set up shop in the 1910s and 1920s. Yet, by the early 1920s, Hollywood had also replaced names such as Screenland to refer to the film colony—its people, businesses, and the dreamlike products it created. As Denise McKenna has described it, "Hollywood became a symbol of the American film industry because filmmakers insinuated themselves socially, culturally, and economically into Los Angeles's infrastructure."[1] Thus, all the unions examined in this volume represent media work in Los Angeles (and therefore in the major studios), though many have larger jurisdictions, meaning they negotiate the contracts of different workers and oversee working conditions in many regions today. These unions have intersecting histories that are made richer by being brought together into a single volume.

Taken as a whole, this collection shows how the unions helped construct a creative class of Hollywood workers. Work is one of the ways that Americans participate in social life and gain social status, and this is magnified in the case of the film industry, which not only contributes to individual fame but also shapes global social and cultural values. This privileged status of Hollywood work has meant that many union organizers, leaders, and members have fought over who could be included within their elite ranks. Yet as the political theorist Kathi Weeks explains, this is a relatively common dynamic across other sectors of work: "Class identities and relations are made and remade as some people are excluded from and others conscripted into work."[2] However, the stakes for limiting membership in ways that favor or exclude particular races or genders are particularly high in an industry that is responsible for telling stories about who we are as a society. As these chapters will show, the unions have been integral in determining who was allowed to work in Hollywood, how workers were trained, and how labor was divided, all while striving to raise the profile of the unions and their professional members.

People today know some of these organizations from their glitzy annual awards celebrations, but the unions' actual importance is in negotiating the Minimum Basic Agreement (MBA) with the Alliance of Motion Picture and Television Producers (AMPTP) on behalf of 367,000 workers in the motion picture and television industry. The unions, through these contract negotiations, have contributed to making media work sustainable in the long term and helped shape the conditions and production cultures of Hollywood. Although the glamour of some Hollywood workers makes them seem exceptional within the American workforce, they are associated with larger international labor unions such as the American Federation of Labor—Congress of Industrial Organizations

(AFL-CIO), along with the Teamsters, LiUNA, and the IBEW, all of which share concerns about fair compensation and safe working conditions.

An array of professional organizations such as the Producers Guild of America (PGA) and the American Society of Cinematographers (ASC), like the unions, provide opportunities for networking, education, and recognition that contribute to the professionalization of media workers. While it can be difficult to discern from the outside, these professional organizations do not function as unions. Though it dabbled in labor representation at points in its history, the ASC is an honorary organization, one of many in the industry that invite elite members of a particular craft to enjoy the privileges of membership. Likewise, although the PGA's name resembles those of the above-the-line guilds, it does not represent producers as workers. Producers historically have been more aligned with studio management than with production labor. They wear multiple professional hats, and in some cases they function as executives, whereas in others they are providing more practical guidance on set, making it challenging to define "producing" as a craft. This has long kept them from unionizing, even though many producers have some of the same grievances about pay and health care that plague the unions.[3] As the number of studio-producer deals has diminished and the work has become increasingly precarious, some producers have unionized as the Producers Union, although the status of that union has not been certified under the National Labor Relations Act (NLRA).[4]

The history of labor organizing in Hollywood is littered with stories like that of the newly formed Producers Union—united workers who were unable to negotiate a contract, or unions that eventually fail due to competing jurisdictions or obsolescence. An alternate version of this collection could cover the histories of the failed unions, from the once powerful projectionists' locals to the struggles of visual effects workers attempting to achieve contracts. As the chapters in this volume will show, there are unique challenges to organizing creative labor that many workers overcame and others did not. The histories of the unions that have endured have much to offer to those in the creative industries who are organizing and to contribute to the decisions that will shape the future of the media industries.

Unions emerged in the U.S. context in the nineteenth century as a reaction to the human cruelty associated with industrialization and the subsequent inequities of the Gilded Age. Philip Dray has called unions a "civilizing influence on politics, government policy, and corporate behavior."[5] They helped to assimilate immigrants into the American workforce and addressed practices such as sweatshops, child labor, exploitation, overwork, and underpayment. Yet, as Dray also points out, this country has always had a disdainful view of organized labor, viewing worker solidarity as counter to American individualism and often akin to communism. In essence, labor unions are viewed in many ways as anti-American. This makes it even more notable that the motion pictures and television shows made in Hollywood, which are the primary means of export-ing and enforcing the "American way of life," are created by a massively unionized workforce.

Although organizing happened concurrently with other unionization move-ments around the United States, Hollywood workers were resistant to involve-ment from existing New York theater unions. As a result, unionization in Hollywood occurred largely in isolation from other industries and unions, which reflects how these unions have been historicized. As the histories unfolding across these chapters show, the stories of the Hollywood unions are highly unique to the forms of labor they represent, but they also resonate with each other and into more common labor sectors in the United States.

Critics, scholars, and media makers alike often parrot the truism that "media is a collaborative art," but this statement is meaningless if we focus primarily on authorship and creative control. Scholarship on industry and labor frequently asserts that an understanding of unions and infrastructure is essential for a nuanced appreciation of textual meaning; building on Denise Hartsough, Thomas Guback, Michael Nielsen, and Michael Chanan, Gerald Horne goes as far as to say that it is not possible to understand movies without engaging with the "basic relation of production," or the collaborative way that Hollywood work-ers labor within a hierarchical system and divide up tasks.[6] However, facilitat-ing this level of nuanced analysis also means that media scholarship must continue to ask questions about Hollywood workers and changes to the work of produc-tion resulting from evolving technology or new understandings of risk and safety.

Despite encouragement from scholars of Hollywood labor and industry, most industrial analyses of films and television shows have continued to focus on authorial contributions of above-the-line talent such as directors, writers, and stars. Similarly, most book-length studies of Hollywood unions focus on those that represent above-the-line talent.[7] New scholarship builds on existing ques-tions and concerns, and in the case of film and television labor, this has created blind spots within both film and media studies and labor studies. Textual and authorial questions guiding media scholars have led to little work on the bulk of Hollywood's labor force, and the exceptionalism of Hollywood's artistic and cre-ative work means that film and television workers do not fit neatly within ques-tions of labor scholars either.

Film and television sets function as *project networks*, to use the sociological term. Film workers, like those in music or construction, come together for a short time to "create custom and complex products or services" before moving to the next project.[8] Each set environment is culturally different, owing to the unique interpersonal dynamics and the particular requirements and conditions of the pro-duction. Workers might perform similar tasks on different film or television proj-ects, but always in service of a (hopefully) unique story or idea.

Hollywood workers move across jobs in similar ways to each other, but the work discussed in each chapter of this volume is very different. Films and television shows have rigid divisions of labor and tasks, yet the work often differs from project to project, making it a form of creativity with constraints. Taken as a whole, it would be impossible to describe commonalities between the mechanics of the work of a writer and a gaffer (lighting technician), but Hollywood workers share a collective goal. Writers, directors, actors, cinematographers, makeup artists, grips, and editors, at every level within their respective departments and whether they are in their first year of working or late in their career, make and execute their decisions to enhance the story they are telling.

The unique nature of Hollywood as a highly unionized cultural center has been a subject of fascination almost since its inception. When Murray Ross set out to write the first history of labor in the American film industry in 1941, the studio system was still thriving, and the unionization of Hollywood was a new reality.[9] He sought to explain how this glamorous center of cultural production became a union stronghold. Subsequent histories mirrored Ross's straightforward and chronological description of the accomplishments and setbacks of the various organizations that set their sights on the motion picture industry. Many of the chapters in this collection incorporate these modes of labor history but also consider how unique conflicts, politics, and culture within the various media crafts have shaped industry conflicts and bargaining priorities.

Despite their centrality to the functioning of Hollywood, there remain significant gaps in our understanding of the roles and histories of the industry's unions and guilds. The Hollywood unions are not homogeneous institutions; rather, they have long histories of jurisdictional battles, competitions with rival unions, and members who have occasionally had heated exchanges about bargaining priorities. Despite internal strife and external conflict, they have supported the industry's workers through the Great Depression, World War II, the McCarthy era, the collapse of the studio system, the rise of television, runaway production and globalization, fights for gender parity and racial equity, the digital revolution, and a pandemic that put production in limbo. The chapters in this collection remedy some of the gaps in knowledge and offer insights into media workers—their vulnerabilities, concerns, and labor conditions. They illuminate how the unions have determined their priorities and interests, particularly in times of crisis.

How Did Hollywood Successfully Unionize?

Hollywood has not always been a union town. When the film industry moved into Los Angeles around 1910, it did so in part to take advantage of the city's open-shop policies and escape the union culture of New York. Despite the best efforts of studio heads and unfavorable conditions for unionization, the Los Angeles film industry would become heavily unionized, while attempts to unionize creative workers beyond those in the theater and radio industries in New York struggled. Changes in U.S. labor culture provided an essential foundation for organizing, but in Hollywood the mobilization of craft identity along with the consolidation of studio interests into the Motion Picture Producers and Distributors of America (MPPDA) and the Association of Motion Picture Producers (AMPP) created conditions that allowed for successful industry-wide unionization. In essence, the studios' decisions to operate as a cooperative oligopoly gave organized labor a single entity to bargain against.

Organizers had many challenges to overcome in Los Angeles. Grace Heilman Stimson's book *Rise of the Labor Movement in Los Angeles* (1955) looks back into the nineteenth century to identify the reasons for the lack of a strong labor movement and the ascendance of the open-shop mentality in the city. She identifies several key historical factors: an agricultural economy, tardy industrialization, economic depressions, physical and psychological isolation, a lack of help from national unions, rapid growth of a transient population, poor local leadership, unstable labor bodies, and the persistent opposition of Harrison Gray Otis's *Los Angeles Times*.[10] It was not until after the depressions of the late nineteenth century and subsequent growth of the city in the 1890s (with the population doubling from 50,000 to 100,000) that the AFL turned its attention to Southern California.

As unions gained ground and began fighting for improved working conditions, they antagonized the once neutral Merchants and Manufacturers Association (M&M) into becoming a powerful anti-union force allied with the *Times*. Instability and dissent among the unions came to a cataclysmic head in 1910 with the bombing of the *LA Times* building and the defeat of the union's political allies, the Socialist Party. According to Stimson, "The immediate and perhaps inevitable result was a trying period of readjustment, of declining membership, of waning vitality."[11] As the chapters in this collection will show, in the film industry, unionization efforts in the aftermath of these events fared no better.

Picking up where Stimson left off, Louis Perry and Richard Perry's *History of the Los Angeles Labor Movement, 1911–1941* (1963) describes the thirty-year period under examination as one characterized by "a painfully slow yet steady increase in strength of the local labor movement."[12] A "dark period" after the bombing was ended by the outbreak of World War I, which led the government to make concessions in exchange for no-strike pledges to guarantee production during the war.[13] Wartime saw union membership in Los Angeles almost triple to 40,000. As membership boomed, the motion picture producers were organizing their first front against the rise of unionism among their craft workers. The wartime gains were heavily nullified as the end of the war brought a new open-shop movement known across the country as the American Plan. Between the end of the war and the enactment of the National Industrial Recovery Act (NIRA) in 1933, studio leadership maintained an open-shop policy and sought to implement changes to how disputes were handled.[14]

The fact that IATSE had been so successful in organizing labor back east (discussed in the introduction to part I of this book) struck fear into open-shop adherents in Los Angeles.[15] As Murray Ross put it, "Hollywood was to become a Trojan horse by means of which organized labor would penetrate antiunion Los Angeles."[16] The establishment in 1916 of the open-shop Motion Picture Producers Association (MPPA, the direct antecedent of today's AMPTP) of seventeen major studios marked "the beginning of a unified labor policy in film production."[17] The open shop meant that the studios were equally open to union and nonunion employees, but whether that was a reality is often a subject of controversy. In her study of women's labor in early Hollywood, Denise McKenna emphasizes that the MPPA's goal was also "to better relations between the film colony and its host city."[18] When the MPPA allied itself with the anti-union M&M, Hollywood leadership showed their intention to ingratiate themselves to the city's open-shop establishment. The MPPA further sought to alleviate labor tensions and fight the rise of labor organizing through the institution of welfare capitalism and company unions, a standard strategy for union busting.

There were obvious financial incentives for the producers to keep unions out of the studios, but the producers also wished to align themselves with the elites of the growing city. The studios were leery not only of unions but also of the working-class connotations of employing union workers in their studios. As McKenna explains it, unions and strikes were working-class expressions and "an association that would be detrimental to the industry's drive for respectability."[19] Studio management's emphasis was on artistic and craft labor, as can be seen through its encouragement of guilds and associations, with their emphasis on training and establishing professional norms (rather than improving wages and working conditions). The quest for legitimacy deepened the anti-union stance of producers and even some workers, who saw themselves as too "prestigious" for unions.

As the 1920s began, the population of Los Angeles was moving toward a million, and motion pictures were the largest industrial employer in the city.[20] The unions continued to fight over jurisdiction as the studios began cleaning up their act in their quest for Wall Street investment. During this decade, the MPPDA took control of the MPPA (which was renamed the Association of Motion Picture Producers [AMPP] and became its West Coast office) and showed much less concern about labor and the local elites, as it focused on a more pressing national public relations campaign in the wake of high-profile scandals.

In 1925, the studios attempted to bypass the unions by setting up Central Casting to handle casting and hiring of extras, as well as the Mutual Alliance of Studio Employees (MASE) for the hiring of craft and technical workers.[21] Two years later, the Academy of Motion Picture Arts and Sciences (AMPAS also known colloquially as "the Academy") was created to, among other things, mediate hiring practices and labor disputes. By creating organizations to manage hiring for low-level, freelance work in some of the unregulated sectors of the film industry, the AMPP was able to stave off unionization for a few more years, but ultimately Central Casting, MASE, and the Academy were unable to resolve all the labor problems in Hollywood.

Despite the AMPP's efforts, several unions threatened to strike in 1926, demanding recognition, a closed shop, wage scales, and other improvements in working conditions. The producers instead offered a corporate welfare program and year-round employment. The threat of a projectionist strike that would cut off box office returns on top of a production shutdown prompted the producers to meet with union officials at the end of the year to forge a plan that would define labor relations in Hollywood for the remainder of the studio system's tenure: the Studio Basic Agreement (SBA). The SBA formally recognized IATSE, the UBC, and the IBEW, among others, as bargaining partners. Although this was a historic win for organized labor against the anti-union and open-shop culture of Los Angeles, this agreement covered only the craft workers (and not even all of them), who had been agitating for the past decade. Writers, directors, and actors would rely on the Academy to settle their disputes for a few more years, while many below-the-line sectors remained without collective representation.

The crisis of the Depression and subsequent New Deal policies inspired nationwide blue-collar organizing, as well as greater interest in unionization for the white-collar and creative workers. The creative workers in Los Angeles and New York offer different narratives for how this interest panned out. Los Angeles motion picture workers organized along craft lines, which emphasized specialized skills, but as Shannan Clark points out, "[a]lthough the majority of white-collar workers in publishing, advertising, design or broadcasting lacked the required craft skills to join these organizations, the nature of their work periodically brought them into contact with their members."[22] In Los Angeles these efforts resulted in the birth of several long-standing unions, including SAG (1933), the WGA (1933), and the DGA (1935) as well as several IATSE locals representing the major crafts. In New York, in contrast, powerful companies such as the Associated Press and Time, Inc. undercut workers and staved off white-collar unionization in publishing, broadcasting, advertising, and design fields by posing legal challenges to win an exemption through the NLRA and buy time to intimidate and fire labor organizers.[23]

This example shows how members of Hollywood's unions—artists working within a glamorous culture industry—were somewhat unique within the context of U.S. unions in the 1930s. Yet they nonetheless followed similar trajectories as other unions in the United States. The successful unionization of the film industry was the result of both the precedent of artistic craft unionization set by the theater unions in New York and the historical factors of the Depression and the subsequent (albeit brief) moment of federal prolabor policies. This unique set of circumstances allowed for the proliferation of unions in Hollywood, but what has made the Hollywood unions truly exceptional is their longevity.

Why Do Hollywood Unions Matter?

Today, the unionization of Hollywood is unique among a vast array of media and information-based industries that have largely fought off labor representation—from Silicon Valley start-ups to digital-born content brands to the massive video game industry. Since 2013, there have been numerous attempts to organize a broader swath of white-collar creative producers in nonunion sectors of media production (such as reality TV), online media outlets (Gawker), media and technology companies (Alphabet), and the video game industry. Although these workers (unionized or not) possess different skills and perhaps are employed in dissimilar areas of media content production, they work in industries with similar profit structures and correspondingly high levels of cultural cachet. As such, those working in nonunionized digital sectors can learn from the successes and challenges of these long-unionized media workers.

Hollywood unions have been historically successful at maintaining their power and influence through myriad political headwinds, including anticommunist sentiments, McCarthyism, neoliberal trade agreements, and the rise of tax incentives in right-to-work states. In the 1930s, Hollywood workers agitated and unionized at the same time as many other workers across the United States, and their reasons for organizing—reasonable hours, breaks, safety concerns, and minimum wages—resembled those of workers in other blue- and white-collar industries. As media distribution changed, however, the bargaining priorities of the Hollywood unions, especially the above-the-line unions, drifted from many of the priorities of the AFL-CIO and the U.S. trade unions.

Prior to World War II, most union organizing in the United States focused on the needs of blue-collar workers. However, when troops returned home and enrolled in college, they joined a changing workforce. Timothy Minchin explains that after World War II, jobs in white-collar sectors grew at a more rapid rate than those in blue-collar sectors, but union leadership failed to see this shift in the workforce as a growth opportunity. This was a strategic focus of the leadership; according to Minchin, "Most affiliates [of the AFL-CIO] concentrated on servicing their members rather than recruiting, a pattern that Meany [the president of the AFL-CIO] did not challenge."[24] Although cultural reasons, such as increasing anti-communist sentiment, contributed to the decline of unionism in the United States, this failure to understand shifts in the labor force had detrimental effects, largely ending "labor's golden era," as Philip Dray describes it.[25]

Mirroring changes in the workforce more broadly, as blue-collar union membership declined in the second half of the twentieth century, white-collar work—and the above-the-line Hollywood unions that represented a similar kind of worker—played a more active role in shaping media work and bargaining priorities. From the 1960s onward, actors and writers struck over residuals as modes of media distribution proliferated, while the below-the-line unions saw their power diminished. The Hollywood unions did align with the labor movement more broadly in what the sociologists Larry Isaac and Lars Christiansen describe as increased attention to issues raised by the civil rights and women's movements.[26] In the 1970s, SAG, AFTRA, the WGA, and the DGA all formed women's committees and minority committees to advocate for social change both within the unions and in Hollywood more broadly. Meanwhile, IATSE, which has been slower to engage with social justice movements, was at odds with the NAACP beginning in the early 1960s.

After decades of effort to remain relevant in the tide of nonunion reality production, outsourcing, and strikebreaking, the unions had the wind at their backs following the COVID-19 pandemic. Amid the sweeping pandemic closures and subsequent labor crises, Hollywood unions provided swift responses. SAG-AFTRA issued prompt "do not work" orders in 2020, and all the unions and guilds worked together to outline safe reopening conditions. When productions resumed and many in other nonessential sectors returned to normal work, they did so with a different perspective on their jobs.

Hollywood workers were not immune to the discontent sweeping the nation. Studios shifted theatrical distribution methods, which impacted remuneration for directors and stars, causing top talent to speak out against studio greed. Although these issues were largely resolved after Scarlett Johansson filed a complaint against Disney, many of the other labor issues in Hollywood were not as easily swept away. In October 2021, thirteen of the fourteen Hollywood locals of IATSE (all but the Animation Guild, whose contract was not up yet) voted to authorize a strike after they failed to reach an agreement on compensation and safe work hours on set. Pay is always a central issue for any (not just Hollywood) negotiation, but the decision to challenge the culture of long hours and no breaks that characterizes most on-set work was noteworthy. As Carl Mulert, a national business agent for United Scenic Artists (IATSE Local 829) said: "People didn't realize how important rest periods were until they actually were getting rest."[27]

Existing unions have found new life, while those in nonunionized sectors are fighting for representation. Despite the strength and longevity of Hollywood unions, it is important to note that unionized Hollywood workers constitute only a fraction of media workers. In the twenty-first century, media companies consist of a broad array of cultural producers and people working at various stages of the distribution chain, many of whom are not unionized. The once clear lines between industries that use organized labor, such as film and TV productions, and those that do not, such as Silicon Valley tech companies, has vanished— bringing questions of who should be represented by media industry unions to the fore. When Apple and Amazon are producing union-made content for their streaming services, it begs the question of why the programmers and UX designers making those streaming services work are not also represented by unions. The tech industry's attitude toward labor often harkens to the Gilded Age industrialists who inspired the formation of the United States' largest unions.

The tide of labor activism has only intensified in recent years with social media's aid in organization and a labor market that has favored workers more than at any time in the last fifty years. Striketober, Strikesgiving, and Strikemas—at the end of 2021, each change of season was memed to account for the surge of labor activism and organizing that unionized new groups of blue- and white-collar workers. Workers at an Amazon warehouse in Alabama; Starbucks employees at a single store in Buffalo, New York; and union members of the Bakery, Confectionary, Tobacco Workers and Grain Millers' International Union voted, organized, and struck for better working conditions and fairer pay during the ongoing COVID-19 pandemic. Although the number of strikes in 2021 seemed significant, when viewed alongside additional reports that two-thirds of Americans were seeking new jobs in the wake of the widespread pandemic closures and layoffs of 2020, they signaled a moment of crisis.[28] The dual strikes of the WGA and SAG-AFTRA that kicked off what many called "hot labor summer" in 2023, followed by hotel worker walkouts in Los Angeles, flight attendant strikes, and, in September, the first trilateral strike by the United Autoworkers Union, indicate that, for once, Hollywood was part of a broader labor movement.

Writers are rarely in the spotlight, but in 2023 they became compelling protagonists fighting for the future of their careers against shrinking wages and replacement by artificial intelligence. Their picket lines became the new Los Angeles hot spots as they were joined by SAG-AFTRA, the DGA, IATSE, and the Teamsters, as well as nurses, flight attendants, teachers, Local 11 hotel workers (who were also on strike during the summer), and other union members across the city. Anna Tsing writes about the importance of these individual stories for understanding movements: "Narratives of capitalism gain their purchase through convincing protagonists—that is, exemplary figures through which we come to understand capital and labor."[29] Tsing's focus is on the liminal figures within capitalism, but we would like to propose the Hollywood unions, which have long negotiated on behalf of a freelance workforce and are at the forefront of negotiating for protections against replacement by artificial intelligence, as another exemplar for understanding contemporary capitalism. The history of unions in the United States is the history of industrialized labor, but the future of unions is media labor.

The Hollywood Unions

The unionization in film and television production that began in the 1910s has been integral to the formation of Hollywood as an industry. Throughout the early twentieth century, the industry was home to several battles over which unions would represent Hollywood labor and how—by craft or by industry. By the late 1940s, the craft approach, in which each craft sector (camera, sound, art, acting, etc.) has its own union, had prevailed in Hollywood, even as the industry approach continued in media industries elsewhere. As such, we take the structure of this book from the industry itself.

We have divided this book into two parts along the industry designation of above-the-line and below-the-line. "The line" creates a divide between creative and technical costs and, as Miranda Banks defines it, establishes "a hierarchy that stratifies levels of creative and craft labor."[30] Above-the-line labor consists of those who negotiate their own salaries on a project-by-project basis, such as actors, writers, and directors. Below-the-line workers have their salaries determined by industry standards often set by unions. Any residuals they receive go to union health and pension funds, any creative compensation being the sense of "fulfillment" they get from using their acquired skills and talents.[31] We recognize that this is a reductive paradigm, and it is often difficult to define these unions as strictly above or below the line, since unions such as the DGA, SAG-AFTRA, IATSE Local 600 (Cinematographers) and Local 700 (Editors) are composed of both above-the-line and below-the-line workers.

This collection focuses on the three guilds that function as unions (the DGA, SAG-AFTRA, and the WGA) and the IATSE craft locals that represent Hollywood film and television workers (fourteen altogether). This is by no means an exhaustive examination of the unions whose members work on Hollywood sets. The unions that are covered in this collection work together to create film and television, were formed during a window of American history when unionization had a greater degree of federal protection, and have continued to thrive in the Hollywood industry. The histories of the DGA, SAG-AFTRA, the WGA, and IATSE are intertwined, and these unions have several shared issues, as well as contract terms. As an example of this, it was the IATSE locals chosen for this volume (minus the Animation Guild) that collectively threatened to strike in 2021.

The story of IATSE in Hollywood is uniquely well covered in the 1930s and 1940s by volumes such as Gerald Horne's *Class Struggle in Hollywood, 1930–1950* and Mike Nielson and Gene Mailes's *Hollywood's Other Blacklist*, but rarely have scholars looked at each individual craft sector, nor has the longer history of IATSE in Hollywood been told. As such, part I begins with a longer introduction that offers a general history of the union in Hollywood. For the many below-the-line IATSE locals, we have created combined chapters to reflect some of the allegiances across crafts and similar or complementary histories. Erin Hill, building on her work in *Never Done*, looks at labor sectors—particularly casting, clerical workers, and script supervisors (Local 871)—that have been "feminized" and therefore struggled to unionize and often found themselves on the outside of IATSE.[32] The highly technologically-mediated and masculinized work on set is covered in two chapters: Luci Marzola's chapter covers both camera (Local 600) and sound (695), and Katie Bird's chapter covers four locals (44, Props and Set

Decorators; 80, Grips and Laborers; 728, Lighting Technicians; 729, Set Painters) that were all part of Local 37 Studio Mechanics in their early history. The artisans working to create everything filmed on set (other than the actors) are covered by Barbara Hall (Art Directors, 800); Adrienne L. McLean (Makeup and Hair, 706), building on her book *All for Beauty*; and Helen Warner (Costumers, 705; Costume Designers, 892). Those laboring at their desks (and, these days, most often at computers) are addressed in Paul Monticone's chapter on the Motion Picture Editors Guild (700) and Dawn Fratini's chapter on the Animation Guild (839). Another chapter should exist alongside these eight on the army of visual effects artists who create so much of what we see in film and television today, but given their lack of unionization at the time of the writing of this book, the visual effects unions (which will likely be formed as industry rather than craft locals) will have to wait until a future iteration.

Part II of this book, on the above-the-line unions, has natural divisions between the three guilds (the WGA, SAG-AFTRA, and the DGA). As Kate Fortmueller's introduction to this part shows, there are common expectations of professionalism, as well as interests in prestige and creative ownership across these unions. These unions have far more common members than found in other unions—yet they have often been at odds. Each chapter in this part emanated from its author's book-length study of the creative labor sectors represented. Miranda Banks's chapter on the WGA expands on her book-length study *The Writers*, Fortmueller's chapter on SAG-AFTRA emanates from her book *Below the Stars*, and Maya Montañez Smukler's chapter on the DGA builds on her work in *Liberating Hollywood*.

These unions are not neutral institutions; they have long histories that include jurisdictional battles, competitions with rival unions, and industry-altering strikes. The scholars who have contributed to this collection consider how labor grappled with division of tasks, hierarchies within unions, separation between crafts, jurisdictional disputes, new production technologies, pushes for diversity, and changes to media distribution. Each chapter can help us comprehend how media labor is performed, how the unions have determined their priorities and interests, and ultimately how Hollywood unions help us to understand film and television with more depth and nuance. Focusing on these histories, this collection illuminates how Hollywood's media production work is organized and how labor structures help inform what audiences see on-screen.

The histories of the Hollywood unions are plentiful, and the challenges faced by the media industries continue to be shaped by the conflicts, struggles, and solutions from past labor activism and negotiation. The details of union activities, which determine duties and compensation, establish professional norms, and help to maintain safe working conditions, may seem to be abstract from the final films and television shows we watch on-screen, but the decisions made during union negotiations shape workers' lives and, in turn, help to define the ways media is made and who can make a living making media.

Notes

1 Denise McKenna in "New Histories of Hollywood Roundtable," moderated by Luci Marzola, *Spectator* 38, no. 2 (Fall 2018): 74.

2 Kathi Weeks, *The Problem with Work: Feminism, Marxism, Antiwork Politics, and Postwork Imaginaries* (Duke University Press, 2011), 9.

3 Stephanie Allain and Donald De Line, as told to Katie Kilkenny, "Producers Guild Presidents to Writers: Why We're with You in This Fight," *The Hollywood Reporter* (hereafter *THR*), May 31, 2023, https://www.hollywoodreporter.com/business /business-news/producers-guild-presidents-writers-1235503629/.

4 Katie Kilkenny, "Amid COVID Turmoil and Low Wages, Feature Producers Form Union," *THR*, May 20, 2021, https://www.hollywoodreporter.com/movies/movie -news/film-producers-unionize-1234956071/.

5 Philip Dray, *There Is Power in a Union: The Epic Story of Labor in American* (Doubleday, 2010), 7.

6 Gerald Horne, *Class Struggle in Hollywood, 1930–1950: Moguls, Mobsters, Stars, Reds, and Trade Unionists* (University of Texas Press, 2001), 35.

7 Virginia Wright Wexman, *Hollywood's Artists: The Directors Guild of America and the Construction of Authorship* (Columbia University Press, 2020); Miranda Banks, *The Writers: A History of American Screenwriters and Their Guild* (Rutgers University Press, 2015); Danae Clark, *Negotiating Hollywood: The Cultural Politics of Actors' Labor* (University of Minnesota Press, 1995); David Prindle, *The Politics of Glamour: Ideology and Democracy in the Screen Actors Guild* (University of Wisconsin Press, 1988).

8 Candace Jones, "Careers in Project Networks: The Case of the Film Industry," in *The Boundaryless Career: A New Employment Principle for a New Organizational Era*, ed. Michael B. Arthur and Denise M. Rousseau (Oxford University Press, 1996), 59.

9 Murray Ross, *Stars and Strikes: Unionization of Hollywood* (Columbia University Press, 1941).

10 Grace Heilman Stimson, *Rise of the Labor Movement in Los Angeles* (University of California Press, 1955), 193.

11 Heilman Stimson, 420.

12 Louis Perry and Richard Perry, *A History of the Los Angeles Labor Movement, 1911–1941* (University of California Press, 1963), x.

13 Perry and Perry, 106.

14 Perry and Perry, 193.

15 Perry and Perry, 319.

16 Ross, *Stars and Strikes*, 6.

17 Perry and Perry, *History of the Los Angeles Labor Movement* 322.

18 Denise McKenna, "The City That Made the Pictures Move" (PhD diss., New York University, 2008), 128.

19 McKenna, "The City That Made the Pictures Move," 216.

20 Kevin Starr, *Material Dreams: Southern California through the 1920s* (New York: Oxford University Press, 1990).

21 Michael Charles Nielsen and Gene Mailes, *Hollywood's Other Blacklist: Union Struggles in the Studio System* (British Film Institute, 1995), 107.

22 Shannan Clark, *The Making of the American Creative Class* (Oxford University Press, 2021), 59.

23 Clark, 86.

24 Timothy Minchin, *Labor under Fire: A History of the AFL-CIO since 1979* (University of North Carolina Press, 2017), 16.

25 Dray, *There Is Power in a Union*, 5.

26 Larry Isaac and Lars Christiansen, "How the Civil Rights Movement Revitalized Labor Militancy," *American Sociological Review* 67, no. 5 (October 2002): 722–746.

27 Gary Baum and Katie Kilkenny, "Inside the Hollywood Labor Rebellion: 'We Have Awoken a Sleeping Giant,'" *THR*, December 17, 2021, https://www.hollywood reporter.com/business/business-news/hollywood-workers-2021-labor-rebellion -1235062315/.

28 "PwC Pulse Survey: Next in Work," PwC, August 19, 2021, https://www.pwc.com /us/en/library/pulse-survey/future-of-work.html.

29 Anna Tsing, "Supply Chains and the Human Condition," *Rethinking Marxism* 21, no. 2 (April 2009): 152

30 Miranda J. Banks, "Gender Below-the-Line: Defining Feminist Production Studies," in *Production Studies: Cultural Studies of Media Industries*, ed. Vicki Mayer, Miranda J. Banks, and John Thornton Caldwell (Routledge, 2009), 89.

31 Matt Stahl, "Privilege and Distinction in Production Worlds: Copyright, Collective Bargaining, and Working Conditions in Media Making," in *Production Studies: Cultural Studies of Media Industries*, ed. Vicki Mayer, Miranda J. Banks, and John Thornton Caldwell (Routledge, 2009), 62.

32 IATSE Local 884 Studio Teachers and Welfare Workers are also among the "feminized" labor fields and the locals in the Basic Agreement. However, this local had less history to pull from and therefore is covered minimally in this volume.

Part I

The Below-the-Line Unions

• •

IATSE in Hollywood

LUCI MARZOLA AND KATIE BIRD

This part of the book tells the histories of the fourteen locals of the International Alliance of Theatrical Stage Employees, Moving Picture Technicians, Artists and Allied Crafts of the United States, Its Territories and Canada (more often called by the first six words of its name, IATSE, or the IA), which represent most of the media craft labor in Hollywood. These workers are often referred to as being *below-the-line*—a Hollywood budgeting term for workers (and also for costs) that are *not* the top creative talent (stars, writers, and directors). This volume uses the industry term *the line* as an organizing principle, even though the bifurcation of media labor into creative and craft sectors is highly reductive and at times inaccurate. As Kate Fortmueller and Maya Montañez Smukler show (in chapters 10 and 11, respectively), the Screen Actors Guild–American Federation of Television and Radio Artists (SAG-AFTRA) and the Directors Guild of America (DGA) straddle the line within their own unions. Likewise, many workers represented by the unions in this part of the book have gained a level of prominence (consider the cinematographer Roger Deakins or the costume designer Ruth Carter) that situates them with the above-the-line talent.

The chapters in this part of the book focus on those who might be called *production workers*—those whose jobs are essential for films and television shows to get made. From camera operators and costume designers to grips and gaffers, these workers do jobs that for the most part exist only in the media, and in most cases are significant professions only in Hollywood and other major media production centers. Also among the ranks of so-called below-the-line workers are those whose work is much the same whether it takes place on or off a movie set. The work of what we might call the basic crafts, such as that done by electricians, carpenters, drivers, and plumbers, requires substantially similar skills whether in or out of a studio. Basic craft workers were more easily incorporated into existing unions such as the International Brotherhood of Electrical Workers (IBEW), the Laborers' International Union of North America (LiUNA), and the International Brotherhood of Teamsters. These workers are *not* the focus of this part of the book, although they intersect with many of these histories (particularly in chapter 2 on backlot labor) and certainly deserve to be addressed more fully in future work for their roles in spreading and maintaining unionization throughout media production.

Through many upheavals and battles, detailed here and in the chapters that follow, production workers would come to be represented by various locals of the IA, a labor union focused on the 168,000 workers in professions that are unique to stagecraft and screen craft. We have chosen to focus the chapters in this part on those specific locals rather than larger unions such as the IBEW or on IATSE locals whose primary jurisdiction lays outside of Hollywood. Yet the history of the IATSE union as a whole gives important context to the individual histories that follow. As such, this introduction presents the common history from which the subsequent eight chapters emanate.

We present these chapters on below-the-line workers prior to those on above-the-line talent in part because these workers have received less attention than their more glamorous co-workers but also because their unions' most important fights came earlier in the history of Hollywood unionization. Speaking about the history of strikes in the film industry, Andrew Dawson recognized that labor activity was more prevalent in below-the-line unions *before* 1950, while the above-the-line unions became more active *after* 1950.[1] This can be seen in the histories in this part, many of which are dense with activity in the early part of the twentieth century.

While the various locals have their own histories unique to their forms of labor and memberships, their craft histories also share characteristics. Throughout the history of IATSE, its leadership has often exploited commonalities and conflicts to consolidate power. The locals all exist within the larger IATSE union, and subsequently, the IA exists within the larger American Federation of Labor and Congress of Industrial Organizations (AFL-CIO). The AFL-CIO (or just the AFL before 1955) presides over and adjudicates disputes between warring unions and locals often over discrete and complicated minutiae of motion picture production and craft jurisdiction. This structure has historically created tension between the guaranteed or perceived local autonomy (home rule) of specific crafts and the power of the IA's collective bargaining agreements to ignore or supersede locals' stated needs. This tension between the power of the locals (individually and collectively) and the IA can be seen throughout the chapters in this part. To mediate these concerns, the AFL-CIO and IATSE have encouraged a more business-like approach to organizing that emphasizes professional issues such as compensation and safety.

Another common concern across the locals, similar to the public discourse of "nepo babies" in the creative class of Hollywood, is that the crafts are rife with generational familial networks. Familial networks (mostly, but not always, white and male) in various crafts reflect similar trends and historical fraternal lineages in other industrial and craft trades where the profession is seemingly "passed on" in the "father-son tradition" or from uncle to nephew.[2] It is not uncommon to find third- or fourth-generation production workers employed in the same craft as their father or grandfather (such as a grip or cameraman or the famous Westmore family makeup artists described in chapter 6). As in other areas of the film and media industries, word-of-mouth reputation is a key factor for finding an apprentice or training position within a below-the-line department, and these crews often tend to work together over years or decades, reinforcing the clichéd mantra that the film crew "is like a family," but historically some crews included actual members of the same family.

These preferences have contributed to, but do not fully explain, the continued racial, ethnic, and gendered barriers to new workers outside of these traditional and insular networks—another common characteristic across the various crafts. The struggles to diversify the media professions exist within every one of the locals, but they look different in each—unique to the particular work being done and the culture that has evolved around it. Some categories of labor have been highly gendered, from strictly male grips and makeup artists to predominantly female script supervisors and ink-and-paint departments. Racial and ethnic disparities are ubiquitous, though more pronounced in some professions than others, as will be seen. IATSE unions have rarely sought to challenge the homogeneous demographic makeup of their rank and file (unless required to do so by government or legal intervention) and had historically preferred to keep membership numbers stagnant until the end of the twentieth century. Failure to meet their own stated goals and members' demands has led to consistent and recurring tensions across unions' history.

With the decentralization of production outside of Los Angeles, hiring customs have also been affected by runaway productions that increasingly use local and rotating location crews for production work. This has added to the common production worker concern over job security, which often causes these workers to look suspiciously toward new members in their ranks. While rank-and-file workers experience short-term unemployment as a perennial feature of their jobs, the threat of long-term unemployment due to the glut of workers in their field makes them less inclined to support membership drives, which unions increasingly need to maintain their power and influence within the industry.

With these common issues in mind, this introduction to part I presents a general history of IATSE's presence in Hollywood. This narrative is indebted to the labor historians Mike Nielsen and Gerald Horne and the union activist Gene Mailes, whose work informs much of this broad history. Despite considerable opposition throughout the early twentieth century, this history shows how and why the IA became the union representing media craft labor in Hollywood. A key question throughout this struggle for supremacy was whether solidarity within Hollywood would operate across the workers of the industry or be divided up between the various crafts. By ultimately siding with IATSE, the workers of Hollywood have largely chosen their individual crafts above all else.

Consolidating Union Power: IATSE in Early Hollywood

IATSE was founded in 1893 and a year later affiliated with the AFL, choosing the relatively young federation of labor unions over the Knights of Labor, ensuring its business-minded labor tactics for years to come. While the Knights were well known as a social reform labor organization concerned more with worker solidarity and socioeconomic reform, the AFL's trade unionism allowed IATSE to focus on campaigns for job security and wages.[3] Concern about the loss of work in the theater would ultimately inspire the IA to consider how to incorporate the new industry of motion pictures in the 1910s. IATSE, like Actors Equity, saw the new industry as a source of opportunities for theater workers. The union first asserted jurisdiction over motion picture machine operators, meaning projectionists for the most part, in 1907. This rather vague term of "machine operators" reflects the ambiguity of work in the film industry during the first decades, and unfortunately these loose terms in an ever-evolving industry would cause problems for unions and locals throughout the twentieth century.

As a theater union, IATSE's growth depended both on large theaters in major cities and traveling shows which previously had relied on non-union workers. IATSE recruited members by advocating for local theater workers to have priority of employment in their region (thus setting up the IATSE tradition of local autonomy or home-rule).[4] By 1911, IATSE had their first successful strike in New Orleans to prevent a theater from hiring non-union workers and within a year had developed a contract specifically for "road men" guaranteeing transport home and two-weeks' pay for shows that closed early. A century later, these negotiations for local and traveling theater crews would continue to inform the unions' position on runaway motion picture production.

The IA rapidly expanded in the 1910s by claiming jurisdiction over scenery, properties, and electrical effects—the elements of stagecraft in motion picture production, along with continued expansion in the theater. IATSE solidified their power over these newly "acquired" workers by supplying studios with workers from existing theatrical locals. However, many current IATSE stagecraft workers were content to make the transition into studio mechanic work, as it offered higher wages, job protections, and better working conditions. According to IATSE, "The movies had another appeal to IA members, especially those on tour: they could go home at night because the movies didn't travel, they could work mostly during the daytime, and they could work nearly every day."[5]

With workers moving between different industries, power increasingly moved away from the locals into the protection of the IATSE presidency and board who could better understand the scope of production work. In 1914, the AFL recognized IATSE's jurisdiction over film projectionists (or Motion Picture Machine Operators) after long jurisdictional disputes in multiple cities with the International Brotherhood of Electrical Workers (IBEW) who was also vying to organize these workers. As a result, the IA could now assert that its projectionists would not be allowed to handle film produced by companies that did not also employ IA studio mechanics. This control of both production and exhibition workers would become a crucial negotiating tool later in the organization's tenure. By 1915, IATSE officially changed its name to the International Alliance of Theatrical Stage Employees and Moving Picture Machine Operators of the United States and Canada, while maintaining the acronym IATSE, signaling how the once locally minded organization of stagecraft workers saw its efforts to center film workers under its governance and protection.

The IA's successful foray into organizing New York-based production and establishing locals around the U.S. would meet new challenges as motion picture production moved further west to the bastion of the open-shop mentality, Los Angeles. As the introduction to this volume details, the move from New York to Los Angeles offered space, sunlight, and freedom from patent restrictions for motion picture producers; but for unions, the move to the West Coast meant an uphill battle to contend with the city's notorious open-shop movement. Despite many efforts from city leadership to keep unions out of Los Angeles, IATSE successfully established its Los Angeles theatrical stage craft Local 33 in 1893 and a motion picture machine operators local in 1908.[6]

In these early years, the city's open-shop policies often brought competing unions together, including IATSE who organized with the building trades unions. IATSE and the IBEW worked together in 1909 to protest anti-union activity at the Regal theater, but such efforts in solidarity were soon thwarted by the Merchants and Manufacturers Association (M&M), which successfully campaigned for an anti-picketing ordinance with the city council a year later.[7] As more and more motion picture production moved to Los Angeles, producers easily trounced labor by increasingly pitting the various unions against one another.

In 1912, with the city growing and home to an increasing number of productions, IATSE Local 33 escalated their unionization efforts. At the time, a core group of workers at the studios were used regularly and told from day to day where to be, while "outsiders" panned at the gates looking for work.[8] The local did not have sufficient membership to meet studio demand, but they made an effort to unite members in solidarity against the studios. According to Mike Nielsen, the producers' fears of labor organization had less to do with these low-level workers than with their concerns about "creative worker" unionization. Yet the discrepancy in the wages between craft workers and stars gave the below-the-line workers leverage, as the studios would be contractually obligated to continue paying the expensive stars should the workers go on strike.

After striking with limited success in 1918, IATSE felt its position was strong enough by 1919 to demand a closed shop, but the ongoing jurisdictional strife meant that other AFL unions supplied the studios with labor, making the efforts unsuccessful.[9] As a result of such ongoing conflict, at the AFL convention in 1921, craft labor in the studios was divvied up between IATSE and various other AFL unions such as the IBEW, Carpenters, Plasterers, Painters, and Plumbers. The divisions caused friction between the various unions and workers and delineated how various forms of labor would be perceived going forward. IATSE was meant to represent stagecraft, something very different than the more commonplace work of a machinist or plumber. The AFL drew this line in the way the work is divided up—IBEW members installed cable, while IATSE members operated lights and cameras; the Carpenters Union built sets, but IATSE retained the prop men. The distinctions separate "real-world" labor from that which was exclusive to the theater and the motion picture industry. These are all below-the-line labor-ers, and yet distinctions were being made with respect to the kind of labor per-formed and its value to the final product.

In the 1920s, the unions continued to fight over jurisdiction while the studios united behind the Motion Picture Producers and Distributors of America (MPPDA), which focused on lobbying, and the Association of Motion Picture Producers (AMPP), the direct antecedent of today's Alliance of Motion Pic-ture and Television Producers (AMPTP), which represented the producers in the emerging labor disputes. In 1925, the studios attempted to bypass the unions by setting up their own Mutual Alliance of Studio Employees (MASE) to manage the hiring of craft and technical workers. This plan, which became known as the "divide and conquer strategy," sought to break up the various unions, provide greater company control over bargaining agreements, and reduce strike threats.[10] The producers' consolidation of control only deepened the labor strife and wors-ened labor conditions. According to the IA international rep Steve Newman at the time, "Conditions here are deplorable. We have more men out of work than we have had at any time since we organized."[11] Newman explained that with MASE as a hiring hall and the first call, fewer and fewer union workers were brought on, and many more were laid off if they failed to renounce their union cards.

Rather than removing the threat of labor, these aggressively anti-union tac-tics brought forth a renewed labor solidarity among the IA and the building crafts. In 1926, all the unions worked together to demand recognition, a closed shop, wage scales, and other improvements in working conditions.[12] The MPPDA and AMPP countered with a corporate welfare program and year-round employment. Forcing the issue further, the IA, the IBEW, the Carpenters, the United Scenic Artists, and others began developing a strike strategy of all four studio unions. The ace in the hole for the unions was an ultimatum threatening a projectionist strike that would cut off box office returns if an agreement was not reached. On November 9, 1926, the Studio Mechanics Alliance threatened a strike by December if closed-shop demands were not met.[13]

Here the association of the motion picture locals with the larger IATSE and AFL organizations proved key, as they were able to threaten both future production and immediate exhibition profits. Fearing further production shutdowns, producers met with union officials in November 1926 to forge a plan that defines labor relations in Hollywood to this day: the Studio Basic Agreement (SBA). The SBA formally recognized the IA, Carpenters, and the IBEW, among others, as bargaining partners. In addition, the SBA stipulated an eight-hour working day and premium wages for overtime, Saturday, Sunday, and holidays. Future agreements (later called the Minimum Basic Agreement or MBA) would be revisited and renewed, and settlements decided by designated committees, the producers (represented by the AMPP), and a single representative from each union.

While calming the uncertainty of the labor disputes, the SBA centralized power with union leadership and removed it from the rank and file. This set the stage for top-down organizational efforts emanating from IATSE and other national, industry-wide organizations over those of groups of workers on the ground. The period to follow, often referred to as Hollywood's Golden Age, would be rife with conflicts between warring ideas about how the industry's labor should be organized and represented.

Union Corruption in Hollywood's Golden Age

The efforts toward studio consolidation that began in the silent era only accelerated following the industrial transition to sound. Likewise, the consolidation of locals under IATSE leadership, formalization of professions that accompanied the SBA, and the financial scare of the early 1930s contributed to an increasingly specialized efficiency model of production. IATSE largely bargained on the studios' terms until the producers instituted a "voluntary" 10 percent wage cut when the effects of the Great Depression began to hit the industry harder. In 1933, the MPPDA and AMPP met in secret to rework the conditions of the SBA that would soon be coming up for renewal.[14] The MPPDA's Will Hays suggested a required eight-week salary cut of 25 to 50 percent for all workers, while Pat Casey (the AMPP labor secretary) suggested 20 percent cuts in pay rates for unionized craft workers. The unions covered under the SBA voted to reject the cuts and renegotiated with the producers for layoffs instead of carrying excess workers on payroll.

The IA's involvement in the SBA limited most locals' ability to independently strike or negotiate with producers, but in 1933, sound technicians from Local 695 working at Columbia Pictures, who had not originally been part of the SBA, declared a strike at the studio demanding a wage scale (discussed at length in chapter 3 by Luci Marzola). Following Local 695's declaration, IATSE called a studio-wide strike across all its eleven affiliated AMPP-member studios. As the strike dragged on through the summer, IA's rank and file grew restless. While the unions listed 6,000 members on strike, nearly half that number left the unions to work on a contract basis with studios.[15]

IATSE's attempt to show its growing power in the studios came up against larger historical forces in an egregious case of bad timing. In the first week of August, President Franklin Delano Roosevelt established the National Labor Relations Board (NLRB); the producers claimed that the IA had violated the terms of the SBA and therefore claimed its provisions were null and void. On August 5, the producers offered a new agreement with the IBEW in a redrawn SBA, granting representation of sound workers to the electrical union. The revised SBA "reduced the daily rate for most SBA groups from $8.25 per eight-hour day to $7.00 per six-hour day, [a] 13.5 per cent increase in hourly rate, but an overall decrease for workers since many of them worked shifts at two different studios."[16]

By the end of the failed strike, the 3,000 remaining workers were willing to sign with whatever union would get them back to work the quickest. Meanwhile, the National Recovery Administration (NRA) established the Code of Fair Competition in the Motion Picture Industry, providing further protections, including a basic minimum wage (forty cents per hour), a six-hour workday, and a thirty-six-hour workweek for studio craft workers, as well as a full day off without pay for every six hours worked in excess. The goal of the code, according to Murray Ross, was to spread "existing jobs among as many of the studio craftsmen as was feasible under the circumstances."[17]

At the same time, in the outer locals of the IA, far from the studio gates of Hollywood, two shady figures were slowly gaining power in Chicago, setting the stage for the most infamous era in Hollywood union history. George Browne had become the business manager of IA Stage Local 2 and began extorting extra dues and fees from stage workers.[18] Getting wind of Browne's scheme, a small-time pimp named William "Willie" Bioff suggested they combine their talents and expand the operation. Soon, the projectionists (the real power source of the IA) were being extorted by the duo. As Browne and Bioff climbed the ranks in Chicago, they were quickly brought into gangster Frank Nitti's criminal network.

Still hurting from the losses of the West Coast studio strikes in 1933 and with almost nonexistent studio membership, a weakened IA squabbled at its 1934 convention and narrowly elected George Browne to the presidency. Browne's first step as IA president was to focus on rebuilding the West Coast studio locals and place the trustworthy Bioff in charge of all studio union business. Despite coming from the theater side of the union, Browne and Bioff recognized the Hollywood workers as the future of the union. As Gerald Horne explained, "Only 16 of IATSE's 950 locals were in Los Angeles, but those in Hollywood were the most powerful."[19]

As in previous organizational efforts, Browne and Bioff understood the efficacy of wielding their control over exhibition to bend the producers to their will. A yearlong strike of projectionists in major cities restored some of IATSE's power and brought most of the major producer and studio heads to an agreement with the new corrupt leaders of the IA.[20] When Browne and Bioff came to the table with the studios in December 1935, they promised a return of the projectionists and a guarantee of no future union disruptions or strikes of studio workers if IATSE was granted a closed shop for studio technical work. A week later, the IA was granted full jurisdiction in sound and a closed-shop agreement with the studios, alongside agreements with the IBEW and the Carpenters. In January, the newly empowered IATSE demanded that all former IA workers return to their pre-1933 unions or risk being blacklisted or having their union cards withheld.[21] These efforts clearly favored power for the union leadership (in the form of the closed shop) over leverage for the workers (by denying them the ability to strike).

Browne and Bioff compelled compliance from studio workers through a variety of strongarm tactics. Moving to consolidate their power over Hollywood labor, Browne and Bioff declared a "state of emergency" in all West Coast studio locals in July 1936, stripping locals of autonomy and outlawing local elections, meetings, and voting. To enforce obedience, Browne and Bioff saturated Hollywood locals with representatives from Nitti's gang. These gangsters were skilled at collecting wage assessments and keeping workers in line so that the Chicago Mafia and IATSE leadership had a steady revenue stream from Hollywood. Surprisingly, very few members of the West Coast local rank and file understood the extent of union corruption and extortion.

Yet, given their aggressive power grabs, Browne and Bioff's reign did meet resistance from some of the rank and file. Splinter groups in the IA and other unions fought off union-producer corruption and cooperated with local workers to demand better pay, working conditions, and safety standards. Most notable was the effort to form the competing Federated Motion Picture Crafts (FMPC), composed of painters, draftsmen, makeup artists, hairdressers, and scenic artists (discussed further in chapter 5 by Barbara Hall). These workers had been shut out of the most recent SBA, as IATSE sought a monopoly over Hollywood craft labor. When the studios refused to recognize the new labor organization, the FMPC went on strike in April 1937. After two months on the picket lines, most of the unions had gained recognition individually, but the FMPC had failed and was dissolved. As Ida Jeter has argued, the FMPC could not compete with the "international union/management coalition" that IATSE had formed with the AMPP members by that point.[22] However, Local 37 propman and communist Jeff Kibre and other IA progressives continued to work to expose IATSE corruption and find an alternative means of representation.[23]

When the LA Central Council passed a resolution calling IATSE "a company union and a scab-herding agency," the progressives got the attention of Carey McWilliams, a prominent attorney who urged the California State Assembly to call for a hearing on the IA's involvement in labor racketeering.[24] The involvement of McWilliams and the state assembly led to a short period of retrenchment and cooling of strong-arm tactics. To reduce suspicion on Bioff, Browne temporarily restored local autonomy to the West Coast studio locals in October 1937 and placed Harold V. Smith and Harland Holmden in charge. After paying off investigators to halt the inquiry, Browne reissued a state of emergency in the studio locals and refused local autonomy. However, he did call off the 2 percent assessment. Browne attempted to improve the union's reputation by officially removing Bioff in 1938, but it was too late for this kind of superficial damage control. Investigators discovered a $100,000 check from MGM's Nicholas Schenk to Bioff, which would break open their extortion scandal for good.

With the corruption of Browne and Bioff coming to light, the progressives made another attempt to form a studio union outside IATSE's control, this time supported by the Congress of Industrial Organizations (CIO), which had recently broken away from the AFL to challenge its dominance. The United Studio Technicians Guild (USTG) was formed in early 1939, aimed at the heart of IATSE's labor strongholds rather than the nonunionized periphery. The group, led by Jeff Kibre and composed mostly of former members of IATSE's recently disbanded Local 37 (which had been divided into five new locals in an attempt to defuse its power), sought to represent cameramen, electricians, prop, and lab workers, among others.[25]

The USTG was able to rally enough support to halt the producers' talks with the IA on a new basic agreement so the NLRB could conduct a vote. Bioff gathered the support of AFL-affiliated unions such as the Carpenters, Plasterers, Musicians, and the Screen Actors Guild; the USTG was supported by the Screen Writers Guild and Herb Sorrell's Painters (in spite of their AFL affiliation).[26] The run-up to the vote saw IATSE circulating red-baiting flyers about "Kibre's Communistic plan," while the USTG distributed "leaflets with mug shots and police records of IATSE executives."[27] The vote came down to 1,967 for the four-month-old USTG and 4,460 for IATSE.[28] The IA had survived another challenge. When IATSE began a purge of the "rebels" from its locals, Kibre agreed to leave Hollywood forever in exchange for a lift on its ban on former USTG members.

It was only a few months later, in early 1940, that the full extent of Bioff's and Browne's criminal activities and Mafia penetration of IATSE were publicly exposed, but it was still challenging to rid the union of their influence, as they both clung on for more than a year. In February, Bioff was charged with income tax evasion, and investigators uncovered a trail of evidence proving payoffs to Browne. The highly publicized trial saw a cavalcade of studio executives, including Schenck and Louis B. Mayer, testifying to being extorted for hundreds of thousands of dollars.[29] Although Browne and Bioff were removed in 1941, many of their leadership remained in power.[30] Richard Walsh, a board member, replaced Browne as president even though Walsh had directly benefited from the payouts. Walsh (who remained president of IATSE for thirty-three years) continued the tradition of placing previous Browne and Bioff henchman into places of power within the studio locals.

While no longer directly connected to the Chicago Nitti gang and the Al Capone syndicate, IATSE continued using many of the same antiworker, pro-producer strategies to control workers for another decade. The association of Hollywood locals with the larger IATSE union had aided in the penetration of unionization in the studios in this era, but the centralization of organization had allowed a few corrupt individuals to control a vast amount of labor in the industry. The producers were willing to comply with these gangsters given that the latter's interest in power often superseded their efforts to improve the working conditions of those they ostensibly represented. Unfortunately, the ousting of Browne and Bioff destabilized the equilibrium of Hollywood unions and unleashed competing forces into an unprecedented era of labor strife and, at times, violence.

Blood on the Studio Lot

The ongoing strikes of the 1930s became even more heated in the 1940s, culminating in bloody riots outside the Warner Bros. studio gates in October 1945. The strife was exacerbated by the addition of the more democratic Conference of Studio Unions (CSU) to the labor scene in Hollywood. Herb Sorrell of the Painters union had been central in the attempted FMPC strike in 1937 and supportive of the USTG in 1939. He formed the CSU, as he did the FMPC, out of the non-unionized studio workers and disgruntled IATSE members who sought to leave the union after the nine-week Disney strike (detailed in chapter 8 by Dawn Fratini). The CSU would become a major player in the strike actions of the 1940s, uniting the Screen Cartoonists Guild, the Screen Office Employees Guild, Lab Technicians Local 683, Machinists Local 1185, and Motion Picture Painters Local 644, as well as the Carpenters and the IBEW. As Mike Nielsen and Gene Mailes contended in the 1990s, "The winners of that time dynastically picked their successors and today's labor structure in the US film industry is based largely on the deals worked out at that time."[31] The conflicts of this era would resonate into subsequent decades far more than anything Browne and Bioff were able to accomplish.

The rise of the CSU led the studios to cozy up to IATSE leadership, whose more centralized organization better suited their ends. Competition between the CSU and the IA studio locals put pressure on IATSE's new president, Richard Walsh, to negotiate a two-year agreement with the studios. Although the new agreement outlined improved provisions for working conditions and a wage increase of 12 to 15 percent over two years, workers felt their leadership had not gone far enough to negotiate a strong contract. Lackluster negotiation tactics and a willingness to sacrifice locals' needs to the benefit of the International were becoming familiar complaints about the IA. However, now IATSE members could do more than complain about their leadership; they could join the CSU, which was agitating and actively vying to replace IATSE.

Labor disputes paused during World War II but resumed with increased fervor in 1945. In March, CSU Painters called a strike, which particularly affected studios such as Warner Bros. that relied heavily on soundstage shooting. Although individual studio workers affiliated with the IA sympathized with the striking CSU workers (and often recognized the picket lines), IATSE leadership saw this as an opportunity to rid themselves of the CSU for good. With the strike ongoing in September, IATSE chartered Studio Mechanics (Local 468) to replace striking CSU workers.[32]

The protracted strike culminated in the October 1945 Bloody Friday riot that erupted between Herb Sorrell's CSU and agitators at Warner Bros.—the most memorable event of the period due to the stark images of bloody violence in the shadow of looming studio buildings. Gerald Horne, in his detailed account of the riots, gathers eyewitness accounts of flying fists, overturned automobiles, studio security throwing tear gas from the roofs, and armed rabble-rousers with cables, chains, and sticks.[33] The strike was settled by the end of October, and CSU members returned to work, but the *Los Angeles Times* labeled it "nobody's victory."[34] The violence of the strikes gave studio bosses grounds to turn to law enforcement and to increase their solidary with each other. Going forward, the studios would almost always negotiate with unions collectively through the AMPP (later AMPTP).

Although the Bloody Friday riot receives a great deal of attention across popular histories of the period, this was only part of ongoing jurisdictional disputes at the height of the studio era. Amid the strike, IATSE also sought to discredit the CSU by using circumstantial evidence to brand it a communist organization. After World War II, any communist sympathies (more acceptable in the days of the Allies and the Popular Front) were seen as un-American. According to Horne, the Communist Party did not initially support the CSU strike and only came around several months into it, but the facts were irrelevant. Once the "Red" label was associated with the CSU, the organization could not shake it. The IA saw how effective these accusations could be and would continue to make claims of communist infiltration to remove local autonomy from several locals, consolidating leadership around the IATSE president.[35]

By 1946, Sorrell and studio leadership had brokered the "Treaty of Beverly Hills" in an attempt to lower the temperature as IATSE and the CSU continued to butt heads. The agreement offered a 35 percent wage increase to both IA and CSU workers and additional increases to certain job classifications. In exchange, the unions agreed to stop striking over jurisdictional claims.[36] Yet movie sets continued to be tense. In the wake of the strike, the AFL attempted to intervene in the jurisdiction disputes—haphazardly dividing duties and awarding "set erection" to IATSE. When the AFL reversed this decision, IATSE leaders fought to keep it, even conspiring with studio heads and Robert Montgomery, the SAG president, to push the Carpenters and CSU Painters off the lots.

FIGURE 0.1 Strikers attempt to stop a scab from crossing the picket line during a labor strike at MGM's West Gate, September 1946. (Courtesy of the Academy of Motion Picture Arts and Sciences.)

In September, the Carpenters struck with the support of Sorrell and the CSU, which led Walsh, Roy Brewer, and IATSE to support the producers in the matter. The studios responded with a lockout of CSU workers. Once again, the studio gates became battlefields, with "open fighting with fists, clubs, stones, and bottles at MGM" and with locked-out CSU members (figure 0.1).[37] Despite high profile support from stars such as Joan Crawford and Gene Kelly, SAG overwhelmingly voted to cross the CSU picket line. The lockout lasted eight months, leaving the CSU mortally wounded. Hollywood was ready to move on from the CSU, and nationally the political climate had changed, with the federal government making it clear it did not support the Hollywood unions' aggressive tactics. Hollywood was under serious scrutiny by Congress, as the House Un-American Activities Committee (HUAC), had begun its public hearings. In addition, IATSE's and the CSU's violent disputes were investigated by a congressional committee chaired by Carrol Kearns that produced the report *Jurisdictional Disputes in the Motion-Picture Industry*. Congress was as flummoxed by the intricacies of Hollywood labor jurisdictions as anyone, and little came of the three hearings, other than an official record of the previous years' events.

With the CSU disintegrated, the various crafts returned to work under new IATSE-affiliated locals.[38] In 1949, the IA won jurisdiction over 16,000 production workers and signed a new five-year SBA with the studios, marking the end to CSU's decade-long challenge.[39] However, this victory came amid weakening studio power in Hollywood. By focusing on these intra-union battles, the CSU and IATSE ignored the major changes happening in the industry. The Supreme Court's 1948 Paramount Decision breaking up the structure of the studio system through its Consent Decrees had shifted production away from the major studios and granted more power to independent producers.[40] The decentralization of production made the IA's hold over studio labor less important precisely at its moment of victory. Nationally, IATSE had lost its most powerful tools, as the Taft-Hartley Act, passed by the Republican-controlled Congress in 1947 in reaction to the major labor actions (including those in Hollywood) of the postwar years, restricted jurisdictional disputes and secondary boycotts. With fewer workers left to leverage and new restrictions on how they could bargain, Hollywood unions had to quickly adjust to the new industrial pressures from television and independent contractors.

Shaking Up Below-the-Line Craft Distinctions

The economists Hugh Lovell and Tasile Carter estimated that the motion picture industry lost around 17,000 workers from 1947 to 1953 largely due to changes in production, exhibition, and distribution, as well as to growth in television and independent production.[41] As studio jobs disappeared, the closed-shop SBA contracts with major producers lost value for workers. Television networks, alongside independent contractors, who produced many network shows, offered steadier and more predictable employment. According to IATSE, television serial and recorded live programs offered a trade-off: "While the pay was low, the work was steady—a fact that was very important to theatrical workers during this time."[42]

To protect expertise and experience in the remaining studio jobs, IATSE introduced the Industry Experience Roster in 1948. In the wake of the Paramount Decrees, the studios not only had jettisoned their movie theater chains but also had significantly pared down their production facilities and, therefore, their full-time workforce. The below-the-line workers of Hollywood were no longer permanent employees of a studio but were increasingly operating freelance, hopping from set to set. When a studio wanted to hire an employee, its personnel department called the Contract Services Administration or the union for a list of workers who had worked in the past 30, 90, and 120 days. Unemployed workers with the greatest number of experience hours had to be selected before workers in subsequent pools could be recommended. While some unions had only two pools of rosters, others had as many as five. Before the personnel office could hire anyone off-roster, it had to exhaust all the available names off studio and industry rosters.

The roster system hearkened back to an earlier form of unionism built on craft solidarity and rewards. However, IATSE was no longer able to sell itself to workers based on a hiring hall mentality alone. The IA had to increasingly advertise its long-term benefits for workers who were no longer tied to specific studios. One of its key changes was to implement a health and pension benefit system that went beyond the "death and sick" funds of the early union, promising more stability and support at the end of a career's worth of work.

In 1945, the IA began organizing broadcast workers in New York, but by the early 1950s, television work was shifting to Hollywood and increasingly shot on film. Many AMPP members began producing television, leading them to eventually merge with the Alliance of Television Film Producers and become the Association of Motion Picture and Television Producers (AMPTP) in 1964.[43] This made it easier for IATSE to organize television workers, given their existing contracts, but the IA also sought to expand their jurisdiction. In 1952, a one-hour strike at four telefilm production companies helped the IA secure some union representations in all ten companies producing films for television and by the end of the year, a quarter of IATSE members worked in television films and programs.[44] Even with these early victories, if the IA thought its preexisting presence in Hollywood would justify its claim over the new audio-visual industry, it was quickly mistaken. Both the IBEW and the newly formed CIO affiliate National Association of Broadcast Employees and Technicians (NABET) fought to retain control of a variety of broadcast workers and engineers.

NABET had a different approach to organizing than the craft-centric IATSE. By 1954, NABET had returned to the flexibility of the 1920s studio mechanic days, in which the various crafts sought solidarity through a single union. According to John Amman, "NABET fit every category of production work into one film local in a structure that is a hybrid between industrial and craft unionism: the structure and philosophy of industrial unionism combined with the skills of craft unionism."[45] NABET continued to redefine the hierarchical and segmented sectors of production craft labor in the 1960s with the introduction of its Association of Film Craftsmen, represented by Local 15 in the East and Local 532 in the West. This group loosened professional definitions, which meant workers could perform several film-related tasks such as lighting, grip work, stage work, and camera operating without infringing on another member's duties. This flexibility was designed for broadcast environments but was later used in independent and low-budget films.

In spite of the challenge from NABET, IATSE had managed to survive the restructuring of the motion picture industry that had come with the Paramount Decrees and the rise of television. The implementation of the roster system, growth of pension and health benefits, and expansion into television were essential for IATSE's survival in post–studio system Hollywood. However, in the coming decades, civil rights movements would put pressure on Hollywood, and the union would be forced to confront how it had long maintained its exclusivity.

The IA in the Civil Rights Era

The roster system was IATSE's coping mechanism for two decades of upheaval, but this system came under increasing fire throughout the 1960s, when it was identified as the primary mechanism preventing diversification of Hollywood union membership. These complaints would culminate in March 1969 at a one-day Equal Employment Opportunity Commission (EEOC) hearing in Hollywood exploring the systemic discrimination against women and minorities in the film and broadcast industry. This occurred only after several years of mostly unsuccessful efforts following a survey by the NAACP that revealed that less than 1 percent of the craft union members were Black.

At that time, in 1963, Herbert Hill, the NAACP's national labor secretary, asserted, "Craft unions in Hollywood systematically excluded Negroes from memberships [sic] and accordingly few have found jobs in such studio jurisdictions."[46] In this case, Hill was able to point to fifteen specific IATSE unions that were "lily-white" including the highly masculinized professions such as grips, projectionists, electricians, cameramen, and sound technicians. Hill accused the film industry of "stalling" on equal job opportunities, claiming there had already been "25 years of 'no tangible gains,' despite many conversations." Inequity had long been on Hollywood's and the NAACP's radar, but these issues were coming to a head in the civil rights era.

The NAACP requested that one crew member of color be added to each crew and admitted into that position's union—a request some union leaders "flatly opposed," saying such a practice would be "contrary to [the] union's pacts" with the industry.[47] The Scenic Artist rep elaborated on the opposition, describing the extensive qualifications needed to join the union or get a job in the field. The common practice in most of these fields was that you had to be in the union to get a job with a signatory company and you had to have a job at a signatory company to join the union. This gatekeeping of the high-demand jobs in the industry dated back to the 1920s as a means of keeping the glut of excess labor at bay.

This effort to add one person of color to every crew was derogatorily labeled "featherbedding" in reaction to the NAACP's assurance that this would not replace anyone on the crew—but just add to it. The cameramen's rejection of the plan had a cascading effect, with "union after union follow[ing] suit."[48] Yet these efforts were not entirely unsuccessful, as the Grips and Lab Technicians, Locals 80 and 683, respectively, both admitted Black apprentices before the end of 1963.[49]

The Industry Experience Roster system was designed to ensure that the studios did not turn to cheaper, inexperienced labor and circumvent the unions altogether. The locals accepted this system because it shifted control of the labor supply to them. A consequence of this structure was that responsibility for diversifying crews was pushed off the studios and producers and onto the unions. As such, this bid for union strength and employment stability then became the means of resistance to diversification. This broader "discriminatory" practice against any nonmembers (as well as against less experienced members) conflicted with a growing and changing industry that was increasingly international, bringing in new talent from the emerging film schools (including women), and producing outside of the major signatory companies.

These demands to welcome new members were also layered onto the fact that employment for all these professions was incredibly volatile throughout the 1960s, with several periods of up to 40 percent unemployment across the industry due to massive upheavals in Hollywood's structure and economics.[50] Runaway productions, the introduction of new unions into the industry, and the rise of nonunion productions meant that IATSE workers scavenged for work multiple times each year in a depleted job landscape. All of this made self-preservation of existing members even more of a priority than usual.

Subsequently, in the IA's 1965 contract, the victories for the union side incentivized studio-era workers to retire. Among the provisions were an increase of $200 per month to pensions, health and welfare coverage for retirees' spouses, hospital coverage, elimination of age requirements in vesting provisions for pensions, severance provisions, and other incentives to retire at sixty-five.[51] In this contract there was also a small acknowledgment of the recently passed Civil Rights Act of 1964—the inclusion of "a non-discriminatory clause"—but the focus was on clearing out the upper tier of the unions' rosters.

In the lead-up to the EEOC's investigation into the IATSE unions, complaints to the NLRB had been lodged on the claim that the roster system was discriminatory and the equivalent of a "closed shop."[52] The pressure to add more people to the roster, both those working outside the unions and those seeking to enter professions that had largely been closed off to them, became dual pressures exacerbated further by declines in overall employment.[53] When the EEOC began its 1969 hearings on the problem of racial diversity in the industry, they were set against IATSE's denials and obstinance. Of the key findings, the commission was able to show how the roster system and training programs were specifically designed to close off access not just to amateur technicians but particularly to women practitioners and male practitioners of color. The IA representatives failed to understand why union application questions about national birthplace, membership connections, and particularly the occupation of one's father would create discriminatory hiring conditions.[54]

The commission found that the training programs and the experience roster were often designed to exclude minorities and women who could not realistically gain the skills required. The EEOC questioned the "very basis for the roster system," arguing that, "Apprenticeship programs to enable people to get on the roster are, at least in some cases, set up with unrealistic standards and requirements, not related to job requirements."[55] This included an example from the 728 lamp operator training program, which required an apprentice to earn 2,100 hours of work experience (almost three months) to even make it onto the lowest tier of the roster.[56] Additionally, the commission demonstrated how nepotism and familial ties to current union members ensured greater access to union technical training for card-carrying members' sons, nephews, and brothers.[57]

After the EEOC's damning report, the Justice Department negotiated a deal with the unions that avoided another painful consent decree like the Paramount

Decrees of 1948. Under the agreement, the backlot unions (such as those for props, grips, and laborers) were given different rules than the more prestigious craft unions (such as those for camera, sound, and editors). The latter unions were asked to make one referral from a minority labor pool for every four referrals made from the general pool.[58] The agreement also explicitly called out "nepotism"—the hiring of friends and relatives—insisting that it could not take precedent over this system.[59] While union leadership agreed to what was essentially a quota system, there was dissent within the rank and file. The very idea of quotas seemed counter to these craft workers' conception of their professions as skilled and talent-based. If they were not in the union because of their unique abilities, then what did that say about them?

The settlement also stipulated that an EEOC officer would assist studios and union reps from 1972 to early 1974 to develop concrete affirmative action policies.[60] Yet little significant action was taken until nearly a decade later. Despite the seemingly major concessions, as Eithne Quinn shows, since these rules were "voluntary" and lasted only two years, they had little impact.[61] Likewise, the backlash to these efforts likely contributed to the retrenchment of exclusionary practices within Hollywood's craft unions. But the results are not entirely to be dismissed, as key craft unions embraced the new quota system. When a few individual IATSE members attempted to rally support to overturn the decision, the business agents for soundmen and cameramen, the industry pacesetters, came out strongly against the group.[62] When the two years of the agreement had passed, only four unions had met the goals set out, but they were the cameramen, sound workers, editors, and costumers—members of the skilled crafts that had been asked to institute referral quotas.[63] While the other unions pitted their experience roster *against* the diversity initiatives, these crafts had sought to shore up their rosters by admitting the new members.

Detailed breakdowns of the unions' demographic discrepancies would not come to light until the 1976 hearings of the California Advisory Committee to the U.S. Commission on Civil Rights and the Commission's follow up hearing in 1977. The purpose of these hearings was to address how studios had made changes following the 1969 EEOC report and subsequent agreements. The U.S. Commission report also offered a more detailed examination of the training programs' failures to attract, recruit, and retain minority and women talent and another scathing indictment of the industry experience roster. The commission made clear that studios had not made large enough gains in minority representation outside of clerical staff. Their hiring practices in the crafts continued to be tied to vague and often discriminatory categories of qualification, including speech, dress, and personality. Commissioner Frankie Freeman pointed out this concern, stating, "I believe you can anticipate the problem. In other words, it is the predominantly white male who makes the judgement."[64] Further testimonials by minority workers at the end of the hearing offered supporting anecdotes of their own experiences of insidious bureaucratic discrimination as well as blatant racism while navigating the unions' training, roster, and hiring practices.

IATSE in the Era of Deregulation

The 1970s and 1980s saw renewed consolidation in the industry, but rather than return to the studio heyday of union contracts, new corporate structures continued to favor the subcontracting system of production to reduce overhead and lessen labor liability.[65] Subcontracting with low-budget, cable, out-of-town, and independent companies often allowed studios and networks to bypass Article 20, which restricted studios from bargaining with contractors without the union. As a result, IATSE, Laborers, Teamsters, and the various building crafts unions held fewer collective bargaining agreements on these enormous sectors of production activity.

Absent the protections of a basic agreement, working conditions deteriorated. According to John Amman, "The industry has seen increased violations of state and federal labor laws, longer workdays (14 to 18 hours per day), employers paying 'flat' wages with no overtime, and employers not fully compensating workers at the end of productions."[66] Since the work was contracted out, studios were insulated from the myriad labor violations that kept production costs low.

In response to what seemed to be unsustainable labor conditions, in 1988 IATSE, the Teamsters, and the IBEW joined the WGA strikes, hoping they might be more successful bargaining while some production was already shut down by higher-prestige players. Earlier that year, the Teamsters and IATSE had attempted to negotiate their shared collective bargaining timelines separately. The Teamsters went on strike in October 1988, joined by the Laborers and IBEW 40. Their gamble did not pay off, as producers saw laborers and drivers as easily replaceable by nonunion workers. When the Teamsters settled with the producers after twenty-four days, they suffered major losses, having received no support from IATSE crafts.[67] Seeing the Teamsters defeated, IATSE made concessions in January 1989, including losses of a five-day workweek, meal and night benefits, and double time on Saturday and Sunday.[68] As Amman explains, rank-and-file workers voted against the concessions, citing specific concerns for older workers, but the contract was ratified anyway.[69] The long-term impact of the lockouts also limited possibilities for labor solidarity and collective action, as future IATSE and Teamsters contracts would expire on different timelines.

With shrinking influence and fewer productions coming out of the Hollywood studios, IATSE turned to membership drives, geographic expansion, and local mergers to bolster its membership numbers and retain its strike power. In the early 1990s, IATSE absorbed the two NABET film locals, ensuring "that every craft associated with the film industry would now stand together under one roof."[70] In 1993, IATSE celebrated its centennial with 74,000 members. The next year, Thomas Short succeeded to the presidency, forwarding the strategy of expansion and consolidation, forming ever-larger (and more power-ful) Hollywood locals, as will be seen in the following chapters. This brought IATSE membership to over 100,000 by 2003, a 42 percent increase in a decade. The expansion of IATSE culminated in 1998 when it officially changed its name to the International Alliance of Theatrical Stage Employees, Moving Picture Technicians, Artists and Allied Crafts of the United States, Its Territories and Canada—while retaining its well-established brand as just IATSE. Federally, U.S. unions lost protections during and following the presidency of Ronald Rea-gan, and trade union membership declined, but IATSE bucked nationwide trends by incorporating a wider range of production workers.

Throughout the late 1990s and into the new millennium, many of IATSE's efforts focused on increasing on-set safety in the wake of high-profile accidents and deaths, such as those on the sets of *The Twilight Zone* (1983), *Top Gun* (1986), and *The Crow* (1994). In 1997, IATSE established the National Safety Commit-tee, followed by the West Coast–based Industry-Wide Labor-Management Safety Committee for Hollywood production.[71] This committee publishes safety bulletins and participates in the Passport Safety Training Program, which cer-tifies members who have completed training. IATSE added the Training Trust Fund in 2009, and the Occupational Safety and Health Administration's "OSHA 10" courses in 2014 to continue training efforts in safety compliance.[72]

The 2015 Basic Agreement with the AMPTP included funding for online safety courses for the first time. This was in the wake of a February 2014 inci-dent on a Georgia-based production in which Sarah Jones, a camera assistant, was killed by a freight train when filmmakers attempted to shoot on a railroad trestle without permission or permits.[73] While IATSE has sought to expand its jurisdiction across the country, it has struggled to gain a larger foothold in right-to-work states such as Georgia and North Carolina, which were the homes of more and more production work.[74] The reliance in these states on less-experienced, local crews can at least in part explain the greater incidence of safety issues on productions outside of the more regulated Los Angeles area.

Safety continues to be a major concern of members working on set—from the use of firearms to COVID-19 protocols to long drives home in the middle of the night after long work hours. The latter issue around the standard state of affairs in media production, with long hours and short breaks, became one of the central issues in the volatile Basic Agreement negotiations in 2021. The pandemic-instigated work stoppage illuminated for many IATSE workers how overworked and sleep-deprived they had been.

#IASolidarity

The IATSE Hollywood locals have never collectively gone on strike. When thir-teen of the fourteen Hollywood locals threatened to strike together in Septem-ber 2021, it was touted as the first such possibility and potentially the largest below-the-line labor action since the violent upheavals of the 1940s. Media attention and social media posts brought public awareness to these workers' complaints of long hours with short turnarounds, ongoing safety concerns, and insufficient compensation in the streaming era.[75] Riding a national wave of union victories and positive attitudes toward labor brought to prominence by the COVID-19 pandemic after decades of decline, IATSE's Hollywood locals seemed poised for a massive win in their negotiations with the AMPTP. The sentiment among members turned out to be stronger than the leadership's willingness to negotiate. While the contract that was narrowly ratified by the membership saw the most significant gains in decades, it was largely viewed as squandering the strong position and goodwill the members had obtained.[76]

The 2021 negotiations were a rare moment of cross-craft solidarity in which all the Hollywood IATSE locals (except the Animation Guild, whose contract was not up for negotiation yet) worked as one. As the next eight chapters will show, the locals have more often focused on the unique needs of their members, creating splintering motivations, jurisdictional disputes, and factionalism. These issues are rife in the following chapters, which follow the structure of the unions themselves in presenting separate histories for each craft area—or strategic groupings. We sought to consolidate the fourteen locals into as few chapters as possible, but they often resisted our editorial intervention. Chapters were added through the process of writing this volume as the unions, like their members, seemed to demand autonomy.

With this spine of a history of the IATSE union in Hollywood to set the scene, the following eight chapters branch off into the various crafts the Hollywood locals represent. Each local represents a different form of labor and a different history of organization. Each has sought solidarity with those within its craft over the industry solidary seen only in particular moments, such as the 2021 negotiations. This points to the importance of the *work* itself when studying unions. The members of the IATSE locals do not see themselves primarily as workers, but first as craftsmen and often as artists with very particular skills that they bring to media production. This has at times put them at odds with each other or, conversely, created unique alignments. As such, the histories overlap and refer to each other frequently, sometimes offering *Rashomon*-like differing takes on the same events. We hope this craft-focused approach serves to tell important stories that have been buried under master narratives, as well as highlighting commonalities and divergences among the crafts and workers in Hollywood media production.

Notes

1   Andrew Dawson, "Strikes in the Motion Picture Industry," in *The Encyclopedia of Strikes in American History*, ed. Aaron Brenner, Benjamin Day, and Immanuel Ness, (Routledge, 2009), 652–664.

2 On the discussion of the "father-son tradition," see U.S. Equal Employment Opportunity Commission, *Hearings Before the U.S. Equal Employment Opportunity Commission on Utilization of Minority and Women Workers in Certain Major Industries: Hearings Held in Los Angeles, Calif., March 12–14, 1969* (Equal Employment Opportunity Commission, 1969), 124.

3 Michael Nielsen, "Motion Picture Craft Workers and Craft Unions in Hollywood: The Studio Era, 1912–1948" (PhD diss., University of Illinois Urbana-Champaign, 1985), 27

4 "125 Years of IATSE," *Official IATSE Bulletin* Q2, no. 660 (IATSE, 2018): 4.

5 International Alliance of Theatrical Stage Employees and Moving Picture Operators of United States and Canada, *IATSE, 1893–1993: 100 Years of Solidarity* (IATSE, 1993), 18.

6 Nielsen, "Motion Picture Craft Workers," 52.

7 Michael C. Nielsen, "Labor Power and Organization in the Early U.S. Motion Picture Industry," *Film History* 2, no. 2 (June 1988): 126.

8 Nielsen, 126.

9 "Make Demands on Film Heads," *Los Angeles Times*, August 28, 1919, II2.

10 Nielsen, "Motion Picture Craft Workers," 107.

11 "125 Years of IATSE," 25.

12 "Studios Will Defy Unions," *Los Angeles Times* (hereafter *LAT*), November 10, 1926, A1.

13 "Predict Labor Move to Cripple Motion Pictures," *Moving Picture World*, November 20, 1926, 144.

14 Mike Nielsen and Gene Mailes, *Hollywood's Other Blacklist: Union Struggles in the Studio System* (British Film Institute, 1995), 11.

15 "The Film Strike Ends," *LAT*, August 25, 1933, A4.

16 Nielsen and Mailes, *Hollywood's Other Blacklist*, 13.

17 Murray Ross, *Stars and Strikes: Unionization of Hollywood* (Columbia University Press, 1941), 134.

18 For a detailed history of this era in IATSE history, see Gerald Horne, *Class Struggle in Hollywood, 1930–1950: Moguls, Mobsters, Stars, Reds, and Trade Unionists* (University of Texas Press, 2001).

19 Horne, 159.

20 Nielsen and Mailes, *Hollywood's Other Blacklist*, 19.

21 Nielsen and Mailes, 20

22 Ida Jeter, "The Collapse of the Federated Motion Picture Crafts: A Case Study of Class Collaboration in the Motion Picture Industry," *Journal of the University Film Association* 31, no. 2 (Spring 1979): 37–45.

23 Larry Ceplair, "A Communist Labor Organizer in Hollywood: Jeff Kibre Challenges the IATSE, 1937–1939," *Velvet Light Trap* 23 (Spring 1989): 64.

24 Horne, *Class Struggle in Hollywood*, 49; Nielsen and Mailes, *Hollywood's Other Blacklist*, 35–36.

25 "USTG Files Petition with NLRB for Bargaining Agent Pact," *Box Office*, July 15, 1939, 26.

26 "IATSE Official Studio Group by Majority Near 2,500," *Hollywood Boxoffice*, September 23, 1939, 41.

27 Ceplair, "Communist Labor Organizer," 72.

28 "I.A. Happenings," *International Projectionist*, September 1939, 23.

29 "Schenck, Bernstein, Mayer Tell of Payments to Browne and Bioff," *Motion Picture Herald*, October 18, 1941, 17.

30 Arthur Ungar, "Bye, Bye Bioff," *Variety*, November 12, 1941), 3.

31 Nielsen and Mailes, *Hollywood's Other Blacklist*, ix.

32 "'IA' Charters Fifth New Local in Strike," *Motion Picture Daily* , September 7, 1945, 1.

33 Horne, *Class Struggle in Hollywood*, 181–182.

34 "Nobody's Victory in Film War," *LAT*, October 26, 1945, 4.

35 Horne, *Class Struggle in Hollywood,* 174.

36 Hugh Lovell and Tasile Carter, *Collective Bargaining in the Motion Picture Industry* (Institute for Industrial Relations, 1955), 23.

37 Horne, *Class Struggle in Hollywood*, 203.

38 Nielsen and Mailes, *Hollywood's Other Blacklist*, 161.

39 "Studios Sign 5-Year Contract for 16,000 IATSE Studio Film Workers," *Variety*, August 17, 1949, 7.

40 For more see Michael Conant, "The Paramount Decrees Reconsidered," in *The American Film Industry,* ed. Tino Balio (University of Wisconsin Press, 1985): 537–573.

41 Lovell and Carter, *Collective Bargaining*, 11.

42 "125 Years of IATSE," 40.

43 The name was changed to its current Alliance of Motion Picture and Television Producers (while remaining the AMPTP) in 1982.

44 "125 Years of IATSE," 41.

45 John Amman, "The Transformation of Industrial Relations in the Motion Picture and Television Industries: Craft and Production," in *Under the Stars: Essays on Labor Relations in Arts and Entertainment*, ed. Lois S. Gray and Ronald L. Seeber (Cornell University Press, 1996), 150.

46 "Negro Spokesman Charges 25-Year Stall on Studio Craft Employment; Scripts Still Stereotype Race," *Variety*, July 3, 1963, 16.

47 "IATSE: No Negro Need Apply," *Variety*, July 31, 1963, 7.

48 "Negroes Want IATSE Memberships: It's 'Featherbedding' Say Lamp Ops; Civil Rights Gets Craft Union Nix," *Variety*, August 7, 1963, 11.

49 "Two IA Crafts Admit Negro Apprentices," *Hollywood Boxoffice*, November 11, 1963, W-1.

50 Dave Kaufman, "Hollywood Unemployment at 42.8%," *Variety*, March 4, 1970, 3.

51 "Pension Road to Pasture," *Variety*, February 3, 1965, 3.

52 "'Experience Roster' & Who Controls It: New Case of Job Poison to NLRB," *Variety*, July 3, 1968, 15.

53 "Coast Unemployment Gloom," *Variety*, July 9, 1969, 7, 20.

54 See testimony of IA representative Josef Bernay, in U.S. Equal Employment Opportunity Commission, *Hearings Before the U.S. Equal Employment Opportunity Commission*, 158.

55 Daniel Steiner, General Counsels Statement, U.S. Equal Employment Opportunity Commission, *Hearings Before the U.S. Equal Employment Opportunity Commission*, 228.

56 Schaeffer testimony, in U.S. Equal Employment Opportunity Commission, *Hearings Before the U.S. Equal Employment Opportunity Commission*, 182.

57 See Eithne Quinn, "Closing Doors: Hollywood, Affirmative Action, and the Revitalization of Conservative Racial Politics," *Journal of American History* 99, no. 2 (September 2012): 466–491.

58 "To Duck 'Consent' H'wood Pledges Racial Quota Hiring; 'Nepotism' K.O.," *Variety*, February 25, 1970, 1, 78.

59 "NAACP Calls Film Crafts Plan OK, If Made to Work," *Los Angeles Sentinel*, March 12, 1970, B.

60 Traylor testimony, in U.S. Commission on Civil Rights, *Hearing Held in Los Angeles, California, March 16, 1977*, (U.S. Commission on Civil Rights, 1977), 120.

61 See Eithne Quinn, *A Piece of the Action: Race and Labor in Post–Civil Rights Hollywood* (Columbia University Press, 2020).

62 "IA Hits Race Pledge Un-Doers," *Variety*, December 30, 1970, 7.

63 "Racial Minority Pact's Future?," *Variety*, April 26, 1972, 5, 22.

64 U.S. Commission on Civil Rights, *Hearings Held in Los Angeles, California*, 35.

65 Susan Christopherson, "Flexibility and Adaptation in Industrial Relations: The Exceptional Case of the U.S. Media Entertainment Industries," in *Under the Stars: Essays on Labor Relations in Arts and Entertainment*, ed. Lois S. Gray and Ronald Leroy Seeber (Cornell University Press, 1996), 91.

66 Amman, "Transformation of Industrial Relations," 140.

67 Henry Weinstein, "Teamsters Reach Tentative Accord with Producers," *LAT*, October 27, 1988, vi.

68 Harry Bernstein, "Hollywood's Craft Workers under Pressure to Take Cuts," *LAT*, January 24, 1989, C1.

69 Amman, "Transformation of Industrial Relations," 128.

70 "125 Years of IATSE," 59.

71 "125 Years of IATSE," 75.

72 "125 Years of IATSE," 102.

73 Hilary Lewis, "'Midnight Rider' Accident: Georgia Gilmmakers Hosting Safety Seminar in Memory of Sarah Jones," *The Hollywood Reporter*, March 28, 2014, https://www.hollywoodreporter.com/news/general-news/midnight-rider-accident -georgia-filmmakers-691911/.

74 Jonathan Handel, "New National 'Right to Work' Bill Threatens Hollywood Unions," *Hollywood Reporter*, February 2, 2017, https://www.hollywoodreporter .com/business/business-news/new-national-right-work-bill-threatens-hollywood -unions-971345/.

75 Jude Dry, "IATSE Considers Strike as Negotiations with Studios Stall over Paltry Streaming Rates," *IndieWire*, September 9, 2021, https://www.indiewire.com/2021 /09/iatse-strike-negotiations-union-1234662902/.

76 Gene Maddaus, "IATSE Contract Ratification Decided by Razor-Thin Vote Margins in Two Guilds," *Variety*, November 15, 2021, https://variety.com/2021/film/news /iatse-contract-vote-razor-thin-margins-1235112711/.

1

Feminized
Production Roles

• • • • • • • • • • • • • • • • • • • •

Uneven Progress, Enduring
Inequality in Female-
Dominated Locals

ERIN HILL

Since 2010, campaigns by three media production professions have highlighted ongoing labor inequities experienced by their members: assistants' #PayUp-Hollywood campaign for a living wage, script supervisors' #ReelEquity campaign addressing gender wage gaps, and casting directors' public campaign for the creation of an Academy Award category for their field. These professions shared a feminized past, in which many of the most difficult and least rewarded production roles were assigned to women. These are still largely understood as "women's work."[1] I have previously written about the *logic of feminization*—in which essentialist notions of gender align with capitalistic, industrial, and economic imperatives to limit women's workplace participation and shape their professional outcomes long after formal gender segregation practices have ended. Unionization is meant to supply its own logic to production systems, operating, at least in theory, as a check against the power of management, and bringing workers higher wages, safer working conditions, and increased job security, among other benefits. It would stand to reason, then, that women and other historically marginalized groups would benefit equally or more than their white male counterparts from this logic of unionization. Yet the opposite is more often the case. Historically feminized fields have unionized later than masculinized professions, and these unionization efforts have met with mixed results—with workers organizing partially, temporarily, belatedly, or not at all.

Explanations of women production workers' uneven progress are difficult to untangle because gender discrimination is insidious and culturally embedded. It takes the form of structuring absences: things *not* said, conditions *not* noted by those present in production spaces, and contributions *not* recognized. Many of the historical causes and conditions that have circumscribed women's labor organizing are similarly indirect:

Women are often introduced to the workforce to disrupt unionization efforts of extant workers.

Women are frequently assigned the most routine, menial, and repetitive tasks left behind when unions codify and separate nearby roles.

Women's aptitudes are not recognized as acquired skills but rather as "natural" functions of their gender.

Women's workplace agency and labor activism must be disguised through feminine performativity, packaged with sexuality, or delivered indirectly through influence.

Women are further marginalized within media production due to their association with work deemed uncreative, unimportant, and invisible.

This chapter accounts for unionization of feminized film and TV production roles through indirect causes, direct actions, and long-term effects. I begin by tracing feminized labor logics from the nineteenth-century managers who first rationalized the hiring of women based on supposed connections between women's traditional domestic roles and low-wage "deskilled" forms of manufacturing, clerical labor, and domestic service. These practices followed women into the rapidly expanding U.S. film industry of the early twentieth century, when reorganizations of studio filmmaking helped to accelerate the feminization process. I then focus on three professions rooted in feminized clerical/administrative labor: clerical workers, script supervisors, and casting workers. I follow these workers' organizing efforts during and after the Hollywood union boom of the 1930s and 1940s, through the freelance era of flexible specialization, to the present. I end by examining recent efforts by women in these clerical/administrative, continuity, and casting professions to address the legacy of the feminized past.

While each specialization's history is unique, each exemplifies common challenges women and other marginalized groups experience in forming and benefiting from unions. Taken together, these labor histories reveal how vestigial feminized labor hierarchies continue to shape the experience of women and other historically marginalized groups in spaces of media production, including the very unions that exist to eliminate workplace inequalities.

Women's Wage Work before "Hollywood"

American manufacturers brought feminized labor inside factory walls in the early nineteenth century, around the time Nicéphore Niépce and Louis Daguerre were capturing some of the first photographic images. Would-be employers of women offered the rationale that women's home roles making family goods might simply be extended to roles making similar goods in factories.[2] Favorable conditions provided a veneer of respectability that initially attracted many working-class, native-born white women, along with immigrant women, to so-called light manufacturing roles involving monotonous, repetitive work on goods formerly fabricated via domestic piecework systems.[3] Racialized labor hierarchies—with jobs segregated according to white supremacist notions of a racial or ethnic group's supposed "natural" skills and aptitudes—existed both alongside and within feminized labor sectors. Typically, managers hired Black and Latina women for work such as industrial farming that was even more painstaking, repetitive, and physically demanding than the work done by immigrant and native-born white women.[4]

White women entered offices in the wake of the Civil War as smaller companies were scaled into vertically and horizontally integrated corporations using principles of scientific management. The nineteenth-century male clerk, an apprentice learning the entire business with the promise of promotion, gave way to the female stenographer and secretary as terminal positions reserved for women. Under such reorganizations, ever-increasing "clerical output"—the intermediate paper records needed to plan the final product—became the link between the "brain" of management in centralized offices and the "hands" of production in so-called deskilled factory roles.[5] Clerical labor was itself deskilled as the writing process was mechanized and feminized via the typewriter, light machinery marketed specifically to women.[6] Between 1879 and 1930, the percentage of female (vs. male) stenographers and typists in the United States rose from 4.5 percent to 95.4 percent.[7]

Women earning wages outside the home were invisibly bound by the nineteenth-century "code of domesticity," an ideology that tied women's class status to the expectations of piety, purity and submissiveness, and positioned work as a way station to marriage and motherhood. These patriarchal notions of gender effectively limited women's investment in sustained careers or secure benefits and abetted employers in refusing them training or promotion, paying women as little as one-third of men's wages and barring them from the workforce once married.[8]

Despite the white patriarchal rationales about protecting white men's jobs, white women's safety, or the home, workplace segregation—not only by gender but also by race, ethnicity, religion, and language spoken—functioned to divide labor against itself, stifling unionization by creating structural competition between groups. Men blamed women when managers hired them to break strikes or drive down men's wages. Women endured hostility, intimidation, and violence from male co-workers in response to their presence in the workplace.[9] They faced managers' ire if they unionized because, as a 1910 government report explained, the moment a woman joined a union, "she diminishes or destroys what is to her employer her chief value," as a source of docile, low-cost labor.[10]

The most successful nineteenth-century women's unions were those that allied with nearby men's organizations, such as the Women's Typographical Union, formed in New York City in 1868, which accepted skilled male workers from Typographical Union 6 and later became a local of that union. However, white men were just as likely to collectivize to keep women or other workers from marginalized groups out of their workplaces—some strikes were called to protest women's entry into the workplace.[11] Even those nineteenth-century women who succeeded in organizing unions faced the problem of securing recognition from male trade unionists or national trade organizations such as the American Federation of Labor (AFL). Some craft unions had rules suspending members for training female workers in their constitutions well into the twentieth century.[12]

By the end of the nineteenth century, as cinema was being invented, nearly all of the 17.3 percent of U.S. women who reported working for wages did so in one of the now-established types of women's labor that would endure for decades, which I subdivide as: domestic manufacturing (12 percent); caring professions (such as teaching and nursing, 11 percent); saleswomen/clerks (9 percent); manufacturing (25 percent); domestic service (33 percent); and agriculture (10 percent).[13] These pre-established categories of women's labor were not immediately incorporated into the nascent film industry due to heterosocial practices imported from popular theater and the idiosyncratic nature of early filmmaking. Many pioneering women of early film found their first jobs in the relatively improvisational atmosphere of early film production, which allowed them to gain experience in different roles.[14] However, the lack of formal boundaries between roles abetted employers in undercutting the wages and job security of skilled craft workers.[15]

During the 1910s, growing motion picture companies looked to scientific management to stabilize the industry and court Wall Street capital.[16] As the film industry grew, mixed-gender sectors such as publicity and casting were claimed by men, while women were relegated to support roles.[17] As their prospects elsewhere shrank, women became associated not with below-the-line craft specialties but with low-paying sectors emerging at the margins of the filmmaking process.

Both managers and unions contributed to increasing departmentalization, specialization of crafts, and the slow, trickling down of the most menial clerical and organizational tasks on set into what became early feminized production roles.[18] The emergence of the production role of script clerk (today's script supervisor) as women's work exemplifies this "trickle-down" effect. Accounts suggest that assistant directors (ADs) and production assistants served as de facto script clerks in early studios, keeping notes on each take for editing and continuity purposes.[19] This procedure persisted in an ad hoc mode until the 1910s, when the role of script "girl" or clerk emerged to track continuity and absorb other clerical production tasks under the rationale that women could "watch the small details better than men."[20] Other feminized production specialties such as the art department secretary (today's art department coordinator) also served as repositories for gender-typed tasks left unclaimed in the process of specialization.

Feminized sectors—as opposed to feminized positions within masculinized departments—typically originated in the first two decades of the twentieth century, with a handful of professionally mobile women. By the 1930s, these transformed into large departments of dozens or hundreds of women restricted to feminized roles and segregated in dedicated floors or buildings. In keeping with white supremacist ideology barring people of color from professions desirable to whites while hiring only people of color in undesirable professions, Black and Hispanic or Latina women primarily worked as janitors, maids, and launderers due to their historical association with those feminized domestic service roles.[21]

Mixed-gender sectors—typically those related to paper planning versus physical production—included story, casting, and publicity departments and were split between typically male midlevel to upper-level manager-executives and feminized support staff. For example, work in studio casting departments was divided between predominantly male casting executives, directors, and associates who allocated actor assets (performers under long-term contracts) across studio slates, and a mostly female workforce of secretaries and clerks who typed and maintained casting's clerical output (actor lists, notes, and memos). Examination of feminized casting director roles is undertaken later in this chapter's chronology, when casting transformed into a freelance, female-dominated role. Meanwhile, casting's feminized lower ranks are discussed as part of the broader collective of clerical workers with whom they unionized.

Organizing Women's Work in the Studio System

By the end of the 1920s, efficient reorganization and early unionization had effectively relegated women to feminized roles. Outside of performers or the rare female scenarist who skipped the secretarial pool by dint of an upper-class or professional pedigree (see Dorothy Parker), female job seekers were funneled into socially acceptable feminized labor categories adapted from other industries. I subdivide these as light manufacture (film patching, negative cutting, inking, painting, machine sewing, beading, embroidery); domestic service (food service, laundry, janitorial); domestic crafts (hairstyling, hand sewing); clerical labor (secretarial, clerical, switchboard); caring professions (teachers, drama coaches, doctors, nurses, massage therapists); and feminized or mixed specializations in planning departments (story analysts/readers, librarians, certain publicist roles). These workers, crucial as a collective, were considered marginal at best to the creative processes at the center of film production.

Women in feminized film industry roles were further marginalized within a production system in which privileges, distinctions, and credit were awarded based on proximity to the creative process (measured in visible, identifiable contributions to finished films) and professional status (elevated by unions, trade publications, awards). The potential for unionization was linked to workers' "hard" technical skills and training, accrued in trade schools or formal apprenticeships. The era's implicit logic made it possible to acknowledge an electrician's training and acquired skills yet overlook the secretary's secretarial certificate or college degree, stenography training, editorial knowledge, and requisite understanding of studio workflow and production systems. Women's work was less likely to be viewed as either skilled or directly related to production for the very reason that it was work done by women. Finally, women's work was defined by its *lack* of identifiable contributions to the final product: that is, clerical workers produced only paper planning and records, while the script supervisor's success was measured by its *lack* of visible contribution to the film image—in the form of errors kept *off* the screen.

Women's managers and production peers also tended to minimize, as the "natural" product of being female, the more universal, soft skills and forms of emotion work invariably demanded of women. Secretarial work required significant interpersonal skills and emotional management to "make friends" for the boss, diffuse conflicts, and quietly fend off sexual harassment.[22] As the set's "professional fault finders," script supervisors needed similar skills to deliver bad news about errors and crew complaints to the director.[23] That women without such skills were soon replaced in these roles evinces the fact that theirs were *acquired skills and competencies* rather than some form of inborn feminine fluency.

The economic consequences of this gendered division of labor are evident in a 1928 *Variety* survey of the "prevailing salaries" across different job classifications. In the report, the low or base pay rate in feminized sectors ranged from $20 (typists) to $35 per week (script clerks). Base pay for masculinized production roles began at $1 per hour (or $40+ per week) for painters, carpenters, and "common laborers"; $75 for set roles such as ADs; and $100 for department heads. Mixed-gender sectors showed the biggest gaps between the lowest- and highest-paid employees (presumably the least senior woman and the most senior man, respectively), such as the scenario writers' pay (low, $25; average, $200; high, $3,500).[24] Thus, in the film industry of the early studio era, the logics of feminization and trade unionism had largely blocked women's prospects from production roles and spaces, as well as from the labor associations and unions that organized them.

The Code of Fair Competition for the Motion Picture Industry became law in 1933, allowing workers to organize and gain federal recognition. As labor organizing expanded during the New Deal and World War II periods, women would join or form unions and, briefly, see their salaries and protections rise. One minor but successful example of women's labor organization was the formation of the studio teachers union in 1938. In these years, jurisdictional disputes between the International Alliance of Theatrical Stage Employees (IATSE) and the Conference of Studio Unions (CSU; discussed in the introduction to part I) would bring most femininized and mixed-gender trades into the organized labor fold.[25] Yet conflicts between the two unions would ultimately result in most feminized specializations returning to independent or nonunion status by 1947.

Script clerks, like ADs, were excluded from the original Studio Basic Agreement despite working the same impossible hours as other crew, often at a flat weekly rate without overtime. One script supervisor recalled working twenty-four hours on, eight hours off, seven days a week for months at Warner Bros. in the 1920s.[26] Another "worked uncomplainingly 26 consecutive hours on one Western" with no expectation of overtime.[27] When 1931 legislation mandated overtime after eight hours, MGM adopted two scales for script clerks so that "girls get a salary of $41 or more weekly when on a picture" where fourteen- to sixteen-hour days were routine "and a much lower rate between pics when they are in stenography department."[28] These continuity workers allied with the independent Assistant Directors Guild, an organization without the power or funding of a federally recognized bargaining agent. In early 1934, the coalition signed a formal agreement with producers, locking in a minimum day rate for script clerks (eight dollars) and "extra" or second ADs (ten dollars) with time-and-a-half overtime.[29] However, West Coast ADs separated from the guild when they joined the Screen Directors Guild in 1937.

The same year, led by Thelma McFate Preece, script supervisors formed the independent Script Clerks Guild (SCG), one of many worker organizations that arose in the absence of an IATSE charter, which sought recognition, wage boosts, a fifty-four-hour week, and overtime after that. Their proposal was variously ignored or stalled by producers for the latter half of 1937 until the Script Clerks, Film Editors, and Interior Decorators petitioned the visiting regional director of the National Labor Relations Board (NLRB) for recognition, at which point producers invited them to the table.[30] They signed a basic agreement in January 1938, only to open new negotiations in February following new wage legislation.[31]

Still unrecognized by producers or the NLRB in 1940, the SCG nonetheless negotiated a new agreement with a guaranteed minimum wage at $55.94 per fifty-four-hour week and $72.04 per seventy-two-hour week on location.[32] While ADs received a bump in their hourly wage after being ruled exempt from overtime under the Fair Labor Standard Act, script clerks were initially ruled nonexempt but limited to forty hours per week to avoid overtime.[33] Script clerks made gradual progress on wages and hours over the next few years, yet they were invariably paid less than the ADs and second ADs.

The SCG increasingly joined with other independent guilds to protest producers' tactics and assert their autonomy in the face of IATSE's threat to assert jurisdiction over all workers "from porters to stars."[34] Seeking greater leverage, the SCG allied with the Hollywood Guild Council, a coalition of independent labor groups including the publicists, readers, set designers, and interior designers guilds, and often stood in solidarity with members of the council. Many of these guilds would later join the CSU coalition brought together by Herb Sorrell in 1941, "out of a sense that IATSE was a tool of the bosses—corporate and mob" and promising "a more aggressive, worker-centric attitude."[35]

Like the script clerks, office workers in planning departments from accounting to publicity had begun to form "white-collar" guilds in the middle to late 1930s. While the mixed-gender publicists and readers formed independent guilds for their specializations, a veritable alphabet soup of unaffiliated guilds emerged to organize the broader collective of office workers. Efforts to organize clerical workers industry-wide were stymied by the emergence of internal guilds at major studios to negotiate between studios and their clerical workers (collectively referred to here as *studio guilds* to distinguish from *independent guilds* such as the SCG). The Warner Bros. Studio Office Employees Guild (WBSOEG), the Paramount Office Employee Association (POEA), and the Twentieth Century-Fox Film Corporation Screen Office Employees Guild (FSOEG) represented clerical units beginning in 1937, and similar groups later formed at Columbia, MGM, Disney, and Loew's.[36] Labor organizers labeled such bodies *company unions* because they represented workers at a single company where organizers were also employed, had no national labor affiliations, and thus lacked independence and leverage. The studio guilds did standardize pay and job classifications, but members lacked solidarity with hundreds of clerical workers outside their own company and relied on their employers' good faith to secure fair contracts.

Then, in December 1939, the independent Screen Office Employees Guild (SOEG) held its first organizational meeting at the Hollywood Women's Club, expecting "to maintain an independent status with complete autonomy."[37] Women were frequently elected to the presidency and seats on the board of the independent SOEG, but male members also held leadership roles.[38] A year later, office employees at Columbia, Universal, RKO, MGM, Republic, Hal Roach and Walter Wanger studios voted in NLRB-mandated elections to reject existing studio guilds and unionize with the SOEG as the AFL-chartered Screen Office Employees Guild Local 1391, which the NLRB recognized as its exclusive bargaining agent a month later.[39] Backed by the AFL and the Hollywood Guild Council, the SOEG would encompass "all office, clerical, secretarial, and accounting employees, office and tabulating machine operators, switchboard operators and messengers," and "casting employees whose work is of a clerical nature."[40]

Excluded from membership were secretaries to major executives, casting directors and assistants, PR/publicity directors, and others that studios contended did not fit the Wagner Act's criteria for "employees" due to their having the "right to hire and fire and a chance to recommend concerning employment."[41] However, the earliest company unions survived this effort: Fox employees continued to be represented by their studio guild until 1946, and the Paramount and Warner guilds continued into the late 1960s.[42]

The SOEG quickly outpaced the studio guilds in terms of gains for workers. In September 1941, after threatening to strike, the SOEG won wage increases above the scales of the remaining studio guilds and a broad array of protections and benefits, including back pay for wage-hour violations, closed-shop status, paid vacations, sick leave, severance pay, a promotion clause, mileage, minimum calls (the minimum number of hours an employee will be paid if called to work), and a joint classification and grievance committee.[43] An 8 percent pay increase in May 1942 gave the SOEG "the highest wage scale for white-collarites in the film industry, shoving them ahead" of the "company unions."[44]

The SOEG also dwarfed its rivals in terms of membership. Counting roughly 2,000 clerical workers at the seven studios in 1941 (to the POEA's 400), the SOEG went on to organize workers in major West Coast film exchanges, the Producers Releasing Corporation, Technicolor, and major film laboratories and by early 1945 was reportedly "moving into radio, intent on adding 700 white collarites" to its 2,500 film workers. By September, the SOEG had swelled to 3,000 members, making it a powerful member of the CSU's coalition.[45] Workers in East Coast studios' financial "home offices" organized into the Screen Office and Professional Employees Guild (SOPEG), an eastern SOEG counterpart, thwarting an IATSE attempt to assert its jurisdiction over all film exchanges nationally.[46] By 1945, SOPEG represented approximately 2,000 employees at "five major producer-distributors."[47]

Then came the CSU strike. In July 1945, SOEG's executive board voted 46 to 2 to recommend that "3000 white collarites stay outside the picket lines."[48] Many SCG and SOEG women supported and participated in the strike, where they balanced activism with pressure to comply with gender norms. As Gerald Horne explains, though radical on labor issues in comparison to the IA, the CSU was not "terribly advanced on gender questions," nearly excluding women from the higher ranks of leadership. Yet "male supremacist ideas among CSU leadership" did not prevent them from depending on "the militance and toil of women workers," featuring scantily clad female strikers in CSU literature and placing female members on the front lines of the conflict even as temperatures rose and violence broke out.[49]

Female strikers, or "glamorous piquettes," quickly became symbols of the strike, photographed picketing in bathing suits or other sexualized, hyperfeminine attire. *Variety* reported on the "eye-catching picketline" of SOEG "bathing beauts on sentry duty" on a summer day outside one studio, quoting Lillian

Hurwitz, then SOEG president, on plans to deploy picketers in shorts and bathing suits elsewhere, explaining "there's nothing like a pretty girl with a generous showing of epidermis to swing the tide in our favor."[50] SOEG women participated in picket line beauty contests and publicity shoots throughout the summer of 1945. *PM New York Daily Magazine* published a photo of June Tracy picketing the Paramount lot in a bathing suit and heels with a sign reading, "Please Don't Cross My Picket Line."[51] Such displays garnered publicity for the strike, disoriented opponents, and were thought to make some visitors less likely to cross the picket.[52]

Women were frequently the architects of such forms of gendered activism, which allowed them to participate in the strike's class struggle without violating long-standing essentialist gender binaries that held women to be the obedient, cooperative, helpful feminine complements to decisional, authoritative, and aggressive men. Stepping outside of this feminine frame might result in social or professional consequences, as in the case of women who were fired for wearing pants to work.[53] In later congressional testimony, Paramount's vice president Y. Frank Freeman implied that the violations of gender norms he had witnessed were the most frightening aspects of the violent, industry-paralyzing strikes, saying, "I have seen women in the picket lines . . . using epithets that I never knew a woman could express or could use. . . . I tell you, it just shakes you from the bottom right on up."[54]

For women of the SOEG who worked in the offices of executives like Freeman, both the ability to strike and the forms of activism available were circumscribed by invisible-yet-real patriarchal boundaries. Strikers in bikinis might be shamed for their risqué attire, for being *too* feminine or sexual, but emulating more masculine forms of protest was arguably a greater taboo. Laurie Pintar compares the gendered contributions of June Tracy to those of Tony Schiavone, a striking carpenter who jumped onstage at a CSU meeting and advocated using the physical force of a thousand picketers to "close Warners tight."[55] These two workers, Pintar explains, "represented highly gendered attempts by workers to empower themselves in their labor struggles against studio producers," whether through sexualized femininity or masculine militancy. Yet while militancy such as Schiavone's has been interpreted as a sign of class consciousness, women's sexualized activism has often been, as Pintar puts it, "dismissed by labor historians as meaningless because it had no apparent connection to traditional understandings of class-conscious behavior."[56]

Despite activists' efforts, the SOEG was hardly a united front. Shortly after the strike authorization, members voted 894 to 666 to ignore the picket lines and keep working, allowing the studios to claim "a semblance of normalcy" with 1,514 members (75 percent) staying on the job while 493 were absent.[57] SOEG was later restrained by a court order from disciplining those who crossed picket lines.[58] Other white-collar guilds similarly waffled, with the Publicists returning to work in defiance of guild leadership.

Female clerical workers, particularly secretaries, had long been cast as the girl Fridays and "work wives" of high-ranking personnel for whom they often worked exclusively and one-on-one, with their loyalty and obligations to "the boss" invariably likened to a familial or marital bond.[59] Script clerks were cast in a similar role as the "director's helper," ally, and mediator on the set. Many relied on long-term relationships with directors and producers for both job security and personal safety on set.[60] This reality bubbled to the surface in script clerk Irma Mae Ross's letter to her boss during the strike. Sounding more like a daughter than an employee, she states, "You have fed me, clothed me, for sixteen years. . . . I Love Warner Brothers."[61] Such relationships, steeped in emotional labor and service, were not switched off as simply as a gaffer's light.

As divisions within CSU deepened, in September 1945, eighteen SOEG members met representatives from five studios and Technicolor to break away from the SOEG and form the Film Office Workers Guild (FOWG).[62] The CSU would later charge the FOWG as a company union, yet the new guild, claiming to represent a majority of the SOEG membership, quickly won recognition from the studios.[63] After the strike ended in 1946, the rival white-collar guilds effectively merged after their members voted to join Local 174 of the AFL-chartered Office Employees International Union (later the Office and Professional Employees International Union [OPEIU]).[64] Local 174 counted 2,400 members in April 1946, when many of them gathered at Hollywood Legion Stadium to adopt its constitution.[65] More than that of the "numerically insignificant plumbers, blacksmiths and steamfitters unions," the loss of "one of the CSU's strongest members" was a blow to Sorrell.[66] The beleaguered CSU would begin to fold later that year.

With the decline of the CSU in the late 1940s and the robust collectivism it represented, "women's already weak position deteriorated further."[67] Following the CSU collapse, the Script Clerks Guild (and later the Script Supervisors Guild) would attempt to affiliate with IATSE several times, only to be rebuffed. The salaries of its predominantly female membership continued to lag behind those of their camera department peers before it successfully affiliated a decade later.[68] The AFL-backed 174 was able to collectively bargain alongside sister unions—IATSE, the Teamsters, and the basic crafts—in the 1950s and 1960s. However, the effects of the Taft-Hartley Act's array of union-weakening measures would slowly destabilize their coalition, further isolating women in feminized trades from fellow unionists.

Feminized Unionization and the Post-Studio Freelancification of Labor

Following the Paramount Decrees of 1948 and economic contractions of forced divestiture, downsizing studios shifted from in-house production, distribution, and exhibition to financing and distributing film projects "packaged" by independent producers and talent agencies. At the same time, both independent producers and studios began branching out into the new medium of television, increasing the number of possible productions and the range of budgets, formats, and schedules. The studios' practice of employing film workers full time was replaced by the "flexible specialization" of labor, in which newly freelance workers were hired on a per-project basis.[69] Work previously carried out in studio planning and craft departments, such as casting or special effects, was outsourced to numerous smaller, more dispersed independent companies.[70] The 1950s through 1970s also saw the creation of new services, filling the void left by the centralized administrative and planning processes each studio carried out in-house, including Entertainment Partners (offering payroll and human resources services), Star Waggons (providing trailer rentals for location production), and Breakdown Services (circulating character descriptions to agents seeking roles for newly freelance actors).

The new flexibility and specialization chiefly benefited employers, who no longer had to pay employees year-round to ensure availability for upcoming productions. The way for such labor arrangements was eased by the Taft-Hartley Act of 1947, federal legislation that sanctioned right-to-work laws and restricted labor unions through an array of measures, including banning jurisdictional strikes, pre-entry closed shops, political strikes, mass picketing, and secondary picketing. Both freelancification and Taft-Hartley complicated labor organizing, creating "a new form of intra-occupational labor market segmentation," based more on differential access to work itself than on hourly wages and altering "the relative bargaining power of employers and workers."[71] These factors pitted workers against each other and undermined union leverage, job security, and solidarity among different unions.

While women benefited from greater career mobility afforded by the freelance era, they were particularly vulnerable to its increased precarity and contraction of organized labor. Script supervisors now worked "picture to picture," securing each job individually, negotiating their own contracts, and endeavoring to please the producers, directors, and executives who might hire them for a future project.[72] Although this was true for other crew members, script supervisors were more vulnerable to the precarity of the times than their Directors Guild of America (DGA) and IATSE brethren. For the next decade, the Script Supervisors Guild, as it was renamed, tried unsuccessfully to affiliate with both IATSE and the DGA.[73] In the meantime, it joined a coalition of AFL-backed locals, including the seventeen IATSE locals, five basic crafts, and two other independent guilds, to reach an agreement with the Alliance of Motion Picture and Television Producers (AMPTP) for a health and welfare plan.[74]

In 1951, East Coast script clerks, along with production secretaries and on-set production assistants were admitted to IATSE Local 161 Assistant Directors, which had formed in 1944. In 1963, when the DGA admitted the masculinized classes of ADs and second ADs, as well as production assistants—who were far junior to script supervisors on set—only script supervisor and production secretary roles remained in the 161, which was thenceforth reported on by various trades as either "161 Script Supervisors and Production Secretaries" or "161 Script Supervisors & Girls."[75] Over subsequent years, the 161 came to represent an entire class of on-set informational manager roles (script supervisors, production coordinators, production accountants, travel coordinators, payroll accountants) that are in large part feminized or female dominated to this day.

In May 1957, West Coast script supervisors "sick of second-class status in the motion-picture industry" finally secured affiliation with IATSE by a unanimous vote of the Script Supervisors Guild's 120 members, and in 1958 they won "belated recognition from the Producer's association" as IATSE Local 871 Script Supervisors.[76] Like its East Coast counterpart, Local 871 would grow to include other dedicated clerical and informational production roles such as production coordinators. Around the same time, in 1960 IATSE also recognized the Studio Teachers union as Local 884, also part of the basic agreement with the AMPTP to this day.

The formation of Local 871, although important for future contracts and raising script supervisors' wages above their pre-IATSE levels, had little effect on the gender wage gap between script supervisors' wages and those of their production peers (ADs and second ADs) doing similar work. The lower wages for women were established in the film industry prior to the unionization drives of the 1930s (as in the 1928 *Variety* report's base pay of seventy-five dollars for ADs vs. thirty-five dollars for script clerks). These basic levels, with women earning one-half to two-thirds the salary of nearby male peers, provided the base for subsequent salary negotiations. The Equal Pay Act of 1963, barring the consideration of gender in determining pay, exempted white-collar executive, professional, and administrative jobs (in which category script supervisors were reclassified in the early 1950s) until 1972. In 1979, Local 871 business rep Ron Chapel confirmed that he had fought for a contractual script supervisors credit in film and TV "crawls" and been denied, adding that script supervisors faced particular difficulties seeking recognition and pay equity because "in the beginning they were all women and this is an industry that has always paid women less."[77] Gender wage disparities persisted and would come to dominate activism by the 871 in the twenty-first century.

OPEIU Local 174 continued to represent clerical workers at the large studios and labs in negotiations throughout the 1950s and 1960s. Yet their actions were circumscribed by Taft-Hartley and undermined by a lack of solidarity from key Hollywood unions. Teamsters, Painters, and Carpenters locals pledged to support a 1953 strike over insufficient pay at CBS, yet while expressing sympathy with strikers' aims, IATSE and SAG ordered members to cross the picket lines in compliance with their contract's "no strike" clause.[78] A planned 1958 strike on behalf of a small clerical unit at National Screen Service Studios, supported by the International Brotherhood of Teamsters (IBT) and others, was called off when "IATSE union members refused to honor the picket line."[79]

In these decades, Local 174's numbers waxed and waned due to withdrawals by the CBS unit in 1957 and the clerical unit at Desilu (formerly RKO), which joined the Paramount Studio Guild in 1967 when the studios merged.[80] Yet their numbers were back to 2,500 in 1979 even though the 174 was no longer jointly negotiating with IATSE. The problem arose because Rob Krug, the 174 business representative, opened Twentieth Century-Fox negotiations early. The studio reported the misstep to the NLRB to have the union "removed from the industrywide umbrella negotiations" being conducted by IATSE on behalf of a coalition of locals.[81] Ruth Benson, the associate business representative, asserted that in separating the 174 from its coalition, the AMPTP "made it clear they considered us second class citizens because we're predominately female" and "have a greater percentage of minorities represented in our union than in any other."[82] The local struck that September, calling management's offer discriminatory, dividing "us from other unions in the industry."[83] Leaders pledged to stay off the job until they were granted parity with the IATSE contract, which gave members dental and vision benefits and a 15 percent raise—well above what the AMPTP had offered the 174 on its own.

While the strike caused "sporadic" telephone service—it was reported that the wives of executives were "pressed into service to do clerical work"—by its second week, leaders expressed disappointment at "not getting the support that had been promised by their sister locals from the IATSE and Basic Crafts."[84] The SAG National Women's Conference Committee made supportive statements, yet a SAG representative clarified that SAG president Kathleen Nolan, in calling on members to back the strike, "was speaking as a person, not as president of the guild."[85] IATSE locals and basic crafts for the most part ignored the 174's picket and continued to work. With ballots on the new basic contract in the mail to IATSE members, one manager expressed that the minimal support for 174 was "a clear indication that the majority is satisfied with the new offered contract."[86] A few days before IATSE's scheduled vote count, Local 174 ended its strike and accepted a contract for a lower salary bump than the initial rejected offer from the AMPTP (a raise of 11 percent versus the IA's 15 percent, without dental or vision benefits).[87] Local 174 leaders accepted what they believed was management's best offer given the local's weak position, in order to get "back to bargaining at the same time as IATSE," an aim that remained elusive.[88]

When Karen Neumeyer was elected business rep in 1980, the 174 represented 2,300 "clerks, data processors, programmers and secretaries," according to the *Los Angeles Times*, which quoted Neumeyer as saying, "Women in the U.S. today make 59 cents for every dollar that a man makes. The non-union woman makes almost a hundred dollars less per week than the unionized woman. We need unions in this industry for secretaries."[89] In 1982, she managed to avert a strike and get members (80 percent female at the time and earning $400 per week on average) the same benefits package as IA and the basic crafts, as well as to secure a "new multi-employer unit with studios." She explained, "I don't expect that we will go back into IA/Basic crafts bargaining unit," because "the strength of your membership is internal."[90]

While Local 174 has continued through today, this 1982 agreement is seemingly the last to have been covered by the major entertainment industry trades of the era, *Variety* and *The Hollywood Reporter*. Certainly, other records survive. Yet the coincidence of this end in trade coverage—of a predominantly female "non-Hollywood" union organizing creative support staff—with Local 174's uncoupling from IATSE's coalition seems like more than pure chance. In the ensuing decades, the 174's membership shrank in proportion to the total number of clerical workers in the entertainment industry. By the 1990s, most clerical workers would shift from large, unionized clerical units at studios represented by OPEIU to smaller nonunionized units in the production companies and facilities to which studios effectively outsourced much of the production process. This trend away from studio-based work was also reflected in the trajectory of the casting profession.

Though casting directors and executives remained on staff at studios throughout the 1950s and 1960s, casting departments shrank as the number of players under contract dwindled. Independent casting companies formed to serve independent productions.[91] No longer able to rely on studio talent divisions to develop and secure a stable of contract players and stars, freelance casting directors began to work with a pool of actors reaching into the tens of thousands, who had to be hired rather than simply assigned as they were in studio days.[92] Two "pioneers," Lynn Stahlmaster and Marion Dougherty—male and female casting directors, respectively—each "set up independent casting shops," where they mentored many of the top contemporary casting directors into the business.[93] They—and Dougherty in particular—are credited with modernizing casting to fit the requirements of the new freelance system, the emergence of television, and post–World War II cultural, artistic, and aesthetic shifts.

Freelance casting combined some of the more gendered aspects of the old process, such as clerical and informational labor (previously done by secretaries in casting departments) and caring labor of developing and nurturing new talent (previously done by coaches in talent departments), with the role of the agent and studio talent scout (both masculinized until the 1950s) in finding and recognizing talented newcomers. In the hands of predominantly female, freelance casting directors, the role took on greater creative dimensions. Rather than an executive distributing actor assets across a studio slate according to established stereotypes and front-office directives, freelance casting directors functioned more like heads of craft departments, who created specialized approach to costumes, set design, and so on for each new film.[94] Dougherty and others would later be credited with ushering in a new era of naturalistic acting style and a generation of unconventional "stars" from Jon Voight to Glenn Close.

Women were normalized as casting directors by the late 1970s, making them acceptable candidates for vice presidents of casting when studios and networks began gender integration of their executive ranks due to legal and political pressure, because "casting was one area of the industry where companies thought it was safe to put women."[95] Yet, creativity and gender integration came at a cost. Casting's lost, studio-era executive status (and pay) was never recuperated. Freelance casting directors, now essential to the creative process of Hollywood Renaissance filmmakers, went unrecognized by an industry that saw them as "technicians rather than artists," conflated them with secretaries, and refused to acknowledge casting "as an autonomous creative process."[96] Taylor Hackford, a former DGA president, explains why casting directors are now credited as "casting by" rather than "casting director," saying, "The reality is you're not a director. And we take exception to being called a director. You're a casting person, 'casting by,' but I do not call them directors, because they're not."[97] It is an odd rationale when the other creative department heads who work closely with directors in preproduction are the art director and the director of photography. More likely decades of explicit discrimination and implicit bias led peers to refuse to use their century-old title.

This diminution also plays into casting directors' professional esteem—they only became eligible for the Emmy in 1989 and are not currently eligible for an Academy Award—as well as their pay. Their reported average base pay in 1928 was $100, in line with that of other male department heads. Yet Dougherty reportedly said that only women could afford to do casting in its freelance incarnation.[98] According to casting director Mike Fenton, in the 1970s the going rate for casting services was $5,000 to $7,000 *per picture* (to be split between multiple casting directors, associates, and assistants). In 1989, Fenton said, the casting director's rate was essentially unchanged. Meanwhile, the pay for ADs had risen to $2,400 per week.[99]

Unlike their peers in production, casting directors did not unionize even after the freelance shift because the AMPTP and studios had long ago "refused to recognize them, labelling them independent contractors" who were thus not eligible for unions.[100] In 1979, Fenton and a group of peers attempted to affiliate with IATSE as the Casting Directors Guild Local 726.[101] However, the union was almost immediately opposed by a rival faction, which publicly assured "producing companies that even if they are IA signatories they are under no obligation to sign with Local 726."[102] The anti-union faction—fifty out of sixty-four of whom were women—bought a two-page *Variety* ad stating that such a union would have a detrimental effect on their casting functions and "the producers, directors and writers with whom we work."[103] Six months later, *Variety* reported that in the face of protest, the 726 had "gone out of business."[104]

Fenton and his peers attempted to move on from the union scrap by founding the American Society of Casting Directors (later changed to the Casting Society of America [CSA]) in 1982. According to the brief history on the CSA website, this was done to establish professional standards and provide members "with a support organization to further their goals and protect their common interests."[105]

According to Fenton, the new organization represented "any port in a storm. . . . [W]e need a group in which we can deal with our mutual interests."[106]

The feeling one gets from both sides of this controversy is that the anti-union faction did not simply fail to grasp the need for a union but rather delayed unionizing as a strategy for maintaining recent creative inroads. The anti-union group feared a union drive would make enemies of the creative elite, whose acceptance they had sought since the field's freelance female domination. By 1997, when Beth Hymson-Ayer became the first female president of CSA, the organization's 300 members had seemingly reached a consensus about the need "to increase the importance and visibility of casting directors" and "pursue health and pension benefits for our members." Hymson-Ayer explored affiliation with IATSE until CSA members voiced a preference for the DGA. Hymson-Ayer agreed that "it would be a dream to join ranks with the DGA" but stated that "in the past the DGA has not been receptive."[107]

Casting directors, associates, and assistants did eventually unionize, but not in the twentieth century, and not with the DGA or IATSE. Instead, in 2005, with the AMPTP insisting on casting directors' independent contractor status and refusing "to grant casters collective bargaining status," casting directors formed "an unlikely partnership with the International Brotherhood of Teamsters Local 399C."[108] The Teamsters had become a staunch ally in recent years, maintaining "that the casters were employees who had an inherent right to be unionized."[109] A few months prior to the NLRB vote to join the Teamsters, CSA leaders sent a letter to the rank and file that attempted to cut through the factionalism of the past, intoning, "We are virtually the only craft in the film and television industry that is not eligible for some kind of union benefit for working members."[110] The NLRB vote was decisive in favor of the Teamsters. Backed by the Teamsters, casting directors threatened "to walk off the job and have teamster drivers and location managers respect the picket line."[111] This show of strength led to the casting directors' first collectively bargained contract, including health care, welfare, and pension benefits, and was overwhelmingly ratified by 95 percent of members.[112]

Casting directors, like script supervisors and assistants, did not immediately catch up to their peers in masculinized professions on becoming union members. Their outcomes in the present show that this process is ongoing and slow, and for the most precarious of the three it has gone backward. Yet workers continue to agitate for change, often with strategies designed to help fellow media workers recognize the structuring absences, invoked throughout this history, that shaped their professional prospects.

Feminized Unionization in Twenty-First-Century Hollywood

Just as we cannot, in the words of the feminist Charlotte Bunch, "add women and stir" to a workforce and assume discrimination stemming from a centuries-old sexual division of labor will be corrected by their mere presence, neither can we assume that, once women are organized, the same discrimination that kept them out of unions will evaporate, or that outcomes for male trade unionists will accrue equally to their female counterparts.[113] The feminized stigma, the vestiges of historical segmentation, the lack of professional esteem associated with women's work all remain embedded in the entertainment industry and its labor unions, contributing directly to persistent imbalances between historically feminized roles and nearby roles in production. Advocacy projects mounted by these professions in the last decade, such as script supervisors' #ReelEquity, assistants' #PayUpHollywood, and casting directors' public pedagogy about casting's history, raise awareness about ongoing gender-based cultural and structural discrimination.

Even after they were accepted into IATSE, organizing alongside more masculinized locals has had its downsides for script supervisors in Local 871, which as of 2018 was composed of 92 percent women. Of all contemporary production trades, the role is perhaps most widely conceived of as "women's work."[114] In recent years, script supervisors and members of other female-dominated IATSE craft unions, have begun to raise awareness about the unique challenges and problems they experience in male-dominated production spaces and cultural spaces, such as IATSE.

In 2018, the 871 commissioned an independent study to "assess gender bias in comparison for four female dominated (clerical/secretarial) crafts involved in film and television production."[115] This study compared worker salaries to those in nearby male-dominated fields and found that "longstanding gender segregation in film and television productions, a past history of gender stereotyping in these crafts, and a current practice of sexual harassment, gender bias and gender stereotyping, all affect Local 871 members' work opportunities and how the industry values their contributions."[116] The study determined that in each of the four feminized 871 professions it considered—script supervisors, production coordinators, assistant production coordinators, and art department coordinators—workers are paid less than those in nearby male-dominated roles that "perform 'substantially similar' work—requiring similar levels of skill and effort, involving comparable responsibility, and performed under similar working conditions." The comparison evinces the long-standing gaps between male-versus female-dominated professions of similar importance within the production hierarchy, with 871 members taking home between $364 and $2,347 less per week than their male-dominated counterparts (table 1.1).

The study also reported rates of female versus male workers' experience or witnessing of sexual harassment in the previous three years (52 percent of women, 39 percent of men, with 13 percent of the women reporting experiencing or witnessing sexual harassment "often"). Respondents viewed reporting procedures as inadequate and attributed the inaction resulting from complaints to "a culture of fear-driven silence" around reporting, and "concern that filing complaints could lead to 'blacklisting.'"[117] The authors of this study argue that

Table 1.1
Overall Weekly Rates of Pay across All Film and TV Productions in 2016

Job Title (% Female or Male)	Rate
Script supervisor (90% female)	$2,574
First assistant director (77% male)	$4,921
Difference	**$2,347**
Production coordinator (66% female)	$2,119
Key second assistant director (65% male)	$3,298
Difference	**$1,179**
Assistant production coordinator (60% female)	$1,294
Second second assistant director (65% male)	$3,114
Difference	**$1,820**
Art department coordinator (80% female)	$1,374
Key assistant location manager (76% male)	$1,738
Difference	**$364**

SOURCE: Pamela Courkos and Cyrus Mehri, "Script Girls, Secretaries and Stereotypes: Gender Bias in Pay on Film and Television Crews," Prepared for IATSE Local 871 by Working Ideal, June 2018, 48, https://www.workingideal.com/wp-content/uploads/2018/06/Secretaries-Script-Girls-and -Stereotypes.pdf.

both the association with the feminized past and gender-based intimidation and harassment may have led to depressed wages; they suggest that production companies, studios, and unions conduct state and federal legal reviews, directing special attention to the California Fair Pay Act, which ensures that gender, race, and ethnicity do not affect compensation.

According to the organizers, the #ReelEquity campaign created to brand the study's findings sought to showcase gender disparities as a necessary first step to combating the issues they face.[118] Inside male-dominated locals, women's problems are often prioritized below issues that concern "all members" and thus are unlikely to be centered by leadership in a union representing such a broad spectrum of trades. Women of color, who experience widespread racial discrimination, are doubly marginalized.

In October 2019, in the wake of activism related to #MeTooHollywood, the hashtag #PayUpHollywood arose to expose workplace exploitation and abuses experienced by media industry assistants. In town halls and op-eds, assistants highlighted the low pay, lack of formal structure for advancement, and unsafe working conditions endemic in these omnipresent, nonunionized roles.[119] Twenty-first-century assistants—a catch-all title for most administrative/clerical/ secretarial support roles—are less likely to belong to unions or to benefit from their protections than at any time since the 1930s. OPEIU Local 174 counts just 1,700 administrative support workers, employed at Universal, Warner Bros, Sony, Fox, Disney, the Cinematographers Guild, and the Motion Picture Health and

Pension Plan.[120] Meanwhile, the entertainment industry has expanded geographically, increased production, and diversified to include television networks, cable companies, streaming services, and so forth.[121] Given the ubiquity of assistants (one or two for every executive, producer, agent, manager, lawyer, director, A-list actor, publicist, department, production office, and so on), a (very) conservative estimate suggests assistants not organized by the 174 number at least 5,000, if not more. More precise accounting for the number of assistants—for the purpose of unionization efforts—is complicated by a lack of oversight, structure, or accountability for these roles, as well as their temporary nature.

No longer able to hire exclusively women for low-paid, low-status jobs without prospects for promotion, many employers frame assistant roles as a quasi-apprenticeship.[122] Just as a Victorian employer dictated his male clerk's working conditions and mobility through the business world, employers hire aspiring film workers as assistants at poverty-level wages, with the promise that "paying dues" in these roles will eventually earn the worker promotion to the elite circles of Hollywood.[123] Contemporary assistant salaries start at between $500 and $1,000 per week, typically without company benefits, overtime, or paid leave. Those who are paid hourly—at the major agencies, for example—have reported being instructed not to report overtime and being punished for doing so.[124] With few exceptions, neither the OPEIU nor any other entity regulates the duration, conditions, or pay of these pseudo-apprenticeships; there is no guarantee the assistant will ever "graduate" beyond these roles.

Unionization remains an elusive goal for these non-OPEIU assistants, whose ubiquity makes them difficult to count or collectivize, and whose aspirations compete with notions of solidarity. Assistants considering collective action are told they will be replaced with eager aspirants and will "never work in this town again."[125] Yet under the #PayUpHollywood banner, assistants have met and shared their stories, created an emergency COVID-19 relief fund, conducted two annual surveys of assistants, and generated steady press coverage around their plight. While public pressure on employers is one clear objective of #PayUpHollywood, its most important product may ultimately be data collection by and counting and collectivizing of assistants—key early steps in forming unions.

Unionizing through the Teamsters has remedied some disparities between casting directors and peers, particularly their much-lamented lack of retirement and health benefits. Yet they remain one of the lowest-paid department heads and are still ineligible for Oscars. Owing perhaps to their proximity to "management" (production's creative elite) and their greater access to the press by virtue of creative proximity to productions, casting directors seem wary of stridently demanding their due or airing grievances via hashtagged calls for change. Instead, their meta-trade discourse focuses on building consensus among their peers. In public-facing interviews and events, casting directors engage in consistent, collegial pedagogy about what some label the "story of casting," highlighting ongoing inequities resulting from the feminized past and asserting the profession's import—a subtler strategy that has nonetheless begun to bear fruit. Two events—the 2013 release of documentary *Casting By* and the 2019 election of casting director David Rubin to the presidency of the Academy of Motion Picture Arts and Sciences (AMPAS)—prompted a fuller articulation of this "story of casting" strategy in the press.

Produced independently of the CSA and directed by Tom Donahue, *Casting By* was quickly embraced by Rubin and fellow casting directors for its history of the profession and mythologization of Dougherty as the "great woman" in casting's heroic journey toward modernization. Dougherty's interventions lend themselves to the sort of lore that has imbued film history's "great men" and esteemed professions with value. At the same time, by exposing the gender-based discrimination experienced by casting directors, *Casting By* implicitly argues the importance of the creative collective over the romanticized trope of the lone auteur, bravely fighting for his vision—invoked by the likes of Taylor Hackford.[126] The film sparked a wave of press lauding casting directors as "the unsung heroes of film" and became the focus of CSA events and public discussion.

Casting directors credit Rubin as an important architect of this pedagogical and persuasive strategy, which he advocated for within the CSA and modeled over years of work serving on various AMPAS committees and its board of governors. Rubin's ascent to the role of president in 2019 prompted another wave of coverage in which fellow casting directors explained the significance of a casting director presiding over an academy that had no casting branch until the 2010s, invariably alluding, again, to the "story of casting." As one profile from 2019 explains, Rubin "recognized that the industry didn't wholly understand casting directors' largely behind-the-scenes role" and sought "to tell the story of how the modern-day concept of the casting director was invented in the '50s and '60s." Consensus-building is explained as a necessary part of "laying the groundwork for casting directors to have their own branch within the Academy," from which Rubin "saw the branch as a perch from which Hollywood could be educated about casting and lobby for the awards eligibility." [127]

In 2013, owing to these combined forms of advocacy through pedagogy, AMPAS created its casting branch. In 2016, it held events—organized by Rubin—celebrating "The Art of the Casting Director" and awarding the first honorary Oscar for casting to Lynn Stalmaster, Dougherty having died in 2011 after the Academy rejected a campaign to award her one in 1996.[128] Though there is as yet no casting Oscar, the prospect has become ever more likely since the strategic telling of the "story of casting" began.

Conclusion

These brief labor histories suggest that workers from marginalized groups experience creative industries, creative collaboration, and collective organizing differently from their white and male peers. Casting directors, script supervisors, and assistants should not have to build consensus around basic equity, convince IATSE of the unevenness of a playing field it referees, or publicly shame their industry into paying them a living wage. Such matters should and likely would have been addressed by Hollywood's unions, had they accepted women, worked continuously on their behalf, and measured union strength by that of their weakest or most vulnerable members.

The past has not passed: whether to lower labor costs, disrupt organizing, or symbolically correct negative public perceptions, today's entertainment industry continues to channel workers into particular pipelines and to extract their labor in *this* but not *that* way according to race, gender identity, and other immutable aspects of who they are. Of course, the female workers portrayed in this chapter—who were and to a degree still are segmented by race, ethnicity, and class—cannot serve as stand-ins for other marginalized workers' facing unique challenges. Rather, their cases suggest further avenues for intersectional research into the dueling logics of labor segmentation and unionization in industrialized creative production.

Notes

1 I use this term to encompass both feminization's gender typing of labor and the hidden, gender-based expectations that accrued to feminized professions once women were on the job. Erin Hill, *Never Done: A History of Women's Work in Media Production* (Rutgers University Press, 2016).

2 Alice Kessler-Harris, *Women Have Always Worked*, 2nd ed. (University of Illiniois Press, 2018), 65.

3 Sharon Hartman Strom, "'Light Manufacturing': The Feminization of American Office Work, 1900–30," *Industrial and Labor Relations Review* 43, no. 1 (October 1989): 60; Clive Edwards, "'Home is Where the Art is': Women, Handicrafts and Home Improvements, 1750–1900," *Journal of Design History* 19, no. 1 (Spring 2006): 11–21.

4 Lois Rita Helmbold and Ann Schofield, "Women's Labor History, 1790–1945," *Reviews in American History* 17, no. 4 (December 1989): 511–512. On African American women's labor, see Kessler-Harris, *Women Have Always Worked*, 92.

5 Lisa Fine, *The Souls of the Skyscrapers: Female Clerical Workers in Chicago, 1870–1930* (Temple University Press, 1990), 12.

6 Marjorie Davies, *Women's Place Is at the Typewriter: Office Work and the Office Worker, 1870–1930* (Temple University Press, 1982), 28–38.

7 Alba M. Edwards, *Comparative Occupation Statistics for the United States, 1870–1940*, Part of the Sixteenth Census of the United States: 1940 (Government Printing Office, 1943), tables 9 and 10, reprinted in Davies, *Women's Place Is at the Typewriter*, 178–179.

8 Sharon Hartman Strom, *Beyond the Typewriter: Gender, Class, and the Origins of Modern American Office Work, 1900–1930* (University of Illinois Press, 1994), 175.

9 Kessler-Harris, *Women Have Always Worked*, 72–73.

10 Quoted in Kessler-Harris, 73–74.

11 On racism, segregation, and organizing, see Kessler-Harris, 79–85.

12 On strikes and objections by male trade unionists, see Kessler-Harris, 73–75.

13 Kessler-Harris, 82.
14 Cari Beauchamp, *Without Lying Down: Frances Marion and the Powerful Women of Early Hollywood* (University of California Press, 1997), 11–12.
15 Michael C. Nielsen, "Labor Power and Organization in the Early U.S. Motion Picture Industry," *Film History* 2, no. 2 (June–July 1988): 122.
16 Karen Ward Mahar, "Doing a Man's Work," in *The Classical Hollywood Reader*, ed. Steven Neale (Routledge, 2012), 83.
17 Female-friendly occupations of the 1910s and early 1920s are detailed in Mertyl Gebhart, "Business Women in Film Studios," *Business Women*, December 1923.
18 Development of early continuity roles into feminized "women's work" in: Hill, *Never Done*, 177–179.
19 "Peggy Robertson Oral History," interview by Barbara Hall, Oral History Collection, Margaret Herrick Library (hereafter MHL), 1995, 55.
20 June Mathis, "The Feminine Mind in Picture Making," *Film Daily*, June 7, 1925, 115.
21 On Latina garment workers, see John H. M. Laslett, "Gender, Class, or Ethno-Cultural Struggle? The Problematic Relationship between Rose Pesotta and the Los Angeles ILGWU," *California History* 72, no. 1 (Spring 1993): 23–24.
22 Script supervisors and emotional labor are detailed in Hill, *Never Done*, 183–187.
23 "Alma Young Oral History," interview by Anthony Slide and Robert Gitt, MHL, 1977, 3.
24 "Studios' Average Pay," *Variety*, February 1, 1929, 3.
25 "About Us," IATSE Local 884, accessed July 29, 2024, thestudioteachers.com/about-us/.
26 "Alma Young Oral History," MH, 4–5.
27 Marjory Adams, "Woman Readers Show Interest in a Hollywood Job," *Daily Boston Globe*, December 20, 1959, A10.
28 "Script Clerk Salaries Save Overtime Check," *The Hollywood Reporter* (hereafter *THR*), September 24, 1931, 2.
29 "Scripters and Assts.," *Variety*, January 16, 1934, 6.
30 "Guild Troubles Again in Spotlight This Week," *THR*, November 1, 1937, 1.
31 "Two Minor Guilds Await Pact Talks," *THR*, January 21, 1938, 2.
32 "All Major Lots Ink Script Clerks Pact," *THR*, April 25, 1940, 2.
33 "Some 6,000 Studio Workers' Status under Nat'l Labor Act to Be Probed," *Variety*, March 12, 1941, 18.
34 Gerald Horne, *Class Struggle in Hollywood, 1930–60: Moguls, Mobsters, Stars, Reds, and Trade Unionists* (University of Texas Press, 2001), 52; "H'wood Crafts in Concerted Move to Thwart Jurisdiction Drive of IA," *Variety*; February 23, 1938, 1, 7; "Guilds Agree on Resolution to Guard Autonomy," *THR*, April 14, 1938, 1–2.
35 Thomas Doherty, "The Crew Strike that Shut Down Hollywood," *THR*, September 28, 2021.
36 "Columbia Pictures Corporation et al, and Screen Office Employees Guild (Ind.)," Cases Nos. R-2035 to R-044 inclusive, National Labor Relations Board, decided October 8, 1940, https://casetext.com/admin-law/columbia-pictures-corp-18; "SOEG Okayed by NLRB to Rep 7 Pix," *Variety*, November 27, 1940), 23.
37 "United White Collar Guild SOEG Tentatively Set Up," *THR*, December 9, 1939, 4.
38 "SOEG Holds Prexy," *Variety*, May 19, 1943, 13; "SOEG Counsels 'Give Top Service,'" *Variety*, July 18, 1945, 27.
39 "Fight White Collar Grab," *Variety*, June 5, 1940, 7, 19.
40 "SOEG Victor in Studios' Balloting: NLRB Election Decides Problem," *RKO Studio News*, November 1940, 2.
41 "AFL Brushoff by NLRB on Pix Clerks," *Variety*, October 16, 1940.

42 "Para. Office Group Signs 2 Year Pact," *THR*, July 11, 1940, 6.

43 "White-Collar Workers Talk Walkout" *Variety*, August 27, 1941, 7; "Studio White Collars Granted Wage Demands," *Variety*, September 10, 1941, 6; "Guilds, Unions Unite in Plea for Probe of Wage-Hr. Law Violations," *Variety*, December 11, 1940, 15; "More Back Pay for White Collarites," *Variety*, October 8, 1941, 7

44 "SOEG Settles for 8%," *Variety*, May 13, 1942, 23

45 "Collarites Move on Radio," *Variety*, January 17, 1945, 7; "Film Guild Unit Breaks Away," *Los Angeles Times* (hereafter *LAT*), September 7, 1945, A2.

46 "Fight White Collar Grab," 7, 19. "White-Collarites' Union Status to Get Airing," *Variety*, December 29, 1943.

47 "SOPEG's New Pact with N.Y. Majors Covers 2,000," *Variety*, July 18, 1945, 27.

48 Horne, *Class Struggle in Hollywood*, 171.

49 Horne, 277–278, 236.

50 "Cheesecake Picketing," *Variety*, August 1, 1945, 9.

51 *PM New York Daily Magazine*, September 2, 1945, reprinted in Laurie Pintar, "Off-Screen Realities: A History of Labor Activism in Hollywood, 1933–1947" (PhD diss., University of Southern California, 1995), 4.

52 *People's Daily World*, September 28, 1945, quoted in Horne, *Class Struggle in Hollywood*, 171.

53 "Around and About in Hollywood," *LAT*, July 7, 1937, 10.

54 *Jurisdictional Disputes in the Motion-Picture Industry: Hearings Before a Special Subcommittee of the Committee on Education and Labor, House of Representatives, Eightieth Congress*, 1st sess., pursuant to H. Res. 111 (Eightieth Congress), 1948, 116.

55 Pintar, "Off-Screen Realities," 4.

56 Pintar, 4.

57 "Teamsters, Collarites, Cross Lines As H'wood Strike Enters 21st Week," *Variety*, August 1, 1945, 9.

58 Horne, *Class Struggle in Hollywood*, 172.

59 See Mervyn LeRoy, as told to Alyce Canfield, *It Takes More Than Talent* (Knopf, 1953), 145–147.

60 Hill, *Never Done*, 186–187.

61 Irma Mae Ross to Warner, October 17, 1945, Box 6, Folder 10, Jack Warner Collection, quoted in Horne, *Class Struggle in Hollywood,* 178.

62 "New Studio Office Guild Forms," *THR*, September 10, 1945, 1.

63 "Film Guild Unit Breaks Away," *LAT*, September 7, 1945, A2; "company unions" resolution in "SPG, SOEG Bolstered," *Variety*, December 12, 1945, 23.

64 "Strike Finally Over," *THR*, October 31, 1945, 14.

65 "OEIU to Hold First Meeting at Stadium," *THR*, April 2, 1946, 15.

66 "Sorrell CSU Hits Skids as OEIU, SEG Score Gains," *THR*, March 8, 1946, 42.

67 Horne, *Class Struggle in Hollywood*, 53.

68 "Script Supervisors Vote IA Affiliation," *Variety*, May 29, 1957, 5.

69 Allen J. Scott, *On Hollywood: The Place, the Industry* (Oxford University Press, 2005), 39.

70 David A. Cook, *Lost Illusions: American Cinema in the Shadow of Watergate and Vietnam, 1970–1979* (University of California Press, 2002), 21–22.

71 Susan Christopherson and Michael Storpor, "The Effects of Flexible Specialization on Industrial Politics and the Labor Market: The Motion Picture Industry," *ILR Review* 42, no. 3 (April 1989): 331.

72 Meta Carpenter Wilde and Orin Borsten, *A Loving Gentleman: The Love Story of William Faulkner and Meta Carpenter* (Simon and Schuster, 1976), 304.

73 "Script Supervisors Vote IA Affiliation," 5.

74 "Draft of Benefits Taking in 25 Worker Groups Being Presented to Major Studios," *THR*, March 25, 1952, 1, 6. At this point, only the white-collar, feminized, or mixed script supervisors, publicists, and story analysts guilds remained from the 1940s.

75 ADs depart, leaving "script clerks" in Local 161 in "N.Y. Assistants Move into Directors Guild," *Variety*, January 8, 1964, 24; reported on as "Script Supervisors and Production Secretaries" in "Local 161, IATSE Opens Offices on 57 St," *Back Stage*, March 6, 1964, 9–10; versus "Script Supervisors & Girls" in: "Script Supervisors & Girls (Local 161) Settle Their Plautus Pay Dispute," *Variety*, January 12, 1966, 3.

76 "Script Supervisors Vote IA Affiliation," 5; Wilde and Borsten, *Loving Gentleman*, 304.

77 Eunice Field, "Script Supervisors Annoyed at Being Blamed for 'Bloopers,'" *THR*, December 21, 1979, 20–21.

78 "Picketing in Full Swing in CBS Offices Strike," *LAT*, May 22, 1953, 9.

79 "Call Off Strike at NSS," *THR*, May 12, 1958, 4.

80 "Hollywood CBS Office Workers Reject OEIU in NLRB Balloting," *Broadcasting, Telecasting*, June 10, 1957, 92; "Par Studio Union Outvotes Local 174," *Variety*, October 4, 1967, 18.

81 Eunice Field, "Union, Producers Caucusing after 6 Hours of Mediation," *THR*, October 4, 1979, 1, 21.

82 Eunice Field, "174 Strike Supported by SAG, NOW," *THR*, October 1, 1979, 1, 3.

83 Eunice Field, "Talks Halt; Local Hits Technicolor following Deluxe," *THR*, September 27, 1979, 1, 4.

84 Field, "174 Strike Supported," 1, 3.

85 Eunice Field, "Striking Locals Still Stalemated; Pickets Remain," *THR*, October 3, 1979, 1, 17.

86 Field, "174 Strike Supported," 1, 3.

87 Eunice Field, "Local 174 Turmoil Has Neumeyer Replacing Krug," *THR*, May 28, 1980, 1, 17.

88 Field, "Local 174 Turmoil," 1, 17.

89 Charles Schreger, "A Woman Leader of a Screen Union," *LAT*, June 23, 1980, G4.

90 Arnold Schmidt, "Last-Minute Agreement Prevents Strike; Local 174 Ratifies Pact," *THR*, October 13, 1982, 1, 4.

91 This transition is detailed in Michael J. Bandler, "Casting Is His Lot," *American Way*, November 1982, 22; "CSA Searches for Respect, Identity in 'New' Hollywood," *Daily Variety*, June 26, 1989, I-32; Dan Holloway, "'Casting By,' Aims to Give Casting Directors Credit Where Due, *Backstage*, July 25, 2013, https://www.backstage.com/magazine/article/casting-aims-give-casting-directors-credit-due-13078/.

92 Hill, *Never Done*, 200–208.

93 Chris O'Falt, "David Rubin Led Casting Directors Out of the Wilderness. Can He Do the Same for the Academy?," *Indiewire*, August 8, 2019, https://www.indiewire.com/2019/08/academy-president-casting-director-david-rubin-oscars-1202164231/.

94 Studio era talent and casting process described in Ronald L. Davis, *The Glamour Factory: Inside Hollywood's Big Studio System* (Southern Methodist University Press, 1993), 91.

95 Mollie Gregory, *Women Who Run the Show: How a Brilliant and Creative New Generation of Women Stormed Hollywood* (St. Martin's Press, 2002), 11.

96 Glenn Collins, "For Casting, Countless Auditions and One Couch, Never Used," *New York Times,* January 30, 1990, C15; references to secretaries by Jane Jenkins, quoted in Jessica Gardner, "And the Oscar Doesn't Go To," *Backstage*, August, 15, 2012.

97 Beth Hanna, "Review: Documentary, 'Casting By' Heralds the Unsung Yet Crucial Art of the Casting Director," *Indiewire*, October 24, 2013, https://www.indiewire .com/2013/10/review-documentary-casting-by-heralds-the-unsung-yet-crucial-art-of -the-casting-director-195419/.

98 Don Shewey, "They Comb New York to Give Its Movies a Special Look," *New York Times*, April 11, 1982, 19.

99 Steve Dyan, "Casting Directors Cast Their Fate with Teamsters," *Variety*, June 24, 2005, 55; Fenton quoted in "CSA Searches for Respect," I-118–I-119.

100 O'Falt, "David Rubin Led Casting Directors."

101 "CSA Searches for Respect," I-118–I-119.

102 "Casting Director Unionism Dispute," *Variety*, December 19, 1979, 5.

103 Unionization goals described in Will Tusher, "More American Actors Sought in O'Seas Pix," *Daily Variety*, September 21, 1983, 1; anti-union ad, "Untitled Ad," *Daily Variety*, March 25, 1980, 32.

104 "Casting Directors 'Union' Ended," *Variety*, November 26, 1980, 16.

105 "A Brief History of CSA," Casting Society of America web page, accessed January 1, 2022, https://www.castingsociety.com/about/history.

106 Will Tusher, "Revamped Casting Assn. Targets Offshore Jobs for U.S. Talents," *Variety*, September 28, 1983, 6, 28.

107 David Robb, "Hymson-Ayer CSA President," *THR*, January 16, 1997, 1, 58.

108 Jessie Hiestand, "Casters in with the Teamsters," *THR*, June 24, 2005, 1, 29.

109 Mary McNamara, "Casting Directors to Seek Benefits," *LAT*, January 14, 2005.

110 Roger Armbrust, "Casting Directors Meet, Talk Strike," *Backstage*, December 17–30, 2004, 26, 37.

111 Jessie Hiestand, "Casters in with the Teamsters," *THR*, June 24, 2005, 1, 29.

112 O'Falt, "David Rubin Led Casting Directors."

113 The quote "You can't just add women and stir" is credited to Bunch in articles by dozens of feminist scholars though the sources cited vary. For example, see "Visions and Revisions: Women and the Power to Change" (NWSA Convention, Lawrence, Kansas, June 1979) and excerpts were published in Women's Studies Newsletter 7, no. 3 (Summer 1979): 20–21.

114 "Script Girls, Secretaries, and Stereotypes" infographic, IATSE Local 871, accessed January 1, 2022, https://www.ialocal871.org/Reel-Equity/Infographic.

115 Pamela Courkos and Cyrus Mehri, "Script Girls, Secretaries and Stereotypes: Gender Bias in Pay on Film and Television Crews," Working Ideal for IATSE Local 871, June 2018, https://www.workingideal.com/wp-content/uploads/2018/06 /Secretaries-Script-Girls-and-Stereotypes.pdf.

116 "#ReelEquity Open Letter to the Entertainment Industry," IATSE Local 871, May 15, 2018, https://www.ialocal871.org/Reel-Equity/.

117 Courkos and Mehri, "Script Girls, Secretaries and Stereotypes," 13.

118 Phone interview by author, Los Angeles, 2018.

119 Nardine Saad, "#PayUpHollywood Explained: Industry Assistants Speaking Out about Their Wages," *LAT*, October 16, 2019; Liz Alper, "#PayUpHollywood Releases Survey of 1500 Entertainment Industry Assistants' Pay, Working Conditions," *Paradise-Delivered*, December 3, 2019; Liz Alper, "I Started #PayUpHollywood & 'The Assistant' Is a Spot-On Look at Our Plight," *Bustle.com*, January 31, 2020, https://www.bustle.com/p/i-started-payuphollywood-the-assistant-is-a-spot -on-look-at-our-plight-21767164.

120 Home page, OPEIU Local 174, accessed, January 1, 2022, https://www.opeiu174.org.

121 MPAA, "What We Do: Driving Economic Growth," Motion Picture Association, accessed January 10, 2022, https://www.motionpictures.org/what-we-do/driving-economic-growth/.

122 Davies, *Woman's Place Is at the Typewriter,* 18.

123 John T. Caldwell, M. J. Clarke, Erin Hill, and Eric Vanstrom, "Distributed Creativity in Film and Television," in *The International Encyclopedia of Media Production*, ed. Vicki Mayer (Blackwell, 2012), 393–419.

124 Nikki Finke, "New Pay Schedule for WME Assistants," *Deadline,* July 29, 2009, http://www.deadline.com/2009/07/more-news-about-wme-assistant-pay/.

125 Erin Hill, "Hollywood Assistanting," in *Production Studies*, ed. Vicki Mayer, Miranda Banks, and John Caldwell (Routledge, 2009), 220–224.

126 Hanna, "Review: Documentary, 'Casting By.'"

127 O'Falt, "David Rubin Led Casting Directors."

128 Chris O'Falt, "'Casting By' Asks Why Casting Directors Are Hollywood's Second-Class Citizens," *THR*, November 1, 2013.

2

Backlot Work

• •

The Working-Class Backbone
of Hollywood's Unions

KATIE BIRD

Before a scene is shot, it must first be put into place by Hollywood's backlot workers. *Backlot workers* is a useful term for the individuals responsible for the physical labor of setting, resetting, and striking the vast array of materials and equipment on set. These workers represent a wide swath of professions and are represented by a variety of Hollywood and craft unions. Backlot workers include industrial labor and basic crafts (drivers, general laborers); building crafts (electricians, carpenters, plasterers); and craft studio mechanics (machinists, grips, electricians, lamp operators, stagehands, property workers, riggers). Today, many of these workers are represented by four International Alliance of Theatrical Stage Employees (IATSE, or the IA) Hollywood locals—Local 44 (Props), Local 80 (Grips, Crafts Service, Medics, Warehouse Workers), Local 728 (Electrical Lighting Technicians), and Local 729 (Set Painters)—that were created after the breakup of the powerful Studio Mechanics Local 37 in 1939. Other backlot workers belong to traditional basic craft unions such as the International Brotherhood of Electrical Workers (IBEW) and the United Brotherhood of Carpenters and Joiners of America (UBC, or the Carpenters). Like the other IATSE unions covered in this volume, the grips, prop workers, lighting technicians, and set painters that are the focus of this chapter do work that is substantially different in Hollywood than in other industries and that contributes significantly to the media produced.

Historically, backlot workers were organized along both industrial and craft lines. Industrial unions such as IATSE unionized workers based on where they worked (i.e., stage, live performance, studio, or exhibition). They faced opposition from more traditional craft unions representing workers whose employment was tied to a longer tradition of materials and practices such as the building and basic crafts (i.e., carpentry, electrical, transportation, and labor). While IATSE ultimately set up craft locals in Hollywood, the early attempts to organize backlot workers employed an industry strategy, as would later organizations such as the National Association of Broadcast Employees and Technicians (NABET).

The history of backlot workers is often positioned less as a case of labor versus management than as one of infighting between various unions. Industrial and craft union leadership fought for control over a mass of workers, giving them little say in union politics. The major industrial unions that competed for and represented these workers included IATSE, the IBEW, the Teamsters, NABET, the UBC, the Laborers International Union of North America Local 724 (LiUNA), and the International Association of Machinists, as well as a whole host of smaller, localized, and independent splinter unions.

Backlot unions, partially due to the perception of the workers as manual laborers and of their contributions as unskilled or less artistic, often have less leverage at the bargaining table than their above-the-line (writers, actors, directors) or even below-the-line peers (editors and cinematographers). As Hugh Lovell and Tasile Carter noted in their survey *Collective Bargaining in the Motion Picture Industry* (1955), "The contribution of the 'back-lot' worker is one of technical rather than artistic skill and, as a general rule, his individual bargaining power is not sufficient to win him concessions above those contained in the union agreement."[1] This notion of backlot labor as replaceable has persisted throughout the history of the film and television industries and has been reinforced by the failure of backlot union leadership to show how specialized craft work is not easily replicated just because it is physical.

What the backlot workers lack in prestige, they make up for in numbers—which can be financially valuable in the case of union dues and politically significant in terms of strike power. The fact that the backlot represents such a large swath of workers has been at the heart of the long history of jurisdictional disputes. As a bargaining unit, backlot workers have been most concerned with their own employment. These unions have focused their efforts on three basic concerns: wages, safety, and job security. These crafts across their history regularly made more than the national averages in wages for similarly physical jobs in other building or industrial crafts, but as is common throughout the Hollywood industry, their employment was often less reliable on a week-to-week or month-to-month basis. Thus, additional wins through collective bargaining for ten cents more an hour, overtime, and location pay were significant gains while percentage wage cuts and hourly restrictions were serious losses.

Rank-and-file workers who worked long physical hours, under hot lights, moving heavy equipment regularly voiced concern about on-set safety. Safety concerns frequently also related to geographic jurisdiction: how far workers needed to commute to locations, sleep, travel, and protections to avoid bodily injury. Finally, rank-and-file backlot workers were most concerned with job stability, which could be improved through closed-shop agreements and seniority protections that guaranteed experienced members first call over less experienced or apprentice members.

The kinds of work performed by individual backlot workers are highly diverse, but the demographic makeup of backlot crafts' rank and file has been historically homogeneous. Most backlot workers have been and still identify as white and cis-male.[2] In early periods of stagecraft and the studio system, the socioeconomic background of backlot workers was primarily working class. The absence of white women and people of color within the backlot ranks was a result of earlier racial and gender segregation policies within the industrial unions. The demographic makeup of the backlot unions today has shifted somewhat (particularly in Latino representation) thanks to challenges by the Equal Employment Opportunity Commission (EEOC) in the 1970s and diversity, equity, and inclusion (DEI) campaigns in the 2010s, but the bulk of backlot workers today remain white and male thanks largely to familial and fraternal nepotism networks that are informally baked into backlot craft training and hiring systems.[3]

In describing such a large array of workers bunched together under the catch-all moniker of "backlot workers," it is necessary to try to avoid the double erasure of their unique crafts and thus their unique labor demands. These workers are some of the least documented in Hollywood history. They did not have their own craft organizations to publicize their artistic contributions or air their grievances, and are barely mentioned in industry trade publications, their own international's *IATSE Bulletin*, or local labor papers such as the *Los Angeles Citizen-News*. The voices of individual workers are also missing from the archives, as there was infrequent communication between the rank and file and the often-enormous international organizations that represented them. As a result, it is difficult to speculate on how workers understood their grievances and needs. This chapter balances the official unions' records of these diverse groups of workers with rank-and-files members' own underrepresented labor concerns to show how backlot workers struggled to form a cohesive front that represented workers' interests to their union and in the face of management.

From Stage Mechanics to Studio Mechanics

IATSE was the first union to attempt to organize motion picture workers, as many early backlot workers were, in fact, theatrical stage workers borrowed by the budding film industry. The stage workers unionized by what would become IATSE in 1886 faced many of the same concerns voiced by backlot workers today, including wage reductions, job threats from nonunion outsiders, and working conditions that involved long working hours and travel-related risks. Early stage-craft workers included stage mechanics, a group of general stage laborers who later specialized in carpentry, lighting, and property work.[4] Like the backlot workers later, stage mechanics were concerned with protections against management who sought to take advantage of their professional instability. IATSE, borrowing from the bylaws of New York Local 1 stagehands, set in place a system of protections that included strict jurisdiction of tasks, an eight-hour working day, pay rates for specific classifications, and provisions prohibiting the practice of using non–stage mechanics (such as actors) for specialized stagecraft tasks.[5]

IATSE Local 33 initially formed as a theatrical local, but by 1911 the Los Angeles–area stagehand union signaled its intent to focus its energies on motion picture workers by declaring their home rule (local authority) jurisdiction across the whole of Los Angeles County.[6] As production companies and studios rapidly expanded, becoming among the largest employers in the city, the new industry quickly exhausted the Local 33 labor supply. Other unions such as the Carpenters tried to help meet the demand for workers, but Local 33 had to open its doors to IA members from other jurisdictions.[7] By 1914, IATSE already faced its first significant jurisdictional dispute over film workers between Los Angeles building trades unions and Local 33.

A year later, Local 33 found that despite its success organizing the new industry in a growing town, the New York–based IATSE leaders sought to dismantle one of the union's earliest tenants of home rule and exert greater organizational control from afar. By 1916, the American Federation of Labor (AFL), which oversaw both IATSE and several of the other craft unions, sent representatives to Los Angeles to help organize the various competing locals. But the power struggles between the basic craft locals, the IA, and the AFL often came at the detriment to rank-and-file workers, who, despite the demands for production labor, still found that employment was "irregular" and often on "short notice," meaning that permanent employment was rarely attainable for individual workers.[8]

The stage workers and carpenters struggled the most to secure consistent or even daily employment. As Mike Nielsen and Gene Mailes explain, "The unions should have been a source of strength for the workers; however, both the AFL craft unions and the IA, in order to gain a foothold in the industry, made deals with the producers to cut wage rates for the studio work."[9] So, while the unions purportedly offered what workers needed—job security, wages, and better working conditions—workers found themselves fighting as individuals for whatever morsels they could get at the morning shape-up at the gates. During the early open-shop period, the stagecraft and building craft workers who would become backlot workers succeeded in being hired by rising in the early hours of the morning and "panning the gates" for day work at various studios. The workers on the lots varied from day to day, and the studio practices and manual work of moving sets, operating lights, setting reflectors and diffusions, and constructing rigging varied across studios.

Studio mechanic workers often found themselves performing a range of jobs under the moniker the "iron-gang." While this term would later come to be used primarily to describe crews of electricians who moved from stage to stage, but did not operate the lights during shoots, at the time it often colloquially stood in for general manual studio workers (including grips, painters, carpenters, lamp operators, and electricians) who were hired and laid off daily.[10] Location work was often the most grueling, as many early film workers performed their tasks outside on the city's streets. As Jim Noblitt, a grip, explained, location work was often more strenuous than backlot work: "On location you're up earlier, and you go to bed earlier because you're so tired. In those days you worked in the sand and the dirt. The equipment was heavy, and you didn't have near the help on location that you had at the studio. . . . Out on location you carried it all. It was very tiresome."[11]

Studio work required a different form of endurance. According to Nielsen, it was not uncommon for a studio worker to eat breakfast at 3:00 A.M. and begin rigging electric and sets by 4:00 A.M. These long days, often without meal breaks, also meant that these workers, "perched on high scaffolding and working in the intense heat given off by the arc lamps, would sometimes pass out under such extreme stress and sustain serious injuries. Without union representation workers who objected to such long stretches without food could simply be dismissed."[12] During this period, the cost of even small infractions such as breaking a piece of equipment could be deducted from a worker's daily wages, and sitting down during the workday could lead to a discharge.[13] But with so many workers to organize and threats from other unions, the various locals were less interested in addressing working conditions and more preoccupied with the politics of amassing membership numbers and jurisdictional control.

Organizing pressure continued after World War I as further wage reductions were justified as part of a larger postwar deflationary trend.[14] The IBEW and UBC ramped up their efforts against IATSE, whose strike in 1918 for union recognition and wage reconciliation was threatened by carpenters who acted as scabs. Seeing little alternative, the IA settled for consistent wages but was not granted union recognition by producers until 1919. However, at the following year's AFL convention, the governing body voted that IATSE had encroached on the building trades' jurisdiction. While IATSE could keep projectionists and electricians, it was forced to relinquish claims over carpenters, plasterers, painters, and other laborers—the first attempt to differentiate who would be represented by IATSE and who would be in traditional craft unions among the backlot workers.[15]

In July 1921, producers blamed skyrocketing star salaries for 12 percent wage cuts and increased hours (from eight- to ten-hour days) for studio mechanics.

As a result, IATSE called 1,200 members to stop working, effectively shutting down production for the remainder of that summer.[16] Rather than appeasing workers, producers saw this as an opportunity to slash their own production budgets and avoid paying higher salaries to talent. Despite IATSE's production shutdown, its workers' needs were not met. In the next two years, the IBEW, the Carpenters, and Painters chartered specific studio locals to unite against IATSE. Each union often had to negotiate far lower on wages for fear that an outside union would easily underbid them. As Murray Ross explains, "It was not uncommon for one local to offer its men at a price somewhat lower than another was asking for artisans of similar qualifications. The unions curried the favor of foremen and managers in order to secure a lion's share of the work."[17] Producers saw the backlot labor as interchangeable and thought it could be performed by any worker from the IBEW, IATSE, Carpenters, or Painters.

Seeing a need to differentiate its specialized labor force and gain headway into motion picture production, IATSE established two newly specific Studio Mechanics locals in 1924: Local 52 (New York) and Local 37 (Hollywood) splintered off from stage work (Locals 1 and 33, respectively).[18] In the same year, the Motion Picture Producers and Distributors of America (MPPDA) and the Association of Motion Picture Producers (AMPP), the trade organizations representing the studios, attempted to remove the union problem altogether by establishing the Mutual Alliance of Studio Employees (MASE) a company hiring hall for craft workers.[19] The AMPP's attempt to create a carefully curated company union led the Studio Mechanics Alliance to threaten a strike in November 1926, leading to the first Studio Basic Agreement (SBA). The agreement recognized IATSE Local 37 along with UBC Local 946, IBEW Local 40, Painters Local 644, and the American Federation of Musicians Local 47.[20]

The SBA calmed some labor uncertainty but ultimately took even more power away from the rank and file in Los Angeles since the studios would negotiate directly with the internationals. As Lovell and Carter explain, the SBA failed to address the working conditions of backlot workers; further, "The basic agreement bypassed local business agents and meant that major decisions were handled by top union and studio officials on the East Coast."[21] By taking decision-making out of the control of the local business reps and the rank and file, Local 37 had no power to initiate local meetings. The inability to address grievances and concerns about labor and wages locally meant large-scale union decisions were often divorced from the realities of workers' lives.

Unions deployed their own ways of using the SBA to manage their workforce, such as developing rotation systems, so that when labor was in high demand, unemployed workers could be hired from the out-of-work books first.[22] In a 1928 renewal of the SBA, an amendment allowed for a "skilled artisans" wage increase and more detailed standards, called the "Mechanics' Wage Scale and Working Conditions."[23] This opened the doors for additional backlot workers' unions, including the 1929 charter of a Hollywood local (what would become the Studio

Utility Employees 724) of LiUNA. However, not all of backlot labor was suddenly unionized under the SBA, resulting in confusion around the "open-shop" status quo as IATSE and others sought a "closed-shop situation."[24]

As part of their recently solidified union status, members were tasked with recruiting others to join. But as the electrician Frank Barenna recounted, such a union drive could be met with open retaliation: "You were very careful not to talk to the wrong people, because you could ask some studio electrician or grip to come to the union and he would turn around and tell the boss and you would find yourself out of a job."[25] Unions found it more advantageous to leverage locations for their union drives, as location scales were higher for union workers than for nonunion workers and more unpredictable in terms of working hours and conditions. By limiting how union members could work with nonunion workers on locations, IATSE and others were able to make union membership more desirable, even with paying dues.[26]

From 1929 to 1939, skilled artisans could make twenty-five cents a day more than the standard nonunion rate of eight dollars. This provided a small but meaningful benefit for unionized workers compared with their nonunion counterparts, who suffered wage reductions in 1927 and 1933.[27] Still, backlot workers had little say in seniority, technology, or the manpower of their crews. This meant that their day-to-day work and safety largely relied on which and how many studio workers were employed (figure 2.1). Ed Rike, a gaffer, described a Warner Bros. lot that "had more help than the other studios, and that made working there easier. There were always plenty of men on the crews."[28] Jim Noblitt, a grip who started at Paramount in 1928 noted, "The studios were all different. Fox was entirely different from Warner Brothers. I think people were more taskmasters at Fox than at Warners. They were more lenient at Warners. There were not as many people walking around to report you."[29]

The shift in local union control from IA Local 33 stage workers to the now dispersed Local 37 Studio Mechanics, the Carpenters, the IBEW, and LiUNA came at the price of brief jurisdictional stability and international control. The lack of local control, home rule, and powerful local business reps also meant that issues of working conditions and job security remained neglected at the end of the decade. The next fifteen years would mean an even more chaotic period of interunion conflict and uncertainty for workers.

Battles for the Backlot Workers

Studio consolidation during and immediately after the industrial transition to sound together with the financial downturn of the early 1930s led to a more efficient production model that shook up business on the studio lot. For backlot workers the addition of new sound workers was central to the conflicts that were to come. Sound workers were initially added to IA Local 37 as backlot workers but were quickly organized into the IA Local 695 sound technicians in

FIGURE 2.1 Grips, electricians, and stagehands perch over the stage and at the edge of the set at the RKO studio. (Photograph: Robert W. Coburn, "Cream of the Stills," *International Photographer* 4, no. 2 (March 1932): 17.)

September 1930 (discussed in chapter 3). But by May 1931, a renewed jurisdictional dispute between IATSE and the IBEW over the sound workers inspired a series of labor actions and a strike aimed at consolidating power over studio labor.

As discussed in the next chapter, Local 695 began the strike at Columbia Pictures, leading the IA to aggressively assert its industry-wide jurisdiction, expanding the strike across its eleven AMPP-affiliated studios.[30] As the strike dragged on through July, the IA's rank and file, including its backlot workers, grew restless. On August 5, the producers offered a redrawn SBA with the IBEW, which "reduced the daily rate for most SBA groups from $8.25 per eight-hour day to $7.00 per six-hour day, [a] 13.5 per cent increase in hourly rate, but an overall decrease for workers since many of them worked shifts at two different studios."[31] By the end of the strike, the 3,000 remaining workers, including 1,250 studio mechanics, were willing to sign with whatever union would get them back to work the quickest.[32]

While the lowest-paid backlot laborers were actually paid sixty cents an hour, the members who made up what were once the studio mechanics (grips, gaffers, electric, carpenters, prop workers, etc.) earned between $1.00 and $1.16 per hour.[33] Additionally, the studios placed foremen on weekly salaries in order to work them unlimited numbers of hours and place them on call for the full seven-day work-week. A later amendment further redefined location wages as set daily and weekly rates for studio mechanics such as grips, gaffers, electricians, and property work-ers to account for the additional time and difficulty of the work.[34]

Meanwhile, the once enormous Local 37 Studio Mechanics' membership was obliterated by the chaos, particularly when the producers granted grip and prop-erty work to the carpenters' union. Within a week, IA members fled or acquired additional union cards in either the IBEW or the Carpenters local to ensure their job security. IATSE's overall membership dropped from 9,000 to 200. The bulk of that lost membership came from the thousands of studio mechanics who deserted Local 37 during the summer of 1933, reducing its membership to a mere forty workers by September.[35]

Backlot workers felt IATSE had gambled on a power grab at the risk of the rank and file, with little concern for what it would mean for its members—even with a healthy union unemployment fund—to weather a strike amid nationwide economic anxieties. Backlot crews who had worked alongside each other for a good part of a decade had been separated by strikebreakers and by divisions across union cards, new and arbitrary craft designations, and the practice of blacklist-ing after the 1933 strikes. Patchwork backlot crews after the summer of 1933 were often composed of randomly selected new union members who had never worked in the trade, scabs without skill, and some experienced old-timers.

Backlot workers were becoming used to being traded among international unions that largely spoke on their behalf. Jim Noblitt, who worked as a grip, described a delicate balance of needing to make good with both the department heads at various studios and the "call steward at the union." Laurie Pintar, refer-ring to this degree of deferential behavior by studio workers, cites an interview with Noblitt as evidence of the union's and studios' "emasculating" force: "People with families had to learn quickly 'whose ass to kiss' to be able to keep working."[36] Perhaps one of the lucky ones, Noblitt also learned to keep up the right acquaintances with department heads who could help put him back to work or give him consistent work amid layoffs and union disputes. Sometimes this meant serving as an IATSE grip one week and doing set construction with the Carpenters the next. In this way, while workers experienced additional and drastic financial and existential precarity, the fact that the chaos of the 1933 strikes had happened recently contributed to a constant atmosphere of insecurity and disruption.

Likewise, the 1933 strike and resulting realignments weakened the resolve of backlot unions. Union officials in the IBEW and UBC, seeing what had happened to IATSE, were reticent to negotiate new working conditions on behalf of their backlot workers, even for the elimination of physically dangerous conditions on set. Meanwhile, IATSE's reduced membership left it, especially Local 37, vulnerable to abuse by those who had designs to restore its once-significant power. As detailed in the introduction to part I, it was under these conditions that the cowed unions and frustrated workers allowed George Browne and Willie Bioff to rise to power and bring their Chicago Mafia ties to IATSE.

Browne and Bioff's influence on the Hollywood backlot workers was particularly significant during their reign over IATSE. In 1936, Browne, as president of IATSE, and Bioff, his representative overseeing the studio locals, declared a "state of emergency" in all West Coast studio locals and staged a shake-up of the organization, effectively stripping locals of all autonomy, and outlawed any local election, meeting, or voting. They saturated IA Local 37 Studio Mechanics in particular with their own representatives (culled from members of the Chicago Nitti gang). Gene Mailes, a former Local 37 Progressive and prop maker, aided by the historian Mike Nielsen, provides a heartbreaking, firsthand account of how the IA's corruption ruined the lives of many studio mechanics. In particular, Mailes describes how Browne and Bioff's mob tactics threatened, humiliated, and sought to destroy Local 37 members who formed various progressive offshoots to fight back against a union unwilling to take care of its own workers. These offshoots included the IA Progressives, the Federated Motion Picture Crafts (FMPC), and the United Studio Technicians Guild (USTG).

The FMPC included the laborers' group the Studio Utility Employees 724 (SUE), whose members Nielsen and Mailes describe as "among the hardest working and lowest paid of all wage earners in the film production industry."[37] SUE laborers made sixty-two cents an hour, with no clear work start and end dates, and no overtime. Not one to miss any opportunity to control workforces, Bioff quickly set up a raid on SUE. Bioff offered SUE members 'Class B' grip memberships and promising them a jump to 82 cents per hour. Nielson and Mailes go on to explain, "As FMPC workers were leaving lots, Bioff's men offered them free IA cards. Several workers accepted the cards . . . a de facto expansion of IATSE's jurisdiction."

On April 20, 1937, a 2 percent levy on workers by studio heads (in addition to the 2 percent assessment for IATSE workers from the union) led to a two-month strike that ended on June 10, 1937. As Local 37's Irv Hentschel of IA Progressives explained in a letter to another union leader, "The recent strike having further exposed the racketeering and complete domination of our local by our officials, had made the rank and file more determined to find the solution to their difficulties."[38] Combined with the strikes, the news of a hearing in the California State Assembly frightened and excited many IATSE workers and put several splinter groups on alert that now was the time to act. Members of SUE voted to work for seventy-five cents per hour, but with an open, nonunion shop. They filed for SUE 724 to be granted jurisdiction over all studio laborers, hoping to block IATSE while the union was weak.[39]

Facing the specter of government investigations, Browne temporarily restored autonomy to the West Coast studio locals at the same time studio producers had already begun cutting down the number of productions and jobs in response to the economic recession of 1938. Jeff Kibre and Herb Sorrell (of Painters Local 644) organized the Studio Unemployment Conference on January 27, 1938, to offer solutions for the 95 percent unemployment crisis.[40] With an absent Bioff and a distracted IATSE, the IA Progressives continued to push for local autonomy at a series of meetings and elections. These campaigns were quickly marred by manipulated votes, false promises, and fear tactics. As Jeff Kibre of the IA 37 Progressives recalled, "Before the meetings intimidation through gang bosses and shop foremen against a vote for autonomy was flagrantly practiced. In the largest organization, Local 37, no free discussion from the floor on the question was permitted. The main issue was so put as to impress the members that a vote for home rule would result in the withdrawal of International assistance breaking of present contracts, and the establishment of open shop conditions. Finally, a standing vote, instead of a secret ballot, was utilized."[41]

Reading a letter from Kibre, Irv Hentschel presented a resolution of IA Progressives' demands at the thirty-fourth IA convention in Cleveland that June. Kibre's letter and Hentschel's testimony—given in front of a tyrannical IA board and an equally hostile audience—outlined the various damages the IA international leaders had inflicted on the West Coast studio locals, specifically Local 37 Studio Mechanics. In addition to workers' lack of participation that had resulted in agreements that failed to "take into account the problems of the industry, and . . . deterioration of working conditions," Kibre's letter also cited the "absence of proper examination to determine qualifications of hundreds of new members."[42]

These new members consisted of Browne and Bioff's henchmen and anyone else on whom they could force a card to increase workforce control and profits. The result, as Kibre bemoaned, was not only that these workers were unqualified for the tasks they would need to perform but also that their lack of expertise and experience potentially endangered the safety and lives of everyone on set. Kibre's laundry list of grievances about the assessments, on-set safety, secret ballots, lack of autonomy, and rampant unemployment (40 to 50 percent of the membership) also drew attention to a shocking trend of declining wages.[43] Craftsman who made $2400 in 1929 were making less than $1500 in 1935 with further declines in 1937, even though there had been hourly rate increases in those two years and the studios were reporting higher profits than they had since the start of the Depression. Grips, electricians, and prop makers often earned even less, averaging between $1,215 and $1,738 in 1938.[44] As Nielsen suggests, the rank and file's "high degree of apathy" over years of mob rule and the history of jurisdictional shakeups may have left them frustrated about the conditions IA Progressives outlined, yet they were unlikely to complain for fear of losing current or future work.[45] Coupled with this indifference and docility, the IA helped scare people away from progressive change by labeling progressives "the 37 white rats" or, even worse, "Communists!"

By 1939, the Progressives were growing in number and appealing to a wider constituency of Hollywood locals (thanks to their role in lifting the 2 percent assessment), and they had the support of Herb Sorrell's Painters local.[46] Employment was rising, and, sensing another Progressive call for autonomy, Browne called another "state of emergency" and moved to divide Local 37 Studio Mechanics into five distinct locals in May 1939.[47] While the Progressives had called for a similar division of craft authority within Local 37 the year before, Browne's intent was to weaken the vigor of the Progressives' call for autonomy and ensure that all leaders of the new locals would report directly to and defend the IA line. The five newly established locals were 44 (Prop Makers), 80 (Grips), 165 (Studio Projectionists), 727 (Utility Workers), and 728 (Electricians). The most susceptible to strong-arming were Locals 80 and 728. Local 80 was governed by a new Browne-appointed board.

Sensing their inability to organize in this new structure, the IA Progressives split from the IA to form the USTG, backed by the Congress of Industrial Organizations (CIO) and led by Howard Robertson, an established gaffer. In August 1939, the USTG requested an election through the National Labor Relations Board (NLRB) to rule on who might organize studio workers, the IA or the USTG. The vote was 4,460 for the IA and 1,967 for the USTG, thanks in part to a promise from Bioff and Browne for a 10 percent wage increase and a closed shop.[48] The aftermath, according to Nielsen, resulted in blacklisting "known USTG supporters," many of whom "never again found work in the studios."[49] Rank-and-file backlot workers wanted an overhaul of IA corruption after Bioff and Browne's removal, indictments, and convictions in 1941, but they were largely disappointed.

Backlot Strikes and IATSE's Ascent

While they were out of the grasp of the crime syndicate, backlot workers under IATSE still faced corrupt officials installed by the previous administration and a labor environment rattled by years of neglect. Labor disputes came to a halt during World War II but quickly resumed as the war wound down. However, the end of the Browne and Bioff era left room for progressive groups to fight for better contracts and labor conditions in the 1940s. In 1941, Herb Sorrell of the

Painters local formed the democratic Conference of Studio Unions (CSU) along-side nonunionized backlot workers and members who left IATSE following the nine-week Disney strike. The CSU would become a major player in the labor actions of the 1940s. The growing power of the CSU meant that IATSE increasingly fought jurisdictional backlot battles against the new organization, including battles of property workers in 1942 and of decorators in 1944, and reinstituting the Studio Mechanics Local 791 to take over electrical workers from IBEW Local 40.[50] The ongoing strikes of the 1940s would both bring together and divide the industry and represented one of the last successes in backlot workers' history.

After the end of the war, the ongoing jurisdictional disputes around backlot set building, woodworking, and prop making continued. On March 12, 1945, the Painters called another strike to maintain decorators among their ranks, which was supported by CSU, Machinists, and Carpenters. In September of that year, IATSE chartered yet another Studio Mechanics local (468). According to IA vice president Roy Brewer, Local 468 would *officially* "absorb workers who don't properly belong in other locals," but unofficially it was clear that these were replacement workers.[51] The most memorable event of the period was the protracted Warner Bros. strike, which culminated in the October 1945 Bloody Friday riot between Herb Sorrell's CSU and the studio.

The jurisdictional disputes during these few years reframed the craft boundaries of backlot workers and their unions for decades to follow. The contestation often revolved around one material—wood—and who had the authority to use it on set. Set erection was granted to Local 946 Carpenters after an agreement in November 1945 between their international representatives and IATSE Local 80 Grips. By December, an AFL committee of three people reversed that contract and granted set erection to Local 80, reverting to an IA/Carpenters agreement of 1925, the provisions of which had previously been discarded.[52] In doing so, the three-person panel failed to review interim agreements and standard working practice, and they ended up taking away work from both groups.

IATSE used the resulting confusion to try to establish further control by creating a new "set erectors" local that took work away from their own grips. As Father Dunne later testified to a congressional committee appointed to settle ongoing labor disputes in the motion picture industry, "If the set erectors had been an old union, it would have been understandable, but it seemed to me obvious that Mr. Walsh [the IATSE president] had established a phony union, and a union which never had existed before, for the precise purpose of frustrating the purpose of this agreement between the grips and carpenters, creating an issue and a controversy that never would have existed in Hollywood."[53] Walsh's newly established union of set erectors was designed to create "hot sets" requiring arbitration (knowingly bending or breaking jurisdictional boundaries to create work stoppages). Thanks to this and the AFL's rash, uninformed decision, the Carpenters responded with a strike. On July 2, 1946, the short-lived "Treaty of Beverly Hills" attempted to ease the jurisdictional disputes by offering a 35 percent wage increase to both IATSE and the CSU and additional increases to certain classifications, as well as outlawing strikes over jurisdictional claims.[54]

Unwilling to accept these conditions, in September 1946 the Carpenters reacted to the recent loss of over 300 CSU jobs with another strike. However, Herb Sorrell and the CSU's backing of the Carpenters helped Walsh and IATSE shore up support from the producers.[55] IATSE offered replacements, and the CSU retaliated with demands around wage and arbitration issues. The carpenter lockout that would follow and the Carpenters' subsequent lawsuits against the IA concealed the underlying collaboration of Walsh and the producers to create many of these "hot sets" that were designed to push the Carpenters and CSU Painters off the lots. As Gerald Horne explains, even "those who did not leave were asked to do so."[56] That these "hot sets" would become the basis for the accounts reviewed by a specially appointed congressional committee later that year illustrates the difficulty of treating even jurisdictional and court cases as objective.

The Taft-Hartley Act of 1947 led to the commencement of hearings of Carrol Kearns's congressional committee, which produced a report titled *Jurisdictional Disputes in the Motion-Picture Industry*. Yet in trying to compare the Hollywood labor disputes to jurisdictional issues in other building crafts industries, the committee was at a loss for how to handle the complicated and often unspoken craft boundaries. At the request of Kearns, the AMPP compiled a portfolio of lot jurisdictional disputes from MGM, Paramount, Columbia, Samuel Goldwyn, Warner Bros, Republic, RKO, Fox, and Universal.[57] The disputes concerned the overlap in grip, carpentry, prop, and electrical work, and where one division started and ended and the next began. Despite holding three separate hearings, the Kearns congressional committee ultimately failed to mediate the complicated disputes.

The jurisdictional battles over the backlot workers continued through the late 1940s. The Carpenters eventually got the AFL to reaffirm principles of the 1946 clarification, but a number of other jurisdictional questions remained, leaving an opportunity for the International Association of Machinists to argue against IATSE for control of motion picture machinists, and for the Teamsters to argue for a specific union local for motion picture garage workers.[58] As explained in the introduction to part I, the CSU was also engaged in a losing battle for membership against IATSE. By the time of the 1949 AFL convention and NLRB elections, the IA had secured a major victory over production work, marking the end to CSU's decade-long challenges.

The 1940s had been a hotbed for union activity, but this period had also signaled a sharp decline in union solidarity. With the 1948 Paramount Decrees and the divorce of studios from exhibition, the IA's hold over its labor force would also become increasingly decentralized as studio work slowed. Additionally, the Taft-Hartley Act similarly restricted the primary tools backlot unions used to maintain control: jurisdictional disputes and secondary boycotts. Investigations into the so-called communist leanings of some of the more progressive independent unions also bolstered the public's unfounded distrust in labor. This was the climate that backlot unions faced as television and independent contractors began to change the media landscape in the 1950s.

New environments of production, from broadcast networks to independent productions, meant union backlot workers had to be more adaptable.[59] IATSE television work was popular for backlot workers and stagehands alike: "For IA stagehands, it was stagecraft transplanted to a TV studio. Networks hired stagehands as well as carpenters, electricians, scenic artists, wardrobe workers, make-up artists, hairstylists and other skilled theatrical technicians to fill these jobs in television."[60] The days of clearly defined craft jurisdictions and skill sets were gone, and many backlot workers had to find their own work by pitching their ability to do multiple on-set jobs for the price of one. While this movement toward generalization and freelancing offered employment possibilities outside the studios, inside the studios, backlot unions attempted to further entrench themselves through specialization.

Challenges to Backlot Workers and Unions

With other job opportunities outside the studios, backlot unions found that workers needed incentives to join the unions. The introduction of the Industry Experience Roster system and pension programs offered one way to attract union participation in an increasingly freelance work environment. The unions also opened their rosters to new members after regulations in the Civil Rights Act of 1964 mandated that employees could not be discriminated against based on race, color, sex, national origin, or religion. The following year, the Contract Services Administration of the Association of Motion Picture and Television Producers (AMPTP) introduced training and apprentice programs specifically designed to address the lack of women and minority representation across craft ranks.[61] Yet, as many younger and inexperienced workers realized over the next decade, the apprentice programs coupled with the roster system often added another hurdle to employment. While the older backlot studio workers finished off their careers attempting to stitch together freelance, broadcast, and roster-based opportunities, the next generation of workers now faced even fiercer competition in training programs, attempting to break into the union, all while trying to attain local work amid the growth of runaway productions that began in the 1950s.

The 1969 EEOC hearing in Hollywood on diversity in the industry revealed how the experience roster reinforced the whiteness of the industry, even if it was challenging to collect accurate employment data for backlot workers. For instance, the EEOC forms asked for departments to list their demographics from 1965 to 1968 based on job classifications the studios did not regularly use, including a division between craftsperson, skilled, semiskilled, and unskilled.

In one testimony, a carpenter is listed as a craftsperson, while a grip may be placed in the semiskilled or unskilled labor category. Thus, the confusion over the EEOC's personnel and demographic classification system ultimately masked the minuscule numbers for minority men, minority women, and white women backlot workers.

Industrial relations department specialists at the participating studios passed the buck of representation to their collective bargaining agreements with unions and the boundaries of the experience roster in particular. IA representatives did not understand why union application questions about national birthplace, membership connections, and particularly about the occupation of one's father constituted discriminatory hiring practices.[62] The commission found that the combination of the training programs and the experience roster was often designed to exclude minorities and women who could not realistically gain the skills required. According to EEOC general counsel Daniel Steiner, "Minorities were previously denied the opportunity to gain the experience to get into pre-ferred positions on the roster or to get on the roster at all."[63] For example, to go through the training program as a lamp operator, an apprentice would have to earn 2,100 hours of work experience to even make it onto the class 3 roster.[64]

Additionally, the commission demonstrated how nepotism and familial ties to current union members through a sometimes conscious and unconscious bias toward a "father-son" craft tradition (almost entirely white and male) ensured greater access to union technical training for card-carrying members' sons, nephews, and brothers. As Eithne Quinn has demonstrated, producers, studios, and unions took little responsibility for proactively following affirmative action policies, instead seeing themselves as arbiters of an "open door" and vague non-discrimination public stances, while offering no institutional mechanism to offi-cially address discrimination or adhere to the law.[65] Anecdotal testimony from the studio industrial department representatives suggested that a handful of Black men and women, Mexican American men and women, and white women worked as grips, carpenters, plasterers, electricians, and lamp operators, but this was not verified by documents in evidence. Further, the testimony does not state whether these workers were employed due to the union roster system; the pro-ducers training programs; or alternative off-roster employment offices such as the Los Angeles Service Center, the Urban League, or the Mexican American Opportunity Foundation, which some studios used when the experience roster was exhausted.

At the 1977 hearing of the U.S. Commission on Civil Rights, minority work-ers described the failures stemming from the 1969 EEOC hearing.[66] David Skeens Walks Eagle, a Cherokee Indian and an actor, described how two quali-fied and on-call Indigenous colleagues had tried and failed to secure grip work in broadcast via IA Stage Technicians.[67] Among other testimonies from Black stage technicians in Local 33, Richard Bryant described the systemic discrimi-nation baked into IATSE: "Blacks who are fortunate or unfortunate, depending on how you view it, being employed by Local 33 are allocated the most undesirable jobs and work situations. The choice of more lucrative situations are [*sic*] reserved for bluebloods; i.e., fathers and/or sons."[68] Additional testimonials from Black workers described going through the minority pool and training programs of the early 1970s only to be met with a mantra of "no work" when they called the union and never received callbacks.

The 1977 hearing also featured representatives from the Teamsters, Laborers, and Plasterers who outlined their various attempts to recruit and retain minority workers and women. Even in these discussions, union reps revealed biases about women's supposed disinterest in performing heavy lifting (Laborers) and placement bias in hiring "attractive women" to drive limousines (Teamsters). However, the basic and backlot crafts had slightly more minority members than other craft locals. Of applicants who applied for and were accepted to the Teamsters 399 roster between 1974 and 1976 when the rosters were open, white women had a 94 percent acceptance rate, and Hispanic men and Black men had a 60 percent acceptance rate, compared with a 70 percent acceptance rate for white men.[69] Acceptance rates may be misleading, however, considering that the minority pool for applications was often startlingly low. White women, Hispanic women and men, Black women and men, and other men of color constituted less than 15 percent of the applicant pool. Of the total applicant pool, Black workers composed only 1 percent. Meanwhile, white men made up 82 percent of new members placed on the Teamsters roster (see figure 2.2). At the same time, Lamp Operators 728 and Grips 80 fared only slightly better in placing male minority workers, while also failing to actively recruit women applicants and offering no

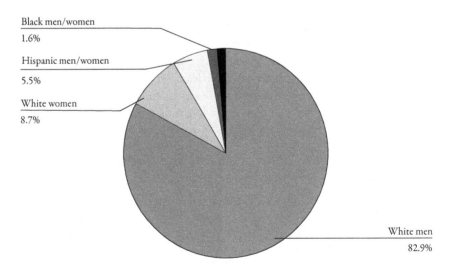

FIGURE 2.2 Percentage of total new roster placements for Teamsters 399, 1974–1977. (Source: U.S. Commission on Civil Rights, *Hearings Held in Los Angeles, Calif., March 16, 1977.*)

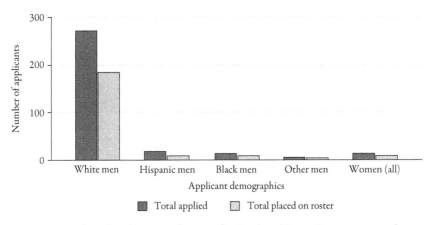

FIGURE 2.3 Number of total roster applications for Combined Lamp Operators 728 and Grips 80, compared with roster placement by demographic, 1974–1976. (Source: U.S. Commission on Civil Rights, *Hearings Held in Los Angeles, Calif., March 16, 1977.*)

positions on the roster to women of color (figure 2.3). By the end of the proceedings, the commission had recommended a full-scale re-evaluation of the training system and removal of the experience roster.

As was clear even during the 1977 hearings, many unions were more concerned with overall employment figures threatened by runaway and independent production than with the welfare or access of its minority rank-and-file aspirants. As IA representative Josef Bernay explained to the commission, the largest menace to union production was the loss of jobs to runaway production.[70] Nearly a decade earlier, IA Locals 728 and 80 (along with the Cameramen's Local 659) announced a picket to protest actors (and thus productions) who left Hollywood to work on runaway production in other states and overseas.[71] Runaway productions not only threatened already weakened backlot local power but also relied on nonunion workers, particularly in the basic crafts.

By avoiding the local home rule jurisdiction of the West Coast, independent productions as well as studios hoped to find cheaper nonunion workers to replace skilled, unionized backlot workers. Thus, IATSE found itself in the same scenario that had inaugurated its union nearly eighty years earlier—how to unionize traveling workers and locals outside the major production centers of New York and Los Angeles. Many of the union's previous collective bargaining agreements could come into play related to travel and overnight work, but the previous traveling workforce did not include backlot studio workers or stage mechanics.

It was here that NABET provided an alternative model. NABET Local 15 in New York City offered, according to John Amman, "a formidable alternative to IATSE for independent producers" by growing the local's membership from the mid-1970s to the 1980s and organizing mid-budget production.[72] IATSE began following NABET's model of catchall craft unionism, using its stage mechanics unions to fill in as studio technicians and mechanics, encouraging a kind of free-lance model of union membership.

Programs such as the class 1 journeyman status in IA Local 33 Stagehands encouraged per diem work not tied to specific studios or companies. While union rates were higher, workers were hired on per diem short-term or daily rates versus longer contracts that could be more costly. According to Susan Christopherson, "In response, unions created and negotiated new institutions which made it possible for these critical functions to be carried on outside the firm and which indirectly enabled the flexible use of labor inputs."[73] These gen-eralized, rather than craft-specific, labor models better suited contract and independent modes of production and also meant that IATSE could use its non–motion picture locals elsewhere in the United States and Canada to begin building labor support.

Labor shifted even further from unionized to nonunion work in the 1980s, constituting a major threat to backlot workers. The combination of runaway productions, corporate mergers, vertical reintegration, and U.S. president Ron-ald Reagan's anti-labor political policies made it difficult for unions to bargain on workers' behalf. Rather than return to the studio heyday of union contracts, new corporate structures continued to favor the subcontracting system of pro-duction to reduce overhead and lessen labor liability.[74] Backlot workers across production industries also faced the threat of automation and redundancy. In the 1970s and 1980s, many sought work in NABET and the IBEW, where workers used new technologies such as the minicam and mobile videotape, rather than in IATSE, where workers specialized in bulky film equipment.[75] At the turn of the twentieth century, unions attempted to ameliorate their situa-tion by further consolidating workers and expanding their outreach efforts in new production locations.

Consolidation and Expansion

In 1994, new pedestal cameras reduced each broadcast camera's labor require-ment from three technicians to one.[76] No longer needing grips to push automated cameras in the studio was only one of the many ways that backlot labor would be transformed just prior to the twenty-first century. As crews consolidated due to the availability of more efficient tools, backlot labor unions reduced their over-head and amalgamated with other unions, growing their labor power. In 1992, NABET Locals 531 and 15 affiliated with IATSE to join the existing locals. Since IATSE had copied many of NABET's techniques for running catchall craft locals, the combination made sense to workers and streamlined their regional jurisdictions and international bargaining agreements. Workers continued to maintain cards in both unions, reflecting uncertainties in the industry and split-ting their loyalties. Many members even risked working nonunion jobs when the pay or opportunity was right.

Backlot unions refocused their attention on organizing more locations, particularly in the northeastern, southwestern, and southern U.S. states. While these campaigns proved easier in the Northeast thanks to stronger building trades and production union culture, additional regional, cultural, and state-by-state anti-union right-to-work laws proved difficult for unions to negotiate elsewhere, particularly in the South. Additionally, unions sought multistate agreements to respond to the surge of new tax breaks for location production and international agreements in Vancouver and Toronto, Canada. Unlike the often nonunionized open-shop work available in many U.S. right-to-work states offering tax incentives, provinces such as British Columbia and Ontario are heavily unionized. The network of larger craft-based locals assisted in these agreements, such as Vancouver-based Local 891 (the largest in Canada and the fourth largest in IATSE), whose membership spiked in the mid-1990s and contained a range of workers, including basic crafts.[77]

During the 1990s and the first decade of the twenty-first century, unions deployed a range of new tactics to expand and support membership. In 1993, a renewal of the basic agreement expanded the reach of West Coast locals into low-budget production, followed in the next decade by cable and later streaming companies, commercials, and reality TV. Another tactic was the establishment of the IATSE National Safety Committee in 1997 and the Craft Training and Safety Committee in 2009. These committees were often run by representatives from the backlot crafts locals, including Locals 728 and 80, who were often responsible for safety on set because of their work with scaffolding, platforms, rigging, and heavy equipment.

Unlike the smaller jurisdictional locals of the studio system days, in recent decades, larger backlot locals have included more than twenty labor sectors, the bulk of which are often construction and studio mechanics such as carpenters, laborers, grips, riggers, and electricians. IATSE's efforts expanded locals to encompass a wider range of workers, which enabled backlot unionization efforts in areas that might not be able to expand or leverage individual jurisdictions. A new openness to the definition of backlot labor and an ability to recruit new members will continue to be crucial as backlot unions look ahead.

What's Next for the "Backlot" Worker?

It is increasingly difficult to parse the parameters of the backlot worker. These individuals still set the scene and take it down again, but very little of this work takes place on the backlot or even under the auspices of studio production. Like their predecessors in stagecraft, backlot workers have performed collaborative work with many colleagues who perform a wide range of physical, mechanical, and specialized tasks. The battle for this group, from the beginning of motion picture history, has evolved: at first the issue was whether they should be unionized; later it became how to distinguish between their tasks.

The return to catchall basic crafts and Studio Mechanics locals since the 1990s has signaled the flexibility of traditional backlot unions such as IATSE, the Teamsters, IBEW, Carpenters, Laborers, and Machinists to reimagine the jurisdictional, regional, and even national boundaries of this workforce. With larger unions and a broader range of bargaining agreements, membership has grown in recent years and reflects a further diversification of talents and tools. While certainly technological and industrial change has reduced employment opportunities in some areas, in other sectors backlot workers have responded to the need for workers to perform expected tasks, such as rigging green screen and setting up large cloud bank LED lights, and unexpected tasks, such as serving as handlers for AI and other automated camera and lighting gear.

At the start of the twenty-first century, labor unions began to market themselves not only to their rank and file but also to the public as a social and business good. The contemporary backlot unions run social media accounts that encourage craft identification, promote their members, and showcase their work on set. Individual backlot workers also have greater public visibility, which allows them to be more engaged with their representatives and their locals through official and unofficial web forums and social media sites. While these outlets provide necessary arenas for worker agency (something that was sorely lacking throughout much of the history of backlot work) and even what John Caldwell has termed "worker industrial snark," these venues have also become unexpected vessels of spec and surplus labor as backlot workers must increasingly promote themselves and their network via social media.[78] As a result, the backlot unions have also had to shift how they address and represent workers' concerns in the public eye. Rather than only running a union on the AFL businesslike model of dues-paying members and industry control, backlot unions use their platforms to promote better working conditions, living wages, and gender and diversity inclusion.

Unions have coupled with production companies to develop quotas and DEI-based training programs to address the nepotistic nature of backlot workers' tight, but still primarily white male, production communities. Where the unions have fallen short, individual workers have also leaned into organizations like the intra-local Caucus of Rank-and-File Entertainment Workers (CREW) and social media campaigns meant to address industry grievances (such as the safety awareness campaigns 12On12Off and Slates for Sarah). As backlot workers face new challenges in technology, industry, and production environments, their unions will likely come to reflect more of the agency, viewpoints, and concerns of their members than they have for much of their history.

The growth in public support of unions in the 2020s, at its highest peak since before the Reagan years, is a positive sign for this so-called lowest echelon of workers whose labor concerns and struggles have often been understated in Hollywood history and often overlooked by their own internationals. However, the biggest threat to backlot workers continues to be nonunionized and casual production. U.S. right-to-work policies and productions in countries where these workers are not organized or protected by local and international labor policies will continue to present significant and ongoing challenges. Open-shop policies, like those that devastated studio backlot workers in the 1920s, continue to push down wages, reduce job opportunities and stability, and impinge on the safety of all workers today.

Notes

1   Hugh Lovell and Tasile Carter, *Collective Bargaining in the Motion Picture Industry: A Struggle for Stability* (Institute for Industrial Relations, University of California Berkeley, 1955), 3.
2   A July 2021 study of Asian and Latino representation in IATSE showed several of the backlot unions to have significant Latino memberships. The four locals focused on here have Latino memberships of 25.4 percent (Local 80 Grips), 25.4 percent (Local 729 Painters), 18 percent (Local 44 Props), and 17.2 percent (Local 728 Lighting Technicians), and Asian members between 2 and 3 percent. The five locals with the highest Latino memberships were all non-IATSE basic crafts. Gene Maddaus, "How Variety Studied the Diversity of Hollywood Unions," *Variety*, July 21, 2021, https://variety.com/2021/film/news/entertainment-industry-diversity-study-methodology-response-1235024157/.
3   For more information on the "father-son tradition," see U.S. Equal Employment Opportunity Commission, *Hearings Before the U.S. Equal Employment Opportunity Commission on Utilization of Minority and Women Workers in Certain Major Industries: Hearings Held in Los Angeles, Calif., March 12–14, 1969* (Equal Employment Opportunity Commission, 1969), 124.
4   Michael Nielsen, "Motion Picture Craft Workers and Craft Unions in Hollywood: The Studio Era, 1912–1948" (PhD diss., University of Illinois Urbana-Champaign, 1985), 27.
5   Nielsen, 28.
6   Nielsen, 56.
7   International Alliance of Theatrical Stage Employees and Moving Picture Operators of the United States and Canada, *IATSE, 1893–1993: 100 Years of Solidarity* (IATSE, 1993), 22.
8   Nielsen, "Motion Picture Craft Workers," 63.
9   Mike Nielsen and Gene Mailes, *Hollywood's Other Blacklist: Union Struggles in the Studio System* (BFI, 1995), 5.
10 Nielsen and Mailes, 5.
11 Sylvia Shorris and Marion Abbott Bundy, *Talking Pictures: With the People Who Made Them* (New Press, 1994),148.
12 Nielsen and Mailes, *Hollywood's Other Blacklist*, 6.
13 "Big Studio Strike Looms," *Film Mercury*, November 12, 1926, 3.
14 Murray Ross, *Stars and Strikes: Unionization of Hollywood* (Columbia University Press, 1941), 7.
15 IATSE, *IATSE, 1893–1993*, 28.
16 IATSE, 29.
17 Ross, *Stars and Strikes*, 10.
18 "Labor in Decline," IATSE, accessed June 30, 2023, https://www.legacy.iatse.net/history/labor-decline.

19 IATSE, *IATSE, 1893–1993*, 30.
20 Laurie Pintar, "Off-Screen Realities: A History of Labor Activism in Hollywood, 1933–1947" (PhD diss., University of Southern California, 1995), 37.
21 Lovell and Carter, *Collective Bargaining*, 17.
22 Nielsen and Mailes, 9; Ross, *Stars and Strikes*, 20.
23 Ross, *Stars and Strikes*, 18.
24 Ross, 21.
25 Nielsen and Mailes, *Hollywood's Other Blacklist*, 9.
26 Ross, *Stars and Strikes*, 22.
27 Ross, 18.
28 Helen Hanson, *Hollywood Soundscapes: Film Sound Style, Craft and Production in the Classical Era* (BFI, 2019): 125.
29 "Sylvia Shorris interview with Jim Noblitt," September 13, 1985, Sylvia Shorris Papers, Margaret Herrick Library, Beverly Hills, CA.
30 "Strike against Columbia Pictures," IATSE, accessed April 13, 2018, http://www.iatse.net/history/strike-against-columbia-pictures.
31 Nielsen and Mailes, *Hollywood's Other Blacklist*, 13.
32 "The Film Strike Ends," *Los Angeles Times*, August 25, 1933, A4.
33 Ross, *Stars and Strikes*, 226.
34 "Maximum Hours and Minimum Wages for Studio Workers," *Film Daily*, December 1, 1933, 10.
35 Nielsen and Mailes, *Hollywood's Other Blacklist*, 13.
36 Laurie Pintar, "Herbert K. Sorrell as the Grade-B Hero: Militancy and Masculinity in the Studios," *Labor History* 37, no. 3 (1996): 392.
37 Nielsen and Mailes, *Hollywood's Other Blacklist*, 26.
38 Nielsen and Mailes, 27.
39 Nielsen and Mailes, 27, 52.
40 Nielsen and Mailes, 37–38.
41 *Combined Convention Proceedings of the International Alliance of Theatrical and Stage Employees and Moving Picture Machine Operators of the United States and Canada*, Volume 2, 1928–1944 (IATSE, 1960), 337.
42 IATSE, *Combined Convention Proceedings*, 337.
43 IATSE, 337.
44 Horne, *Class Struggle in Hollywood*, 50.
45 Nielsen and Mailes, *Hollywood's Other Blacklist*, 38.
46 Nielsen and Mailes, 53.
47 "Local 37 Now No More as 6,000 Film Workers Absorbed by Five IATSE Unions; Dicker for Basic Agreement," *Variety*, June 21, 1939, 5.
48 Nielsen and Mailes, *Hollywood's Other Blacklist*, 61.
49 Nielsen and Mailes, 62.
50 "Ask Conciliation Service to Intervene in Strike," *Film Daily*, August 29, 1944, 10.
51 "'IA' Charters Fifth New Local in Strike," *Motion Picture Daily*, September 7, 1945, 1.
52 Nielsen and Mailes, *Hollywood's Other Blacklist*, 134.
53 *Jurisdictional Disputes in the Motion-Picture Industry: Hearings Before a Special Subcommittee of the Committee on Education and Labor*, House of Representatives, 80th Cong., 1st sess., pursuant to H. Res. 111, 1948, 410.
54 Lovell and Carter, *Collective Bargaining*, 23.
55 Nielsen and Mailes, *Hollywood's Other Blacklist*, 134.
56 Horne, *Class Struggle in Hollywood*, 200.
57 *Jurisdictional Disputes in the Motion-Picture Industry*, 468–507.

58 "Studio Mechanics Union Hearing Set," *Los Angeles Times*, September 21, 1948, 17.

59 For more on the transition of some backlot workers to broadcast work, see Susan Christopherson, "Flexibility and Adaptation in Industrial Relations: The Exceptional Case of the U.S. Media Entertainment Industries," in *Under the Stars: Essays on Labor Relations in Arts and Entertainment*, ed. Lois S. Gray and Ronald Leroy Seeber (Ithaca, NY: Cornell University Press, 1996), 103; IATSE, *IATSE, 1893–1993*, 51–53; and John Amman, "The Transformation of Industrial Relations in Motion Picture and Television Craft Industries: Craft and Production," in Gray and Seeber, *Under the Stars*, 150.

60 "TV Wages Low, but Work Was Steady," IATSE, accessed June 30, 2023, https://www.legacy.iatse.net/history/tv-wages-low-work-was-steady.

61 U.S. Equal Employment Opportunity Commission, *Hearings Held in Los Angeles, Calif., March 12–14, 1969*, 223.

62 Josef Bernay testimony in U.S. Equal Employment Opportunity Commission, *Hearings Held in Los Angeles, Calif., March 12–14, 1969*, 158.

63 Daniel Steiner, General Counsel's Statement in U.S. Equal Employment Opportunity Commission, *Hearings Held in Los Angeles, Calif., March 12–14, 1969*, 228.

64 Arthur Schaeffer testimony in U.S. Equal Employment Opportunity Commission, *Hearings Held in Los Angeles, Calif., March 12–14, 1969*, 182.

65 Eithne Quinn, "Closing Doors: Hollywood, Affirmative Action, and the Revitalization of Conservative Racial Politics," *Journal of American History* 99, no. 2 (September 2012): 466–491.

66 Lorenzo Traylor testimony in U.S. Commission on Civil Rights, *Hearings Held in Los Angeles, Calif., March 16, 1977* (U.S. Commission on Civil Rights, 1977), 120.

67 David Skeen Walks Eagle testimony in U.S. Commission on Civil Rights, *Hearings Held in Los Angeles, Calif., March 16, 1977*, 137.

68 Richard Bryant testimony in U.S. Commission on Civil Rights, *Hearings Held in Los Angeles, Calif., March 16, 1977*, 138.

69 See 1974 and 1975 Roster appendix in U.S. Commission on Civil Rights, *Hearings Held in Los Angeles, Calif., March 16, 1977*, 152–154.

70 See Josef Bernay testimony, in U.S. Commission on Civil Rights, *Hearings Held in Los Angeles, Calif., March 16, 1977*, 105.

71 Murray Schumach, "3 Unions to Picket 'Runaway' Actors," *New York Times*, May 26, 1962, 13.

72 Amman, "Transformation of Industrial Relations," 151.

73 Christopherson, "Flexibility and Adaptation in Industrial Relations," 103.

74 Christopherson, 91.

75 Amman, "Transformation of Industrial Relations," 131.

76 Suzanne Gayle Harris, "New Camera Cuts Costs for Sitcoms, but Some Aren't Laughing," *Los Angeles Times*, December 27, 1994, 3.

77 "Interview with Dusty Kelly," in *Voices of Labor: Creativity, Craft, and Conflict in Global Hollywood*, ed. Michael Curtin and Kevin Sanson (University of California Press, 2017), 261.

78 John Caldwell, "Spec World, Craft World, Brand World," in *Precarious Creativity: Global Media, Local Labor*, ed. Michael Curtin and Kevin Sanson (University of California Press, 2016), 45–46.

3

Sound and Camera

• •

The Pacesetters on Set
and in IATSE

LUCI MARZOLA

In 1929, Hollywood cameramen and sound workers were at war with each other. In the pages of their chief publication, *American Cinematographer*, the cameramen declared this moment "the war of the talkies."[1] Over the early decades of motion picture production, cinematographers had established themselves as the chief studio technicians, but these new sound engineers, with their educational pedigrees and sensitive equipment to which every apparatus in the studio needed to conform, threatened to usurp the position of the cameramen. While the cameramen had built their status through industrial rhetoric about their skills, knowledge, and artistry, the sound engineers had quickly joined the ranks of organized labor—something that the cameramen had up to that point rejected.

This chapter's pairing of camera (IATSE Local 600 now, but 659 for most of its history) and sound (IATSE Local 695) unions is not arbitrary, as these two unions stand apart from their International Alliance of Theatrical Stage Employees (IATSE, or the IA) craft peers in many ways—having been formed prior to the organizational efforts of the 1930s and often serving as bellwethers among the Hollywood locals. Likewise, these two forms of labor are at the core of on-set production: there is nothing to see without the camera workers, and there is nothing to hear without the sound workers. This centrality in motion picture production is deeply connected to their respective unions' leadership roles in labor organizing. As such, they set precedents for other IATSE locals to follow. Even more so than other unions (except for the editors and animation guilds), 659 and 695 represent labor that had no analogue before the advent of the motion picture industry. Theater has no equivalent of the cameraman or the sound recorder. This made incorporating particularly the cameramen (who worked in the field for decades before sound arrived) into existing union structures a challenge. As they worked to form an identity for their profession, many in their ranks resisted the idea that organized labor would be part of that. This struggle and conflict within the fields lasted well beyond the establishment of Locals 659 and 695 and still resonates today.

The histories of sound and camera workers parallel those of others in Hollywood who struggled to decide whether to identify as artists, craftspeople, or laborers. As Patrick Keating has shown, early on the cameramen were eager to be perceived as artists more so than technicians, believing this would elevate them to being seen as equals with directors and others in the creative class.[2] The sound workers came into the industry as equals to the camera workers on set and thus wrestled with many of the same ideas about identity. Yet their backgrounds in engineering and the ultimate diminishment of their status on the set (after cinematographers reasserted their authority) allowed them to settle more easily into an identification with labor, but it was not always clear who should represent them.

Camera and sound workers have collaborated and clashed on set, in labor negotiations, and in union meetings throughout their histories. In the 1920s, the camera workers resisted attempts at labor organization and were thrown into flux by the incursion of sound. Their resistance to union representation put them on a separate path from their colleagues through much of the 1930s, before they aligned in the battle against both the Conference of Studio Unions (CSU) and the corruption of the national leadership of IATSE. The 1940s saw separate fights over jurisdiction: 659 with the first cameramen, who preferred the American Society of Cinematographers (ASC), and 695 with both the International Brotherhood of Electrical Workers (IBEW) and the larger IATSE union over those handling sound equipment. As the studio system declined, the two unions often found themselves fighting the studios together to improve employment conditions. The fights around television and diversification likewise found the former foes often working on the same preservationist, reactionary side. Throughout this chapter, the two histories converge and diverge while the locals remain the core of motion picture and television production in Hollywood.

Organizing Cameramen in the Silent Era

In 1911, David Hulfish observed four distinct professions in motion picture work— the author, the producer, the salesman, and the photographer—the last being the sole technician in charge of all the various technologies of motion pictures.[3] As production work became more complex and divided, the cameramen described themselves as technical *and* creative workers, developing a hierarchical system in which the first cameraman was aided by one or more second cameramen (who operated cameras) and an assistant cameraman (who carried and maintained equipment). By the mid-1910s, directors began asserting more authority, particularly by using the growing trade papers to gain recognition for their roles. Famously, in 1913, when D. W. Griffith was trying to leave Biograph and move into features, he took out an ad in the *New York Dramatic Mirror* claiming responsibility for more than 400 films and all the success and innovation of the studio's output, leaving out the contribution of cameraman Billy Bitzer.

Around the same time, the American Federation of Labor (AFL) gave IATSE jurisdiction over motion picture workers, but it had little success in organizing. Instead, cameramen organized as the Cinema Camera Club (CCC) in New York and then as the Static Club in Los Angeles. The industry had grown enough and the professions in it had become defined enough for individuals to seek out a community of colleagues, if not a union. Even though the CCC was not a union, because of the producing companies' leeriness of labor organizing, "Anonymous notices were sent out to as many cameramen as it was possible to reach, with a request that they reply to a certain office in the Tribune Building."[4] However, their secrecy was unnecessary, as little was thought of the organization when it went public the next year.

By 1915, the CCC had 120 members, but it operated mostly as a social club.[5] The two coastal organizations merged in 1917, setting the groundwork for the ASC. By 1918, most prominent filmmakers and their crews had migrated west to work in Los Angeles, and the East Coast orientation of the CCC no longer seemed fitting as membership waned. On December 21, 1918, the club held a meeting of select members in Los Angeles in which to dissolve and reorganize as the ASC two and a half weeks later. Through these changes, the goals of the organization remained focused on community and education.

While IATSE set up a camera operators union (Local 557) in the more labor-friendly city of New York in 1920, on the West Coast, the profession was defined by members of the ASC in the pages of *American Cinematographer*. The front of one of the magazine's first issues featured an essay by Mack Sennett cameraman Fred W. Jackman titled "The Cameraman as He Is," in which he extolled the ASC for "elevat[ing] the public's estimation of the value and importance of their duties."[6] He explicitly places this in opposition to "an organization with a Union charter, which seeks to estimate the art of the cameraman as the level of unskilled labor." This idea, that a union would lower the status of the cameramen while an honorary organization would elevate them to be equals with "writers, artists, sculptors or musicians," as Jackman put it, was pervasive throughout the silent and studio eras and made many wary of unionization. Ironically, a quarter of a century later, Jackman would once again serve as ASC president, negotiating the surrender to IATSE over representation of the cinematographers.

In late 1921, at an AFL meeting focused on disputes in the growing motion picture industry, IATSE gained explicit jurisdiction over cameramen in the Hollywood studios. According to the historian Mike Nielsen, "The cinematographers were at the top of the chain of employment in the craft sector of the production process. . . . To afford maximum job security to its members, IATSE needed to bring all such decision-making technicians into their fold."[7] Yet the cameramen remained hesitant to join IATSE; even assistant cameramen were organized into an ASC-affiliated Junior Cameramen's Club. The choice between the honor of the ASC versus the potential for stability and improved working conditions with IATSE was easy for the first cameramen attracted to the prestige of the ASC, even if it was difficult for their crews.

The ASC stood firmly against the unionization of the cinematographers throughout the battles for the first Studio Basic Agreement (SBA), going so far as to render union members ineligible for membership in its organization.[8] In "An Open Letter" in *American Cinematographer*, ASC's president Daniel B. Clark explained that the cinematographers were not against unions "as a matter of policy or principle," as they had proved "the salvation of the calling of the projectionists."[9] However, the cinematographers did not want to be considered among the ranks of such workers, as he regarded the cameraman's work "as individual and distinctive to such a degree that it cannot be stereotyped into a set basis for a wage scale." Clark instead advocated for the "independence and self-government" of his organization away from any labor union.[10]

The ASC continued in its resistance to the union even after the studios signed the SBA, expanding its organization by creating categories for special process cinematographers, Akeley camera specialists, news cameramen, still photographers, and second cameramen, thereby swelling membership to almost 300. While the editorial line presented in *American Cinematographer* focused on the unification of the "Cameramasters" of Hollywood, this occurred in the direct wake of the SBA and as IATSE was forming the cameramen's locals, indicating that the ASC was protecting its status as the representative body for the cameramen.[11]

IATSE established New York cameramen's Local 644 in 1926 and began working on a West Coast branch. Hollywood cameramen began meeting in the home of Alvin Wyckoff, who would become the Los Angeles union's first president. Seventy-five cameramen signed applications for IATSE membership as a Hollywood branch of Local 644. The application was taken by Roy Klaffki (fresh off shooting Erich von Stroheim's *The Wedding March*) to the IATSE convention in Detroit, where it was approved by IATSE and the 644 leadership. The Hollywood cameramen were given their own separate charter for Local 659 on August 1, 1928. An MGM lawyer, Howard Hurd, became the first business representative, and Loew's executive Nicholas Schenck established the jurisdictional borders between the two unions. Chicago Local 666 was created the following year, splitting the country between the three locals, an arrangement that lasted until the 1990s.

In spite of the ASC's efforts to thwart the success of the union, within a month 659 (which called itself the International Photographers, even though its jurisdiction was the western United States) claimed nearly 600 members, which was 95 percent of all first, second, assistant, and still cameramen working in Hollywood.[12] This rapid and seemingly painless incorporation of the local into the studios (due in large part to the SBA) may have given the leadership the false impression that the issue of representation for the camera workers was settled; it was not. The newly formed Academy of Motion Picture Arts and Sciences (AMPAS), controlled by the producers and administrators of the studios, negotiated a contract with the expanded ASC in 1928, clearly preferring to work with a selective honorary association operating in Hollywood rather than a local with ties to the largest labor union in the nation. Once again, the ASC, with support from the Association of Motion Picture Producers (AMPP) and the Academy, argued that it elevated the cameramen's status closer to the creative "above-the-line" labor of the industry—a persuasive argument for the first cameramen.

In spite of these efforts, the membership in and influence of IATSE Local 659 only grew after it signed the second SBA in November 1928.[13] This led the next administration of the ASC to disavow its interventions into labor representation. In a private letter, Joseph Dubray explained to a fellow ASC member that the aims of the two organizations were completely separate: the union handling the "physical welfare" of the cameramen, and the ASC "remaining the academic and educational society which it has always been."[14] His language implied that the very recent attempts to thwart the unions and negotiate on behalf of its members were to be forgotten.

The Coming of the Soundmen and the Great Depression

Less than two years after the release of the first part-talkie, *The Jazz Singer* (1927), IATSE began setting up Local 695 to represent sound engineers. Likewise, postproduction sound film editors were brought into IATSE's lab workers Local 683 in early 1929. Sound workers were flooding into Hollywood from places such as Western Electric, where they would have been represented by the IBEW. Seeing a threat from the IBEW as its numbers increased, IATSE set up 695 in 1929 and incorporated the local on September 15, 1930, to represent those who worked on set recording audio. Unlike the cameramen who were inventing a new field, these engineers brought skills from radio, telephony, and other fields with more established avenues for training and labor organizing.

The cinematographers' initial contempt for the sound engineers emanated from the engineers' interference with the camera *and* their lack of status in Hollywood. The sound engineers, being new in the motion picture industry, had yet to form any kind of equivalent society to the ASC. As such, they were represented collectively only by their IATSE local, which gave them the appearance of "mere" technicians rather than elite artists. This exaggerated the sense of hierarchy between the two positions from the cinematographers' perspective, making it even more outrageous that they should have to cater to this new department. James Lastra argues that the sound engineers capitulated to the cinematographers too easily; thus, "the status of soundmen in Hollywood was much lower than it should have been."[15] Despite this lower status for the soundmen within the production hierarchy, when it came to labor struggles, the more unified sound workers generally stood on an equal footing with their camera colleagues.

When the Great Depression hit the industry with production slowdowns and cut hours to avoid layoffs, the few IATSE locals that had managed to gain a foothold in the studios pushed back. Although Locals 695, 659, and 683 were still fighting for recognition, they convened to reject the studios' proposed salary cuts, arguing that the studios were violating the terms of the Basic Agreement.[16] Even the political headwinds in labor's favor could not compete with the financial realities of the early years of the Depression. By the end of 1931, the studios were asking the cameramen to take massive pay cuts.[17] Although craft workers mostly avoided wage cuts in 1932, overall wages and salaries went from $156 million in 1931 to $50 million in 1933, in large part due to slowed production and talent cuts.[18]

By 1933, IATSE felt it had enough indispensable presence in the studios to begin a more aggressive fight. In March, 8,000 union workers in the studios refused massive pay cuts, nearly leading to a work stoppage.[19] A compromise, which allowed the locals to take in nonunion workers and move to arbitration, favored the unions and further emboldened them. A few months later, when the producers attempted to take a 20 percent pay cut to Locals 659, 695, and 683, the union heads insisted that recognition of the sound and lab unions was a precondition for any negotiations.[20] The producers likely saw this as an opportunity to weaken the presence of unions within the studios and stem the tide that was looming due to the newly elected progressive administration in the White House.

The tensions boiled over at Columbia Pictures, where Harry Cohn was determined to "abolish all union labor from its studios."[21] On July 15, the sound technicians walked off the lot over a promised and delayed new contract and pay raise. The producers' negotiator, Pat Casey, refused to talk to 695's representative Harold Smith on the grounds that the union "did not have jurisdiction" since Columbia did not recognize the union and had not signed the SBA. Casey tried to meet instead with the IBEW, the union that had represented sound workers when they began arriving in the studios from other industries. However, Smith assured Casey that only seven sound technicians out of hundreds working in the studio were still represented by the electricians' union. Casey's refusal to negotiate led IATSE to authorize a strike of sound workers at all eleven major studios on July 22, leading Warner Bros. (and likely many other studios) to fire their sound department en masse the same day.[22]

Facing a complete work stoppage because of an unrecognized union, most of the studios (including Paramount, Metro, Fox, United Artists, Warner Bros., and

Universal) advertised for scab labor to take over sound recording. When the scabs showed up for work on Monday, July 24, IATSE claimed a violation of the SBA and called for a general strike that would include cameramen, projectionists, editors, lab workers, grips, props, set dressers, and special effects workers. Columbia, Hal Roach, RKO, Fox, and Paramount shuttered production the next day. While Warner Bros. and MGM soldiered on with scab labor (or, as Louis B. Mayer called it, "every man and woman who wants to work"), sound equipment manufacturers ERPI and RCA grew alarmed at the idea of "incompetent" nonunion workers manning their tools. Both sound and camera work had become highly technical, making production nearly impossible without trained, experienced workers. Far from being an inconvenience to work around, the 6,000 striking workers proved themselves essential to the basic functions of Hollywood studios.

If the strike had continued, it likely would have been *the* key moment in labor organization in Hollywood history. However, the newly formed National Labor Board (later renamed the National Labor Relations Board, or NLRB) intervened to end the strike in August. The studios successfully argued that IATSE's efforts were in fact "out of sympathy with the campaign of the President to speed business to normalcy." *Hollywood Filmograph*'s Harry Burns called the strike "the height of stupidity" because it threatened "to upset all the good work that has been done up to date."[23] IATSE had overplayed its hand and lost the struggle for public favor.

IATSE not only failed to gain the participation of fellow unions such as the Carpenters and Joiners, Teamsters, Musicians, and IBEW but also tested the solidarity of its own Hollywood locals. Though the *leadership* of the cameramen's Local 659 firmly supported the strike, the effort angered many cinematographers by lumping them in with "lesser" professions. The move ruptured the precarious coalition in the local, causing dozens of top cameramen to abandon the union, while the ASC negotiated a ten-year deal that required first cameramen working at AMPP companies to be ASC members. The deal, officially signed on September 6, gave "all cameramen, whether members of ASC or not, the benefit of wage scales and working conditions," returning to the rates under the SBA that IATSE signed with the studios.[24] After taking on this labor negotiation, the ASC membership ballooned once again to 400, with a Junior Division for seconds, assistants, and stills men swelling the society's ranks.[25] At the same time, IATSE's membership within the studios dropped from 9,000 to fewer than 200, which *Variety* referred to as the "desertion" of the union, particularly, it noted, by the cameramen.[26]

The "Golden Age" of Labor Strife

The Golden Age of the Hollywood studio system saw both the sound and camera workers negotiating the rising power of IATSE under the corrupt leadership of George Browne and Willie Bioff. The Roosevelt administration's National Recovery Administration (NRA) had its work cut out organizing much of the motion picture industry for the first time, but the NRA concluded that "both sound and cameramen were amply taken care of."[27] Yet these workers' representation was hardly settled. The cameramen fought over who should represent their interests: the American Society of Cinematographers or IATSE Local 659, while the sound workers likewise considered different forms of representation that would delineate their work while resisting the IA's oversight.

The Cameramen's Local 659 attempted to rebuild after the failed strike, forming a 100-person steering committee tasked with reorganizing the union and slashing overhead. They would now have executive and committee members representing all levels of work: second, still, assistant, and newsreel cameramen, not just the first cameramen who had largely fled to the ASC.[28] There were brief discussions at this time of merging the union with the ASC, but the talks quickly fizzled out due to lingering resentment over the ASC's opposition to the strike.[29]

After the coming of sound, the first cameramen adopted the title director of photography (DP), furthering their association with the above-the-line workers. Given that, the new, more democratic structure of 659 did not sit well with many of them, and some ASC members began circulating a petition in late 1935 to designate the society as their "sole representative for negotiations of wage scale agreements [and] working conditions."[30] Over 500 cameramen signed the petition, signaling their growing discontent with the IATSE local, yet the ASC failed in its attempt to take over representation of the camera crew. While the ASC negotiated a contract with the major producers for exclusive representation of the first cameramen (or DPs) in late 1935, all other camera workers (seconds, stills, etc.) returned to the IATSE local.[31]

The split between the DPs and their crews, the former represented by the ASC and the latter by Local 659, seemed inevitable. More significantly, it was favored by many DPs, including the co-winner of the first Academy Award for cinematography, Karl Struss. In 1934, Struss began a personal crusade against the union, launching a lawsuit against the International Photographers and soliciting contributions to his cause from other prominent ASC members, including Charles Rosher (his *Sunrise* co-cinematographer), James Wong Howe, and Gregg Toland.[32] Among his many concerns, Struss distrusted the union due to the corruption at the top of the IA throughout the latter 1930s and early 1940s (discussed in the introduction to part I), which was widely felt among the ASC membership.

While the split had some logic given the divergent needs of workers of differing status, IATSE leaders (and mob affiliates) George Browne and Willie Bioff were not ready to give up on the first cameramen. The DPs, with their high status and control over large portions of the set, were seen as key to winning over the entirety of Hollywood's below-the-line labor. In 1938, Local 659 filed a petition with the NLRB seeking collective bargaining designation "for all photographic work" at the studios.[33] Though the NLRB saw many jurisdictional disputes from the motion picture industry at this time, *Variety* considered the fight over the cameramen as the "most important."[34] When the ASC sought to renew its contract with the studios for another five years, IATSE loudly demanded "the return of jurisdiction over first cameramen," to no avail.[35]

These efforts to strong-arm the DPs into returning to Local 659 were led by the union's business representative, Herbert Aller, and President Hal Mohr, who also held a spot on the ASC's board. While Mohr assured the AMPP that most of the ASC favored the local and were already members, it is clear there was dissent even within the society's leadership. In October 1939, the ASC members once again rejected a proposed merger with Local 659; they instead supported a measure to form their own separate local within IATSE.[36] Aller made it clear to the IA leadership that such a proposal would be unacceptable. Rather than trying to win over the DPs, they forced them to join 659, insisting all IA members resign from the ASC.[37]

While the two organizations battled, the cameramen themselves seemed unwilling to sacrifice either organization. The ASC board assured Fred Pelton of the AMPP of the unwillingness of the DPs to join a union "with the balance of the photographic craft."[38] The board cited the huge differences in salaries, potential poor participation if forced to join, and the supposed preference of the second and assistant cameramen (due to fear of embarrassment in front of their bosses). The ASC pleaded its case once again to the IATSE leadership for a separate charter, but it was once again denied—vowing to continue its efforts while 659 pledged to continue recruiting members from its ranks.[39]

The dispute between the ASC and 659 came to a head in the early months of World War II. Several ASC members joined an attempt to create an alternate union sponsored by the IBEW, Local 1318, "exclusively for First Cameramen of the Motion Picture Industry."[40] The ASC pleaded its case in a full-page ad in *The Hollywood Reporter* describing the aggressive tactics of the "Bioff-Browne crowd" and its regret at any "inconvenience" caused by the ongoing conflict.[41] The ASC's attempt at gaining industry favor came as the jurisdictional disputes were heating up. Warnings against dual card-carrying led to Dewey Wrigley's expulsion from the ASC for taking over a Fox shoot from Virgil Miller without approval from the board.[42]

At this point, months into the much more pressing world war, ASC president Fred Jackman called for a sixty-day truce, at the end of which the ASC agreed to abandon the merger with the IBEW and join with 659.[43] The agreement constituted a near-total victory for IATSE and 659, which was granted jurisdiction over first cameramen, elimination of the no-strike clause, and the ASC's guarantee that it would "forever relinquish all rights as a collective bargaining agent."[44] In return, 659 had to admit all first cameramen "without reservation and condition," including members who had long since moved into process photography such as Farciot Edouard and Jackman himself. The DPs were given special status within the local, but they had in essence lost their efforts to be separate from the crews that worked under them. Jackman was hardly surprised, though regretful, a month later when Struss resigned from the ASC board, his efforts having clearly failed.[45]

Surprisingly, the ASC's attempts to represent labor in this era were not confined to the cinematographers, as it also became involved with representation of sound workers. In January 1934, the sound workers met at the Writers Club to determine who would represent them under the NRA code—the IBEW or IATSE. A large contingent chose neither and voiced their intention to affiliate with the American Society of Cinematographers, in what *The Hollywood Reporter* called a "bombshell."[46] Like the cinematographers, many in the sound departments resented IATSE's failed strike of the previous summer, yet they were unwilling to see themselves as mere electrical workers" (the IBEW received the fewest votes). While the ASC affiliation failed to gain enough support, many soundmen remained skeptical of both IATSE and AFL leadership.

Finding little recourse from within, the independently minded sound workers who had favored ASC affiliation left 695 en masse to form the American Society of Sound Engineers, taking their business rep Harold Smith with them.[47] The goal of the new organization, which immediately claimed 200 members, was to get away from "jurisdictional disputes and labor union difficulties" by remaining unaffiliated with a larger international.[48] Yet they still needed to combat the IBEW contract and now had an enemy in IATSE Local 695. Having Smith, a well-known Bioff-Browne associate, as their advocate while operating outside the jurisdiction of the AFL seemed to have broken the stalemate. A deal was quickly negotiated, moving all electricians to the IBEW (out of IATSE Local 37) and all sound workers back to Local 695 with Smith returning as their representative.[49] When the IA scored its victory over the IBEW in representing Hollywood labor at the end of 1935 through Bioff and Browne's strong-arm tactics, soundmen were carved out of the deal to be dealt with in arbitration.[50] Through a series of shady, closed-door "negotiations," IATSE Local 695 became the sole union representing sound workers in Hollywood by mid-1936.[51]

With representation seemingly settled, the power and influence of Local 695, firmly in the pocket of the Bioff-Browne regime, quickly grew. Harold Smith led the charge in supporting the continuation of international supervision over local autonomy. While the cinematographers were fighting to be independent of any larger union, the sound workers were embracing the oversight and the collective power that came with centralized leadership. Smith's loyalty led the IATSE leadership to elevate him to being their West Coast representative.

Local 659's camera crew membership and its representative Herbert Aller stood alongside Harold Smith and the sound Local 695 in support of the IA. These unions, along with the Lab Workers 683 and Technicians 37, altogether representing 12,000 workers, constituted the IATSE stronghold within the studios. This consolidation of power did not go unquestioned, as affiliates of the Congress of

Industrial Organizations (CIO), which had just broken from the AFL, filed charges in 1938 with the NLRB of unfair labor practices by IATSE, which they justifiably argued was attempting to set up a company union. As a countermeasure against the suit, Local 695 led an effort with the NLRB to gain official recognition for IATSE as "sole bargaining agency" for their local—followed by similar petitions from the cameramen, lab workers, and technicians.[52]

The NLRB was unmoved, and the IATSE leadership backed off in early 1939, returning local rule to the four unions in exchange for a request that the board dismiss the charges of company unionism.[53] Smith and Aller had risen to leadership through cooperation with Bioff and Browne, but the loss for IATSE gave them more power over their locals. While Smith had proved his loyalty to the regime, Aller used this increased independence to separate himself, even calling for Smith's resignation.[54] Smith clung to his job at 695, but he was forced to step back from his position as the West Coast representative of the IA as part of the Bioff-Browne regime lowering its profile in the wake of investigations.[55]

In a maneuver to enlarge 695 and gain greater autonomy from IATSE, Smith moved aggressively for full control over sound workers in every corner of Hollywood. Local 695 already had contracts with the major studios, so Smith turned his sights to the "independents," strong-arming Republic and other smaller studios into exclusive contracts with 695.[56] The local's strike against Republic in April 1940 lasted approximately one hour, ending with a phone call from Bioff ordering its members back to work.[57] In spite of the pushback from the IA leadership, 695 succeeded in securing a contract with thirty-seven independent producers with a new minimum wage, a four-man crew minimum, and total jurisdiction over sound workers.[58]

The removal of Bioff and Browne and the beginning of World War II led to a period of calm in the labor sector of Hollywood—particularly for the sound and camera workers. The soundmen signed a new two-year contract in 1942 with little negotiation, and Smith's contract was extended "past the duration of the war," whenever that would be.[59] Likewise, 659 had won its battle with the ASC for the cinematographers and had gained the membership of every first cameramen, but for thirty holdouts, by mid-1943.[60] During the war years, the locals enjoyed relative peace and autonomy from the IA as significant numbers of its members left the studio for the battlefield.

Throughout the war, the new IATSE president Richard Walsh (a Bioff-Browne associate) worked to rebuild the IA and reassert its control over the Hollywood locals. The last two holdouts in this effort were the cameramen and the soundmen, represented by strong, entrenched representatives in Herbert Aller and Harold Smith, respectively. The War Labor Board repeatedly supported the two locals' efforts to maintain their autonomy from the IA.[61] Ultimately, the IA leadership would use their jurisdictional fight against the CSU (detailed in the introduction to part I) to consolidate its authority over the locals. During the CSU strike and ongoing upheavals from 1945 to 1947, the IA leadership threatened to take over any local that got out of line, but Smith and Aller acted together in defiance. Throughout his firsthand account of these events, Gene Mailes consistently pairs Smith and Aller together as powerful agents more concerned with their own job security than with member welfare.[62] Despite the loyalty these reps had engendered in their decades with their respective locals, this would be a last gasp for local autonomy.

With the slow dissolution of the CSU in the late 1940s, IATSE had prevailed over below-the-line labor in Hollywood. The labor issues that would arise in the postwar era and beyond for Locals 659 and 695 would largely center on various efforts to broaden their scope, including through new technologies, diversification of the workforce, and the expansion of the jurisdictions for both unions.

The Postwar Technological Shift

The postwar reorganization of the industry saw not only the breakdown of the vertical structure that defined the studio era but also a realignment of the division of labor that had prevailed since the silent era. Both Local 659 and Local 695 initially saw diminishing employment for their members in the wake of the Paramount Decrees and the subsequent decline of motion picture production, but the members increasingly turned to the new medium of television for work. By 1954, Aller estimated a quarter of 659 members were working behind the camera in television, while 695 claimed 60 percent of its members were in TV by the end of the decade.[63]

Television ushered in new picture and sound technologies, which created new jurisdictional questions. Throughout the 1950s, more and more television programming was being captured on videotape rather than on film stock. At the same time, sound recording, in both film and television, was transitioning from optical recording to magnetic tape. These changes in the fundamental tools being used by camera and sound workers led to new battles, even within IATSE. In the early 1960s, when IA president Richard Walsh sought to establish a new tape contract with the studios, both 659 and 695 were adamant that their contracts covered tape already and fought off Walsh's attempt to circumvent them.[64]

Likewise, the new medium brought with it new unions with which the IATSE locals had to compete for work. The National Association of Broadcast Employees and Technicians (NABET) began as an NBC company union and affiliated with the CIO in 1951. NABET operated across the industry rather than taking the craft local approach of IATSE. As the work of the NABET members in television, particularly in camera and sound departments, increasingly resembled motion picture work, 659 and 695 sought to absorb its members.

What started in the mid-1960s as friendly talks turned into raids on NABET-represented crews at the networks. Locals 659 and 695 felt that anyone doing camera and sound work in Los Angeles should be under their jurisdiction, no matter the medium. When the AFL and CIO merged in 1955, NABET and

IATSE fell under the same umbrella organization, but Aller and Thomas Carman (who moved into 695's leadership after Harold Smith was ousted for embezzlement) seemingly did not care.[65] Aller and Carman admitted their open defiance of the AFL-CIO, and both claimed that IATSE had given them tacit permission to raid NABET with Aller claiming, "Walsh hasn't told me to stop."[66] In May 1967, the two locals claimed to have gathered 678 signed cards from NABET technicians working in Los Angeles studios. Carman and Aller sought to take their efforts to the NLRB for approval, but they were shot down by the AFL-CIO leadership.[67] While their ambition to take over all NABET work in Hollywood was thwarted, they continued to fight the incursion of the rival union's workers in their territory into the 1980s.[68]

It was undeniable that particularly in the realm of sound, the job, not just the technology, had changed. The incorporation of sound recording into the camera in studio work eliminated the traditional role of the sound recorder, one of the four union-required soundmen on the set. In one example at Columbia, the recorder was loading tape at the beginning of the day, unloading at the end, and sitting in the sound shop the rest of the day.[69] On other sets, the sound mixer was taking on extra duties by working with the tape cartridges. This technological change also led to conflict between 659 and 695 (as well as the Film Editors Local 776, discussed at length in chapter four) in the early 1970s, with the cameramen accusing 695 of raiding and overstepping its jurisdiction. In retort, the 695 representative accused both unions of allowing their members to do sound work in highly personal terms, claiming, "Jerry's [659] members do my sound work all over town, and Walsh allows them to. As for Lehners [776], his editors do my transferring in soundwork in backyards, basements and other clandestine places."[70]

The fighting among the locals was halted when members realized President Walsh was negotiating directly with the studios without their consent. The camera and sound workers united in opposition to Walsh's negotiations over videotape with the Alliance of Motion Picture and Television Producers (AMPTP) in 1973, accusing him of violating the Labor-Management Relations Act of 1947.[71] This cooled the tension between the two unions, leading to an agreement between them (which was later amended to award tape editor jurisdiction to Local 776).[72] With Richard Walsh retired from IATSE leadership after more than thirty years, Frank Segers opined in *Variety* that the "craft-splintered" structure of IATSE had been to its detriment in the shift to tape, which blurred such distinctions.[73] The three unions continued to squabble about differences between their work with videotape well into the 1980s.[74] The same issues between 695 and 776 would be ignited with the turn to digital audio in postproduction in the 1990s.[75]

The Roster System and the Civil Rights Era

Fights over tools on set defined the sound and camera unions after World War II, but they were not the only issues radically transforming the unions.

Both unions had long been dominated by white men, perhaps more so than any other professions in Hollywood. The maintenance of this narrowly defined workforce was perpetuated by the adoption of the Industry Experience Roster system in the wake of the Paramount Decrees. However, the civil rights and women's rights movements and the internationalization of the motion picture industry would push the two locals to change their ways, often against their will.

Along with other IATSE locals, 659 and 695 introduced a roster system in the late 1940s as an answer to the freelancification of their member workforce. The Industry Experience Roster was designed to ensure continued employment for experienced union members over those who might enter the industry in this time of flux. As discussed in the introduction to part I, the roster system helped IATSE locals and their members survive the decline of the studio system, but prioritizing employment for experienced workers hindered efforts to diversify the industry in the 1960s.

An unintended (or perhaps intended) consequence of this new structure, in which the unions had at least some control over who got jobs, was that it became the union's responsibility to diversify crews. In 1963, when the NAACP requested that one crew member of color be added to each crew (and admitted into that position's union), the cameramen "flatly opposed," saying this would be "contrary to [the] union's pacts" with the industry.[76] The cameramen's rejection of the plan had a cascading effect, with "union after union follow[ing] suit," as was often the case when Local 659 took a position.[77] While other professions made progress in diversifying their memberships with these efforts, the lack of progress among the camera and sound workers was noted, with the NAACP Hollywood–Beverly Hills chapter "narrowing" its sights on those two remaining "discriminatory crafts." Herb Aller of 659 waged a public battle against the NAACP and its accusations of discrimination, dismissing the NAACP's Herbert Hill as a "rabblerouser."[78]

Aller was fighting these accusations and threats against the union for discrimination at the same time there was increasing attention on the problem of the experience roster system. While the two are "unrelated," it is hard to separate the struggle for diversification from the larger issue of the unions acting as gatekeepers into industry employment. These events set at least some of the context as the Equal Employment Opportunity Commission (EEOC) held hearings on the problem of racial diversity in the industry in 1969. After the EEOC's damning report, the Justice Department negotiated a deal with the unions to avoid another painful consent decree like the Paramount Decrees of 1948. Under the agreement, the craft unions were asked to make one referral from a minority labor pool for every four referrals made from the general pool.[79]

While there was backlash to these efforts, the results are not entirely to be dismissed, as there was a marked change in approach from Locals 659 and 695. When a few IATSE members attempted to rally support to overturn the decision, the business agents for soundmen and cameramen came out strongly against the group.[80] Likewise, when the two years of the agreement had passed, only four unions had met the specified goals, but they were the cameramen, sound workers, editors, and costumers—the skilled crafts that had been asked to institute referral quotas.[81] While the other IA locals challenged the diversity initiatives by emphasizing the strength of their experience roster, the cameramen and sound workers had strengthened their rosters with the addition of new members.

In 1972, Local 659 became the first IATSE local to sign an agreement that allowed all minority trainees (along with members already in groups 2 and 3) to join group 1, the top tier of the roster. Anyone new at that point would have to enter through the lower groups.[82] In this way the local was able to appease the Justice Department while ensuring the continued favoritism toward existing members—at least over future new members. This was hardly the end of the diversity problem, as the growing issue looming in the background was the complete absence of *any* women members.

About six weeks after the minority agreement was signed, bringing all existing members and trainees into group 1 and closing the door behind them, a class action lawsuit was filed in federal court by Sandra Lee Kaplan, who had been trying to enter the cameramen's local for two years.[83] Another six weeks later, before the court could make a decision, 659 admitted Bri Murphy as its first ever female member, ensuring Kaplan would not gain that pioneer status by force of the courts—she was admitted about a week later.[84] It would be another couple of years before 695 would also be confronted with claims of gender discrimination within their union and the sound profession. Maureen Madery had served as assistant business agent for Local 695 but was denied membership in the union.[85] Additionally, she was underpaid compared with men in the same position. She filed charges in 1976 and was fired a year later when the union emerged from one of its many periods of trusteeship. The court ruled in her favor, giving her a small settlement, but it did not reinstate her job or give her a union card.

Despite the valiant attempts to preserve the Industry Experience Roster system, it began to deteriorate, in no small part due to these efforts to open the professions to a wider population. In early 1974, the Supreme Court declined to review the DC Appeals Court's decision to uphold the NLRB's determination that the Local 659 industry roster system was discriminatory.[86] The NLRB ordered the local to "stop enforcing the roster system in a discriminatory manner," but it left enforcement in the hands of future complainants. The incredibly fragile employment situation of minority and women camera and sound personnel made it nearly impossible for them to be the ones to enforce the decision. Rather, it was independent filmmakers, such as Andrew Davis (who made his name as a blaxploitation cameraman before becoming the director of films such as *The Fugitive*) and Tak Fujimoto (who had already begun working with Jonathan Demme) who launched a class action lawsuit against Local 659 in 1975 and helped to diminish the role of the roster system.[87]

Expanding Jurisdictions

Through myriad fights with the AMPTP and the IA, the sound and camera unions have grown over the decades in different ways. While 695's expansion involved incorporating workers with new expertise in an ever-changing technological landscape, 659 has increased its jurisdiction over cameramen geographically. Many of these developments were brought on by the rise of runaway production in the postwar era. Local 659 representative Herb Aller became chairman of the AFL's Film Council on runaway production in 1954.[88] The local took an aggressive stance against international production and staged a boycott and picketed runaway productions in 1960.[89] While such tactics were quickly deemed counterproductive, the concerns about work moving out of Hollywood were salient for the camera and sound crews. While a DP would likely be hired from among 659 members, his crew might be picked locally. This was true whether in Europe or in New York, the center of more productions with the rise of location shooting.

As early as 1956, a floor fight broke out at the IATSE convention over Local 659's request that production crews be "allowed to travel and work anywhere in the U.S.," wiping out the three-way split in jurisdiction established in the late 1920s.[90] The effort was rejected by a three-to-one margin after extensive debate. The separate jurisdictions for 659 (Hollywood), 644 (New York), and 666 (Chicago) had caused only minor headaches during the studio era, when Hollywood productions were shot mostly on the studio backlots, but the shift in the industry toward location shooting transformed this from an irritation to a major problem.

In the 1970s, the issues of regional jurisdiction and the incursion of prominent foreign-born DPs caused consternation for 659. It went back and forth with the New York union, with members of Local 644 complaining they could not come to Hollywood, but then blocking members of Local 659 on Hollywood productions that did location work in New York.[91] While the IA Basic Agreement allowed Hollywood crews to go anywhere in the United States without violating jurisdictional agreements, 644 saw the increasingly mobile 659 members as an invasion into their territory. On the other hand, the New York–based 644 crew on the Warner Bros. film *Going in Style* (1979) was disallowed from finishing the twelve-week shoot when the production moved to Las Vegas for its final week.[92]

The structure set up during the studio era, which also limited foreign members, could not account for the increasingly complex constellation that made up modern film crews. For example, when Haskell Wexler had to drop out of the Robert Redford film *Brubaker* (1980), the production hired the French cinematographer Bruno Nuytten for the Ohio-based shoot with a crew supplied by Local 666 in Chicago.[93] Local 659 fought against granting of permits to foreign DPs such as Nuytten, also denying Vittorio Storaro's request to join the *Reds* (1981) production for its one-week stateside shoot.[94] The producers attempted to tack Storaro's work onto the end of his shoot on Francis Ford Coppola's *One from the Heart* (1981), for which he was granted an exception, but they were denied.

The protests, boycotts, and walk-offs on these productions were indicative that the geographic division of the camera locals made little sense in the poststudio era. As a New York union official said during the *Going in Style* dustup, "It looks like there is more chance for New York camera crews to get reciprocity with England than with its [*sic*] own nation on the West Coast." Once again, there were calls to merge the three locals into one national local. While they continued to clash over productions such as *Ghostbusters*, in 1984 the members of 644 voted for the merger. But they disagreed on how to go about it, given that Local 644 was not a part of the Hollywood unions' Basic Agreement with the studios.[95] The talks leading to the merger began in earnest in 1988 but took the better part of a decade to resolve. Jurisdictional battles were waged until the bitter end, with confusion over the jurisdiction of Minnesota on the Coen brothers' *Fargo* (1996), which New York "believed" was theirs.[96]

When a district court judge denied the 644's last-minute injunction, the merger finally came through in May 1996, with 659, 644, and 666 united into the national IATSE Local 600. Local 659 had called itself the International Photographers Guild since its inception, but at least now it was a national union (the first in IATSE, followed in 1997 by Local 800 Art Directors, in 1998 by Local 700 Editors, and in 2023 by Local 839 Animators). A year and a half later, the merger was complete when the members ratified their first national contract with the studios.[97]

The 695 sound union did not experience the same move toward a national local, and to this day it is still geographically bound to the Los Angeles area. However, it has expanded its membership as the tools of the trade have evolved. Perhaps because of 695's rebel spirit (which dates to the bombastic leadership of Harold Smith), more and more technical workers joined their ranks seeking the local's protection. This is despite the fact that the local has frequently clashed with the IA leadership (and almost as frequently been forced into trusteeship).

In 695's aggressive battle in the late 1970s to maintain three-man sound crews on all productions, the IA repeatedly refused to provide aid, instead denying strike requests, negotiating behind its backs, and attempting to cajole the local into compliance by putting it in trusteeship.[98] While the AMPTP filed complaints against 695 with the NLRB for "harassment," the members continued their push for home rule, ratifying a network newsreel contract without IA oversight.[99] Every attempt to stamp out the union's efforts led them to double down. When representative Jack Coffey was suspended for a year (not for the first time) as part of the trusteeship, he fought not only to return but also to run for IATSE president (which he did repeatedly, always losing narrowly).[100] Coffey and other leaders' dogged determination in one area ultimately prevailed, resulting in the restoration of the three-soundmen crew in 1979.[101]

Despite 695's precarious status within the IA, media workers repeatedly voted to join its ranks—likely recognizing the ways the union had served its members in recent decades. They were joined by Local 789 Cinetechnicians in 1979, the video technicians of Compact Video Sales in 1981, and Local 165 Projectionists in 1987. The 1990s saw volatility in the leadership that led to another bout of trusteeship. IA leadership took advantage of this period of weakness, moving nearly half of 695's members to the Editors Guild (Local 700) and the Lab Technicians Local 683 (now part of 700).[102] This effectively ended the sound local's run as one of the more powerful unions in Hollywood. Today, according to its website, the union "proudly represents the finest technicians in production sound, video assist, video engineering and studio projection," still expanded well beyond the initial jurisdiction only in on-set sound.

The changes to Local 695 reflected the IA's focus in recent decades on consolidation of locals in Hollywood to increase their size and power. While the mergers within 695 have a logical focus on recording and playback technicians, this effort has led to less obvious pairings. A particularly odd move was the merger of the Publicists Guild of America (IATSE Local 818) into the cameramen's Local 600 in 2002. In what *The Hollywood Reporter* referred to as a "shotgun wedding," the IA leadership "mandated" the merger, claiming there were overlapping interests such as "the fact that still photogs and publicists frequently work together."[103] This justification strains logic but fits with IATSE's overall mission of folding smaller Hollywood locals (the publicists numbered around 400) into larger ones to increase their strength.

The Ongoing Battles

In 2021, *Variety* released a massive study of racial diversity among the IATSE locals, using Asian and Latino surnames to capture a rough estimate of the representation of these populations. As with the NAACP's studies of Black representation in the 1960s, the camera and sound unions came out near the bottom. Unlike many of the other locals that acknowledged their shortcomings, 695 and 600 bristled at the study's conclusions, with the sound spokesman calling the method "racist and inaccurate" and the publicist for the cinematographers calling it "flawed."[104] Nonetheless, the study showed that these core locals fell behind the other unions in expanding their memberships beyond the white men who had founded them nearly a hundred years earlier.

With progress yet to be made, IATSE Locals 600 and 695 continue to represent the key technical personnel on set in Hollywood productions. With the expansive growth of postproduction in recent decades, the need to have highly skilled craftsmen and technicians *on set* to capture live sounds and images may have become a smaller part of the process, but they are no less central.

Notes

1 See "To Hell with Photography! What About Sound?," *American Cinematographer* (hereafter *AC*) 9, no. 9, December 1928, 4; Frank Lawrence, "The War of the Talkies" *AC* 9, no. 10, January 1929, 11, 13, 25.
2 Patrick Keating, *Hollywood Lighting: From the Silent Era to Film Noir* (Columbia University Press, 2009).
3 David S. Hulfish, *Motion-Picture Work*, (American School of Correspondence, 1913), 76.
4 H. Lyman Broening, "How It All Happened," *AC* 2, no. 19, October 1921, 13.
5 "Goodbye 'Static' Club," *Cinema News*, November 1917, 10.
6 Fred W. Jackman, "The Cameraman as He Is," *AC* 1, no. 4, December 1920, 1.
7 Michael Nielsen, "Motion Picture Craft Workers and Craft Unions in Hollywood: The Studio Era, 1912–1948" (PhD diss., University of Illinois at Champaign-Urbana, 1985), 138.
8 Foster Goss to Edwin DuPar, August 7, 1926, Edwin DuPar Member File, ASC Collection, Margaret Herrick Library, Beverly Hills, CA (hereafter ASC Collection).
9 Daniel B. Clark, ASC, "An Open Letter," *AC* 7, no. 5, August 1926, 8.
10 Daniel Clark, "The A. S. C. and the A. F. L.," *AC* 8, no. 8, November 1927, 11.
11 Silas Edgar Snyder, "Editorial—The Voice of the A.S.C.," *AC* 8, no. 6, September 1927, 5.
12 "Defines Attitude of Cameramen's Union," *Motion Picture News*, September 29, 1928, 1000.
13 "Studio Agreement," *International Photographer* 1, no. 1, February 1929, 1.
14 Joseph Dubray to Edwin Dyer, December 12, 1928, Edwin Dyer Member Files, ASC Collection.
15 James Lastra, *Sound Technology and the American Cinema: Perception, Representation, Modernity* (Columbia University Press, 2000), 171.
16 "Big Labor Meet Sunday," *The Hollywood Reporter* (hereafter *THR*), December 12, 1931, 1–2.
17 "Labor Situation Acute," *THR*, December 16, 1931, 1, 3.
18 Nielsen, "Motion Picture Craft Workers," 156.
19 "No Production Shut-Down," *Variety*, March 14, 1933, 5, 25.
20 "Prod.-IATSE Meetings Break Up in Deadlock," *THR*, May 18, 1933, 1, 2.
21 "Production Recovering from Strike of 6,000 on West Coast," (*Motion Picture Herald* hereafter *MPH*), July 28, 1933, 10. Quotations in the next two paragraphs are also from this source.
22 WB Sound Personnel Files, Box 2819B, Warner Bros. Archives, University of Southern California. Other studios likely did the same, but we have evidence only from Warner Bros.
23 Harry Burns, "Strike Threatens to Upset the Entire Industry," *Hollywood Filmograph* 13, no. 29, July 29, 1933, 1, 3.
24 "ASC's Wage Act Brings on Further Dissension in Lens Unit of IATSE with Militants Reported Using Ax," *Variety*, October 17, 1933, 4.
25 William Stull to George Benoit, February 22, 1934, George Benoit File, ASC Collection.
26 Hugh Lovell and Tasile Carter, *Collective Bargaining in the Motion Picture Industry: A Struggle for Stability* (Institute for Industrial Relations, University of California, 1955), 17.

27 "Soundmen Claim They Will Get Scale They Struck For; Point to the Code," *Variety*, December 12, 1933, 7.
28 "Steering Committee of 100 to Guide New Union Set-Up," *THR*, February 21, 1934, 7.
29 "ASC-Union Merger Off," *THR*, May 9, 1934, 1, 5.
30 "A.S.C. Asking Final Say-So," *Variety*, December 11, 1935, 12.
31 "IATSE's Move for All Labor," *Variety*, December 25, 1935, 5.
32 Karl Struss to Mr. Leonard M. Smith, June 19, 1934, Karl Struss File, ASC Collection.
33 "Photographers Union Opposes ASC Claims," *Motion Picture Daily* (hereafter *MPD*), October 24, 1938, 1, 2; "Tension between SAG and Independents," *Boxoffice*, October 29, 1938, 17.
34 "Ready Docket for NLRB Hearings on Squawks Affecting 15,000 in Pix," *Variety*, January 4, 1939, 30.
35 "IATSE in Two New Jurisdiction Fights," *MPD*, July 7, 1939, 1, 6.
36 "IATSE Seeks Film Studio Control by Takeover of Cinematographers," *Variety*, July 12, 1939, 6; "Raises, Not Cuts, Talent Demand; New AFL-CIO Fight Near in East," *MPH*, October 14, 1939, 48; "Labor Council Formed to Deal with Producers; Bioff Head," *Boxoffice*, October 14, 1939, 66.
37 "I.A. Demands Cameramen's Jurisdiction," *MPD*, November 26, 1940, 4.
38 Letter: Board of Directors ASC to Fred Pelton, MPPA, October 25, 1941, Charles G. Clarke Collection, Folder 33, ASC Collection.
39 "ASC Wants Own Charter," *Variety*, July 23, 1941, 29.
40 Statement, October 1, 1942, IBEW Local Union No. 1318, "First Cameramen of the Motion Picture Industry," Karl Struss File, ASC Collection.
41 "The Case of the Cameramen" (ad), *THR*, August 6, 1942, 22.
42 "ASC Gauntlet to IATSE Members," *Variety*, August 12, 1942, 25.
43 "Fight Continues on Cameraman Status," *MPH*, September 5, 1942, 38; "ASC Votes to Join IATSE Coast Local," *MPD*, November 16, 1942, 1, 8.
44 Agreement between ASC, Inc., and Local 659 of the IATSE, December 10, 1942, ASC miscellaneous, f.638, ASC Collection.
45 Fred Jackman to Karl Struss, December 15, 1942, Karl Struss File, ASC Collection.
46 "Sound Men in Muddle," *THR*, January 9, 1934, 1, 4. According to *The Hollywood Reporter*, the vote was 448 for Local 695, 93 for the ASC, and 9 for the IBEW. "IATSE Goes into Action," *THR*, April 2, 1934, 1, 5.
47 Mike Nielsen and Gene Mailes, *Hollywood's Other Blacklist: Union Struggle in the Studio System* (British Film Institute, 1995), 42.
48 "New Sound Men's Group Swinging into Action," *THR*, May 4, 1934, 6.
49 "IATSE and IBEW to Trade Off Their Differences," *THR*, June 26, 1934, 5. Yet, a year later, in 1935, history repeated itself, with Local 695 again complaining of the IBEW's interference with the sound workers. "I.A. Resumes I.B.E.W. Fight," *International Projectionist* 9, no. 3, September 1935, 22; "Start New Coast Union," *MPD*, November 2, 1935, 4.
50 "IATSE Wins Out in IBEW–Hollywood Studios Showdown; IA Closed Shop," *Variety*, December 11, 1935, 5, 12.
51 "Soundmen Now under IATSE Jurisdiction," *MPD*, April 1, 1936, 2. See Nielsen and Mailes, *Hollywood's Other Blacklist*, for more on Bioff and Browne.
52 "IATSE Asks Bargaining Agency Certification," *Film Daily*, October 14, 1938, 2; "Four Coast Locals Seek Certification," *MPD*, October 14, 1938, 1, 5.
53 "Majors Cited for NLRB Violations, Unions Given Autonomy by IATSE," *MPH*, February 4, 1939, 36; "Unions Ask Dismissal," *MPD*, February 21, 1939, 3.

54 Nielsen and Mailes, *Hollywood's Other Blacklist*, 53.
55 "Smith, Resigned Coast Rep. of IATSE, Questioned by Rose," *Film Daily*, May 31, 1939, 6.
56 "Indies Given Week's Time to Raise Soundmen's Pay," *Film Daily*, March 18, 1940, 1, 7.
57 "Bioff Halts Republic Strike in One Hour," *MPD*, April 8, 1940, 2.
58 "37 Indie Hollywood Producers Sign New Minimum Wage Agreement with IATSE Sound Technicians 695," *Variety*, November 6, 1940, 15.
59 "Soundmen Agree to Terms by Producers," *Variety*, April 22, 1942, 22; "Field to Himself," *Variety*, December 23, 1942, 10.
60 "Photogs Local Rounds Up All Pic Lensers," *Variety*, June 2, 1943, 23.
61 "WLB Gives Okay to Local Autonomy for Soundmen, Rebuffs IA's Int'l," *Variety*, January 17, 1945, 11; "RWLB Voids IATSE Photographers' Pact," *MPD*, July 27, 1945, 5.
62 Nielsen and Mailes, *Hollywood's Other Blacklist*, 113.
63 "Vidpix Avert Crisis for Coast Unions; Hypo Employment from 25 to 60%," *Variety*, May 19, 1954, 41, 44; "Hollywood in a Television Boom," *Broadcasting*, October 26, 1959, 88–89.
64 "Lampmen Rue IA's Talks with Studios for a Tape Pact," *Variety*, October 16, 1963, 4; "IA Locals Rebuff Walsh in Bid to 'Tape Up' Major Telefilmeries," *Variety*, July 31, 1963, 64.
65 "Coast Technicians to Try Suspended Execs on Funds Rap," *Variety*, April 4, 1951, 7; "Sound Local's New Faces," *Variety*, March 9, 1955, 22.
66 "IATSE Shed Role as Intervenor, Makes Own Bid for Grab vs. Nabet," *Variety*, May 3, 1967, 44.
67 "AFL-CIO Stops IATSE Romance with Units of NABET on Coast," *Variety*, August 9, 1967, 46.
68 "2 IATSE Locals Join for Fuss with NABET," *Variety*, August 6, 1980, 58; "NABET Scores Win over IATSE in N.Y. WOR Election," *THR*, May 9, 1983, 1, 10.
69 "About New Tools & Old Jobholders," *Variety*, May 10, 1967, 11.
70 "IATSE Locals' Vidtape Battle Wide Open Via Defy by Soundmen," *Variety*, January 26, 1972, 45.
71 "3 IATSE Unions File Charges vs. 74 AMPTP Films," *Variety*, June 6, 1973, 44.
72 "IA Photogs, Sound Men Settle Intro Hassle over Videotape Jobs," *Variety*, October 10, 1973, 4.
73 Frank Segers, "Videotape and Jurisdiction" *Variety*, January 9, 1974, 101, 104.
74 "Editors, Soundmen Settle Long Fight over Jurisdiction," *Variety*, December 9, 1987, 4, 87.
75 "Unions Smooth Digital Edit Feud," *THR*, June 12, 1996, 1, 8, 42.
76 "IATSE: No Negro Need Apply," *Variety*, July 31, 1963, 7.
77 "Negroes Want IATSE Memberships," *Variety*, August 7, 1963, 11.
78 "IA's Herb Aller Chides NAACP's Rabblerousing," *Variety*, July 13, 1966, 1, 54.
79 To Duck 'Consent' H'wood Pledges Racial Quota Hiring," *Variety*, February 25, 1970, 1, 78.
80 "IA Hits Race Pledge Un-Doers," *Variety*, December 30, 1970, 7.
81 "Racial Minority Pact's Future?," *Variety*, April 26, 1972, 5, 22.
82 "Cameramen Fully Okay Minorities Plan of Justice," *Variety*, December 27, 1972, 18.
83 "Class Suit Calls Camera Union 659 Hostile to Frails," *Variety*, February 7, 1973, 7.
84 "659's 1st Gal Member," *Variety*, March 21, 1973, 5; "Gal Makes IATSE with Judge's Help," *Variety*, March 28, 1973, 7.

85 "'Secret' Madery Settlement Gives Her $19,000, No Job, No Card," *Variety*, January 17, 1979, 30.

86 "659 Roster Rule Loser; But What Does It Change?," *Variety*, January 30, 1974, 4.

87 "Photogs Testing IATSE Seniority," *Variety*, December 10, 1975, 33; "10 Photogs, in Class Action, Say Unions, Employers Exclude Them," *Variety*, December 17, 1975, 30.

88 "Coast Council to Probe Peck on O'Seas Films," *Variety*, September 15, 1954, 3, 61.

89 "Photographers Abandon 'Runaway Film Boycott," *MPD*, October 14, 1960, 4.

90 "IATSE to U.S.: Cancel Divorcement! Claims It Hurt Whole Industry," *Variety*, August 29, 1956, 15.

91 "N.Y. Cameramen Cannot Work in Hollywood," *Variety*, March 10, 1976, 36; "Cameramen: 'West Coast Is All of U.S.,'" *Variety* 294, no. 7 (Mar 21, 1979): 7, 36.

92 "'Style' Camera Crew Walks Off," *THR*, August 9, 1979, 1, 21.

93 "Union Hassle May Erupt over French Cameraman's Hire," *THR*, March 22, 1979, 1, 25.

94 "Coast Crafts Aided in Fight on Visas to O'Seas Workers," *Variety*, November 12, 1980, 3, 42; "Storaro Can't Wind Camera Work on 'Reds,'" *Variety*, June 3, 1981, 7, 42.

95 "Photog Locals Talking National Union Merger," *THR*, July 3, 1984, 1, 33.

96 "N.Y. IATSE Local Sues to Block 3-Way Merger," *THR*, March 6, 1996, 4, 86.

97 "Focused Camera Local Clicks on 1st National Pact," *THR*, February 10, 1998, 4, 8.

98 "Three-on-Crew, or Face a Fine: Soundmen Rule," *Variety*, March 31, 1976, 22; "Local 695 Breaks with IA Tradition," *Variety*, May 26, 1976, 5. "Looks Sure Three-Man Sound Crew Demand to Be Cancelled as IATSE Trusteeship Moves," *Variety*, December 8, 1976, 4.

99 "IATSE Sound Local Ratifies Network Newsreel Contract," *Variety*, March 9, 1977, 60.

100 "Say 695 Gripes Galore Is 'Harassment,'" *Variety*, March 7, 1979, 7.

101 "Most West Coast Productions Are Back to 3-Soundmen Crew," *Variety*, November 21, 1979, 5, 40.

102 "IATSE Shores Local in Shift," *Variety*, October 9, 1997, https://variety.com/1997 /biz/news/iatse-shores-locals-in-shift-1116674653/.

103 "State of a Union: The Publicists Guild of America Faces a Year of Change after Merging with the Cinematographers Union," *THR*, March 20, 2002, S-1, S-2, S-4.

104 Gene Maddaus, "How Variety Studies the Diversity of Hollywood Unions," *Variety*, July 21, 2021, https://variety.com/2021/film/news/entertainment-industry -diversity-study-methodology-response-1235024157/.

4

Postproduction

• •

Working behind the Scenes
and at the Forefront of IATSE

PAUL MONTICONE

Over the summer of 2021, talks between the International Alliance of Theatrical Stage Employees (IATSE, or the IA) and the Alliance of Motion Picture and Television Producers (AMPTP) on a new Basic Agreement stalled, and, by the fall, it was possible to imagine a confrontation between the craft workers and their studio employers. As a crucial strike authorization vote approached, Hollywood's most deliberately self-effacing workers were uncharacteristically visible. Local 700 hosted a rally at its Sunset Boulevard headquarters where cross-craft solidarity found expression in slogans painted across car windshields and hoods. The editor-hosted rally and these homemade, mobile billboards reached beyond the Los Angeles craft community; images of them circulated widely on social media, and these same images often served as the lead illustration for national news reports on the outcome of the vote. By an overwhelming majority, Hollywood's locals authorized a strike, giving IATSE's negotiating team leverage to extract further concessions from the studios and producers.

The Motion Picture Editors Guild (MPEG), or IATSE Local 700, one of four national unions among the IA's film and television locals, was formed in 1998, after the merger of the Hollywood and New York City editors guilds.

Over the subsequent years, the 700 absorbed several other locals representing postproduction workers; it now stands as the second-largest local in IATSE, bringing together picture and sound editors, laboratory workers, Foley artists, and story editors. Notably absent from this postproduction union are visual effects workers, whose occupational lineages and worldwide geographic dispersal have left them as-yet unorganized.

MPEG and its predecessor organizations have, much like the workers they represent, occupied a crucial yet often overlooked place in the history of media production. The skilled artisans and craftspeople who have labored over Moviolas and developing tanks, in editing bays and at digital audio workstations, have benefited from a guild that has worked quietly and efficiently, though often forcefully and independently from Hollywood's other production unions, to advance the unique needs of postproduction workers. Whether measured by size or by gains won for its members, MPEG is a successful union. Yet, its historical achievements also reveal the limits of business unionism, which too often leads to narrowly focusing on one's own interests over broader solidarity and relying on collective bargaining progress to achieve enduring workplace gains. With the 2021 negotiations with the producers, however, MPEG began to take on a more public and assertive role in industry labor relations, leading the more conservative factions in IATSE to negotiate more forcefully.

MPEG previously contributed to setting the agenda for the Basic Agreement in 2018 and was the lone holdout in ratifying the agreement. Cathy Repola, the guild's newly promoted national executive director and representative on the International's negotiating team, dismissed that deal, which the other locals supported, as "totally, unnecessarily unacceptable" and encouraged her local's members to reject it.[1] IATSE president Matt Loeb and his allies reacted by unleashing a torrent of invective and abuse, characterizing Repola as "selfish, divisive, and irresponsible" and pursuing her own leadership ambitions.[2] But—despite these very public, personal attacks—Repola simply continued to reiterate her concerns with the tentative agreement and won the trust of not only her membership but also the rank and file of other locals. As an IA member told *IndieWire* at the time, "Every time they go after her 10 times harder than they ever stood up to the AMPTP, it just confirms our worst fears about leadership."[3]

The central issues in the 2021 contract were much the same as those Repola flagged for her membership as inadequately addressed in 2018: health and pension benefits were underfunded, new-media residuals were not collected, and turnaround time between the end of one shift and the beginning of the next was inadequate. Although Local 700 stood alone in rejecting the 2018 Basic Agreement, MPEG and Repola had laid down the marker for the 2021 negotiations, through which IATSE's broader membership sought to ameliorate the issues the guild's executive director had previously highlighted.

The emergence of the Editors Guild as a labor agitator is both characteristic and atypical of Hollywood's postproduction unions through their nearly

100-year history. The Editors Guild and its postproduction union predecessors have previously found themselves pushing against the International's leadership, but rarely have their actions synchronized with those of other production workers. Whether working from a building on the studio lot nearer the executive offices than the soundstages or from home editing suites, editors have always been at a physical remove from other production workers. The quasi-mass-production workers of early labs exhibited a distinctive pattern in early organizing, while studio editors found themselves comfortable within an organization often derided as a company union. At the height of labor militancy, lab workers emerged as a progressive force, while editors watched the strife of the mid-1940s from the sidelines.

As the studio system disintegrated, editors—at least those who were white and male—were well served by a mode of business unionism that did not have to confront runaway production, saw increased work from television production, and could comfortably assert the right to Minimum Basic Agreement (MBA) contract ratification against IATSE. MPEG's oppositional stance did not extend to technological change, in which area it was on the same, producer-friendly page as the IA, and this posture, which has not served all postproduction workers equally well, helped spur the organization's recent growth into the industry's second-largest local. As a new generation of postproduction workers find themselves in a larger, more diverse membership body, opportunities for solidaristic labor actions increasingly present themselves, as they did in the 2021 Basic Agreement negotiation.

The Forgotten Origins of Postproduction Labor Unions

The Motion Picture Editors Guild was not chartered as an IATSE local until 1944, nearly two decades after IATSE affiliates were recognized under the Studio Basic Agreement (SBA) of 1926. Today's guild marks its significant anniversaries from the 1937 founding of the Society of Motion Picture Film Editors, an independent union that directly preceded and was reorganized into MPEG. But there were even earlier attempts to attain labor representation for editors. The Laboratory Technicians Local 683, a union that MPEG absorbed in 2010, had just succeeded in bringing editors into its ranks when the disastrous 1933 strike led to IATSE's temporary expulsion from the studios and personal setbacks for many rank-and-file participants. Among them was Ralph Winters, then a young assistant, who recalled his participation in the strike as a folly of youth and "a part of my life I don't want to even remember."[4] Nor, it seems, does MPEG, which has written this brief marriage of lab and editorial workers out of the guild's prehistory and instead traces its lineage to the Edited By club, which was more professional society than union and operated for only a few months in the late 1920s.[5] Nevertheless, the history of editors' labor organizing is intertwined with that of lab workers.

Analogies between the Hollywood studio system's mode of production and assembly-line mass production are more convincing as rhetoric than description, unless, as Charles Musser has argued, we expand our definition of cinema's industrial processes: "Cinema became a form of mass production not because of the way that a picture was made . . . but because multiple prints could be struck and assembled, rapidly circulated, and repeatedly shown."[6] The film lab was the first stage at which cinema took on features of mass production, among them the types of semiskilled labor one might find in a factory. The laboratory workers waded "wet and uncomfortable" among developing tanks, hauled racks of film to large drying drums, hunched over workstations in crowded inspection and assembly rooms, and otherwise worked "from morning until night with only the light from a dark lantern to guide their activities."[7] They did some of the most repetitive and grueling work in the film industry.

Here was the film industry's functional equivalent of manufacturing workers. They existed at a crucial phase in cinema's industrial process and could, as Laurie Pintar put it, create "a productive bottleneck if they chose not to work."[8] Labor organizers on the East Coast realized this, and in July 1920, just months after organizing into IATSE Local 614, the Motion Picture Craftsmen's 2,100 members walked out of thirty-eight labs in the New York City area, striking for recognition, a 35 percent wage increase, and a forty-four-hour workweek. Beyond these bread-and-butter issues, the strikers demanded a union-made label be affixed to negatives and prints to ensure union workers were engaged at each stage of the process, from photography through to projection. Although the expected sympathy strike from the cameramen's local never materialized, the strike achieved higher wages and fewer hours for Local 614's members. But the potential for industry-wide solidarity represented by the trade-seal privilege was not realized. This limited victory proved Pyrrhic as the sector began relocating to the West Coast, following the client base to the new production center and likely seeking the same employer-friendly labor climate.[9]

Even accounting for the region's hostility, the unionization of postproduction workers in Hollywood proceeded slowly, as several factors conspired to leave lab technicians overlooked in labor's early efforts. First, labs fell between the cracks of the major labor groups attempting to organize Hollywood. On one side, the American Federation of Labor Buildings Trades viewed the studio carpenters, painters, and electricians as a foothold in the notorious citadel of the open shop, but no existing subset of organized labor in Los Angeles took an interest in lab workers—the proximate trades, such as chemical or electrical manufacture, were just beginning to appear in the region.[10] On the other side, IATSE sought first to organize studio crafts that had analogues in the theater, and studio technicians whose jobs were without precedent in other entertainment fields fell "between the lines."[11]

If not from above, agitation for a union could come from below, but the rank and file of the Los Angeles labs were not the militant children of Jewish garment sweatshop workers who "absorbed union history from their parents," as Gene Mailes recalled the originators of the New York City lab local.[12] Instead, the Los Angeles labs, like many workplaces in the boomtown, were staffed by recent transplants from the Midwest, the type of American worker for whom "mobility became a surrogate for collective action."[13] For example, the sound editor Milo Lory, as an adolescent recently arrived from Indiana, worked alongside his mother and brother at Standard Laboratory, and then at a series of smaller labs where he could work across departments, learning the full process of film development and finishing in the small firms that served studio directors and producers by printing dailies and tinting and toning samples.[14] The conditions of a decentralized, fragmented industrial structure that primarily aided the studios' production needs and flexible work roles militated against unionization until the late 1920s.

Milo's brother David followed a different path and departed Standard for the regular employment of the newly built Paramount laboratory. His trajectory typified the changes that would ultimately facilitate the founding of a lab union: as the decade progressed, Hollywood's lab sector centralized, expanded capacity, and rationalized labor. Studios increasingly brought their lab work in-house, and Consolidated Film Industries bought out most of the independent firms. The production of distribution prints moved to the West Coast, signaling Hollywood's transformation, as Luci Marzola puts it, from "an oversized location shooting destination" to the industrial center.[15] Part and parcel of these developments were the increasing rationalization and automation within the labs: as larger plants predominated, more workers were assigned to single tasks; newly built labs even incorporated assembly lines. With the coming of sound, the alchemistic developer, the "old hand craftsmen" who worked through intuition and experience, was displaced by automatic developing machines (figure 4.1).[16] As the gap between developers and other skilled technicians narrowed, a key barrier to solidarity eroded, and the feasibility of establishing standard wage scales created a powerful incentive to act, as did shifts that ran eighteen hours without overtime pay. In 1929, David Lory, along with an organizer from New York, obtained a charter from the American Federation of Labor that was soon transferred to IATSE.[17]

From its first year, Local 683, the Laboratory Workers Union, sought to bolster its numbers by recruiting studio film editors. Technological change and consolidation were similarly proletarianizing this craft. Where the silent-era editor had worked alongside the director assembling the image track, now the two interacted during the screening of production dailies so that editing could proceed piecemeal as principal photography continued. This speedup was a result of the sound transition, which multiplied the steps needed to complete a final edit of a work print for the lab's negative cutters. Turning in an initial cut within days of production wrapping enabled sound effects and music editors to complete their work before the final sound mix.

FIGURE 4.1 Film-developing machine at MGM, undated. Employee unidentified. (Courtesy of the Academy of Motion Picture Arts and Sciences.)

This increasing subdivision of labor expanded the ranks of editing departments, often with assistants who had previously worked in the labs, and a generational split developed as the new entrants sought fixed minimums and overtime pay.[18] The older, more established editors continued to view their work as akin to that of the writer or director, and those who worked year-round on the larger lots doubted the benefit of "union hours."[19] This resistance broke down as larger studios adopted the practice of dismissing editors between assignments and Fox launched a six-month training program to turn "college boys" into "expert cutters."[20] After ensuring equal representation on the local's board in the summer of 1931, 80 percent of Hollywood's 350 editors and assistants joined Local 683's 3,000 lab members.[21]

Local 683's existence as a labor organization representing all postproduction was brief, undone by the broader strategic errors of IATSE even before any incompatibility between the varied crafts could arise. During the first wage-and-hour conference in which editors were included, the producers refused to recognize that contingent of the membership, continuing their policy of keeping their most crucial workers out of the SBA. Attesting to the importance of editors, however, the producers affirmed the same basic wage and hour rules attained by parties to the SBA. We cannot know whether the editors would have remained affiliated with laboratory technicians because the 1933 strike, discussed in the introduction to part 1 and chapter 3, broke the union. When newly elected IATSE president William C. Elliot backed Sound Local 695's wildcat strike, many of Local 683's members joined in sympathy—and came to regret it, as in the case of Ralph Winters—but others crossed the picket line and advanced their own careers. The experience soured Hollywood's editors on IATSE for the next decade and established a tendency toward autonomy and self-preservation that would reappear throughout the guild's history.

Postproduction Unions under the Studio System

The IATSE-affiliated craft unions were not kept out of the studios for long. With the Wagner Act (1935), national policymaking overran many of the open shop's fortifications. More important, as the studios began expanding output in the mid-1930s, producers sought the stable supply of able personnel that unions could provide. This more favorable terrain for labor, however, did not benefit Hollywood's locals as much as it did the IA and the criminal syndicate that had seized control of it in 1934. When it returned to the studios in early 1936, IATSE, as Denise Hartsough has put it, "metamorphized suddenly from a nearly extinct outcast in Hollywood to a large, powerful, leading union."[22] This sudden change in fortune was underwritten by an unspoken agreement described by Carey McWilliams in the *New Republic*: "Browne and Bioff policed the 12,000 members of the IATSE for the producers and the producers policed the same members for Willie and George."[23]

When the Browne-Bioff regime ended in 1941, what followed was not a full reform of the organization but another era of heavy-handed International control under the new leadership of IA president Richard Walsh and its Hollywood representative Roy Brewer. Until the end of the studio era, Hollywood's craft workers were simultaneously squeezed by both their studio employers and their own International, which colluded with the producers to contain labor costs and rank-and-file militancy.[24] While many craftspeople profiled elsewhere in this part of the book rebelled against these conditions and joined the succession of organizations that emerged to challenge the IA, the labor organizations of postproduction workers charted their own paths through the challenges of the era.

The former core of Local 683, the laboratory employees, appear to have benefited from IATSE's ability to corral the independent labs with bicoastal operations, such as Consolidated, and the smaller independent firms in Hollywood.[25] These workers did not consider alternative affiliations, such as the Federated Motion Picture Crafts (FMPC), and were initially obedient followers of the IA under the local leadership of David Lory, who became both president and business representative of the 683 in 1939. As the Browne-Bioff scandal unfolded, a slate of progressive reformers challenged Lory and took control of several positions within 683. Perhaps responding to pressure, Lory tried to lead the union in a more assertive direction, pulling 683's members from Technicolor in support of the Screen Cartoonists Guild's efforts to organize Disney. But he ultimately stepped down when the membership insisted on negotiating their own basic contract. In so doing, 683 succeeded in becoming the first Hollywood local to negotiate its basic agreement without the interference of the IA's East Coast negotiators.[26] After Lory stepped down, Russell McKnight, a negative cutter at Columbia and the progressive editor of the guild's newsletter, *Flashes*, succeeded him as 683 president and, after World War II, would lead the 683 into more direct conflict with IATSE's leadership.

Laboratory workers gradually asserted their independence from the IA, but film editors kept IATSE at a remove from their earliest days. Spurred on by the Supreme Court's decision in *NLRB v. Jones & Laughlin Steel Corp.*, the editors, like many unorganized sectors, sought to form a labor organization, but they chose not to affiliate with their previous local, with some editors now feeling aligning with lab technicians was "kind of beneath them."[27] When IATSE attempted to claim jurisdiction over editors, the Society of Motion Picture Film Editors (SMPFE) safeguarded its independence by threatening intervention by the National Labor Relations Board. Instead, the SMPFE's founders modeled their new organization on the American Society of Cinematographers (ASC), with the film librarian Edmund "Eddie" Hannan and editor Frederick Y. Smith—both of MGM—getting the ASC's bylaws from John Arnold, head of the studio's camera department.[28] Founded in May 1937 with nearly 600 picture and sound editors, assistants, apprentices, and librarians from all the majors and the largest independents, the SMPFE was a hybrid organization, intended to function as both honorary craft organization and labor union, but, as Katie Bird has observed, it "failed to successfully be either."[29]

As to the SMPFE's failure as a union, it is clear that Smith, the group's second president, was most interested in the SMPFE's potential to elevate the status of editing as a craft, an ambition he pursued when he founded the American Cinema Editors (ACE) in 1951, and it is doubtful whether he was even philosophically in favor of organized labor.[30] But picture editors constituted only about one-fifth of the membership, and the selection of the head of MGM's film library as inaugural president indicates the existence of some obligation to improve conditions for the assistants, apprentices, and other classifications. The society went on to negotiate its own deals with the studios, in 1939 and 1942, which won raises and reduced workweeks. The SMPFE's primary failure as a labor organization pertains to its status as a "company union" tolerated, and likely encouraged, by the producers in order to channel workers' energies in the least threatening direction (of course, this characterized most IA unions in the Browne-Bioff years).[31] That editors, of all the crafts, should have ended up in such an organization owes to the place of these workers in the studio hierarchy and production process. When the studio-era director moved on to his next assignment, the editor reported directly to studio executives. The major editor-executive collaborations of this era—for example, Barbara McLean with Darryl Zanuck,

Margaret Booth with Louis B. Mayer—were indicative of this change. As a "company union," the SMPFE seems to have done reasonably well by its members, even as it served the primary purpose expected by the producers—to minimize solidarity between sectors of workers.

Frustrating solidarity among workers is a long-standing criticism of the AFL's brand of craft unionism, which is an embedded feature of IATSE: as a whole, it is quasi-industrial, insofar as "entertainment" is a coherent industry, but it is none-theless internally segmented along craft lines.[32] These structural impediments to solidarity could be overcome, but only through the concerted efforts of committed organizers, and under ideal circumstances. This is evident in the Lab Technicians Guild under the progressive presidency of Russell McKnight. That 683 was a "vertical" local meant there was a pocket of industrial unionism within the craft-oriented IA. Whereas workers on soundstages or location were scattered among several unions, the laboratory workers, from foremen to shipping clerks, were all in the same guild, and, unlike in the SMPFE, no aristocracy of artisans existed atop the membership. Local 683 was thus fertile ground for reformers espousing democratic unionism and home rule. Under McKnight's editorship, the local's newsletter, *Flashes*, became an important venue of worker education and a democratic forum reflecting the interests of the rank and file. It is worth noting that while many mixed-gender unions excluded women from prominent organizational roles, 683—the first IATSE local to admit women—was, under its progressive leadership, recognizing the contributions of women members who were active on 683 committees and, in the case of Fox lab technician Fawn Farrar, as a delegate to the 1942 IA convention.

By the time the Conference of Studio Unions (CSU) struck for recognition, 683's membership had been, as the business agent John R. Martin later observed, "taught the principles of unionism" and so frustrated Walsh and Brewer's efforts to break the strike.[33] McKnight's columns increasingly excoriated IA leadership, especially when Brewer ordered IATSE members to work outside their jurisdictions to break strikes. The 1,800-member guild slowed the processing of release prints to force the Treaty of Beverly Hills in July 1946 and later voted to support the CSU in the lockout that began that October, explaining its decision as a stand in support of "the principle of honest, American trade unionism, in unions democratically controlled and run."[34]

In the intervening months, the IA had prepared to help the studios avert the slowdown, having recruited strikebreakers to fill in at labs, and declared the local in a state of emergency. When Brewer tried to take control, he found the 683 offices fortified and under guard, and so brought a $50,000 suit against the local, demanding it turn over the books, property, and offices to IATSE. The rank and file were, as much as the local, ground down in a war of attrition; while carpenters and painters could find work offering commensurate compensation, laboratory technicians' skills were too specialized to be of use outside the film industry. Those who walked out of studio laboratories or film vaults might only find alternative employment in retail or hospitality positions. Given the difference in pay between being a vault clerk and a clothing store clerk, a lab worker took on a great burden when striking and would eventually, as one strike participant recalled, decide "to get back into that craft at all costs."[35] After a year, McKnight and 683 withdrew from the strike, their resources "entirely exhausted."[36]

The newly christened Motion Picture Editors Guild, conversely, had no qualms about crossing the picket lines. The editors saw the CSU action as a distant jurisdictional squabble having nothing to do with them and were happy to follow the advice of their new International. The circumstances by which the SMPFE was chartered as IATSE Local 776 in August 1944 are not clearly documented. Oral histories with longtime editors attribute this development to a generational changeover, as many longer-serving editors joined the armed services and were replaced by a younger generation with no memory of the 1933 strike and warmer feelings toward trade unions.[37] In addition to this, the American Federation of Musicians (AFM) claimed jurisdiction over music editors, which may have led the SMPFE to seek the protection of the AFL-affiliated IATSE.[38]

More motivating to the rank and file, however, may have been broader changes in the structure of the production sector: as independent producers proliferated, the independent quasi union had difficulty enforcing its contracts and now saw advantages to affiliating with other labor organizations.[39] While the SMPFE served editors well during the studio system's most consolidated form, IATSE offered a means to ensure compliance with minimum agreements as the industry began to decentralize. As to MPEG's conduct during the CSU strike, insight we have into the mindset of editors of the time suggests most such workers were generally inattentive to labor politics and happy to follow the lead of the International that was improving their material conditions.[40]

The Postwar Successes and Failures of Business Unionism

With its defeat of the Conference of Studio Unions (CSU), IATSE consolidated its position as the sole labor representative for Hollywood's technicians and artisans. According to the labor historian Andrew Dawson, "The consequence of the IA's postwar supremacy was the creation of a profoundly conservative union incapable of facing up to the technical and organizational changes brought about by the advent of television."[41] As noted throughout this volume, IATSE locals were often at odds with the International, and, if the demise of the CSU left workers with no broader labor alliance to join, tensions between the two levels of the organization remained.

During this era, editors, like many film workers, transitioned to an employment structure characterized by freelancing and flexible specialization, and Local 776's brand of business unionism served its (white, male) postproduction members well amid these industrial changes. Indeed, as the union took over essential supports—most notably health and retirement benefits usually provided, for most of the U.S. workforce, by the firm—it "indirectly enabled the flexible use of labor inputs" by guaranteeing producers access to a "skilled and specialized workforce without long-term employment contracts."[42] The collective bargaining system's capacity to deliver gains for workers depends on the harmonization of capital and labor interests that cannot be sustained when resources grow scarce, and by the 1970s, editors were at the forefront of efforts to democratize a process that had outsourced worker collectivity to a "priestly order of arbitrators, mediators, and conciliators."[43] This did not spell the beginning of a new phase of worker militancy in Hollywood, but it was symptomatic of how tenuous and limited labor's mostly favorable position was.

With the postwar decline in movie theater attendance, the studios entered a period of retrenchment, during which their payrolls dropped from their postwar high of 24,000 to barely one-half that by the mid-1950s.[44] The lab technicians, who regained their IATSE charter in 1953, were particularly hard hit as studios shuttered their in-house labs and subcontracted the work to Technicolor and Consolidated. By the end of the 1960s, most feature editors had been turned out of their plum salaried positions on studio lots and were working in a freelance market, finding work with postproduction houses that would provide subcontracted services for projects made on a per-film basis. The editors who ran these firms were often former studio employees who now took on the new role of managing a business and clients, acting as intermediaries between producers and workers.[45]

Technologies such as flatbed editing tables were introduced to the editing suite during this period and enabled editors to work alongside directors, facilitating "strong relationships with filmmaker clients that could lead to recurring work and the prospect of a stable career."[46] Studios themselves retained editors to carry out the constant stream of postproduction work for their distribution businesses. Many of the departed feature editors were replaced on the studio lot by those working in telefilm, an area over which MPEG quickly established jurisdiction.[47] Therefore, MPEG, and its coffers, grew substantially—membership nearly doubled to 1,800 by 1980—and the total number of studio workers was not much diminished, although they now worked in television.[48] Freelancers, however, represented a greater proportion of its membership, especially among the top tier of workers (feature picture editors). Amid these changes to the composition of its membership, the MPEG's core functions changed correspondingly.

The affiliation of MPEG with IATSE in 1944 largely ended the organization's ambition to function as a craft society. Editors' workaday interests were overseen and safeguarded by the business representative John Lehners, a holdover from the SMPFE days who remained with the guild until 1972.[49] During these thirty years, he became an important labor official in Hollywood, serving as head of the AFL Hollywood Film Council in 1958 and chairing a committee of three local business agents who drafted the initial list of basic contract demands in 1960.[50] MPEG increasingly centered on facilitating employment through management of the roster, establishing and coordinating portable benefits, such as the Motion Picture Health and Welfare Plan in 1952, and ensuring adherence to the Basic Agreement as the AMPTP parties to the collective bargaining agreement subcontracted work out to smaller service firms. These years were the height of business unionism, with the MPEG members making gains through the orderly, legalistic collective bargaining process that defined labor activity after the passage of the Taft-Hartley Act in 1947.[51]

By the early 1970s, negotiations with the AMPTP, and relations between MPEG and IATSE, grew increasingly fraught. The issues of autonomy and home rule remained dormant until IA president Walsh signed a video production agreement with producers that ensured jobs for his members but came with low rates. Lehners led the other locals in speaking out against Walsh's signing a "secret videotape agreement" without the involvement or approval of the affected locals.[52] And yet Lehners remained close to the Walsh administration, as he had throughout his tenure. The 776 business agent customarily seconded Walsh's nomination at every IATSE convention, but, in 1972, dissatisfied with Walsh's AMPTP negotiations on their behalf, the MPEG board passed a resolution instructing Lehners not to second Walsh at the upcoming convention. When he persisted, 776 refused to renew his contract, forcing him into retirement.[53] It replaced him with an industry outsider, Jerry Lennon, a union professional who had worked with the Los Angeles teachers and municipal employees.[54]

Heading into the 1973 MBA cycle, a "loose coalition" of Hollywood locals formed to "assert a degree of independence from the New York international, and not to accept a Walsh-dictated piece of paper."[55] By the end of the year, MPEG joined two other locals—the lab technicians (683) and studio projectionists (165)—in refusing to sign the negotiated agreement and suing their own international, charging that the IA's constitution forbade the practice of adopting an MBA without the ratification of the membership that would work under the agreement.[56] MPEG refused to sign the 1973 MBA, and in the next negotiations, the three locals voted to authorize a strike if not granted a cost-of-living adjustment.[57] Walter Diehl, the new IATSE president, whose administration began with statements in support of local autonomy, granted the strike sanction, and the ranks of the AMPTP broke. Universal's Lew Wasserman and Sid Sheinberg, reluctant to delay production at the industry's busiest studio, negotiated a deal directly with IATSE, agreeing to a raise that amounted to 52 percent over the forty-two-month life of the contract.[58]

With the restive locals having been granted concessions, Diehl withdrew the strike sanction, but not without causing some controversy in Hollywood. Though the contract offered the largest wage increase in IATSE history, and one that the remaining AMPTP member companies were willing to accept in the MBA, no cost-of-living adjustment or work-week reduction was included.[59] Holding to its demand, the 776 voted down the contract, but, when the other

Hollywood locals voted to ratify, it was forced to accept the deal.[60] MPEG had won the right for membership to vote on ratification, but autonomy from IATSE did not mean the guild could operate independently of the industry's other locals.[61]

Even the heyday of business unionism excluded many workers from its generous bargain with employers. Asked about the role of the union in bringing women into the profession, Marjorie Fowler said, "No. Hell no!" and went on to quote Lehners undermining a female editor on his roster: "Well, you don't want a women, do you?"[62] While 683's progressive president had addressed his membership as "brothers and sisters," in MPEG, as in other sectors of the postwar economy, business unionism tended to view women workers as impediments to full employment for male breadwinners. This attitude preceded MPEG's 1944 affiliation with IATSE and had roots in the formation of the Society of Motion Picture Film Editors.

Several of the organization's early members were women—from pioneers such as Margaret Booth and Barbara McLean to assistant editors such as Mary Steward—but this did not ensure them prominent positions in the union or that their employment conditions were of much concern. Steward later recalled a meeting with an unnamed SMPFE official: "With his feet up on his desk, he told me, 'My dear, we don't get jobs for girls.'"[63] At a structural level, the increased complexity of sound editing produced a job classification and promotion system that were encouraged by the union and had the effect of frustrating the advancement of women in editorial departments. As such, those who held positions of prominence at the height and in the waning days of the studio system had, in most cases, begun their careers in the silent era.[64]

Women editors benefited from the erosion of the studio hierarchy. Verna Fields, for example, had left her career to start a family but re-entered as a freelance sound editor for television. Others, such as Ann Rutledge, succeeded in starting their own postproduction houses.[65] Flexible specialization, which rewarded editors who could manage clients with whom they worked much more directly, resonates with Erin Hill's findings that poststudio casting directors discovered essentialized gendered competencies served them well in the new employment environment (see figure 4.2).[66] A generation of women editors, whose individual success owed little to the MPEG's old guard, thus stood ready to take on positions within the guild when the postwar consensus fell apart. The gains made by prominent women editors during the New Hollywood era soon shaped the craft's labor organization, with Bea Dennis's election as MPEG's first woman president in 1980.[67] More women presidents followed— Carol Littleton (1988–1991) and Lisa Zeno Churgin (2002–2010)—and eventually the executive director post would come to be held by Cathy Repola in 2016, when she succeeded Ron Kutak, the executive director who had steered the MPEG through an era of extraordinary technological change and organizational consolidation.

FIGURE 4.2 Film editor Dede Allen in the cutting room, October 26, 1982. (Courtesy of the Academy of Motion Picture Arts and Sciences.)

Technological and Organizational Convergence

Beginning in the 1970s, technological change became the primary force driving MPEG's membership growth, which accelerated in the last decade of the twentieth century as postproduction workflows and then labor groups rapidly converged. As the national political environment presented labor with an increasingly hostile terrain, MPEG strengthened representation among nonunion freelancers and facilities by reducing the waiting period to attain full-fledged editor classification from eight years down to five (in 1979), then eliminating it altogether (in 1989). The popularization of flatbed editing systems such as the KEM made editors less dependent on assistants, thus disrupting the profession's existing system of promotion.[68] Just over a decade later, the multiplication of boutique postproduction shops in the wake of digitization would only heighten the need to focus on grassroots organizing and membership drives.[69] But more than enlisting new members, it was the organizational consolidation spurred by MPEG's expanding jurisdiction that most contributed to the guild's long-term viability. That MPEG was the beneficiary of these changes was not inevitable but was helped along by the guild's pivot toward education and reskilling.[70] These victories, however, often came at the expense of workers in other locals—the gains of Local 776 were often the losses of Locals 683 and 695 (the latter discussed in chapter 3 as well).

The arrival of audiotape and videotape production to Hollywood not only reignited tensions between the locals and the International but also set off a jurisdictional struggle between Hollywood locals. Tape's potential for television production had been apparent to the unions covering the networks, the National Association of Broadcast Employees and Technicians (NABET) and the International Brotherhood of Electrical Workers (IBEW), and their flexibility around craft distinctions enabled them to quickly organize workers at NBC, ABC, and CBS.[71] Tape technology did not threaten to displace celluloid in image making, but it did alter production practices within specific craft areas, to varying outcomes on the affected locals. The transition to magnetic tape recording in sound, for example, was delayed until the technology was adapted to the workflow that had been established, in the decades prior, around optical soundtracks, but there were nonetheless efficiencies gained that had notable consequences for industry workers. Local 683's members saw a straightforward displacement—magnetic sound left labs with half the negative to develop, and tape transfer and duplication work did not replace these hours—but the effect on Sound Local 695 was more complicated and provided a valuable opportunity for MPEG.

Recording devices such as the Nagra III enabled producers to reduce sound crews. While 683's membership simply dwindled in the face of technological change, Local 695 fought the erosion of work under its aggressive business agent John Coffey, who spent much of the 1970s trying to maintain a minimum three-person production sound crew. In an attempt to boost membership, Coffey also tried to use 695's unionization of an independent production facility to claim jurisdiction over all uses of tape—not only for sound recording or mixing—which the camera, editing, and projectionist locals took as incursions into their territories.[72] Coffey's efforts not only raised the ire of other locals, but they came at the expense of shoring up 695's control, through the sound mixer classification, of sound's most rapidly expanding area. By the time Coffey realized his error, MPEG had established a hold over sound postproduction. The reintroduction and popularization of multichannel sound entailed increased roles for the sound editor and soundeffects editor, and the emergence of new professional identity, the supervising sound editor; all represented diminutions of 695's rerecording mixers' role.[73]

On 695's broader tape claims, a protracted dispute that went to the IATSE board determined that tape jurisdiction would fall along pre-existing craft lines; MPEG, which had been investing in training courses for its members, was granted control of tape editing.[74] While 695 was viewed as standing in the way of technological progress and selfishly claiming other locals' workers, MPEG was assisting in maintaining a skilled, trained workforce for producers. This became increasingly central to the International, beginning under Diehl's successor, Alfred DiTolla, who addressed the 60th Biennial Convention: "We must educate and train ourselves to make sure our services become necessary and indispensable to employers."[75] MPEG was an early adopter of training programs, beginning with courses in the 1950s, and became a frequent partner with producers in programs covering videotape editing (1976), then nonlinear editing (1995), and finally digital audio workstations (1996). As an enthusiastic participant in the IA's educational program, the guild was rewarded by the International with expansions of jurisdictional boundaries.[76]

In this respect, MPEG's fortunes evoke another major development during this era: conglomeration. As the studios combined into larger entities, the industry's labor organizations followed suit. Under President Tom Short, IATSE adopted the view that "locals themselves are strengthened when they become larger through mergers."[77] Combining locals into larger entities could create more formidable bargaining units and facilitate the sharing of knowledge about new technologies. At the beginning of Short's tenure, in 1994, MPEG counted just over 3,000 members. In 1997, 700 postproduction sound workers, including rerecording mixers, were transferred from 695 to MPEG. A year later, MPEG's Los Angeles and New York branches—Local 776 and Local 771, respectively—were merged to form a new, national local, IA 700. This new entity absorbed New York's postproduction sound workers from Local 52 (1999); story analysts, who composed Local 854 (2000); and Foley artists (2006). Finally, the remaining 1,000 members of lab workers Local 683 became members of the Editors Guild (2010).[78] By the end of the 2010s, MPEG included over 6,000 members, was the second-largest Hollywood local (after the Cinematographers Guild), and comprised vastly more work classifications than it had previously.

Adequately representing workers whose interests can conflict with one another's has proved a challenge. This became evident as postproduction underwent its digital transition in the mid-1990s. As noted earlier, MPEG ensured its members remained vital to producers by investing in continuing education programing for new technologies, but this did not preserve the work hours of craftspeople whose place in the postproduction task structure has been altered by those new technologies. The shifting status of the sound editor and postproduction mixer in the wake of the digital audio workstation (DAW) is an instructive example. Given the affordances of DAW software, the sound editor's job responsibilities have expanded, from preparing audio tracks for the mix to creating a preliminary mix ("premixing"). This reduces the time needed in expensive mixing suites, as well as the work of rerecording mixers to that of "problem solvers for the integration of dialog and music."[79]

Since sound editors are paid at a lower rate than mixers, and mixers are not compensated for their lost income or hours toward their health and pension benefits, producers reap the benefits of increased productivity, enabling them to complete films and shows with fewer resources devoted to postproduction.[80] The postproduction crunch has been exacerbated by digital production's ever-increasing shooting ratios and file-based recording's disruption of the traditional task structures that integrated production and postproduction; in some cases, editors are now having to "figure out the entire post workflow."[81] This deterioration of working conditions has occurred even as MPEG's jurisdiction over postproduction work has expanded.

Facing technological change outside of its control, MPEG invested its resources not in protecting the task structure of existing work classifications but in ensuring its members were trained to supply producers with a skilled workforce. Rather than maintaining a closed roster or a strict advancement structure to limit the supply of such labor, MPEG has sought to organize a postproduction workforce that has made its way from the studio lot to postproduction houses and now to small boutique firms. MPEG has been aided by an International that has helped swell its ranks with worker classifications transferred from locals that were shrunk (695) or shuttered entirely (683).

With the notable exception of computer-generated visual effects, which has yet to successfully unionize, Local 700's bargaining unit now comprehensively covers postproduction work.[82] These transformations, and MPEG's and IATSE's posture toward them, have produced winners and losers among the guild's many classifications. But the enlarged membership base and eroded craft distinctions have also produced something more akin to an industrial or sectorial union, with its potentials for solidarity and confrontation with increasingly consolidated media conglomerates.

Postproduction Unions in the Contemporary Media Industries

Over the last decade, the rapid growth of internet-delivered video has further sped up postproduction work, enabled work from home, and created a subscription-model home-video window which has made the residuals that fund IA workers' benefits vexingly difficult to calculate. These issues, largely unaddressed by the 2018 MBA, led MPEG to object to that agreement. More locals joined them in objecting in 2021. Like many workers in the wake of the COVID-19 pandemic, IATSE's rank and file was more willing to hold out for concessions than they had been three years earlier. The round of negotiations that followed the strike authorization produced increases to wages for the lowest-paid workers. But the overall package was greeted with skepticism by bargaining-unit members whose activist impulses were more widely shared throughout the IA: rumblings of a rejection were heard across IATSE's fourteen Hollywood locals. In the end, and despite the wind seeming to be at the back of labor nationwide, the deal with the producers was ratified, much to the disappointment of many of IATSE's rank and file. This anticlimactic resolution may be attributed, at least in large part, to Local 700. As the modest objectives identified at the outset of collective bargaining had been attained, Repola didn't feel she could press her, or the membership's, advantage without compromising their integrity and instead advised that the MPEG's members support the contract.[83] The MPEG vote proved decisive in securing the overall outcome.

IATSE's ratification vote resulted in a split between the rank-and-file membership's "popular" vote and the IA's "electoral" vote system, which apportions delegates among IATSE locals based on their membership sizes and awards them, in a winner-take-all fashion, to whichever side carries the vote within the local. Second only to the Cinematographers Guild in size, the MPEG, having absorbed most other postproduction guilds over the past twenty years, now boasts a roster of over 8,000 members, which secures it about 20 percent of all delegates. When ratification narrowly won the MPEG's vote by 52 percent to 48 percent—a slim margin of only about 270 votes—this sent all of its eighty-odd delegates to the ratification side, which, in turn, tipped IATSE to accept the contract. A popular vote in which ratification lost 49.6 percent to 50.4 percent produced a delegate victory of 256 to 188. The voting system that produced this undemocratic outcome—which one IATSE reformer, making the connection to U.S. presidential elections, derided as "an archaic voting method with a shameful history"—was itself the hard-won, democracy-expanding outcome of MPEG-led advocacy and litigation in the 1970s.[84] This voting system, which was a modest reform within the prevailing business unionism, proved inadequate amid the grassroots fervor of IATSE's new generation.

In 2021, MPEG was *simultaneously* prescient and willing to confront the IATSE leadership over the core MBA issues *and* ultimately willing to endorse a deal that, given the grassroots mood, amounted to granting concessions to the producers. As guild members, editors have often found themselves marching to a different beat than other locals in Hollywood's labor community. Isolated from the "shop floor" concerns of and camaraderie shared by on-set workers, MPEG's membership found itself relatively aligned with its producer bosses under the studio system and later director-clients as that system disintegrated. This has sometimes been to the detriment of the broader Hollywood labor community, but it has almost always been to the benefit of the industry's editors. As technological change has eroded occupational boundaries and brought postproduction workers into closer contact with each other (and other IA craftspeople), new possibilities for labor activism have begun to present themselves.

Notes

1   Carolyn Giardina and Jonathan Handel, "Editors Guild Publishes Reasons Why Members Should Vote 'No' on IATSE Contract," *The Hollywood Reporter* (hereafter *THR*), August 1, 2018, https://www.hollywoodreporter.com/movies/movie-news/editors-guild-publishes-reasons-urging-members-vote-no-iatse-contract-1131555/.
2   David Robb and Dominic Patten, "IATSE President Accuses Editors Guild Leader of Violating Federal Labor Law," *Deadline*, August 16, 2018, https://deadline.com/2018/08/hollywood-unions-fight-iatse-editors-guild-labor-law-accusations-1202447178/.

3   Chris O'Falt, "The Two Months That Changed a Union: Inside IATSE's Awkward Attempt to Crush an Insurgency and Avoid a Strike," *IndieWire*, September 11, 2018. https://www.indiewire.com/2018/09/iatse-agreement-avoid-strike-matthew-loeb-cathy-repola-1202001279/.

4   *An Oral History with Ralph Winters*, interviewed by Jennifer Peterson, Academy Oral History Program, Margaret Herrick Library, Beverly Hills, California (Academy Foundation, 2000), 124.

5   For the guild's account of its founding, see Jeff Burman, Christopher Cooke, and Michael Kunkes, "The Great Society: The Beginnings of the Editors Guild," *CineMontage*, May 15, 2017, https://cinemontage.org/great-society-beginnings-editors-guild/.

6   Charles Musser, "Pre-classical American Cinema: Its Changing Modes of Film Production [1991]," in *Silent Film*, ed. Richard Abel (Rutgers University Press, 1996), 101–102.

7   On working conditions in early labs, see Richard Koszarski, *An Evening's Entertainment: The Age of the Silent Feature Picture, 1915–1928* (University of California Press, 1994), 155–159; Luci Marzola, *Engineering Hollywood: Technology, Technicians, and the Science of Building the Studio System* (Oxford University Press, 2021), 49–52.

8   Laurie Caroline Pintar, "Off-Screen Realities: A History of Labor Activism in Hollywood, 1933–1947" (PhD diss., University of Southern California, 1995), 340–341.

9   On the first lab technician's local, see "Film Laboratory Men Strike Claiming Alliance's Backing," *Variety*, July 23, 1920, 38; "Moving Pictures: Laboratory Men Go Back to Work Pending a Compromise," *Variety*, August 6, 1920, 30.

10 Murray Ross, *Stars and Strikes: Unionization of Hollywood* (Columbia University Press, 1941), 6–11; John H. M. Laslett, *Sunshine Was Never Enough: Los Angeles Workers, 1880–2010* (University of California Press, 2012).

11 Marzola, *Engineering Hollywood*, 88–89. The motion picture lab's predecessor—photographic manufacturing—was an unorganized sector, owing largely to the success of Eastman Kodak's corporate welfare policies in staving off unionization. See Sanford M. Jacoby, *Modern Manors: Welfare Capitalism since the New Deal* (Princeton University Press, 1998), 57–94.

12 Mike Nielsen and Gene Mailes, *Hollywood's Other Blacklist: Union Struggles in the Studio System* (British Film Institute, 1995), 63

13 Mike Davis, *Prisoners of the American Dream: Politics and Economy in the History of the US Working Class* (Verso, 1986), 60–61.

14 Milo Lory, interview with Irene Atkins, 1970, American Film Institute/Louis B. Mayer Oral History Collection, 1–17. See also *Oral History with Ralph Winters*, 6–7.

15 Marzola, *Engineering Hollywood*, 56.

16 Lory interview, 16.

17 "Pictures: Lab People on Coast Asking AFL Charter," *Variety*, August 28, 1929, 7; "Lab. Workers Unionized," *Billboard*, October 12, 1929, 20.

18 "Film Editors' Union Seems Near at Hand," *THR*, March 25, 1931, 4.

19 "Cutters in Rattle over Union Charter Issue," *THR*, January 20, 1931, 3; "Cutters Divided on Unionization," *THR*, April 20, 1931, 3.

20 "Fox School for Cutters Cutting Cutters' Time," *THR*, June 19, 1931, 3; "Pictures: Cutters Are Hot Again for Union as Jobs Given to Collegians," *Variety*, June 23, 1931, 25.

21 "Cutters, Lab Workers Agree on Rep. Basis," *THR*, July 9, 1931, 1.

22 Denise Hartsough, "Crime Pays: The Studios' Labor Deals in the 1930s," in *The Studio System*, ed. Janet Staiger (Rutgers University Press, 1995), 238.

23 Carey McWilliams, "Racketeers and Movie Magnates," *New Republic*, October 27, 1941, 534.

24 Hartsough, "Crime Pays," 226–250.

25 "Eastern Labs in IATSE," *THR*, August 30, 1937, 1, 15.

26 "Lab Local Wins Contract from Producers: Other Doors Open," *THR*, August 19, 1941, 1, 4.

27 Lory interview, 37.

28 *An Oral History with Fredrick Y. Smith*, interviewed by Douglas Bell, Academy Oral History Program, Margaret Herrick Library, Beverly Hills, California (Academy Foundation, 1994), 179–184.

29 Katie Bird, "The Editor's Face on the Cutting Room Floor," *Spectator* 30, no. 2 (Fall 2018): 9–19.

30 By 1970, Smith complained that "unionism takes a talented man and puts him the middle strata. It takes the lazy, inefficient person and brings him up to the same level as the talented person." See Mike Steen, "Film Editor: Fred Y. Smith," in *Hollywood Speaks, an Oral History*, edited by Mike Steen (G. P. Putnam's Sons, 1974), 314.

31 As Dunne summarized it in his exposé, "Film companies buy up studio workers' bargaining rights for $200,000 per year." See George Dunne, *Hollywood Labor Dispute: A Study in Immorality* (Conference Publishing Company, 1950), 14–15. Even then, racketeer-ruled IA would have to cut workers in on the deal when threatened by other labor federations.

32 On craft and industrial unionism, see Davis, *Prisoners of the American Dream*, 3–51.

33 *Jurisdictional Disputes in the Motion-Picture Industry, Hearings Before a Special Subcommittee of the Committee on Education and Labor Pursuant to H.Res. 111*, House of Representatives, 80th Congress, 2nd Session (Government Printing Office, 1948), 750.

34 Quoted in Pintar, "Off-Screen Realities," 380. On the 683 facilitating the Treaty of Beverly Hills, see Nielsen and Mailes, *Hollywood's Other Blacklist*, 140.

35 Nielsen and Mailes, *Hollywood's Other Blacklist*, 153–154.

36 Pintar, "Off-Screen Realities," 430.

37 *An Oral History with Rudi Fehr*, interviewed by Douglas Bell, Academy Oral History Program, Margaret Herrick Library, Beverly Hills, California (Academy Foundation, 1992–1993), 460–470.

38 "Petrillo Plans to Pull Film Music Cutters Out of SMPFE," *THR*, March 28, 1944, 1, 4.

39 Lory interview, 16.

40 "Film Editors Get New Closed Shop Contract and Pay Hikes," *THR*, April 4, 1945, 1, 3.

41 Andrew Dawson, "Strikes in the Motion Picture Industry," in *The Encyclopedia of Strikes in American History*, ed. Aaron Brenner, Benjamin Day, and Daniel Ness (Routledge, 2009), 659.

42 Susan Christopherson, "Flexibility and Adaptation in Industrial Relations: The Exceptional Case of the U.S. Media Entertainment Industries," in *Under the Stars: Essays on Labor Relations in Arts and Entertainment*, ed. Lois S. Gray and Ronald L. Seeber (Cornell University Press, 1996), 103–104.

43 Davis, *Prisoners of the American Dream*, 63.

44 Tino Balio, *The American Film Industry*, 2nd ed. (University of Wisconsin Press, 1985), 402.

45 Benjamin Wright, "The Auteur Renaissance, 1968–1980: Editing," in *Editing and Special/Visual Effects*, ed. Charlie Keil and Kristen Whissel (Rutgers University Press, 2016), 106.

46 Wright, 106.

47 "TV-Films: Film Editors Ride TV Gravy Train," *Variety*, September 21, 1955. About two-thirds of editors were doing work related to television, whether series or TV edits of features.

48 Motion Picture Editors Guild, *75th Anniversary Celebration, 1937–2012*, program, October 6, 2012, 21–28, Author's Collection.

49 See "Lehners New SMPFE Rep," *THR*, December 4, 1940, 4; "John W. Lehners Dead of Cancer," *THR*, January 4, 1977, 8.

50 See "Lehners AFL Council Chief," *Variety*, October 29, 1958, 19; "Three IATSE Chairmen Are Named to Draw Up Basic Union Demands," *Motion Picture Daily*, August 30, 1960, 6.

51 For a discussion of collective bargaining in U.S. industrial relations, see Davis, *Prisoners of the American Dream*, 63.

52 "IATSE Convention," *International Projectionist* 39, no. 8 (August 1964): 10

53 "Film Editors Oust Lehners as Biz Agent; Other Unions Squawk," *Variety*, October 4, 1972, 6; Bill Elias, interview with the author, October 7, 2021.

54 "Pictures: From Teacher Unionism, Jerry Lennon to Editors," *Variety*, August 15, 1973, 3.

55 "Hollywood's Labor Negotiation Maze: Will Locals Actually Buck Walsh?," *Variety*, January 10, 1973, 7.

56 Dave Kaufman, "Say Walsh Tramples on Their 'Home Rule,' Hollywood Locals Sue, Ask IATSE Pay Damages," *Variety*, December 5, 1973, 4.

57 "Pictures: Studios to IA Eds: 'We're Settled'; Lennon: 'We Never Signed,'" *Variety*, October 9, 1974, 34.

58 "Pictures: Rebel Editors 'Explore Litigation' against IATSE Crafts Pact Okay," *Variety*, October 15, 1975, 24

59 "Pictures: Diehl Cancels Strike Sanction, Coffey Enraged; Smith Hails Pact, Keeps Hollywood Competitive," *Variety*, September 10, 1975, 3, 26.

60 "Pictures: Discontented Eds' Local Ratifies; Now Talks Exit of Alliance," *Variety*, April 14, 1976, 33, 35.

61 For a detailed account of this event, see Jay Beck, "A Quiet Revolution: Changes in American Film Sound Practices, 1967–1979" (PhD diss., University of Iowa, 2003), 229–285.

62 *An Oral History with Gene Fowler Jr. and Marjorie Fowler,* interviewed by Douglas Bell, Academy Oral History Program, Margaret Herrick Library, Beverly Hills, California (Academy Foundation, 1990), 19. Lehners was similarly quoted in the *Los Angeles Times* in 1940: "Women cutters are 'resented' by their male colleagues." Dee Philip K. Sheuer, "Lady Film Cutters: A Vanishing Profession," *Los Angeles Times*, April 21, 1940, C3.

63 Edward Landler, "Post-production Pioneers: The Guild's Earliest Members—West Coast," *CineMontage*, September 1, 2012 https://cinemontage.org/post-production -pioneers-guilds-earliest-members-west-coast/.

64 See Karen Ward Maher, *Women Filmmakers in Early Hollywood* (Johns Hopkins University Press, 2006), 200–202.

65 See Evelyn Rutledge, interview with Irene Atkins, 1970, American Film Institute/ Louis B. Mayer Oral History Collection, Los Angeles, California, 303–304.

66 See Wright, "Auteur Renaissance," 109–110; Erin Hill, "Re-casting the Casting Director," in *Making Media Work*, ed. Derek Johnson, Derek Kompare, and Avi Santo (NYU Press, 2014), 142–164.

67 "Pictures: Woman President for Editors Guild," *Variety*, December 24, 1980.

68 Wright, "Auteur Renaissance," 105–106; Beck, "Quiet Revolution," 275.

69 Benjamin A. Wright, "Sound from Start to Finish: Professional Style and Practice in Modern Hollywood Sound Production" (Ph.D. diss., Carleton University, 2011), 330.

70 This corresponds to developments in the broader labor movement. As the neoliberal consensus solidified in the 1980s, organized labor faced an increasingly hostile judiciary and administrative state, which emboldened employers to claw back gains labor had won through collective bargaining, a system of industrial relations that was revealed to be contingent and fragile. Under these conditions, organized labor devoted increasing attention to education and skills as it became harder to secure a greater share of material benefits from employers. On the decline of collective bargaining, see Davis, *Prisoners of the American Dream*, 102–153.

71 Frank Segers, "Videotape and Jurisdiction; Have NABET & IBEW Bested Craft-Splintered IA Caution?," *Variety*, January 9, 1974, 101.

72 "IATSE Locals' Vidtape Battle Wide Open via Defy by Soundmen," *Variety*, January 25, 1972, 45.

73 Beck, "Quiet Revolution."

74 Frank Segers, "Pictures: Videotape Issue as IATSE Labyrinth," *Variety*, August 18, 1976, 5.

75 IATSE, *I.A.T.S.E. 1893–1993: One Hundred Years of Solidarity*, 88, Authors Collection.

76 "SMPTE, IA Plan Course In TV Tape Editing," *THR*, December 30, 1959, 10.

77 IATSE, *Official Bulletin*, no. 660 (2018), 70, https://iatse.net/wp-content/uploads /2021/05/IATSE-2nd2018_web.pdf.

78 The preceding timeline of mergers is from Motion Picture Editors Guild, 75th Anniversary Celebration, 25–28.

79 On the transition, see Wright, "Sound from Start to Finish," 321–347.

80 Stephen Andriano-Moore, "The Motion Picture Editors Guild Treatment of the Film Sound Membership: Enforcing Status Quo for Hollywood's Post-production Sound Craft," *Labor Studies Journal* 45, no. 3 (September 2020): 273–295.

81 The editor Rob Kraut, speaking at an MPEG organizing meeting, is quoted in John Caldwell, *Specworld: Folds, Faults, and Fractures in Embedded Creator Industries* (University of California Press, 2023), vii–viii.

82 On the challenges of organizing visual effects workers, see Michael Curtin and John Vanderhoef, "A Vanishing Piece of the Pi: The Globalization of Visual Effects Labor," *Television and New Media* 16, no. 3 (2015): 219–239; and interviews with visual effects artists Dave Rand, Mariana Acuña-Acosta, and Daniel Lay and union official Steve Kaplan in *Voices of Labor: Creativity, Craft, and Conflict in Global Hollywood*, ed. Michael Curtin and Kevin Sanson (University of California Press, 2017), 204–260.

83 Cathy Repola, "Moving Forward," *CineMontage* 10, no. 4 (Winter 2021): 13.

84 Carolyn Giardina and Katie Kilkenny, "IATSE's Big Divide: 'Status Quo' Studio Deal Roils Membership," *THR*, November 17, 2021, https://www.hollywoodreporter.com /business/business-news/iatse-deal-membership-divide-1235048898/.

5

Art Direction

● ●

The Drive to Unite Hollywood's
Designers and Artists

BARBARA HALL

In September 1943, the director Irving Pichel penned an article for *Action*, the studio magazine at Twentieth Century-Fox, praising the work of the personnel in the art department. "I do not wish to imply that all writers, producers and directors ignore the importance of background in their pictures," Pichel wrote, "but it is true that most of us fail to recognize the Art Department as one of the major collaborators along with writer, producer, director, cameraman and players in the creation of a picture."[1] Pichel's observations were no doubt welcomed by his colleagues in the art department. Though they were staffed by a unique cross section of trained architects, talented draftsmen, and gifted artists, the studio art departments were chronically undervalued, both within the industry and in the general discourse about Hollywood filmmaking. While certain figures such as William Cameron Menzies and Cedric Gibbons became well known, most art directors worked below the radar, practicing their remarkable craft without fanfare, assisted by an army of equally underappreciated set designers, illustrators, sketch artists, model makers, scenic painters, and other craftspeople. Not surprisingly, the history of the unionization efforts of these workers has also been underdocumented. *Stars and Strikes* (1941), the first in-depth study of labor organizing in the film industry, includes only the briefest reference to the art department crafts, and even books on production design rarely discuss the challenges these creative workers faced in their pursuit of their right to organize. The goal of this chapter is to reclaim this piece of labor history by exploring what was at stake for these art department workers, documenting their various efforts to organize, and examining how they addressed the tensions and contradictions that arise when creative artists collaborate in an industrial setting like the Hollywood entertainment business.

Defining the Craft

While scenic design has been an intrinsic part of moviemaking since the days of Georges Méliès, cinema art direction in Hollywood is often traced to 1914, when feature-length films began to gain in popularity in the United States and abroad.[2] That year, Wilfred Buckland, an accomplished theatrical scenic designer who had been celebrated for his work with the impresario David Belasco, was recruited to move to Los Angeles to design and build sets for the movie producer Jesse Lasky and the director Cecil B. DeMille. At the time, Buckland had strong opinions about the possibilities of cinema, telling *Motion Picture News*, "Too many picture productions of the present day are only commercial photographs, accurate and clear in detail, but with no artistic value or meaning. I am entering the motion picture field, because that field offers what the stage does not—an opportunity to create new methods of production to take the place of those which we have outgrown."[3] According to some accounts, Buckland—who had exercised so much creative control in the theater that he expected the same freedom in Hollywood—underestimated the strong opinions and personalities of his new employers and frequently clashed with DeMille when it came to having a say on the overall look of their collaborations.[4] Nevertheless, Buckland's influence during his early years in Hollywood was groundbreaking, especially in the area of lighting. It was Buckland who convinced DeMille and Lasky to move from the tradition of filming with daylight to using theatrical Klieg lights to illuminate sets, an innovation that came to be known as "Lasky Lighting" and led to a major shift in production practice.[5]

Although Buckland is widely regarded as the first motion picture art director in Hollywood, a number of other groundbreaking designers came to filmmaking either before Buckland or around the same time, including Ben Carré, Joseph Urban, Anton Grot, Hugo Ballin, and Robert Brunton. In a *Photoplay* article from 1916, Alfred A. Cohn wrote about the recent emergence of the art director (also known at that time as the technical director) and the way this relatively new position was changing how films were made. Describing the art director/technical director as the "wise guy of the studio" and a "well-read and much-traveled individual," Cohn emphasized the level of knowledge and sophistication that an art director could bring to a production.[6] In fact, as feature filmmaking became the norm in the late 1910s, the art director was often spoken of as equal in importance to the director and the cinematographer, with influence not only on how sets were designed and built but also on how scenes were staged, lit, and photographed. For instance, the *Photoplay* article noted that the art director is "equipped with a wide knowledge of picture conditions; knows what the camera will do and what it will not; and is an expert on color values as translated into the black and white of the screen."[7] As the historian Beverly Heisner has pointed out, during this period the art director was also appreciated for his singular ability to create a sense of verisimilitude, a quality that became even more important to viewers as their expectations for realistic filmed entertainment grew.[8] Interestingly, even at this early stage, it was acknowledged that this authenticity was brought to the screen not only by the art director's own knowledge and expertise but also by a reliance on historical research. The *Photoplay* article mentions that at least one studio had already established a "well organized research department" equipped to supply art directors with illustrations and other visual materials.[9] The author was most likely referring to the research library at the Lasky Studio, which was established in 1914 by Elizabeth McGaffey, a pioneer in production research for motion pictures.[10]

Of course, not all members of the crew were equally comfortable with the art director assuming such an influential position in the production hierarchy. According to Kevin Brownlow, there was some resentment directed at early art directors from the carpenters and prop men who had previously overseen set construction, and even some directors were not sold on having to defer to an art director's vision.[11] As the movie business continued to expand, however, and the studios consolidated their control over production, the demand for elaborate built environments increased. Now, art directors not only were employed on every important film but also began bringing in trained support staff to help handle the load. This included draftsmen (also known as set designers) with architectural training to make detailed construction drawings of the sets; architectural model makers to build 3D miniature mock-ups for choosing camera angles and lenses; and illustrators, often with art school backgrounds, to create sketches and presentation drawings. This influx of personnel from the art and architecture worlds led to a new professionalization of art direction and established a foundation for the studio art departments that would become the norm in the 1920s.[12]

Professionalizing the Art Director

The late 1910s were a period of labor unrest in Los Angeles, with the studios battling workers demanding unionization, but several motion picture professions avoided conflict by forming what were sometimes called cooperative organizations, as opposed to unions or guilds. These fraternal groups included the Motion Picture Directors Association, established in 1915, and the American Society of Cinematographers, founded in 1919. Following in their footsteps, the Motion

Picture Art Directors' Association was formed in late 1919, and by early 1920 it boasted 100 members and was already planning its first major event, a dinner dance to be held in June of that year at the Alexandria Hotel in Los Angeles. There is little documentation available about the society, but a souvenir program from the dinner dance details the gala event. The program includes a statement of the association's purposes, which expresses not only how art directors viewed their own profession at that point in time but also how they felt about the prospect of making demands on the studios for fair compensation:

> We, the Art and Technical Directors of the Motion Picture Industry, in order to insure due prestige and recognition for our profession, to better existing conditions and to assure the producers of our help and co-operation in securing competent men of recognized standing and experience as designers and executors of settings, scenic and lighting effects, and desiring to stand on our merits, do hereby organize ourselves into an association for the above stated purposes, the maintenance of a circulating library and suitable club rooms where we can meet for the exchange of ideas, hold lectures, etc., thereby helping us as individuals and making us more valuable to the producing companies with whom we desire to co-operate at all times for the betterment of production in general.
>
> It is not the desire of this body to at any time enter into controversy regarding compensations, but we aim to so improve our profession that our worth will be appreciated and our services adequately rewarded in proportion to the other elements of the industry.[13]

Although the Motion Picture Art Directors' Association was mentioned in the trade papers off and on through 1920, its activities seemed to be very limited following the dinner dance, and by 1923 it appears to have become inactive. In fact, it is likely that its members simply moved over to another organization, one that would have much more staying power: the Cinemagundi Club.

Formed in 1924 by a group of sixty-three prominent art directors, including Leo "K" Kuter, William Cameron Menzies, Ben Carré, and Anton Grot, the Cinemagundi Club supported some of the same goals as the association but couched them in a broader context of artistic achievement and comradeship.[14] In the preamble to the organization's bylaws, the founders espoused lofty ideals, stating, "From all countries, Artists and Artisans foregather in Hollywood to serve the world with their talents through the Motion Picture. To the end that these creative minds may find friendliness and good fellowship, and meet on common ground, we do hereby create the Cinemagundi Club."[15]

Given the pervasive anti-labor atmosphere in Hollywood in the early 1920s, the elite members of the new organization were careful to position the group as a professional society rather than a nascent labor union that was going to begin making demands on employers. The Cinemagundi founders promoted the idea that the club's goal was to bring together like-minded artists to socialize while discussing issues that affected them, with an emphasis on elevating motion pictures to an art form and calling attention to the accomplishments of its members. In 1926, the Cinemagundi Club incorporated and offered stock options to its members, a move that allowed the group to purchase property on Beachwood Drive in Hollywood.[16] The building at that location was renovated into the organization's clubhouse, where meetings, art classes, soirees, and other get-togethers were held for members and their guests. Though the club remained a mostly social organization, the idea of supporting the work of Hollywood's many artists was taken seriously by the membership. In fact, many of the club's original members supported the formation in 1928 of the League of Art Directors and Associates (LADA), the first organized unionizing effort by art department workers.[17]

The League of Art Directors and Associates

If during its early years the Cinemagundi Club focused on networking and professional development, the League of Art Directors and Associates was equally clear about its mission to improve working conditions for all art department employees and was not afraid to associate itself with the labor movement. From the beginning, LADA was committed to bringing together many different artists and artisans, from art directors and draftsmen to costume designers, set dressers, illustrators, sketch artists, and special effects men.[18] These workers organized LADA partly in response to the craft unionization efforts of the 1920s that resulted in the first Studio Basic Agreement (SBA) in 1926. The five unions that signed on to the SBA, including the International Alliance of Theatrical Stage Employes (IATSE) and the International Brotherhood of Painters, Decorators and Paperhangers, represented a number of below-the-line crafts, but most were not art department jobs. Given this inequity, it is not surprising that a group like LADA was formed with the express goal of addressing issues such as wages, hours, and working conditions in different art- and design-related crafts.

There were also other reasons why art department workers chose this moment to organize. As the studio system became firmly entrenched in the 1920s, settings for motion pictures became more elaborate and complex, and the art departments at each studio were called on to create ever more challenging sets on soundstages and backlots, often with limited budgets. Studio art departments became tightly structured to manage this workload, with a hierarchy resembling that of an architectural firm. Pridgeon Smith, one of the leaders of LADA, made this comparison in a letter to the president of IATSE, claiming art department personnel's relationship to the studio was "approximately that of the Architect to his client, i.e. consultation with the client, a critical examination into his particular needs and requirements, and then professional advice and active service in solving the problem."[19] In this system, a supervising art director served as a link to studio management and oversaw the labor of a staff of unit art directors, draftsmen, illustrators, model makers, and assistants who were assigned to work on specific productions.[20]

The detailed plans generated by the art department were the first steps in a process that involved many other departments and hundreds of studio employees, including painters, carpenters, set builders, special effects men, set dressers, researchers, scenic artists, and property men (figure 5.1). Many of these below-the-line employees were covered by the SBA, but those who were not, including the members of the art department, were subject to long hours and low wages. As the set designer and union organizer Edward Gilbert explained in a 1947 hearing, "The need for collective bargaining became evident to art department workers. The studios frowned on organization in our departments and showed their displeasure by discriminating against those who talked organization."[21] The production designer Robert Boyle, who started out as a draftsman at Paramount in 1933, recalled that when he "came into the business we were working seven days a week and working long hours, and it was miserable. And that was why we started the unions. Not so much for the money, although that was certainly part of it, but for the working conditions." Boyle added, "We very often slept right there on the drafting tables. Get about three or four hours sleep, get up, continue drawing. Oh, it was brutal. You learned a lot, but it was brutal."[22]

From the beginning, LADA was attuned to all these concerns. In a forward-thinking survey sent to members in May 1929, respondents were asked to weigh in on a number of issues that would be on the table when negotiating with the studios, including screen credit, overtime pay, weekend and holiday work, and vacation days.[23] However, despite the enthusiasm of its leaders and a fast-growing membership spread over a number of crafts, the League of Art Directors and Associates proved to be short-lived once its leadership made it known that it intended to either operate as an independent union or obtain a charter from IATSE. These plans were quickly shot down by the International Brotherhood of Painters, Decorators and Paperhangers, which controlled Local 235, the West Coast affiliate of United Scenic Artists, the theater workers union that had jurisdiction over the entertainment industry in New York.[24]

The Brotherhood of Painters included motion picture scenic artists in its West Coast membership, and it was determined to parlay its foothold in Local 235 into control of all art department personnel in the Hollywood film industry. Starting in the spring of 1929, letters and memos from the leadership of the Painters, as well as the heads of the American Federation of Labor (AFL) and IATSE, made it clear that LADA members were expected to join Local 235. On July 19, 1929, William F. Canavan, the president of IATSE, wrote to Pridgeon Smith and flatly denied his request for an IATSE charter, claiming that it would "involve us in a jurisdictional dispute with several other trades." Demonstrating a distinct misunderstanding of the work of LADA members, Canavan added, "It seems to me that there are already sufficient organizations in the motion

FIGURE 5.1 Storyboard illustration of the work of an art director, c.1940. (Courtesy of the Art Directors Guild.)

picture industry to fully cover the modeling and other similar work of this nature that have already been conceded as belonging to the Plasterers' Union; wardrobe department employees to the Needle Workers; painters of any description to the Scenic Arts organizations; men making any sort of stage setting to the Studio Mechanics Alliance, etc."[25] In reply, Smith attempted to explain to Canavan that the LADA members all needed to be in one organization because of the collaborative nature of their crafts, writing that "to separate these departments, and these workers, upon an arbitrary basis is to work a great and unnecessary hardship."[26]

Despite multiple appeals to the organizations involved, LADA was not able to survive as an independent union. Faced with no other option, the LADA leadership acquiesced, and the process of joining Local 235 got underway in January 1930. Later that year, however, the Brotherhood of Painters decided to split Local 235 into two groups, moving the set painters and paperhangers into a new local (644) and leaving the art department personnel (also identified as the "professional" group) with the original charter, with the local now known as "Two-Three-Five United Scenic Artists."

Unfortunately, Two-Three-Five was never given the opportunity to negotiate a contract with the producers and received little support from its affiliate, the Brotherhood of Painters. The situation was summed up in a remarkable letter, written in June 1931, from Pridgeon Smith to William Green, the head of the AFL, which detailed the poor treatment that the group endured in trying to convince the producers to give them due consideration. The letter suggests that the producers and their representative, Pat Casey, colluded with the Internationals Committee (made up of the five signatories to the SBA) to deny the members of Two-Three-Five a contract. Describing a meeting that was scheduled for February 5, 1931, Smith wrote, "Chicanery and machination on the part of the Producers coupled with treachery and betrayal by those in whom their confidence had been placed, defeated the efforts of men honestly and sincerely striving to advance the cause of organized labor on the Pacific Coast."[27]

Although Two-Three-Five continued to be listed in the annual *Film Daily Yearbook* through 1934, there is no indication that it was affiliated with a labor organization or actively pursued a contract with the producers after 1931. Nevertheless, its address at 2560 North Beachwood Drive, the home of the Cinemagundi Club, suggests that there was still solidarity among art directors and an interest in collective bargaining. This became clear in 1937 when many of the remaining members of the Cinemagundi Club became founding members of the Society of Motion Picture Art Directors (SMPAD).

With Franklin Delano Roosevelt's election in 1932 and the establishment of the National Recovery Administration the following year, labor organizing became an even greater priority for workers struggling to make a living in the movie industry. Since 1929, the Academy of Motion Picture Arts and Sciences (AMPAS) had positioned itself as an impartial arbiter of labor disputes in Hollywood, but within a few years workers were beginning to doubt AMPAS's motives, leading to an exodus of members from the organization. In 1932, this disillusionment resulted in the creation of a new group called the Federated Motion Picture Crafts (FMPC). The FMPC was a coalition of unaffiliated worker groups that included scenic artists who had broken away from the

Painters Local 644, as well as the members of the struggling Local 235.[28] According to a *Hollywood Reporter* article from 1934, the federation also included employees from many different job categories, including assistant directors, upholsterers, script clerks, plumbers, bill posters, and motion picture airplane pilots.[29] Despite much labor unrest around this time, however, the studios had little incentive to negotiate with the loose-knit federation, especially once Roosevelt's National Industrial Recovery Act was found unconstitutional by the Supreme Court in 1935. But the FMPC's formation during this time and the participation of several groups of art department craftspeople demonstrate how committed these workers were to organizing and collective bargaining.

Two years later, however, the tide turned following the Supreme Court's upholding of the sweeping National Labor Relations Act (NLRA). Also known as the Wagner Act, the NLRA outlawed the tactics commonly used by management against union organizing and encouraged workers to form their own bargaining units for dealing directly with their employers. Immediately following the decision, in April 1937, the dormant FMPC resurfaced as the leader of a renewed effort to bring new voices into the Hollywood labor conversation. As it had before, the federation brought together a coalition of unaffiliated crafts that were not covered by the SBA in order to initiate a more local and democratic approach for studio employees. Within the roster of workers again taking a stand were several art department groups, including set designers, scenic painters, and illustrators, many of whom had chosen to affiliate with Local 621 of the Brotherhood of Painters.[30]

When the Hollywood producers refused to negotiate with the FMPC, these groups and their allies went on strike on April 30, 1937. As Ida Jeter showed in her landmark study of the strike and its ramifications, the response orchestrated by IATSE, the studios, and various outside anti-labor groups was swift and violent.[31] IATSE, which was pushing to represent all below-the-line crafts in Hollywood, refused to recognize the FMPC and actively moved to squash the strike, and the Screen Actors Guild, which at first planned to join the walkout, backed out when the studios agreed to ratify its first contract.[32] Even though they were outnumbered, the workers were fired up. In an FMPC bulletin published on May 28, 1937, striking set designers were described as being "strong for the Federation and unified to the man," especially once they learned that the studios were recruiting draftsmen from architectural firms to do the work of the strikers. In the colorful account, the writer stated, "The studios have picked up a few punks here and there, and with the aid of a few rats who crawled back into their holes in a few of the drafting rooms, there seems to be every reason for the fact that in at least one major studio, not one blue print has been made from a drawing executed by these poor saps who thought they could carry on where our set designers left off."[33] Nevertheless, the strike was short-lived, and the FMPC was dissolved in early June, with many of the remaining strikers negotiating for higher wages in exchange for joining existing locals. However, other workers doubled down and continued to build their own organizations. In fact, Gerald Horne has argued that even though the FMPC strike was not successful, it had a galvanizing impact on the independent union movement and laid the groundwork for the formation of the Conference of Studio Unions (CSU) in 1941.[34]

This call to action certainly seemed to inspire the art department craftspeople who had been involved in the strike. Soon after the dissolution of the FMPC, several new independent craft groups were formed, including the Society of Motion Picture Artists and Illustrators, the Screen Set Designers, and the Society of Motion Picture Interior Decorators (SMPID). Each group proceeded to begin negotiating directly with the studios and made significant inroads, culminating in the Screen Set Designers' initial contract in 1939. That successful negotiation made the Screen Set Designers the first independent art department union to secure an agreement with the Association of Motion Picture Producers (AMPP).[35]

A New Deal for Art Directors

In May 1937, a few weeks after the conclusion of the FMPC strike, fifty-nine employees from the various studio art departments came together to establish the Society of Motion Picture Art Directors. When it was initially formed, the SMPAD included art directors, assistant art directors, and chief draftsmen, as well as the supervising art directors from each studio, including Cedric Gibbons of MGM and Hans Dreier of Paramount. From the beginning, the art directors seemed wary of getting caught up in the jurisdictional battles then being fought in Hollywood and asserted that they wanted to operate independently. In fact, according to the minutes of the first meeting, chaired by Bernard Herzbrun, the group resolved to "form themselves into an unincorporated association for the purpose of representing themselves in all matters between themselves and their employers and in order that they shall not be represented by any other organization or body of men."[36]

Early minutes and memos indicate that the founding members of the SMPAD were confident that they would soon be recognized by the studios, and they made plans to have negotiations handled by several supervising art directors who, as heads of the art departments at the various companies, were accustomed to working with studio management. A board of directors and officers were elected, and several meetings were held in the summer of 1937 under the leadership of the society's first president, Stephen Goosson, who was then the supervising art director at Columbia. However, the SMPAD hit a roadblock almost immediately when the motion picture studios refused to recognize it as a bargaining agent for their employees, forcing the society to engage an attorney and file a petition against each studio with the National Labor Relations Board (NLRB).[37] In their responses, the studios asserted, among other dubious claims, that they were not "engaged in the exhibition of motion pictures" and that "the provisions of the [National Labor Relations] Act delegating to the Board the power to determine the appropriate unit were unconstitutional."[38] In its July 1939 decision in favor of the SMPAD, the board noted that the case was complicated by competing claims on the art directors from Harold Davis, the business agent for United Scenic Artists, Local 621, and representatives of the IATSE. Both groups claimed jurisdiction over the art directors, as well as the set designers, illustrators, and scenic artists, and objected to the formation of the SMPAD as an unaffiliated labor organization. In its decision, the NLRB noted that Pat Casey, the chief negotiator for the studios, used these jurisdictional disputes as another reason to refuse to engage with the SMPAD.[39]

The battle for recognition crippled the SMPAD for two years, but eventually the NLRB sided with the fledgling organization, decreeing that it was the representative for its workers in five studios (based on the number of employees who were already members of the society) and ordering elections at three studios where it did not hold a majority of members.[40] These elections were held in August 1939, and all three resulted in the SMPAD being recognized as the sole bargaining agent for the art directors, assistant art directors, chief draftsmen, and supervising art directors at the eight companies. Once the dispute was finally settled in the SMPAD's favor, the society again started meeting regularly and began working on a draft agreement to present to the producers.

When it reconvened in August 1939, one of the first actions the board of directors undertook was a revision of the society's bylaws. The most significant change was to the membership status of supervising art directors. In an overview of the SMPAD written in 1950, attorney William Whitsett explained that the supervising art directors were given the status of "inactive members with no right to vote, to hold office, or to attend meetings."[41] Clearly, after the events of the previous two years, the members of the society had realized that department heads with close ties to studio management might not fully understand the needs of workers during contract negotiations. With the supervising art directors sidelined, the membership of the SMPAD included only art directors, assistant art directors, and chief draftsmen (who were also known as art directors in charge of the drafting room).

Unfortunately, with or without the supervisors, the process of negotiating and signing its first agreement with the AMPP turned out to be prolonged and extremely taxing for the young organization. An early draft of the proposal from the society shows that in addition to setting minimum wage scales and terms for vacations, sick leave, severance, and travel, the society was hoping to guarantee equal screen credit for supervising art directors and unit art directors and wanted the professional acronym SMPAD to follow the name of any member of the society credited on-screen. Among other ideas, the negotiating committee also asked that art directors be allowed to make rough drawings and sketches in the course of their work, and that an art director be assigned to every film.

The committee also stipulated that unit art directors not be required to work on more than two films concurrently.[42]

In the end, however, the society was forced to give up on many of those initial proposals. The minutes from that period show that the producers refused to compromise on core terms such as job descriptions, credits, and minimum rates, and used a variety of stalling techniques to prolong the negotiations, including canceling or postponing meetings. Stan Rogers, one of the members of the negotiating committee, later recalled that the producers' representatives "refused to meet on any points. Everything we presented to them, they absolutely refused to meet."[43] This was confirmed by reports from the guild's attorney, Leonard Janofsky, who led the negotiating team. At a membership meeting held on July 8, 1941, Janofsky read a summary of the progress of negotiations and then stated that "he believed that it is the best practical deal that can be obtained from the producers at the present time."[44] After numerous meetings where the latest version of the contract was read to the membership and then counterproposals were drafted in response, the members finally voted to approve the agreement in August 1941.

A review of the executed 1941 contract shows that some of the SMPAD's requests were granted, but that much of what it had hoped for was not achieved. Instead of the society's proposed starting weekly minimums of $275 for art directors and $150 for assistants, the contract established a starting minimum of $125 per week for art directors and $90 per week for assistant art directors, with only more experienced art directors guaranteed up to $175 per week. The contract did promise a screen credit to unit art directors when they worked on a film but stipulated that an art director did not necessarily need to be employed on pictures that were shot entirely "with natural outdoor background and without sets" or if standing sets were going to be used without structural changes. The contract also stated that producers could ask for a certain number of temporary work permits for nonmembers each year, which meant that the society would be a limited version of an open shop, as opposed to the union shop that it was hoping to establish.[45] Not surprisingly, within a year, members of the SMPAD were already questioning the terms of the agreement and arguing for a return to the negotiating table, with some advocating for joining a union that could give them more bargaining strength.

Strength in Numbers

Throughout its early history, the SMPAD tried to increase its membership ranks and was frequently in conversation with the other art department groups about possible affiliation. As each group within the art department formed its own union and started to establish its goals and demands, there was a sense that it would be mutually beneficial to join forces under one umbrella that would encompass all the art-related crafts, much like LADA had in 1929. Shortly after the SMPAD was reactivated in 1939, it went on record as supporting the United Studio Technicians Guild (USTG), a coalition of unaffiliated labor groups led by Jeff Kibre and backed by the Congress of Industrial Organizations (CIO), which was presenting itself as an alternative to the domination of IATSE.[46] Kibre's efforts were quickly shot down, but the idea of joining forces continued to percolate among the art department workers. For instance, in November 1941, the *Los Angeles Times* reported, "The four motion-picture art organizations comprising the Screen Set Designers; Society of Motion Picture Interior Decorators; Society of Motion Picture Artists and Illustrators and the Society of Motion Picture Art Directors will celebrate their 25 years of association on Wednesday at the Cafe Caliente, Olvera St. at a stag dinner."[47] This informal alliance soon developed into a serious discussion of affiliation among what came to be known as the Four Art Groups. During this time, the SMPAD also had meetings with a nascent organization known as the Inter-Guild Council.[48] Toggling between affiliation with other art department workers versus above-the-line creatives like the directors and screenwriters, who were part of the Inter-Guild Council, demonstrates that the art directors were still trying to determine where they belonged in the studio hierarchy, and whether affiliation with other groups would improve or hamper their professional status.

In 1942, the issue of officially uniting with the other art department crafts was again brought to the forefront. At a meeting on August 4, the SMPAD members in attendance debated the merits of affiliating with another union versus staying independent. The discussion centered on whether the SMPAD should join forces with the recently organized Local 1421 of the Painters and CSU, which then included set designers, illustrators, and set decorators. Some art directors argued that there were advantages to being backed by a major union organization, citing as proof the fact that the set designers, hourly workers represented by the Painters Union, now in some cases earned more than art directors, who were paid a weekly salary.[49]

By 1943, the possibility of affiliating with Local 1421 became so appealing that the SMPAD formed a committee to investigate the issue. In the meeting minutes from that time, it is clear that many SMPAD members felt that the contract that the society agreed to in 1941 was unfair, especially the wage scales, and they became more vocal about the need for increasing their power and influence by joining with a major labor organization like the Painters Union. But while there was agreement on the need to act, there was still debate about the best way to proceed. Some members were in favor of requesting a separate charter from the Painters Union, while others thought that a merger with Local 1421 was the only way to gain the strength in numbers they needed to stand up to the Producers Association. Finally, in July 1944, the SMPAD passed a resolution supporting affiliation with Local 1421, with the stipulation that the society could maintain some degree of independence within the local.[50] There were some sticking points, including conflicts over job classifications, notably the definition of the title "production designer," which was claimed both by the art directors and by illustrators in Local 1421.[51] This disagreement, as well as a growing feeling from the Local 1421 leadership that the SMPAD was using the threat of affiliation as a bargaining chip in their upcoming negotiations with the producers, led to a standoff. After months of detailed negotiations, the SMPAD recommended discussions of affiliation be suspended in December 1944, stating, "The Board believes that a proper basis for affiliation with Local 1421 by the Society of Motion Picture Art Directors cannot be arrived at [at] this time."[52] Ultimately, the "strength in numbers" argument that would have united all the art department workers into one union appears to have bumped up against long-standing concerns about the art director's position in the traditional production hierarchy. The SMPAD renegotiated its contract in 1946 and at that time was able to secure more favorable terms, including a significant wage bump.[53]

The mid-1940s brought labor strife to previously unseen levels in Hollywood. In 1945, soon after the decision to affiliate with the SMPAD was tabled, Local 1421's jurisdictional showdown with IATSE over the fate of the set decorators came to a head. The ensuing strikes led to unprecedented labor unrest in the industry that lasted several years and fomented deep divisions between studio employees. The SMPAD had an anti-strike clause in its contract and so did not get directly involved with the conflict, although members were assured they did not have to cross the picket lines if they felt threatened or in danger.[54] They also were advised that they could refuse to do any work that should have been done by a striking worker. For instance, during the strike, IATSE pressured its members not only to cross the picket lines but also to perform the work of the strikers. Many refused, including Local 44 prop masters working at Warner Bros., who at one point walked off the job rather than follow the order to perform the duties of the striking set decorators.[55]

Although most of the labor unrest took place in 1945 and 1946, it would be several more years before the jurisdictional issues at the heart of the strikes were resolved and all the members of the CSU-affiliated unions were able to return to work. During this time, the Screen Set Designers, Illustrators, and Decorators (CSU Local 1421) continued to fight for its right to represent its members, even though many of them had signed cards with other locals in order to return to work.[56] In 1949, a group of studio-based set designers, model makers, illustrators, sketch artists, and assistants, motivated to find a solution that did not involve affiliating with IATSE, approached the SMPAD about joining forces and organized a vote that overwhelmingly favored affiliation. However, when the SMPAD filed a petition with the NLRB requesting permission to bring those workers into the society, IATSE intervened, claiming that the SMPAD could not represent these employees because some of its members were their supervisors in the art department. In a lengthy brief filed with the NLRB, the society's attorney, William Whitsett, pointed out that many unions in Hollywood included supervisory employees, and that denying the request in this case would have a chilling effect on the ability of motion picture industry workers to freely organize and participate in collective bargaining.[57] However, the NLRB sided with IATSE and denied the petition, putting an end to the latest affiliation effort in a decision that cemented IATSE's almost complete control over Hollywood's below-the-line craft unions.

Following the NLRB decision, and once Sorrell and the CSU had been driven out of the industry (as detailed in the introduction to part I), IATSE moved to organize the art department crafts that were not yet under its umbrella by launching several new locals. This process had started as early as 1945, when IATSE chartered Local 790, then known as Motion Picture Studio Art Craftsmen. According to testimony offered during a congressional hearing investigating jurisdictional disputes in the movie industry, Local 790 was originally formed to represent "set designers, painters, and scenic artists," though it later came to include only illustrators and matte artists.[58] Many of the intended members still had an allegiance to Sorrell and Local 1421 and so chose not to join Local 790 initially, though it was key to IATSE's strategy to gain jurisdiction over those crafts in the future.

Another IATSE local formed around this time was Local 816, chartered in 1949, representing scenic painters and title artists. After briefly striking out on their own in the 1930s, scenic artists had eventually rejoined the Painters Local 644 in 1942, but in many ways that affiliation did not address the unique talents of this group of artists who specialized in painting the monumental scenic backdrops used in so many studio films. The formation of a separate local specifically focusing on their craft allowed the scenic artists to gain more stature and recognition within the industry. The advent of television was especially game-changing for scenic artists, whose skills were suddenly in higher demand due to the theatrical nature of live television programs, which often called for multiple painted backdrops. In a document titled "A Short History of Scenic Artists," member W. A. Jackson praised the affiliation with IATSE, especially in terms of its negotiation of regular wage increases, and the fact that contracts were signed not only with the movie studios but also with independent companies, title art studios, and all major television producers.[59]

The last holdouts among the art department were 150 set designers, sketch artists, and model makers still loyal to Local 1421, referred to in a 1950 *Los Angeles Times* article as a "lost tribe of Hollywood motion picture employees."[60] By this time, the members of Local 1421 had been working without a contract for nearly five years. In July 1949, they had been given the green light by the NLRB to negotiate with the AMPP on an industry-wide level, but the producers continued to refuse to engage with them.[61] Following the NLRB decision against affiliation with the SMPAD, the Brotherhood of Painters revoked Local 1421's charter, and IATSE moved to form a new local for set designers and model makers. Despite a last-ditch effort by a group of designers to establish a new unaffiliated society, an election held in July 1952 handed a decisive victory to IATSE, and the set designers and model makers joined the newly chartered Local 847 in September 1952.[62] In the meantime, the Society of Motion Picture Art Directors continued to operate as an independent guild representing the interests of art directors, assistant art directors, and chief draftsmen.

Elevating the Craft of Art Direction

Since its founding, the Society of Motion Picture Art Directors not only had been interested in negotiating with the studios on wages, credits, and working conditions but also had been concerned with raising the profile of art directors and calling attention to their important creative role in the filmmaking process. As a result, the SMPAD went to great lengths to promote itself and its members. As early as 1939, before the society had even secured its first contract, it formed a publicity committee charged with building recognition for the work of art directors in the movie industry by getting articles placed in national magazines, organizing exhibits, reaching out to universities, and working with studio marketing departments.[63] But this was an uphill battle, given that art direction was thought of as technical and less than glamorous. For instance, in a 1941 article in the *Los Angeles Times*, Philip K. Scheuer wrote, "Your art director is usually quiet, well-mannered, soft-spoken, married to a non-pro and dressed like a conservative business executive." He went on to praise the work of Hollywood's art directors, while admitting that he did not fully understand what they did. According to Scheuer, "It is they, as someone pointed out last week, who are responsible for the APPEARANCE of a motion picture—everything an audience sees outside of the actors and physical movement. I'd never realized it before myself. True, a line of credit does reach the screen: Art direction by _____. But who and what, actually, is this art director?"[64]

One tactic that brought some positive attention their way was to nod to the past, which surely was the thinking in 1941 when the SMPAD hosted a testimonial dinner for the pioneering art director Wilfred Buckland. At the event, Buckland was toasted by some of the leading figures of the time, including William Cameron Menzies and Cecil B. DeMille, as well as by members of other unions.[65] In 1946, the society engaged the services of the respected publicist Henry Rogers to place positive mentions of the craft into the trade papers and popular press. Norman Lowenstein, who was hired as the business agent for the SMPAD that same year, issued regular reports to the membership in the early years of his tenure, and often the focus of those updates was the progress of the publicity campaign.

In 1949, the society honored film pioneers Cecil B. DeMille and Jesse Lasky for their contributions to cinema, and the following year, on October 12, 1950, it voted to present a new award, the SMPAD Medal for Distinguished Achievement, to Cedric Gibbons, the longtime head of the MGM Art Department. In his letter to Gibbons telling him about the award, Lowenstein wrote that the members of the society had voted "unanimously" to honor Gibbons in this way.[66] Certainly Gibbons, who by that point had won seven Academy Awards for art direction, was one of the most famous members of the craft, and presenting him with this honor did generate positive publicity for the SMPAD. It would be interesting to know, however, whether all the members of the society really supported the award, given that Gibbons was a department head and was not considered a hands-on designer.

The SMPAD also tried to raise its profile by engaging with the public. In 1950, it announced that it would begin giving annual awards to "manufacturers in the fields of home furnishings and home decorative fields," which resulted in commendations to products such as refrigerators and flooring.[67] In addition, the society put together what was billed as the "first exhibit in Hollywood history showing the public what art directors do in the making of motion pictures." Held at the Santa Monica Art Gallery beginning in March 1955, the show featured eighty-five exhibits, including spotlights on sets from *Rear Window*, *High Noon*, and *Bad Day at Black Rock*.[68] Two years later, in 1957, the SMPAD announced that its members would be "willing to supply original sketches of homes designed for various movies, enabling the new home builders to have exact replicas of what they have seen on the screen."[69] All of these activities were undertaken in order to raise the profile of art directors both within the industry and with the general public.

One of the most ambitious projects launched by the SMPAD during these years was the publication of a magazine. Originally launched in 1951 as the *Society of Motion Picture Art Directors Bulletin*, the newsletter was reimagined later that year by editor Leo "K" Kuter as *Production Design*, a journal showcasing the work of SMPAD members. The articles ranged from features on the art direction of *An American in Paris* and *A Streetcar Named Desire* to technical treatises on designing for live television, the use of three-point perspective, and the challenges of underwater shooting. Other articles explored associated fields, such as animation, research, and costume design, or celebrated the work of seasoned veterans like Stephen Goosson or newcomers like John DeCuir. Unfortunately, the magazine was short-lived, with only ten issues published between October 1951 and August 1952.[70] It stands, however, as a particularly interesting example of Hollywood professionals celebrating and documenting their own contributions to the filmmaking process.

The Arrival of Television and a Shifting Industry

Like every other craft union, the SMPAD had to address the arrival of television. As TV production began to move from New York to the West Coast, the SMPAD added a television section in 1949 and began actively recruiting nonunion members working in TV in Los Angeles to assure that they were not organized by another union.[71] Once the section was established, the society began negotiating on these employees' behalf with the television networks, which at that time were not covered by the Basic Agreement. Even though television design came to represent a growing proportion of the membership's work throughout the 1950s and 1960s, the society did not officially add "television" to its name until 1967, when it became the Society of Motion Picture and Television Art Directors.

It was the television section of the SMPAD that finally gave women art directors a way to make inroads into the male-dominated profession. The first woman invited to membership in the SMPAD, Rita Glover, came in as a television designer in 1949, as did several others in the 1950s and 1960s. Other women, like the accomplished TV art director Jan Scott, began their careers in New York, where they belonged to Local 829, United Scenic Artists. However, there continued to be a barrier in place for women as art directors on feature films. In fact, in 1955, when *Variety* reported that Ruth Sobotka, an artist and scenic designer, would be the credited art director on the upcoming film *Clean Break* (released as *The Killing*), directed by her husband Stanley Kubrick, the trade paper made a point of adding that she would be "the first femme to be given such pic billing, according to the records of the Society of Motion Picture Art Directors."[72] Sadly, Sobotka's achievement did not fling open the doors to the profession: Polly Platt, the first woman film production designer in the union, was not invited to membership until 1971.

Progress for women in the other art department locals was also glacial, though a few illustrators, set designers, and scenic artists did begin to show up on membership rolls in the 1950s and 1960s. For instance, Virginia Johnston, described in a 1955 newsletter as one of "three members of the fair sex in the scenic craft," was not only an active member of Local 816 but served on its board of directors from 1954 to 1969.[73] In 1960, Camille Abbott joined Local 790 as an illustrator and storyboard artist, and it was later noted she was just the third woman to be inducted into the union. Abbott went on to become a leader in the local, serving as secretary-treasurer for forty-two years.[74] Dianne Wager, who joined Local 847 in 1964, was one of the first female set designers in the union, and went on to become an art director as well.[75]

Unfortunately for women joining the ranks of the SMPAD, the slow progress in gender parity came at a time when the landscape for art directors in motion pictures was changing rapidly, with a steep increase in overseas location shooting leading to growing concerns about job stability and the future of the industry. In 1958, Serge Krizman, the president of the SMPAD, weighed in on the runaway production controversy in a speech to the Motion Picture Industry Council. According to *The Hollywood Reporter*, Krizman argued that "most U.S. pictures with foreign backgrounds can be made in Hollywood, with the exception of some locations that require absolute authenticity." The story goes on to say that Krizman "estimated that of about 50 pictures made by Hollywood producers abroad last year, 20 could have been made locally without loss of production values (see figure 5.2).[76] In addition, as Merrill Schleier showed in her study

FIGURE 5.2 Despite an increase in runaway production in the 1950s and 1960s, many films continued to be shot on Hollywood's soundstages. For *Marlowe* (1969) scenic artists created a stunning painted backdrop of nighttime Los Angeles to complement a partially built terrace set. (Courtesy of the Art Directors Guild.)

of *Giant* production designer Boris Leven, there was a significant shift in the 1950s from the structured studio art departments to a freelance model, where production designers were hired to work on feature film projects independently.[77] This reorientation of the studio system, with workers dispersed across television and lower-budget independent films as well as big studio productions, also led to stresses within the art department. For instance, throughout the 1950s, there were significant jurisdictional disputes between the members of the SMPAD and Local 847, representing set designers. The leaders of SMPAD frequently tangled with Zeal Fairbanks, the business agent for 847, over employment practices and jurisdiction on independent productions, and even suggested that Fairbanks had deliberately undermined the efforts to bring the set designers into the society in 1950 in exchange for his leadership position in the local.[78] At the same time, the set designers were concerned that art directors for independent films were producing working drawings and enabling producers to eliminate the need for employing set designers on their productions. Similar concerns were raised by the members of Local 790, which represented illustrators and matte artists, leading to a somewhat strained relationship among some art department personnel, despite the collaborative nature of their work.

Affiliation with IATSE

With all the other members of the art department under the IATSE umbrella, along with related crew such as construction, painters, props, set decorators, and location managers, the leaders of the SMPAD finally decided that it was in their best interest to consider affiliation as well. In February 1958, a group of representatives from the society traveled to an IATSE meeting in Tulsa to explore the idea of applying for an autonomous charter with the International. In a detailed memo, Norman Lowenstein and Leo Kuter reported that the group met with international president Richard Walsh, who enthusiastically endorsed the idea and even offered to help resolve the ongoing jurisdictional disputes with Local 847. According to the report, Walsh "stated that the Society represents a 'Loose-end' (and that he intended no dimunition [sic] of importance by the use of the term) of the production end of the business, and accordingly even if he could see no advantage to be gained by our inclusion in the I.A. other than that fact, this fact was sufficient to want us invited in."[79] Clearly, the IATSE was interested in cementing its control over below-the-line workers in Hollywood, and bringing the art directors into the fold would be an important step toward that goal. Following the meeting with Walsh, the board started discussions with the other locals and with the national office of IATSE. However, negotiations with the other locals continued to be challenging, and IATSE president Walsh and negotiator George Flaherty were forced to intervene to broker a compromise.[80] The decision to move forward was cemented in 1959 when 85 percent of the membership voted in favor of affiliation. Finally, the charter establishing the SMPAD as IATSE Local 876 was signed in January 1960. This put the SMPAD on an equal footing with the other IATSE locals representing art department workers.

Over the next forty years, the SMPAD and the other art department locals maintained their own identities as they, and all other workers in Hollywood, weathered profound changes to an industry moving from a studio-based model to one dominated by independent production and television. Almost all art department workers now fell under the various IATSE Basic Agreements, which were renegotiated every three to five years. Yet the locals were also continually struggling to increase wages and improve working conditions for their own members, which often proved challenging due to the studio downsizing and corporate takeovers that characterized the entertainment industry in the 1960s.

The Art Directors Guild

In 1971, the Academy Award–winning production designer Gene Allen became the executive director of the Society of Motion Picture and Television Art Directors, a position he held for the next twenty-seven years.[81] Known as a tough and pugnacious negotiator and administrator, Allen raised the profile of the guild during his tenure by also serving as president of AMPAS, head of the Motion

Picture Industry Film Council, and vice president of IATSE. When Allen retired in 1997, it was noted that among his accomplishments were negotiating the single-card credit for art directors and production designers, significantly increasing the minimum salaries for all job classifications, and obtaining national jurisdiction for art directors. [82] During Allen's tenure, production design, especially in feature films, also began to gain more recognition thanks to a new appreciation among critics for the work of contemporary designers such as Richard Sylbert, Ken Adam, Polly Platt, and Dean Tavoularis.[83]

Allen's retirement in 1997 inspired a revitalization of the SMPAD that resonated throughout the organization. In an issue of *Trace*, a new member-driven newsletter, the shift was characterized as a "revolution," and 1997 was described as "the year 876 awoke."[84] Over the next decade, the society held its first Excellence in Production Design Awards; established a film society and a hall of fame; began publishing a membership directory; set up a scholarship fund; launched *Perspective*, a journal celebrating production design; and began regularly participating in exhibits, trade shows, and other outreach activities. In 1999, after several years of lively debate, the membership voted to change the name of the SMPAD to the Art Directors Guild (ADG). Throughout this period, the ADG continued to join forces with other IATSE locals to advocate for safer working conditions and reasonable hours, and to lobby for tax credits and other incentives to counteract runaway production, which was continuing to severely affect the Hollywood industry.[85]

In the late 1990s, at the instigation of IATSE leadership, the society also began talking to the other art department locals about coming together as one union. In 2003, Local 816, representing scenic and title artists and graphic designers, merged with the ADG, a move that was approved by both locals and increased the size of the ADG to more than 1,600 members.[86] At that time, the guild was awarded a new IATSE designation, becoming Local 800, and changed its name to the Art Directors Guild & Scenic, Title and Graphic Artists. In 2005, the guild purchased the building in Studio City where it had been renting offices for several years, for the first time providing the organization with a permanent home.

In 2008, the guild went through another merger. This time, the ADG joined forces with Local 790 (Illustrators and Matte Artists) and Local 847 (Set Designers and Model Makers) to form what would again come to be known as simply the Art Directors Guild. The merger was instigated by the IATSE in 2006, and the three locals were given a year to complete the process. But unlike the 2003 merger with Local 816, which had not faced any significant resistance, the 2008 merger was a different matter. After so many attempts in the early years to join forces, the set designers' and illustrators' locals had come to value their independence, and many of their members wanted to remain separate from the ADG, whose members in many cases were their supervisors in the art department. Whereas IATSE objected to an almost identical merger in 1950, this time the IATSE leadership called for and approved the action, dismissing concerns from the smaller locals that their members would be disadvantaged by belonging to a union run by art directors and production designers. The merger did eventually come about, but only after the two smaller locals, under the leadership of the business agent Marjo Bernay, took the fight all the way to the NLRB and filed suit in federal court.[87] Their appeals were denied, however, and the two groups were merged into the guild, an uneasy alliance that precipitated a restructuring of the organization.[88]

Since 2008, the four former locals have been joined together as one union, representing most of the workers who create the visual environments for movies, television programs, streaming content, broadcast TV, and commercials.[89] In addition to the IATSE Basic Agreements, the guild regularly negotiates and enforces more than twenty contracts that cover broadcast, streaming, and commercial work performed by guild members, as well as agreements with scenic shops and selected theatrical venues. The structure of the guild respects the autonomy of the four original locals, with independently elected councils for each craft and representatives from each group on the board of directors and the board of trustees. In 2016, following complaints from members who felt that the guild was not following protocol in its hiring of senior management, the guild was ordered by the Department of Labor to hold elections for the positions of executive director and associate executive director, roles that in the past had been appointed and approved by the board of directors. In the election, the longtime executive director Scott Roth, who had succeeded Gene Allen in 1997, was defeated by Chuck Parker, an ADG member and working production designer.[90] Parker was re-elected to a third term in 2022, after having led the guild through the COVID-19 pandemic and a contentious Basic Agreement negotiation that almost resulted in an IATSE-wide strike in October 2021. In 2023, the guild again faced challenges as it helped its members navigate the work stoppages that resulted due to the Writers Guild of America (WGA) and Screen Actors Guild–American Federation of Television and Radio Artists (SAG-AFTRA) strikes that paralyzed the industry.

Even during this difficult period, however, Local 800 has continued to move forward, thanks to leadership from ADG president Nelson Coates and a core group of active members who volunteer their time on more than a dozen committees, including Young Artists; Diversity, Equity, and Inclusion; and Professional Development. The guild also provides its members with a wide range of educational offerings, including training in and discussion of the latest technological advances in the field, with many of the classes being led by peers. In addition, the guild has greatly increased its outreach activities in recent years, regularly presenting at Comic-Con, Lightbox, and Siggraph; organizing panels and exhibits at local colleges and universities; and offering programs like the Production Design Initiative to encourage up-and-coming designers and artists to pursue careers in the art department.

As this overview of the history of the Hollywood art department unions has shown, the creative workers who now make up the ADG have fought long and hard to secure the rights they are now guaranteed under their collective bargaining agreements. This has been challenging not only because of a system that regularly tried to minimize the power and influence of these below-the-line workers but also because of the nature of the art department's labor, which has frequently been misunderstood and undervalued. Fortunately, that narrative has begun to change. In October 2023, the Production Designers Collective, an online community of art department professionals, organized eleven days of live and remote events that shone a spotlight on film and television design around the world.[91] In more than 200 screenings, tours, exhibits, seminars, and workshops, participants celebrated every facet of production design as an art form and a craft and brought to center stage the designers, artists, and visionaries who have too often been relegated, literally and figuratively, to the background.[92] This kind of advocacy and community-building among the creative profession-als of the art department, along with the strong commitment to fairness and accountability that continues to exist within the Hollywood labor community, suggests that union workers, including the artists and designers of the ADG, are going to continue to have a voice in the rapidly changing entertainment land-scape of the 2020s and beyond.

Notes

1 Irving Pichel, "The Art Department," *Action*, September 1943, 3–4.
2 Some scholars have argued that scenic design was an important element in early filmmaking, and that perhaps the contributions of those early set designers, construction men, and decorators have been overlooked in favor of the narrative that links art direction to the emergence of feature filmmaking. See Lucy Fischer, "The Silent Screen 1895–1927," in *Art Direction and Production Design*, ed. Lucy Fischer (Rutgers University Press, 2015), 23–47.
3 "Art and Pictures United by Buckland," *Motion Picture News*, May 30, 1914, 48.
4 John Hambley and Patrick Downing, *The Art of Hollywood: Fifty Years of Art Direction* (Thames Television, 1979), 13–14.
5 Jack Grant, "Hollywood's First Art Director," *American Cinematographer*, May 1941, 219, 238–239.
6 Alfred A. Cohn, "The Art Director," *Photoplay*, August 1916, 43–46, 177.
7 Cohn, 46.
8 Beverly Heisner, *Hollywood Art: Art Direction in the Days of the Great Studios* (McFarland, 1990), 16.
9 Cohn, "Art Director," 46.
10 Mary Mallory, "Hollywood Heights: Hollywood's First Studio Librarian, Elizabeth McGaffey." *The Daily Mirror*, May 1, 2023, https://ladailymirror.com/2023/05/01/mary-mallory-hollywood-heights-hollywoods-first-studio-librarian-elizabeth-mcgaffey/.
11 Kevin Brownlow, *The Parade's Gone By . . .* (University of California Press, 1968), 239.
12 Heisner, *Hollywood Art*, 25.

13 Program for First Annual Dinner Dance, Motion Picture Art Directors' Association, June 26, 1920, Folder 499, Leo "K" Kuter Papers, Margaret Herrick Library, Academy of Motion Picture Arts and Sciences, Beverly Hills, California (hereafter Kuter Collection).

14 The inspiration for the club's name was said to be the Salmagundi Club, an exclusive "sketching society" in New York City.

15 Preamble to the Cinemagundi bylaws, May 1, 1924, Art Directors Guild Archives, Studio City, California (hereafter ADGA).

16 Cinemagundi minutes, March 3, 1926, Folder 454, Kuter Collection.

17 This backing for LADA is evident from several trade paper articles from the time that indicate the Cinemagundi Club supported an independent charter for an art directors union. See, for instance, "Not Paperhangers," *Variety*, September 18, 1929, 5.

18 Telegram from Pridgeon Smith to William Canavan, June 8, 1929, ADGA.

19 Letter from Pridgeon Smith to William Canavan, June 27, 1929, Folder 525. Kuter Collection.

20 For a detailed description of the structure and operation of the studio art departments, see Heisner, *Hollywood Art*, 25–40.

21 Testimony of Edward M. Gilbert, *Jurisdictional Disputes in the Motion-Picture Industry, Hearings Before a Special Sub-committee of the Committee on Education and Labor, House of Representatives* (August–September, 1947), 509.

22 *An Oral History with Robert F. Boyle*, interviewed by George Turner, 1993, AMPAS, 247.

23 Note and survey from Hugh Reticker to members of the League of Art Directors and Associates, May 1, 1929, ADGA.

24 The corresponding union in New York was Local 829, United Scenic Artists, which included both stage and film designers and artists. Formed in 1897, United Scenic Artists was briefly affiliated with the IATSE but in 1918 was taken over by the Brotherhood of Painters and became Local 829. In 1999, the membership voted to affiliate again with IATSE. The local has jurisdiction over theater, film, and television production in the New York area.

25 Letter from William Canavan to Pridgeon Smith, July 19, 1929, Folder 525, Kuter Collection.

26 Letter from Pridgeon Smith to William Canavan, July 21, 1929, Folder 525, Kuter Collection.

27 Letter from Pridgeon Smith to William Green, June 1931, Folder 525, Kuter Collection.

28 Local 235's affiliation with the FMPC is confirmed in an undated draft agreement between the two groups located in Folder 459 of the Kuter Collection.

29 "Revolt against Casey," *The Hollywood Reporter*, April 25, 1934, 1, 6.

30 Gilbert testimony, 509.

31 Ida Jeter, "The Collapse of the Federated Motion Picture Crafts: A Case Study of Class Collaboration in the Motion Picture Industry," *Journal of the University Film Association* 31, no. 2 (Spring 1979), 37–45.

32 Jeter, 42.

33 *Federated Motion Picture Crafts Strike Bulletin*, May 28, 1937, Folder 460, Kuter Collection.

34 Gerald Horne, *Class Struggle in Hollywood: 1930–1950: Moguls, Mobsters, Stars, Reds, and Trade Unionists* (University of Texas Press, 2001), 51.

35 Gilbert testimony, 509.

36 Minutes of the first SMPAD meeting, May 6, 1937, ADGA.

37 Decision Certification of Representatives and Direction of Elections, National Labor Relations Board, July 22, 1939, ADGA, 3.

38 Decision Certification, 3

39 Decision Certification, 13.

40 Decision Certification, 16–17.

41 William Whitsett, Petitioner's Brief, in the Matter of Columbia Pictures Corporation et al. and Society of Motion Picture Art Directors, Petitioner, National Labor Relations Board, 1950, ADGA, 10.

42 Producers–Art Directors Society Basic Agreement—Draft, 1939, ADGA.

43 Transcript of Special Membership Meeting of the Society, August 4, 1942, ADGA, 8.

44 General Membership Meeting Minutes, July 8, 1941, ADGA.

45 Agreement with the Society of Motion Picture Art Directors, August 4, 1941, ADGA.

46 "'Big Five' Favors CIO Technicians," *Motion Picture Herald*, September 23, 1939, 30.

47 "Film Art Groups Plan Celebration," *Los Angeles Times*, November 30, 1941, A2.

48 Minutes of the Board of Directors, SMPAD, December 11, 1939, ADGA.

49 Transcript of Special Membership Meeting of the Society, August 4, 1942, ADGA, 8.

50 Minutes of Board Meeting, Society of Motion Picture Art Directors, July 19, 1944. ADGA.

51 The production designer credit was first given to William Cameron Menzies in 1937–1938 for his work on two David O. Selznick productions. However, the credit came to prominence when Selznick awarded it to Menzies for his major contributions to the overall visual design of *Gone with the Wind* (1939), for which Menzies was given an honorary Academy Award.

52 Minutes of Quarterly Meeting of the Membership, Society of Motion Picture Art Directors, December 5, 1944, ADGA.

53 Agreement between producers and the Society of Motion Picture Art Directors, December 16, 1946, ADGA.

54 Letter from Alexander H. Schullman to Wanda Cade, March 26, 1945, ADGA.

55 Horne, *Class Struggle in Hollywood*, 168.

56 In 1939, IATSE had claimed jurisdiction over the set decorators and assigned them to the newly chartered Local 44, the local for property men. However, most decorators instead opted to remain with or join the independent Society of Motion Picture Interior Decorators, which was formed in 1937 and affiliated with Local 1421 in 1942. After the 1945–1946 strikes, set decorators were once again routed into Local 44, where they remain today, despite their close collaboration with the art department.

57 William Whitsett. "Petitioner's Brief, in the Matter of Columbia Pictures Corporation et al. and Society of Motion Picture Art Directors, Petitioner," National Labor Relations Board, 1950, ADGA.

58 Gilbert testimony, 96.

59 W.A. Jackson, "A Short History of Scenic Artists," undated, ADGA.

60 "Lost Tribe of Studio Employees Discovered during NLRB Inquiry," *Los Angeles Times*, July 20, 1950, 21.

61 "NLRB Says Industry-Wide Bargaining Should Be Followed in Hollywood," *Variety*, July 6, 1949, 6.

62 "Film Workers Pick IATSE as New Bargaining Agent," *Los Angeles Times*, July 30, 1952, 20.

63 General Membership Meeting Minutes, SMPAD, June 4, 1940, ADGA.

64 Philip K. Scheuer, "Town Called Hollywood," *Los Angeles Times*, March 9, 1941, C3.

65 Grant, "Hollywood's First Art Director," 219.

66 Letter from Norman Lowenstein to Cedric Gibbons, June 12, 1950, Folder 175, Cedric Gibbons and Hazel Brooks Papers, Margaret Herrick Library, Academy of Motion Picture Arts and Sciences, Beverly Hills, California.

67 "Coast Art Directors Set Annual Awards," *Variety*, July 5, 1950, 7.

68 "Film Art Directors Stage First Exhibit for Public," *The Hollywood Reporter*, February 21, 1955, 3.

69 "Designs of Film Homes to Be Given Builders," *Los Angeles Times* (August 5, 1957), B10.

70 All issues of *Production Design* are available through the Media History Digital Library: https://mediahistoryproject.org/reader.php?id=productiondesign00soci.

71 Report of Television Committee, SMPAD, March 2, 1949, ADGA.

72 "New York Sound Track," *Variety*, October 19, 1955, 4. While it does reflect the situation for women art directors after the 1920s, the society's statement overlooks the work of several women art directors active during the silent period, including Una Nixson Hopkins and Natacha Rambova.

73 816 Quarterly Bulletin, First Quarter 1955, ADGA, 1.

74 "Lifetime Achievement: Camille Abbott," *19th Annual Art Directors Guild Excellence in Production Design Awards Program*, January 31, 2015, 17.

75 "Hall of Fame: Dianne Wager," *20th Annual Excellence in Production Design Awards Program*, January 31, 2016, 27.

76 "SMPAD's Krizman Hits Foreign Filming Trend," *The Hollywood Reporter*, July 14, 1958, 3.

77 Merrill Schleier, "Postwar Hollywood, 1947–1967," *Art Direction and Production Design*, ed. Lucy Fischer (Rutgers University Press, 2015), 73–96.

78 Norman Lowenstein and Leo Kuter, report on meeting with IATSE officials, February 28, 1958, ADGA.

79 Lowenstein and Kuter, 3–4.

80 Letter from Norman Lowenstein to Richard F. Walsh, September 23, 1958, ADGA.

81 Gene Allen was known for his frequent collaborations with the director George Cukor. Along with Cecil Beaton, Allen won an Academy Award for color art direction on *My Fair Lady* (1964).

82 The single-card credit on feature films and TV movies not only was important for raising the profile of the art director, but the guaranteed placement in the position just before the cinematographer credit created a long-sought-after parity with the work of other department heads.

83 See, for instance, Bart Mills, "The Brave New Worlds of Production Design," *American Film*, January–February 1982, 40–43, 45–46.

84 "The Revolution: Year Two," *Trace: The Art Director's Newsletter*, January/February 1998, 10.

85 Victoria Paul, "Crew Call: Hollywood," *Trace: The Art Director's Newsletter*, September 1999, 1.

86 "Merger Announced for Art Directors Guild IATSE Local 876 and Graphic Artists IATSE Local 816," IATSE, May 23, 2003, https://iatse.net/merger-announced-for-art-directors-guild-iatse-local-876-and-scenic-title-and-graphic-artists-iatse-local-816/.

87 The dispute and its resolution are summarized in Institutional Reorganizational Plan Mergers Locals 790, 847, and 800, Case 2:08-cv-04517, Respondent's, IATSE, Position Statement and Offer of Evidentiary Proof (2008), ADGA.

88 Jay A. Fernandez, "Art Directors Guild Restructures," *The Hollywood Reporter*, February 26, 2009, https://www.hollywoodreporter.com/business/business-news/art-directors-guild-restructures-79953/.

89 As of 2023, the positions represented by the ADG include art directors, assistant art directors, electronic graphic operators, graphic artists, graphic designers, illustrators, matte artists, model makers, previs artists, production designers, scenic artists, score box operators, set designers, storyboard artists, supervising art directors, title artists, and visual consultants.

90 David Robb, "Art Directors Guild Election: Chuck Parker Upsets 19-Year Incumbent Scott Roth," *Deadline*, June 29, 2016, https://deadline.com/2016/06/art-directors-guild-election-chuck-parker-beats-scott-roth-upset-1201781464/.

91 For more information on the Production Designers Collective and its range of activities, see its website at https://www.productiondesignerscollective.org/.

92 An overview of the wide range of programs presented during Production Design Week can be found at the event's website: https://productiondesignweek.org/program/.

6

Makeup and Hair

• •

Forgotten Folks and
Famous Experts

ADRIENNE L. McLEAN

In general terms, the labor history of studio-era makeup and hairdressing is not dissimilar from that of other below-the-line crafts, such as costume and set design, whose initial identities came from outside the industry and whose practitioners were never sure whether they were of value to their employers as mechanics or artists.[1] On the one hand, makeup and hairdressing were crucial to the creation both of characters in narrative films and of stars and potential stars, and by the 1910s, according to the historian Richard Koszarski, "star prominence [had become] the single most important factor in determining a film's box-office success."[2] But, on the other hand, the adoption of theatrical traditions of various kinds by the nascent film industry meant that actors were assumed, if not required, to apply their own makeup and dress their own hair as they would for the stage. Only when the film close-up showed everyone, from practitioners to audiences, that on a giant screen theatrical training might matter less than whether an actor already physically resembled the role he or she was playing did makeup and hairdressing gradually become film-specific crafts, a circumstance that also derived from Hollywood's idealization of glamour and the distorting tendencies of many film stocks that required special cosmetics and even hair colors to counteract.

However, for a number of complex reasons that I have examined elsewhere, Hollywood itself, throughout the studio era, would often underplay the importance of makeup artists and hairdressers to the looks of its stars, male stars in particular, especially if the makeup was of the straight or so-called beauty variety rather than the virtuosic or transformative character makeup designed to make an actor look different than his or her fans might expect.[3] In 1938, *Variety* went so far as to call makeup artists and hairdressers "the more or less forgotten folks among the film industry's technical divisions," asserting that it was the increase in the use of Technicolor that suddenly made producers "makeup-conscious." Studios had begun "swelling budgets for both personnel and equipment for facial painters and hair dressers" and investing "in new quarters for the workers, more modern gadgets and really scientific lighting."[4] But "makeup-consciousness" was also likely raised by the unionization of the crafts in 1937, the year that the major studios became essentially a closed shop.

Comparatively few of Hollywood's below-the-line craftspeople were ever well known to the film public, of course, although it was somewhat unusual that even makeup and hairdressing department heads were rarely given screen credit until the late 1930s, and then not consistently. There was not even an Oscar category for makeup until the 1980s, with "and hair styling" added to it only in 2012.[5] But the men whose names did appear from time to time in studio-era credits or in fan magazines and trade and technical journals, such as the Westmore family and their "rouge pot dynasty" (a father and ultimately six sons) or Max Factor and his cosmetics and wig salon and factory, did their best to become famous themselves. They traded on their film work to appeal to female spectators' desires to "look like the stars" by purchasing the multiple lines of eponymous beauty products and consuming the "expert" advice the men or their corporations marketed. These "famous experts" and their ambitions, as well as their collaborative, if not collusive, attempts to organize all the practitioners of the crafts from the late 1920s on, would also greatly affect how the International Alliance of Theatrical Stage Employees (IATSE or the IA) Local 706 was structured and chartered, especially in relation to gender. In contrast to the culture more broadly, in which women wore makeup and men did not (or were not supposed to), and in which makeup and hairdressing, even as businesses, were almost exclusively associated with femininity and women's concerns (or "swishy" men), the Westmore brothers and the Factor corporation worked to ensure that they and their collaborators and employees would dominate the crafts at all the Hollywood studios, and that makeup artists, though not hairdressers, would be required by union regulations to be male.[6]

Ironically, as makeup artists—a term used in the industry since the early silent era, for women as well as men—took over the craft that women had been successfully practicing for years, male department "chiefs" also helped to make the several larger unions that initially incorporated makeup and hairdressing into among Hollywood's most diverse in gender terms. For despite, or perhaps because of, the fact that the Westmores (like Max Factor, who was not properly a studio worker but a subcontractor) began their careers as hairdressers and wig designers rather than makeup artists, all labor unions whose membership included the two crafts would formally mandate not only that makeup artists be male but also that hairdressers, while operating under the authority of men, had to be female.[7] Most important, this gender bifurcation was codified once more in the 1937 constitution of IATSE Local 706, the Make-Up Artists and Hair Stylists Guild, and remained the case for thirty-plus years (however, women makeup artists now outnumber men in the union and have for several decades). In other words, large numbers of hairdressing women helped swell the membership roster of *all* the unions in which makeup artists and hairdressers were located at various times during the studio era, and any exceptions to this gender distinction (all were presumed to be white and heterosexual as well) only prove the rule. Although Hollywood often used *makeup* as shorthand for both crafts, then, the two also had separate identities—identities that are implicated in the struggles over who would be allowed to work on films and their stars for as long as the studios and their labor structures existed.

The saga of how makeup artists and hairdressers ended up with their own union is not always easy to trace because of the characteristic paucity of studio documents pertaining to day-to-day filmmaking processes, and because the union currently has other things to do than answer questions from outsiders. But primary research is also made more complex because of a corresponding surplus, as it were, of ballyhoo generated by the outsize personalities and self-aggrandizement of the Westmores and Factor's corporation. These men's advice columns and opinions, as well as advertisements for their products, can be found in decades of promotion and publicity material. But a comparatively large number of women were working as studio makeup artists, and even "chiefs" or executives, before 1937, and there are tantalizing signs of their struggles to retain their titles and responsibilities in labor negotiations, as well as of hairdressers seeking their own separate self-representation. Even when the women's own efforts are lauded in fan magazines and the like, this material is harder to find when it occurs in articles with titles like "Miracle Men at Work."[8]

In the rest of this chapter, I first discuss how the ambitions of the Westmores and Factor led to the creation of the first professional Hollywood-based makeup organization, the Motion Picture Makeup Artists Association (MPMAA). Although other craft organizations certainly contained members whose identities might be known to audiences through promotion and publicity—costume or set designers, for example—evidence suggests that the Westmores took the lead in organizing makeup artists and, by the mid-1930s, hairdressers in order to consolidate their own authority as nationally known "experts" and to become department heads across several studios at once. Then I explore how this organization, as well as other unions that the MPMAA joined or was affiliated with, interacted or intersected with the chartering of Local 706, which remains the representative of all card-carrying makeup artists and hairdressers/stylists in the film and television industry today.[9] Finally, I turn to the practices and policies of Local 706 that were carried over from other organizations, and how the criteria for eligibility and the union's goals and responsibilities toward its members have functioned since the end of the studio era.

Good Feeling between the Boys

The MPMAA was founded in 1926 through a collaboration between Max Factor and the Westmores (although each would take credit for it separately). The fact that the association had a membership of close to fifty upon its founding tells us how many makeup men were already at work in Hollywood near the end of the silent era, despite later (and erroneous) claims by the Westmores that they were the first studio makeup artists in history.[10] Max Factor had arrived in Hollywood in 1908, the Westmores in 1920, and both sets of men—the women in their families were excluded from the family's public existence—initially gained the attention of the film industry because of their expertise in hair and wigs. Indeed, by Perc Westmore's later admission, the Westmores had little knowledge of makeup and cosmetics, much less of how film stock rendered them visually, when they began to work on actors in the early 1920s, first in salons and soon, whether upon the recommendation of star clients or the family's own aggressive self-marketing, at a number of studios.[11] In other words, the MPMAA seems to have been founded partly to help the Westmores and Factor fill the gaps in their knowledge and increase the men's value to producers.

The MPMAA's membership rosters were published annually in the *Motion Picture Almanac* between 1930 and 1937, but there is little information available about how the group functioned internally. A brief column in *International Photographer* in mid-1929 comments on the "remarkable growth" of the "unique organization" in "only two years" and describes its "beautiful headquarters" in the Max Factor building. The column adds that at weekly meetings "demonstrations are given by the various members to the extent that each artist helps the other in solving the problems relating to their particular branch of the industry," such that the organization's growth has been "conductive of good feeling between the boys."[12] We cannot now know precisely why almost all of the U.S. labor organizations related to motion picture makeup ultimately ceded complete control to these "boys," limiting women's contributions either to body makeup—everything below the neck but also, sometimes, ears, but on women only in either case—or hairdressing.[13] Even the union itself has no written history on the issue. Instead, as former Local 706 president Sue Cabral-Ebert put it to me, "It's all storytelling. (Why would men write down stories that make them look like jerks?) The version we always heard was that the women were hair stylists on a shorter guarantee of hours so they could go home and get dinner ready, and the male makeup artists would get the overtime and watch the set."[14]

It is not clear how male makeup artists were recruited into the MPMAA, whether by invitation (the ASC's modus operandi since its founding in 1919) or petition, much less how women ultimately joined "the boys" as hairdressers, given that the fairly large number of women makeup artists and "chiefs" then working in Hollywood do not appear on published membership lists either. What *can* be documented is that many of the MPMAA's members, and most certainly the Westmore brothers, were working by the early 1930s to make it into the governing body of studio makeup artists across the industry. But by 1929, "all members of the Association," *International Photographer* reports, were already also members of another Hollywood labor organization: Local 235, United Scenic Artists, which the MPMAA likely joined to acquire some sort of authority that it could exert in negotiations with studios over wages and conditions.[15]

As readers of this volume know, the open-shop plan had prevailed in Hollywood until the Studio Basic Agreement (SBA) was negotiated and signed in 1926, from which "small crafts"—such as makeup and hairdressing—were excluded, whether as individuals or as separate organizations.[16] While this also helps to explain the affiliation of the MPMAA with a member union of the SBA such as United Scenic Artists—which was itself an "autonomous" local of the Brotherhood of Painters, Decorators and Paperhangers of America—I have found no information about the process by which the affiliation occurred, or whether it was a decision made with the agreement of or in spite of the Westmores and Max Factor, who housed the makeup association's meetings until the two dynasties split from one another around 1935.[17]

The constitution of the Brotherhood, which applied to United Scenic Artists, was written in 1905 and amended at least seventeen times, likely well before Local 235 joined or was created. But by September 1929 it refers to "the art of make-up and all its various effects" as a craft under the Brotherhood's jurisdiction.[18] Although the rationale for and precise steps by which this happened remain unclear as well, in August 1930, United Scenic Artists was divided into two organizations: a "professional" group that retained the original charter named Two-Three-Five, and a "labor group" that was rechartered as Motion Picture Painters Local 644 of the larger Brotherhood (hereafter referred to, in common parlance, as the Painters). Most later accounts, and that of Local 706 today as well, maintain that makeup artists and hairdressers were members of Local 644. But at least in the early 1930s (as the 1931 "Working Rules" of Two-Three-Five laid out), makeup artists, body makeup "girls," and hairdressers all remained members of the originally chartered organization.[19] More will be said later about how the categories were defined and regulated and by whom, but for now the important fact is that in the early 1930s, the Painters were either not receptive to, or were unable to assume authority over, makeup and hairdressing.

A 1932 article in *Hollywood Filmograph* (a weekly trade paper for actors), for example, notes that "the union"—which it does not name—had demanded that "members of the makeup artists organization walk off of a Radio pictures location owing to the fact that men were employed who were not members in good standing."[20] The article claims that the association as a group was "split wide open" that year when Perc Westmore and his twin brother, Ern, along with "certain [other] members," refused to strike and decided that they were *"through with Local 235 since the Motion Picture Make-up Artists are not recognized by the producers, as are other crafts of the local, and they openly defied representatives of the union, and continued to work on the location"* [italics in original]. I do not know more about the particular events *Hollywood Filmograph* describes, but certainly the article's subheading, "ERN AND PERC WESTMORE FIGHT TO MAINTAIN POSITION WITH THEIR CO-WORKERS," should be kept in mind in light of how these competing factions were ultimately brought together within the same union, even as the Westmores, or their fame, were clearly resented by some of their rank-and-file colleagues.

An Organization of Our Own Choosing

Many organizations, including the Academy of Motion Picture Arts and Sciences itself, were jockeying in 1933 to "represent and co-ordinate the various branches of the motion picture production industry in their activities and relations with each other."[21] But, as did workers in many other crafts at the time, makeup artists wanted to form their own labor organization, and in June 1933 some thirty-eight men—including all four of the then working-age Westmore brothers—sought to make the MPMAA their official labor representative rather than Local 235. As the men wrote:

> We, the undersigned . . . hereby declare; that we accept this Association as our representative in the preparation of a Code of Ethics and Regulations, covering the salaries, hours, and working conditions, of our profession, and which is to be presented to the Motion Picture Industry, or the representatives of same, or to the Federal Government, noting under the rights given us in Section Seven of the Industrial Control Act, as signed by President Roosevelt, in which we are given the privileges of collective bargaining with our employers, through an organization of our own choosing, and with representatives of our own choosing; and on [*sic*] our own free will and without restraint or coercion, we hereby declare that it is our desire to be represented by the Motion Picture Make-Up Artists Association, and by no other individual and/or any other group or organization.[22]

The next day, the same paragraph accompanied two pages of signatures of forty-five women, but with the "organization of [their] choosing" now called the Motion Picture Hairdressers Association (with "Motion Picture" typed above the line on both pages, as though it were inserted later). There appear to be no minutes of whatever discussion led to what may have been the first Hollywood craft organization with an all-female membership (nor is it clear what the women's status had been previously vis-à-vis the MPMAA). However, Michael Westmore, whose father, Mont(e), was the oldest Westmore brother and an executive makeup artist before his death in 1940, told me that he thought Perc was "involved with making many of the rules, especially 'men-makeup artists/women-hairstylists.'"[23] This would be an especially ironic state of affairs given not only the Westmores' original training but the fact that their own beauty salon, the House of Westmore, which opened to compete with Max Factor's in 1935, employed women makeup artists, among them Perc Westmore's fifth wife.

If I do not know of any other craft union that officially restricted its membership to women, I can note, first, that the 1931 "Working Rules" of United Scenic Artists already had divided makeup artists (and body makeup "girls") and hairdressers on the basis of gender; and second, that by December 1933 the new women's organization had its own letterhead identifying itself as the Studio Hairdressers Association (the name change perhaps an attempt to assert at least some degree of agency against their governing makeup-men masters). Moreover, the women officers were negotiating on their own with the Association of Motion Picture Producers (AMPP) about hours and salaries, pointing out in a letter that the new organization represented "over 45 out of approximately 60 persons engaged in this profession."[24] The address of the Studio Hairdressers Association, however, was then the same as that of the MPMAA, in the Max Factor building. And given the way makeup and hairdressing departments had been practically organized by that point, it would appear that hairdressers were still employed at the pleasure of the makeup executives who remained their bosses.

This early attempt to create a separate instrument by which makeup artists and hairdressers could negotiate on their own with the studios is interesting both with respect to the *Hollywood Filmograph* piece from 1932 and as an example of the precise form of labor organization that the studios were seeking to avoid, through which one small organization (the League of Art Directors was another) could threaten to or actually disrupt productions across the industry. However, studios frequently granted small wage increases through such organizations since the salaries of below-the-line personnel represented a comparatively negligible percentage of any film's production costs.[25] Decades later, the MGM makeup artist and executive William Tuttle recalled that the MPMAA also had dues that supported a secretary, which helped it to function much like the union would later, where "studios could call and give out calls to people and they would contact them."[26]

Signally, during an earlier March 1933 walkout of makeup artists ordered by Local 235 in response to the studios' "wage waiver"—the across-the-board wage reduction in purported response to declining profits and the effects of Roosevelt's bank holiday—*Hollywood Filmograph* again wrote that several makeup "heads" had returned to work in defiance of the walkout and were "ordered removed from the union roster as violating the union's orders."[27] This, then, would seem to have helped throw at least some makeup artists toward the Painters and Local 644. Were the June documents an attempt to separate the MPMAA from both Local 235 *and* Local 644? And given that the originals of the signed statements were found in the archives of the current union, were they ever delivered, and if so, to whom? Jack Dawn, then a studio makeup artist who became MGM's department head in 1935, also reported in a telegram to General Hugh S. Johnson from 1933 or 1934 (the dates of Johnson's tenure in Roosevelt's New Deal administration) that two competing organizations were threatening to keep him from working if he joined the other. Since Dawn had signed the 1933 document, one assumes that the MPMAA was one of the organizations and that either United Scenic Artists or the Painters, both of which were under the jurisdiction of the larger Brotherhood, was the other.

Despite any dissension between makeup artists and whichever union was representing them, however, or among makeup artists themselves, neither makeup artists nor hairdressers seem to have materially participated in IATSE's failed strikes against the studios in summer 1933, after which it withdrew from the SBA. But IATSE was readmitted in 1936 as producers realized the benefits of colluding with its henchmen, mobsters Willie Bioff and George Browne, who promised the producers that they could keep laborers from striking—and productions moving smoothly—as long as IATSE was given, historian Mike Nielsen writes, "complete control over the key workers in the industry."[28] The studios had already offered the Painters the right to rejoin the SBA if they ceded the makeup artists and hairdressers to IATSE. Instead the Painters and several other smaller crafts—among them makeup and hairdressing as well as disparate categories ranging from plasterers and painters to studio plumbers and cooks—organized themselves into the democratic and worker-led Federated Motion Picture Crafts (FMPC).[29] Since producers took IATSE's side and refused to bargain with the FMPC, the collective called a strike against most of the major studios in April 1937.

That makeup and hairdressing are mentioned in many accounts contemporary to the six-week FMPC strike is partly because of the Westmores' fame and their public refusal to join their rank-and-file colleagues by claiming that, in contrast to the workers who populated the departments that the brothers ran (at the time Perc Westmore was at Warner Bros., Wally at Paramount, Mont at Selznick, and Ern at Twentieth Century-Fox), they were not "labor" but "management." A column by Louella Parsons reported that two non-Westmore executives—Jack Dawn at MGM, and Dorothy "Dot" Ponedel, who had been a Hollywood makeup artist since the early 1920s and was working alongside Wally Westmore at Paramount—also refused to strike.[30] But the Westmores were singled out, and the House of Westmore was vandalized, with police reports indicating that "the sabotage was committed on the belief the firm was supplying nonunion makeup artists to replace striking makeup men."[31] The perpetrators, who were never identified, poured creosote on the furnishings as well as drapes and carpeting of the salon and caused what news reports claimed was $10,000 to $20,000 in damages.

The way that the FMPC strike played out suggests that significant divisions remained between executive makeup artists, several of them Westmores, and the workers who "manned" the picket lines. Because the Westmores refused to abide by the rules of the FMPC, and many of their followers defected and were quickly offered IATSE union cards, the new federation was doomed from the start (some makeup artists and hairdressers did resist IATSE's overtures, however).[32] The labor historian Murray Ross, writing less than five years out from the strikes, claimed that makeup artists as a group proved "unreliable" as strikers, and that some of the violence was sparked by the firing of a female extra from the Screen Actors Guild who had defied the strike by obtaining a card from IATSE to work (quite successfully, one imagines) as a makeup artist (which also challenged the men's authority in the field).[33] Further urgency for resolution was likely prompted by the fact that, as the strike deepened during the production of several big-budget Technicolor films, *Variety* reported that the studios "dispatched calls for auxiliary make-up artists and extra girls were enlisted as hairdressers. Producers claimed the situation was well in hand and that the strike would not interfere with production schedules."[34]

The demise of the FMPC in June 1937 was followed by IATSE's chartering of Local 706 as Make Up Artists and Hair Stylists later that year.[35] But in the interim, IATSE appears to have put the makeup artists into another union, Studio Makeup Artists, under the jurisdiction of Local 37, Studio Mechanics, which had been one of the only IATSE "backlot" locals prior to the strikes.[36] Although I could find little information about Studio Makeup Artists as such— Local 37 is discussed at length in chapter 2 of this book—the two organizations must have been contiguous given that Local 706 would retain the same president and secretary. Moreover, Dot Ponedel's application to Studio Makeup Artists in September 1937 ("he" having "fully complied with the requirements" for membership) was stamped "approved" on November 1, literally the same official date as Local 706's charter.

To complicate matters further, Dot Ponedel noted on her application to Studio Makeup Artists that she *already* belonged to a different organization, Local 731, which, she wrote, was called "Make-up Artists." About all I could discover about that organization comes from a January 1936 *Variety* squib that refers to the fact that "Motion Picture Hair Stylists Guild and Make-up Artists have amalgamated as Local 731," which also gives a list of "reelected" officers—all of them women, though all were studio hairdressers rather than makeup artists.[37] Perhaps Local 731, which was under the jurisdiction of the Painters rather than IATSE, also divided the FMPC strikers; I assume this is what Murray Ross is referring to when he writes that one of the Painters' "imaginative business agents" in 1934 suggested that the union "absorb" the makeup artists "even though," in Ross's words, "their brushes moved over faces instead of walls."[38] But this anecdote does not jibe with the fact that makeup artists—and hairdressers, whom Ross does not mention—already had been members of United Scenic Artists.

It does appear, however, that some makeup artists as well as hairdressers were working to leave Local 235 before 1937, with the MPMAA, in whole or in part, leading one way and, whenever it was created, Local 731 leading the other. The latter and its female membership also indicate that there were attempts to counter the male dominance of makeup as a craft even if ultimately, and unfortunately, they proved futile in institutional terms or were rendered moot by IATSE's studio-sanctioned organization of makeup artists and hairdressers into a single union (figure 6.1).[39]

Closing the Shop Door

In contrast to the MPMAA, once Local 706 was successfully chartered and accepted into the SBA as the representative of all studio makeup artists and hairdressers, the Westmores appear not to have served as officers. (Not until 1965 was a Westmore—Monty, Mont's son and Michael's brother—elected as secretary-treasurer.) And while for a single year, 1938, a hairdresser, Carmen Dirigo, served as vice president, thereafter no woman appears publicly as a union officer until the 1970s. Indeed, while the Westmores all retained union memberships throughout their careers, they mostly would continue to sign executive contracts with the studios and to run departments that were now populated by union laborers over whose careers they exerted substantial influence. More to the point, many of the rules and much of the structure of the new union—including its gender divisions—were those of the original organization the Westmores and Factor had founded, and that had been further codified in the rules of Locals 235 and 644.

Again, before 1937, although men dominated the ranks of makeup "chiefs," several women, such as Lillian Rosine at MGM and Dot Ponedel at Paramount, were listed on studio rosters as department heads, with other women routinely working as studio makeup artists. As Nellie Manley, a signatory to the 1933 hairdressing document who later became a head hairstylist at Paramount, put it, "Before the days of the union Paramount used to have four girls who did only face makeup. When the union was organized, all the makeup artists were men, and all the hairstylists were women."[40] (Manley does not indicate what became of those "girls," nor do I know whether she was including Ponedel on her list.) But after 1937, with a vanishingly small number of exceptions, the only women allowed to join Local 706—and hence to work on films and in studio departments—were hairdressers and body makeup women, with neither group given the honorific "artist" like the men were. (According to her obituary in *Variety* in 1979, Rosine continued to work at MGM until 1948, most likely as a nominal body makeup woman.)[41] Ponedel had been admitted to Local 706 immediately, but once her Paramount contract was terminated following unionization, she was told that she was now limited to "performing body makeup." Not until 1940 did the union, after Ponedel's strenuous petitioning,

FIGURE 6.1 *Top,* MGM makeup department in 1928, showing both women and men as makeup artists and hairdressers. (Bison Archives and Hollywood Historic Photos.) *Below left,* Dot Ponedel, the only woman makeup artist in Local 706 during the studio era, with Paulette Goddard in the 1930s. (Courtesy Meredith Ponedel.) *Below right*, hairdresser Leonora Sabine with Betty Grable in 1937. Sabine was one of the officers of the short-lived women's union Local 731. (Bison Archives and Hollywood Historic Photos.)

grant her a "temporary permit" to "make up faces of women in the makeup departments of the various motion picture studios."[42] Even this was on a stand-by basis and required that a journeyman makeup artist—the gendered *journeyman* signifying, as it did for other crafts, a successful apprenticeship or otherwise meeting the qualifications for membership in a union—be "in charge of the company on the set."

Prior to 1937 there are also a few references to male studio "hair stylists" in fan magazine beauty columns, but perhaps because of the overlap between Factor and the Westmores as hairdressers and wigmakers by training (union regulations allowed makeup men to apply hairpieces and wigs to male actors, and certain kinds of wigs to women), gender seems to have posed fewer problems for the men.[43] Larry Germain was admitted to Local 37 and then 706 as a hairdresser in April 1937, although he apparently remained the only male hairdresser in the union through the 1970s and had few screen credits until the 1950s. Sydney Guilaroff, undoubtedly the most famous hairdresser in all of classical Holly-wood, was made "head of the hairdressing department" at MGM in the mid-1930s and never joined any labor organization while signing executive contracts that also gave him screen credit on hundreds of films from 1938 on.[44] (He later crowed that the credits were an "innovation [that] was recognized by the indus-try as a historic breakthrough.")[45]

Although the charter of Local 706 included "hair stylists"—Guilaroff's pre-ferred term—from the beginning, women continued to be referred to as hair-dressers in most contexts, and not until the mid-1940s did they begin to appear in some screen credits as well. (Carmen Dirigo's 2007 obituary states that she was the first credited hairstylist; I assume this means the first *female* credited hairstylist, which is hard to substantiate but makes historical sense.)[46] And it was only in 1942, when women were actively being urged to work outside the home, that Dot Ponedel—who, like Guilaroff, had a number of high-powered star clients who demanded her services in *their* contracts—was, at last, granted a permanent union membership card as a makeup artist rather than a body makeup woman or a hairdresser.[47]

Once the gender restrictions were in place, for makeup artists and hairdress-ers the major employment categories and hierarchies during the studio era were marked by whether one worked on stars and featured players ("first-class" or, later, "key" makeup artists and hairdressers) or on lesser performers, including extras and bits (the "second-class" makeup artist, or, by the 1940s, simply the ordinary "makeup artist" or "hair stylist").[48] The MPMAA had not taken apprentices at first but seems to have done so in the 1930s. A three-year makeup apprentice pro-gram was put into place from the first union contracts in which the (male) recruits were paid low weekly salaries that increased if they successfully com-pleted each six-month session, likely modeled on the apprentice program of United Scenic Artists. In all the makeup artist categories, there were journey-men who had passed the union's exams and were members in good standing, and "auxiliaries" who worked under supervision as apprentices. Unfortunately, there was no equivalent program for hairdressing during the studio era, so women were not called journeymen but "assistants."

As had been the case since the crafts' involvement with United Scenic Artists, the union relied on the self-funded licensing and testing required for women to work in local beauty parlors, so that they arrived in departments already trained in styling, design, cutting, and every other skill a film might require, including caring for wigs, toupees, and other hairpieces.[49] In contrast, the training of makeup artists was, and always had been, more ad hoc—many began as actors, some as office boys or mailroom clerks; others came from any number of fields, from department store illustration to mortuary work. Thus, makeup apprenticeships enabled the men to be trained into their positions regardless of their qualifications, although in the 1930s having some background in what was amorphously termed *art* was increasingly touted as a useful prerequisite. Cinematographers had been calling themselves *artists* since the mid-1920s, and it made sense that makeup *artists* would also begin to take the term more seriously, and to deploy it to separate themselves from, as well as elevate themselves above, their female colleagues or their own previous public image. In other words, they wanted to ensure that, as Jack Dawn told his MGM protégé William Tuttle, makeup men would be known and treated as "artists, *not* mechanics."[50]

Apprenticeships were also a way for a department head to maintain his hegemony throughout the industry. Ultimately, Perc Westmore claimed to have trained some "sixty-five or seventy men in the profession" in addition to "all [his] brothers"; he also stated that the union allowed one apprentice for every five journeyman.[51] It is likely that other makeup chiefs also trained "dozens of apprentices," as Fox's Ben Nye did, over the years.[52] Not until the 1960s was a studio apprenticeship program for hairdressers finally instituted, just as departments were being shuttered—MGM's closed in 1969—and all such apprenticeships, for makeup artists as well, discontinued.

A Tight and Jealous Craft

Makeup and hairdressing, like other studio crafts, had of course been given considerable "wage tilts," in *Variety*'s patois, by unionization (as they had by joining Local 235 years earlier). Yet the terms seem less than ideal to us now given that the accepted workweek ranged from forty-eight hours for "first makeups, assistants and apprentices" to sixty hours a week for "key men." Nevertheless, this was an improvement over the conditions set by the Motion Picture Industry Code in 1933, in which makeup artists and hairdressers were put in the class of laborers who could be asked to work any number of hours because time limits might "hinder, reduce or delay production."[53]

Not surprisingly, wage scales were connected to gender as well in the studio era, both in earlier organizations and in Local 706. Labor contracts stipulated that makeup artists be paid the most, of course, followed by hairdressers and, below them, body makeup women; even a "head body make-up woman," an "optional" category at the discretion of a producer on any film, had a minimum pay less than that of any journeyman makeup artist or even a hairdresser.[54] If a makeup artist temporarily substituted for a department head, he—or she, if the "head" was a supervising hairdresser—would receive either higher weekly pay or a bonus, but neither option could exceed the pay of the executive in question.

Finally, there were "senior" and "junior" groups of makeup artists and hairdressers based on number of years in the union, with junior members to be laid off first.[55] Indeed, for many below-the-line workers in Hollywood, unionization ended up replacing some of the stress and anxiety of exploitative salaried employment with that of "casualization," in which they were hired for a specific film production (and if lucky rehired for new ones) rather than being employed on salary year-round. Workers were also now at the mercy not only of department heads but also of studio production schedules and genre preferences—historical epics and big-budget musicals and their large casts employed far more makeup artists and hairdressers than the average drawing room comedy, for example.[56]

Yet the stresses even of casualization were clearly worse for some than others. For as was the case with other unsalaried craft workers, many makeup artists and hairdressers did remain affiliated with one or another studio for a number of years—even if they still had to "stick close to the phone," as studio and star hairdresser Ginger "Sugar" Blymer writes in her memoir, so they "wouldn't miss that all-important call."[57] To conform to holiday release schedules and the like, studios planned their production year well in advance, and by the mid-1930s the number of craftspeople required for any given production, large or small, would have been possible to estimate and employment offered, with the union also maintaining lists of auxiliaries to add to the journeymen assigned to films or to stars themselves. A preliminary budget sheet for a 1953 Twentieth Century-Fox baseball film, *The Kid from Left Field*, shows that the executive Ben Nye recommended one key makeup man for twenty-two days plus "extra help only as needed"; one key hairdresser but "only as needed"; no body makeup woman at all; and supplies and expenses that were a little more than 10 percent of the overall budget amount computed.[58] In this scenario, only the key makeup man was assured of employment, and for less than a month, which replicated the situation for many "modern" films with smaller casts.

Nevertheless, a cooperative journeyman makeup artist or hairdresser who could do a job well and was familiar with a department's routines, schedules, and work practices might effectively remain in more or less steady employment at one studio for decades. Although obituaries in trade papers might later state that someone had been "a makeup man at Warners for [the] past 25 years"—as *Variety* did about Walter Rodgers in 1951—the fact remains that most nonexecutive union craft employees were subject to periods during which they did not work and therefore received no pay.[59] And if you displeased an executive or a co-worker with more seniority or of a higher grade, or conversely were so good at your job that you fomented their jealousy, then employment could be contingent on elements that had nothing to do with talent or ability. (Dot Ponedel was regularly sabotaged by her male competitors.)[60]

Since studio-era union contracts did not protect against job insecurity or contain written provisions for how far in advance an employee would be notified of termination (and an executive could fire anyone "for cause"), workplace politics could still be demoralizing. According to Michael Westmore, for example, his uncle Perc was often a generous and supportive boss, but he also "had the power to control many situations, even to the extent of blackballing an individual from the film business."[61] Not surprisingly, then, a 1942 profile of Maurice Seiderman, the uncredited makeup artist who created the remarkable makeup for and on Orson Welles in *Citizen Kane* at RKO in 1940, refers to makeup as a "tight and jealous craft." The article lays out the difficulties Seiderman faced even to become an apprentice when he arrived in Hollywood in 1936 with twelve years of stage makeup experience, among them being accused anonymously of "unspecified unethical conduct." Seiderman's "mysterious sins were mysteriously forgiven," and he was admitted to the union as a journeyman without an apprenticeship, only when Mel Berns, RKO's makeup chief since 1933, refused to fire him.[62]

Despite what seems now like basic job insecurity at all but the executive level even after the chartering of Local 706, makeup and hairdressing appear never again to have participated in public labor activism involving the studios. In November 1937 a strike was called at Columbia, according to *Variety*, because "makeup artists were being laid off and small-bracket actors instructed to make up themselves. Walkout was ended after one day ... when studio agreed to the demands of the IATSE that sufficient makeup men be employed to take care of the work."[63] Makeup artists and hairdressers are not mentioned in accounts of the violent labor strikes that rocked the Painters and other unions in the mid-1940s, nor of the various postwar investigations by the House Un-American Activities Committee and their aftermath.

While some studios experienced more frequent turnover of department heads, several executives remained in place for decades—including, among others, Perc and Wally Westmore at First National/Warner Bros. and Paramount, respectively, and eventually their younger brother Bud at Universal; Jack Dawn and William Tuttle at MGM; Mel Berns at RKO; Ben Nye at Twentieth Century-Fox; and Clay Campbell at Columbia. These executives at times had to mediate difficult situations that the union's regulations helped to support if not create, such as when MGM's white hairdressers, according to the dress designer Helen Rose, refused to work on Lena Horne in the 1940s. Rather than get into a dispute with the union, Sydney Guilaroff not only took over and did Horne's hair himself but also hired one of Horne's friends to be her hairdresser on the set and "made the union accept her," in Rose's words (see figure 6.2).[64]

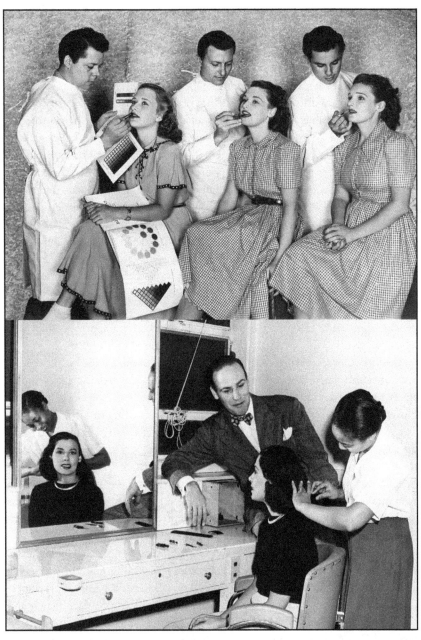

FIGURE 6.2 *Top,* publicity photo of Perc, Wally, and Bud Westmore with the Lane sisters in 1939. *Below,* Sydney Guilaroff with Lena Horne and Noelia (Nolelia) Kyle in 1946. Guilaroff never joined Local 706 but enabled the first Black hairdressers to become members in the 1940s. Both images from the Margaret Herrick Library, Academy of Motion Picture Arts and Sciences.

As is the case with all forms of palace intrigue, then, villains and heroes are often the same individuals depending on one's relationship to them. Jack Dawn, according to William Tuttle, "was always firing people," but he would often bring the same person back after two or three days.[65] In addition to providing glimpses into the interplay of talent, skill, studio politics, and sexist and racist power structures in makeup and hairdressing as crafts, such stories help support the contention made by several Hollywood labor historians that by the mid-1940s many if not all of the below-the-line crafts had become entities to which the "tight and jealous" label could be attached. Murray Ross, writing in the early 1940s, indicated that the effects of craft unionization on Hollywood had been ambivalent at best, although he cautioned, "It is very difficult to draw general conclusions from the study of labor-management relations in the studios. The diversity of behavior exhibited by the various unions and guilds makes any generalization precarious."[66] For Ross, the issue had become "the shrinkage of employment opportunities" in the industry precisely because of the regulations governing employment categories that unions so assiduously maintained, and because "the craft unions have made every effort to limit the supply of labor in the industry.... They charge high initiation fees and membership dues and levy occasional special assessments. They have established a very low ratio of apprentices to journeymen, hoping that the number dropping out will exceed the number entering the local. These policies have contributed to a decline in membership and to a rise in the average age of members.... This perpetuates an aristocracy of studio craftsmen."[67]

This problem would become even more pronounced in the postwar era, when television was initially seen by the studios, or some of their department heads, as a threat. Wally and Bud Westmore, for example, did not want to allow television shows to film on their studios' lots, which perpetuated the "aristocracy" and the corresponding decline in union membership that Ross described. Sugar Blymer, who began her career as a studio messenger at MGM in the early 1950s and then became a stock clerk in Tuttle's makeup department, was urged by her colleagues to become a hairdresser in the early 1950s. Because there was no studio apprenticeship for her craft, she had to pay for and complete cosmetology school at night—a process that took six years—while working a full-time job and raising her children in addition to working a requisite number of hours on film and television productions.[68] When Blymer applied to Local 706 in 1959, she noted, "They hadn't taken anyone into the union for more than seven years."[69] She even had to wait an extra month to be sworn in because the union could not muster a quorum for her first union meeting. The situation became even more dire following the demise of the studio system; in the opinion of the makeup artist Ben Nye Jr., whose apprenticeship had been in his father's department, "I think the people we have coming in today are talented, they're fine people. There's just nobody to teach them.... The system doesn't exist to pass it down anymore. We need an apprenticeship program. Who's going to finance it? The studios used to."[70]

Cadillac Plans for Worker Bees

As is well known, the studios themselves, or rather their real estate and sound stages, did begin the shift to television production by the end of the 1950s, but the disappearance of all apprenticeships along with the lavishly appointed departments of the past meant that makeup artists, too, now needed to be previously trained, whether at a salon or beauty school or through personal diligence, in order to be hired for jobs or to join the union.[71] In the words of Sue Cabral-Ebert, a member of Local 706 since 1978 and its president from 2003 to 2018, "self-reliance" and being "strong and resourceful" and even "being able to find work on your own" are now normative characteristics for show business labor.[72] As one anonymous makeup artist put it in 2017, "There's nothing worse than having no control over your destiny week by week. My friends who are salaried don't understand how I cope. . . . I don't either! I lose my mind. . . . You're helpless. All you can do is remind people that you exist. . . . You're at the mercy of others. You're contingent labor." In her words, makeup artists had become "worker bees," because there was no time or money now for the "divas" of old.[73]

As is true for many if not most show business unions these days, the catch-22 for membership in Local 706 remains that one cannot join without work experience, but it can be difficult to acquire work experience without a union card. To quote the anonymous makeup artist again, there are currently three avenues to becoming a member, which include working thirty days on a film or television show that "flips partway through the production to become a union signatory" (which can be "terrifying," since the production might be shut down altogether); the "60/60/60," which requires sixty production days a year on a film, television show, and/or music video, three out of five years in a row, which "breaks down to five or six days a month"; and, finally, to do "ninety union commercial days in a year." But the "biggest challenge," as the union itself admits, is that "your days don't roll over into the next calendar year. They expire. So it could take years and years to join if you fall short annually."[74]

There remain substantial benefits to union membership, however. From 1937 on, all of Hollywood's craft unions had set "minimum call" pay standards for a day or a week of employment; instituted rules about when a call could be canceled; and laid out requirements for mealtimes, overtime, weekend, "on-call," and holiday pay and the hours and conditions for location ("near-by" or "distant") versus studio shooting.[75] By the mid-1940s, a paid vacation plan had been instituted for Local 706, based on the number of days worked in the preceding year, with the maximum being 12 twelve vacation days—including Saturdays—and granted only to people employed for over 240 days. Early in the 1950s, health insurance and pension plans were negotiated and added to the union's contracts.[76] All these benefits, especially the last, remain "spectacular": "You can have a family. You can have a partner or a spouse or children or other dependents all covered, virtually for free. It is remarkable. . . . But the problem is that you've got to earn those hours every year. And you start at zero each year. If you work more than eight hundred hours in a given year you can bank up to four hundred hours. . . . But any more than that, you just lose the hours."[77] What a current representative of the union calls its "Cadillac health plan" is also now accompanied by a generous pension and an "individual account plan," a lump sum paid upon retirement, "100% by producers. Can't get better than that."[78]

How all of this will play out in the future is hard to judge. The commercial film and television industries only fitfully resemble the "factories" of the studio era; there are no longer permanent departments located in California whose only purpose is to design and craft the production of characters and stars, on and off the screen, for hundreds of films a year. Because of the enormous increase in runaway productions and to lure them back to the state where so many members continue to live, in 2014 Local 706 became active in crafting the California Film and Television Tax Incentive. However, runaway productions continue as other states also create tax incentives for filmmakers (Georgia's made that state the third largest production hub by 2023). So the union has had to come up with other creative, if controversial, ways to employ its members. Besides broadening the categories in which its members can accrue work hours, it instituted another catch-22 policy to include "super-low-budget union movies at rates that would never have existed even a couple years ago," according to the anonymous makeup artist, which means that "highly skilled craft workers are earning not too much more than fast food jobs for the privilege of working near home."[79] Local 706, represented by Cabral-Ebert and supported by the California Labor Federation, also united with hairstylists in salons and schools in 2018 to defeat legislation that would have eliminated the requirement of a cosmetology license to work in certain functions of salons, a license that, Local 706 maintains, helps to maintain the quality of its applicants.

At least those who want to become, or remain, makeup artists and hairstylists in the modern entertainment marketplace face fewer hard institutional barriers today than did their "forgotten" forebears. The gender restrictions had disappeared by the 1970s, and IATSE included a diversity, equity, and inclusion (DEI) statement in its 2021–2024 Basic Agreement in order partly to recruit more artists of color, which has increased union membership numbers across the board.[80] Unlike their predecessors during the studio era, makeup artists and hair stylists can aspire now to winning industry awards and other forms of professional recognition of their work. In contrast to the single film or television show that can win an Oscar or an Emmy, the Make-Up Artists and Hair Stylists Guild Awards, an annual event presented by Local 706 starting in 1998, includes categories for feature films, television, commercials, music videos, live theater, children's and teen programming, and daytime television, representing the range of labor opportunities for union members now beyond commercial feature films.[81] (These awards are open to nonunion artists too, although only union members can vote.)

The COVID-19 pandemic that began in 2020 complicated the lives of all entertainment workers enormously, but ironically, it greatly increased the participation in Local 706 member meetings since they could be attended remotely. Other elements, however, arguably indicate the continued relevance of the "tight," if not the "jealous," adjectives applied to the crafts as they are practiced today, especially given the competition that all workers continue to face. I end with a statement from the office administrator of Local 706 that, while written in 2022, would have been familiar in sentiment to any Hollywood craft laborer from the 1930s on: "The culture of the business is you have to fiercely defend your position or risk losing it to another. That is not just our union, but the industry itself. . . . That is the reality, you keep your mouth shut and keep your jobs within your group so you all keep working."[82]

Notes

1 Patrick Keating engages this dichotomy in relation to cinematographers in the first chapter ("Mechanics or Artists") of his study *Hollywood Lighting from the Silent Era to Film Noir* (Columbia University Press, 2010).
2 Richard Koszarski, *An Evening's Entertainment: The Age of the Silent Feature Picture, 1915–1928* (University of California Press, 1990), 71.
3 This chapter is a condensation and updating of material I explore in more detail in Adrienne L. McLean, *All for Beauty: Makeup and Hairdressing in Hollywood's Studio Era* (Rutgers University Press, 2022), esp. chaps. 2 and 3.
4 Quotations from "Makeups' Prestige Up," *Variety*, October 24, 1938, n.p., clipping file ("Makeup"), Margaret Herrick Library (hereafter MHL), Academy of Motion Picture Arts and Sciences (hereafter AMPAS), Beverly Hills, CA.
5 Two special Oscars for disguise-based character makeup were handed out in the 1960s. For a list of all Academy Awards in the category, see the appendix to Adrienne L. McLean, ed., *Costume, Makeup, and Hair* (Rutgers University Press, 2016).
6 With very few exceptions, the U.S. beauty industry itself had been developed and was maintained by "immigrant, working-class, or black women" (Kathy Peiss, *Hope in a Jar: The Making of America's Beauty Culture* [University of Pennsylvania Press, 1998], 5). There is no mention of Hollywood's male "experts" in academic histories of beauty parlors in the United States such as Julia A. Willett, *Permanent Waves: The Making of the American Beauty Shop* (New York University Press, 2000), or Julia Kirk Blackwelder, *Styling Jim Crow: African American Beauty Training During Segregation* (Texas A&M University Press, 2003).
7 Factor and his company (he died in 1938) supplied most of the cosmetics and wigs used by studio departments across the industry until the 1960s.
8 See, e.g., Adele Whitely Fletcher, "Miracle Men at Work," *Photoplay*, August 1939, 14–15, 78.
9 The terms were largely synonymous in the studio era, with women primarily called hairdressers even when they designed a style, as they all could do because of their salon training.
10 For more of this history see McLean, *All for Beauty*, esp. chap. 1.
11 Perc Westmore in Mike Steen, ed., *Hollywood Speaks! An Oral History* (G. P. Putnam's Sons, 1974), 258–261.
12 "Make-Up Artists Progress," *International Photographer*, March 1929, 5.

13 A "revised constitution" of Local 706 dated February 16, 1957, states "Applicants to Make-Up Artists craft must be male.... Applicants to Body Make-Up craft must be female.... Applicants to Hair Stylists craft must be female and licensed by the California State Board of Cosmotology [sic]." The race of applicants is not mentioned. John Truwe Papers, "Make-Up and Hair Stylists Local 706–1957," MHL, AMPAS.

14 Email to the author, July 17, 2018. Cabral-Ebert told me that the historical archives of Local 706 are "only one box of stuff."

15 "Make-Up Artists Progress," 5.

16 Murray Ross, *Stars and Strikes: Unionization of Hollywood* (Columbia University Press, 1941), 13.

17 The most useful source of material about Local 235 has been the papers of a Hollywood art director, Leo "K" Kuter (hereafter LKKP), MHL, AMPAS.

18 *Constitution of the Brotherhood of Painters, Decorators and Paperhangers* (Haywood Pub., September 1929), 41–42, LKKP, MHL, AMPAS.

19 "Working Rules, Two-Three-Five, Hollywood, United Scenic Artists of America," 6–7. The booklet's first page states "Effective September 15, 1931." LKKP, MHL, AMPAS.

20 Quotations from "Union Trying to Force Issue with Make-Up Artists," *Hollywood Filmograph*, May 21, 1932, n.p.

21 "By-Laws, Article 1," *AMPAS Bulletin* no. 14 (June 22, 1933): 1. Margaret Herrick Library Digital Collection, https://digitalcollections.oscars.org/digital/collection/p15759coll4/id/1697/rec/60.

22 Original documents cited in this and the subsequent paragraph are from the files of Local 706 in Los Angeles, sent to me by Sue Cabral-Ebert.

23 Michael Westmore, email to author, January 28, 2019.

24 Letter, Local 706 archives, dated December 27, 1933.

25 According to *Film Facts* in 1941, as cited in a June 1946 paper by Evelyn Wright, "Labor Relations in Motion Picture Production" (available in the Online Archive of California, http://oac-upstream.cdlib.org/ark:/28722/bk0003z6p8h/), "the labor cost of craftsmen is only 5% of the total cost of a picture" (8).

26 William Tuttle, corrected typescript of AFI oral history, 1975–1976, William Tuttle Papers, MHL, AMPAS, 122.

27 "April Third Will Be the Deadline for General Walkout," *Hollywood Filmograph*, March 25, 1933, 1.

28 Mike Nielsen and Gene Mailes, *Hollywood's Other Blacklist: Union Struggles in the Studio System* (British Film Institute, 1995), 18–19. Nielsen wrote the sections from which I quote.

29 Much of this information is from Ross, *Stars and Strikes*; Edward Newhouse, "Hollywood on Strike," *New Masses*, May 18, 1937, 6–7; Hugh Lovell and Tasile Carter, *Collective Bargaining in the Motion Picture Industry: A Struggle for Stability* (Institute of Industrial Relations, University of California, 1955); Ida Jeter, "The Collapse of the Federated Motion Picture Crafts: A Case Study of Class Collaboration in the Motion Picture Industry," *Journal of the University Film and Video Association* 31, no. 2 (1979): 37–45.

30 Louella O. Parsons, "Hollywood Buzzes with New Topic about Movieland's Big Strike as Film Players Are Forced to Don Own Make-up," *San Antonio Light*, May 4, 1937, scrapbook no. 19, Perc Westmore Papers (hereafter PWP), MHL, AMPAS.

31 "Sabotage in Movie Strike," *Des Moines Register*, May 5, 1937, n.p., in scrapbook no. 19 of the PWP, which contains a number of clippings about the vandalism and the strikes.

32 "Federated Rejects Peace Plan by Vote of 640–276," *Film Daily*, June 2, 1937, 1, 8.

33 Ross, *Stars and Strikes*, 199.

34 "See Film Peace This Week, SAG, IATSE Not Backing FMPC," *Variety*, May 5, 1937, 1–2.

35 The text from the original charter of Local 706 was provided to me by Kathryn Sain; while it instructs that the charter be dated November 1, 1937, it was signed on October 21, 1937.

36 I am taking the information about Studio Makeup Artists and its status within Local 37 from Dot Ponedel's application to the group on September 13, 1937 (a copy was provided to me by her niece Meredith Ponedel). On Local 37 itself, see "The War for Warner Brothers" on the IATSE webpage: https://www.iatse728.org/about-us/history/the-war-for-warner-brothers.

37 "Beauticians Unionize," *Variety*, January 29, 1936, 3.

38 Ross, *Stars and Strikes*, 193.

39 Some women hairdressers also attempted to establish their independence through publicity. See their remarks in "Studio Hairdressers, The Stars You Don't Know," *Evening Sun* (Baltimore), September 16, 1936, 20.

40 Nellie Manley in Steen, *Hollywood Speaks!*, 284.

41 Lillian Rosine obituary, *Variety*, September 5, 1979, n.p., Rosine clipping file, MHL, AMPAS.

42 Correspondence between Dot and the union cited in Susan Cabral-Ebert and Meredith Ponedel, "And the Answer Is . . . [Dorothy Ponedel]," *The Artisan*, Winter 2007, 14. Local 706 began to publish this quarterly in the 1960s.

43 I assume this from the United Scenic Artists' 1931 "Working Rules," given that so many other of their "rules" persisted into Local 706.

44 Sydney Guilaroff and Cathy Griffin, *Crowning Glory: Reflections of Hollywood's Favorite Confidant* (General Publishing Group, 1996), 57–59. Local 706 did grant him a "life member" card in the 1970s.

45 Guilaroff and Griffin, 89.

46 Carmen Dirigo obituary, *Los Angeles Times*, August 26, 2007, n.p., in Dirigo clipping file, MHL, AMPAS.

47 See Dorothy Ponedel and Meredith Ponedel, with Danny Miller, *About Face: The Life and Times of Dottie Ponedel: Make-Up Artist to the Stars* (BearManor Media, 2018). Dot Ponedel remained the only female makeup artist in the union during the studio era.

48 See Jeanne North, "Do You Want a Job in the Studios?," *Photoplay*, May 1931, 68–70, 116–20, which gives pay scales and employment categories. The rest I base on facsimile reproductions from the archives of Local 706 reproduced in *The Artisan*. For IATSE categories and wage scales effective October 1, 1937, see *The Artisan* 8, no. 4 (2012): 14; for "Wage Scales, Hours of Employment and Working Conditions" ("Effective between January 1, 1947 and December 31, 1947"), see *The Artisan* 9, no. 3 (Summer 2013): 38.

49 The 1931 "Working Rules" of United Scenic Artists stipulated a "State license" and the ability to conform to "all laws of the Cosmetology Act" (7). On the extensive rigor of salon training, see Frances A. Macmullen, *Practical Science of Beauty Culture* (Hollywood Publishing, 1937).

50 William Tuttle interview, August 12, 1976, DeGolyer Institute of American Studies, Southern Methodist University, Dallas, Texas, 18 (my italics).

51 Perc Westmore in Steen, *Hollywood Speaks!*, 262.

52 "A Tribute to Ben Nye, Sr.," n.d., n.p., Ben Nye clipping file, MHL, AMPAS.

53 See the "Motion Picture Industry Code" ["submitted yesterday . . . to the NRA"], *Film Daily*, August 24, 1933, 6–7. In the 1931 working rules of Local 235, women had been prohibited from working "more than eight hours in any 24-hour period, except as provided by the laws of the state in which the work is performed" ("Working Rules," 8).

54 Body makeup ceased to be a separate classification in 1999; now all makeup artists are allowed to do body makeup. Sue-Cabral Ebert, email to the author, July 12, 2018.

55 Wright, "Labor Relations in Motion Picture Production," 28–34.

56 See Anthony H. Dawson, "The Patterns of Production and Employment in Hollywood," *Hollywood Quarterly* 4 (Winter 1949): 338–353.

57 Ginger "Sugar" Blymer, *Hairdresser to the Stars: A Hollywood Memoir* (Infinity Publishing, 2000), 25.

58 "Makeup Dept. Budget" signed by Ben Nye, *The Kid from Left Field* (1953), Leonard Goldstein Papers, MHL, AMPAS.

59 Walter Rodgers obituary, *Variety*, April 25, 1951, n.p., in Jack L. Warner Collection, Cinematic Arts Library, University of Southern California, Los Angeles.

60 See Ponedel and Ponedel, *About Face*, 60.

61 Michael Westmore, email to the author, August 18, 2018.

62 Henry A. Reese, "Merlin of the Movies," *Saturday Evening Post*, February 28, 1942, 22–23, 37–38.

63 Ralph Roddy, "Labor Picture in Hollywood," *Variety*, January 5, 1938, 54.

64 In James Gavin, *Stormy Weather: The Life of Lena Horne* (Atria Books, 2009), 107–108.

65 William Tuttle interview, 24.

66 Ross, *Stars and Strikes*, 218.

67 Ross, 202–203.

68 All from Blymer, *Hairdresser to the Stars*.

69 Blymer, 24.

70 Quoted in Alexandra Brouwer and Thomas Lee Wright, eds., *Working in Hollywood* (Crown, 1990), 233.

71 Makeup schools began "popping up," in Sue Cabral-Ebert's words, in Los Angeles in the 1970s. Today the most "notable" are Elegance International, MUD (Makeup Designory) and the Cinema Makeup School; all teach "everything from runway to advanced prosthetics." Sue Cabral-Ebert, email to the author, August 1, 2018.

72 Sue Cabral-Ebert, email to the author, August 3, 2018.

73 "Anonymous, Makeup Artist," quoted in Michael Curtin and Kevin Sanson, eds., *Voices of Labor: Creativity, Craft, and Conflict in Global Hollywood* (University of California Press, 2017), 83, 85.

74 "Anonymous, Makeup Artist," in Curtin and Sanson, 86–87.

75 Wright, "Labor Relations in Motion Picture Production."

76 See "In Memoriam" [Howard Smit], *The Artisan* (Summer 2009), 16.

77 "Anonymous, Makeup Artist," 87–88.

78 Kathryn Sain of Local 706, email to author, October 20, 2022.

79 "Anonymous, Makeup Artist," 84.

80 See *The Artisan* (Winter 2023), 9.

81 Sue Cabral-Ebert, email to author, May 23, 2023. Cabral-Ebert was instrumental in founding the Make-Up Artists and Hair Stylists Guild Awards in 1998. The awards were discontinued after 2003 for financial reasons but became an annual event in 2012 in partnership with Ingledodd Media, which publishes *The Artisan*.

82 Kathryn Sain, email to author.

7

Costumes and Wardrobe

• •

Gender and the Invisible Labor
of Costume Departments

HELEN WARNER

When Jennifer Johnson, a BAFTA-nominated costume designer (*I, Tonya*), received a production designer's pay slip in error, it revealed a difference in pay of $1,000 per week. Both Johnson and the production designer were department heads, working on the same feature, and yet Johnson was paid significantly less.[1] This was not an isolated incident. The disparity between costume designers' pay and that of individuals with other below-the-line roles is well documented in the trade press. The current president of Local 892, the Costume Designers Guild (CDG), Salvador Perez, attributes this to long-standing gendered assumptions about the kinds of work costume designers undertake, stating, "Costume designers are 85% women. Production designers are 85% men. We are working for hire. They build. We are two department heads doing what I think is an equal job. But because we are mostly women, we are getting paid less and I think that's something that needs to be addressed as part of this movement."[2] The movement mentioned by Perez refers to the #CDGpayequity and #nakedwithoutus campaigns launched by the CDG's pay equity committee. The committee was set up ahead of the 2021 contract negotiations between the CDG and the Alliance of Motion Picture and Television Producers (AMPTP), and, in aiming to end to gender pay bias, it sought to right some historical wrongs.

The CDG argued that this pay inequality is the result of historic patterns of gender and racial discrimination built into the industry (as Erin Hill discusses in chapter 1), which resulted in a failure to recognize costume design as important creative labor. Unlike art directors, there is no official requirement for a studio to hire a costume designer.[3] This is a relic from Hollywood's infancy, when producers relied largely on rental companies or stars and extras to supply their own wardrobes. Even when formalized as a role following the growth of film production in the 1920s, costume design did not gain cultural legitimacy. As Elizabeth Nielsen notes, "In the early days of the Hollywood studio system, the costume department was a favorite place for studio bosses to place 'girlfriends' and inept relatives for whom they could find no other job in the studios."[4] The legacy of this practice, which dismisses the craft of costume work, can be observed in the attitudes of some producers who continue to hold costume designers in poor regard. For example, in a 2018 article in *Variety*, then executive director of the CDG Rachel Stanley, remarked, "In my own career, I've been told several times by producers, 'My wife could do your job.'"[5]

Such quips demonstrate a lack of recognition of costume design as skilled work and render invisible the assistant costume designers, illustrators, wardrobe supervisors, key costumers, costume coordinators, and tailors who bring a costume to life. The relative invisibility of costume workers extends into film histories. Attempts to reconstruct and recover histories of costume design are compounded by their erasure and marginalization within motion picture archives. As Deborah Nadoolman Landis (former president of the CDG) notes in her history of costume illustration, "For costume scholars, there is a mountain of motion picture material that one must sift through for the precious footnote on costume design."[6] Record keeping from the unions in the early years is haphazard, and the industry's preoccupation with forecasting and future returns often results in the "indiscriminate dumping" of historical files.[7] While prominent designers such as Edith Head donated material to motion picture archives, the histories of lesser-known designers and costumers, the majority of whom are freelance, are particularly difficult to recover. Consequently, histories of costume continue to be partial and fail to fully capture the complexities of the profession, including the collaborative nature of the work.

In what follows, I trace these "precious footnotes" to reconstruct the history of International Alliance of Theater Stage Employee (IATSE) Locals 705 and 892 that have shaped the culture of the profession. In doing so, this chapter seeks to provide a corrective to existing histories by bringing those marginalized to the fore, as I detail the formation of the distinct organizations designed to represent those who design costumes (Local 892) and those who make them (Local 705). I consider the consequences of the division between design and wardrobe and the ways in which gendered assumptions about labor and value have not only structured these professions along unequal lines but also hampered efforts to collectively organize.

The Design Team and the Wardrobe Team

In *Hollywood Costume Design*, David Chierichetti aims to capture the significant contribution costume designers made to the "visual language of motion pictures."[8] His compendium of significant costume designers in the studio era is often viewed as the first attempt to make visible the labor of those working in costume. In his introduction, however, he acknowledges that, in addition to the designers singled out in his work, there are "thousands of expert seamstresses, cutters and fitters, milliners and wardrobe men and women, working long hours with little reward, [that] made the brilliant concepts reality."[9] The importance of this collaborative process is echoed by Landis, who claims that "a costume designer shares authorship with a team of talent in the costume department."[10] Despite this understanding of costume as a collective endeavor, there are strict divisions between the design team and the wardrobe team, reflected in the fact that they are represented by different locals. For the purposes of clarity, within this article, the design teams include costume designers, assistant designers, and illustrators (members of Local 892), and the wardrobe team includes all costumers involved in the manufacture and organization of all costumes (members of Local 705). The catchall term *costume departments* refers to both design and wardrobe. The trade unions played a crucial part in constructing these divisions of labor when they established job classifications and pay scales in the late 1920s. To understand the significance of these divisions, and what they mean for the reputation of those working in costume, it is necessary to delineate the roles and responsibilities of those working in design and those in wardrobe.

For modern pictures in the 1910s, actors were expected to provide their own costumes, but for historical films studios had to make or rent them. D. W. Griffith's *Intolerance* is thought to be the first picture in which all the costumes for cast members and extras were designed. Griffith hired Clare West, who reportedly also designed the Klan outfits for *The Birth of a Nation*, to design *Intolerance*. West is considered one of the first costume designers (at that time her title was studio designer). In 1918, she was hired by Famous Players-Lasky (which would become Paramount) and designed ten films for Cecil B. DeMille. During this time, West not only designed the costumes but also ran the wardrobe department, hired workers, and took care of the budget. When West left Paramount in 1924, she was replaced by Howard Greer, who assumed the position of chief designer and would only undertake designing duties. The budgets and the general running of the wardrobe department fell to Frank Richardson, who would become head of wardrobe (a position he would hold for over fifty years). This model became standard in the studio era.

The chief designer was typically responsible for designing a star's costumes, while an assistant may have designed those for a film's other leading female actors. Costumes for men and for extras were typically organized by the wardrobe team and involved renting from costume houses or reusing existing stock. The chief designer was the only worker to receive a credit, if indeed a credit was given, which likely read "gowns by . . ." Few working in costume during this time received fame or notoriety, although a select few would become household names; Travis Banton, later replaced by Edith Head (Paramount), Orry-Kelly (Warner Bros.), Walter Plunkett (RKO), and Gilbert Adrian (MGM). Adrian, often considered the most famous designer of the era, was reportedly "treated like a star" and marketed as such by studios' publicity departments.[11] However, this treatment was typically reserved for men working in costume design (with the exception of Head). Assistant designers, sketch artists, and wardrobe teams rarely achieved recognition.

The wardrobe department was organized into two sectors: manufacturing and finished wardrobe. Manufacturing (or custom-made) included cutters, fitters, tailors, beaders, milliners, shoemakers, and so on, who were responsible for the research, fitting, production, cleaning, and aging of costumes. Finished wardrobe staff included costume supervisors, costumers, checkers, stock clerks, and so on. This department was responsible for analyzing scripts; selecting clothing from rental shops, retail outlets, or studio workrooms; and ensuring that all actors were dressed and ready for set at the appropriate time. Both manufacturing and finished departments were divided along gendered lines, with separate men's and women's tailors/seamstresses and costumers responsible for the manufacture and fitting of male and female actors' garments, respectively.

Often, as was the case at Paramount, men and women in finished wardrobe worked on separate floors of the studio. Most heads of wardrobe at the time were men (with the exception of Vera West at Universal, though significantly she was never officially given the title of head), and men's costumers and tailors were paid more than women's costumers and seamstresses. Consequently, the urge to politically organize was driven by the women in the department who, among other things, were keen to establish equal pay for comparable work. The costumer Agnes Henry recalls of the time: "Personally, I felt that ladies' wardrobe was just as important as men's. With ladies, there is more required in putting everything together than there is with men—especially when you consider how Hollywood focuses on women and their role in being beautiful. When I could vote for equal pay, I put my hand up."[12] Thanks to the costumers union, the equal pay of tailors and seamstresses was achieved in 1945, though it was not until the 1970s that women in finished wardrobe would receive equal pay with men's costumers. According to Elizabeth Nielsen, "The union played a large part in developing a sense of professionalism among the costumers. It gave them better wages, conditions, and a sense of self-respect which costumers never had enjoyed in the pre-union days."[13] Part of this success was due to instituting job classifications and policing roles to ensure that studios hired appropriately skilled workers.

This division of labor more or less continues in 2023, and costume locals are similarly divided between those tasked with design (Local 892) and those working in wardrobe (Local 705). Local 705 has a diverse membership of over 2,300 and represents more than thirty-five membership classifications, from costume supervisors to manufactures to cleaners.[14] The CDG (Local 892) is the smaller of the two, with just over 1,200 members. It represents three membership classifications: costume designers, assistant designers, and costume illustrators. In order to comply with current union guidelines, the costume designer hires their assistant costume designer and sketch artist/illustrator (if necessary) from Local 892. A costume supervisor (from Local 705) is also typically selected by the costume designer, although the designer is prohibited from selecting set costumers or workroom crews from Local 705. This is the remit of the costume supervisor. The costume supervisor is a more managerial position and is responsible for the overall running of the wardrobe department to avoid unnecessary delays in production. The assistant costume designer (a member of 892), if the production requires such a role, answers to the costume designer and must not take direction from the supervisor. The illustrator works with the costume designer and the director to create sketches that will be passed to those in the wardrobe team to construct.

It is clear that the institution of pay scales and role classifications by the locals served to professionalize costume departments and secured better working conditions for those in design and wardrobe. However, it is also clear that this division of labor requires strict policing. For example, locals have revisited the role descriptors of costume designers (Local 892) and costume supervisors (Local 705) several times across their history to ensure that the responsibilities of the two roles remain separate.

The History of Locals 705 and 892

Elizabeth Nielsen's article "Handmaidens of Glamour Culture" provides the most comprehensive account of Local 705's formation. Using interviews with key personnel from the Golden Age of Hollywood, it remains one of the few academic accounts to reconstruct its history and make visible those whose names would have otherwise been forgotten. Nielsen's interview with the costumer Georgina Grant (MGM) reveals that those with the poorest working conditions began to organize first (figure 7.1). Shop supervisors in manufacturing felt threatened by the prospect of union organizing, since they, as department heads, had a good deal of power. Therefore, it was the cutters and fitters within the workroom who would meet in their homes in secret, facilitated by Grant.

In 1929, nineteen men and women from finished wardrobe departments established the first motion picture costumers' union as part of the American Federation of Labor (AFL). During this time, studios and costume rental houses were open shops, making it very difficult to organize and secure workers' rights (figure 7.2). It was only against the backdrop of the New Deal legislation that the costumers' union would gain any significant power when it came to collective bargaining. Consequently, in 1937, after the Federated Motion Picture Crafts

FIGURE 7.1 MGM ladies wardrobe workroom, featuring Georgina Grant (ca. 1940). (Courtesy of Motion Pictures Costumers Union.)

FIGURE 7.2 Western costume men's wardrobe workroom. (Courtesy of Motion Pictures Costumers Union.)

(FMPC) strike, the union gave up its AFL charter to join IATSE as Local 705.[15] At this time Local 705 represented only the finished department. It was not until 1941 that the manufacturing department would join, followed by the costume house employees, who joined in 1944.[16]

In the earliest days of Local 705, Sheila O'Brien, who worked her way up in studio wardrobe and costume departments, was one of the strongest advocates for workers' rights. O'Brien began as a seamstress at Paramount, before moving to finished wardrobe at MGM and eventually becoming a costume designer in 1950, designing all of Joan Crawford's pictures (except *Torch Song*) for the next decade. During her time in the wardrobe department, she was incredibly active in Local 705, joining their negotiating committee in the 1930s and serving on the executive board for many years. O'Brien's contribution during this time cannot be overstated, and among her peers she was known for "being tough when it's necessary for business."[17] It was during her tenure that costumers in manufacturing successfully agitated for equal pay between tailors and seamstresses. Such was O'Brien's commitment to workers' rights that she would go on to found the Costume Designers Guild in 1953.

O'Brien, along with Marjorie Best, Renie Conley, Elois Jenssen, Leah Rhodes, Howard Shoupe, William Travilla, and Michael Wolfe, set up the guild with the aim of advancing "the economic, professional and cultural interests of its members."[18] Significant names in Hollywood such as Edith Head and Walter Plunkett would join shortly after. Although the guild gathered momentum as an organization, it did not originally participate in collective bargaining with producers. It was not until 1976, with a membership of around 100, that it would become affiliated with IATSE as Local 892. O'Brien is often credited with turning the guild into Local 892 and would become its first business agent, a position she held until her death in 1983. Despite the significant role she played in establishing the guild, and in securing fairer working conditions for its members, she did not run for president until 1975. According to Chierichetti, she was "determined to never let it become a one woman show."[19]

Following the decline of the studio system, the importance of both locals significantly increased. As Prudence Black and Karen de Perthuis note of this period, "Hollywood no longer meant a long-term contract but the insecurity of working freelance along with diminished responsibilities, a lowering of status, and shoestring budgets."[20] In the late 1960s, as studios sold their backlots to stay afloat, they also auctioned off wardrobe warehouses and many historical props and costumes. Long-term contracts became increasingly rare, and a number of independent features made during this transitional period did not use a costume department at all (e.g., *Easy Rider*). While costume supervisors and department heads were spared the most devastating effects of the cuts, the majority of those working in costume found themselves in an extremely precarious position.

The new era of short-term contracts brought with it issues for union members and the locals themselves. To manage financial instability in the post-studio era, freelance costumers and designers were required to become more flexible in their pursuit of employment. The ability to be geographically mobile was necessary in order to take on projects in both Los Angeles and New York. Moreover, the ability to move between mediums became a financial imperative, with many seeking to design for the stage as well as for film and television. The most precarious workers made the decision to move between the design and wardrobe teams, a practice that remains commonplace today. For example, assistant costume designers and illustrators are not required for every production and consequently often fail to qualify for pension or health plans. Illustrators are in a particularly precarious position. They are paid hourly, but unlike their hourly paid colleagues in Local 705, if hired, they can often secure work only for a day or week. Consequently, a number of assistant costume designers and illustrators also took on work as costumers. To do so, however, requires multiple memberships to different locals given their specific regional and occupational jurisdiction.

To work on productions based out of Los Angeles, designers needed to belong to the costumers union, Local 892. To design for film in New York, or to design for the stage, they needed to belong to the United Scenic Artists Union, which was, until 1999, affiliated with the Brotherhood of Painters, Decorators and Paperhangers of America (later to become the International Brotherhood of Painters and Allied Trades). To work as part of the wardrobe crew for the stage, costumers needed to belong to IATSE Local 786 and to work in film and television in Los Angeles, they needed to belong to Local 705.

The contemporary climate within which freelance designers and costumers must operate therefore brings with it several obstacles. The logistical and financial challenges of moving from place to place notwithstanding, there were also concerns that those with more experience on the West Coast were being "discriminated against" and losing out on opportunities on the East Coast (and vice versa).[21] In addition, the financial challenges of paying multiple union fees for some of the lowest-paid and most precarious workers is not to be underestimated, even with the introduction of a "dual membership" for Locals 705 and 892 in an attempt to reduce costs. These challenges pose a problem not only for individual members but also for the locals themselves. This issue has created some difficulties in ensuring that roles remain separate, an area that requires constant policing and has been revisited multiple times throughout the locals' histories. In minutes from a CDG meeting in 1973, the existing definition of a costume designer was replaced with more specific guidance about the precise duties of those belonging to 892 and 705, explaining that no member of 705 should sketch any costumes, and no member of 892 should be involved in the fitting. In addition, a clause was included that indicated a Local 705 costume supervisor may oversee an entire production if it was costumed from existing garments. A formal agreement has since been drawn up, yet there remain concerns that there have been breaches.[22] In 2014, there was an accusation from Local 705 that Local 892's description of an assistant costume designer encroaches on the duties of a costume supervisor.[23] Moreover, the clause that allows productions with no "made-to-order" costumes to reduce their budgets by hiring only a Local 705 costume supervisor has generated some animosity from within the CDG. Sue Moore, who acted as the supervisor for *Jurassic Park* and *The Lost World* without a designer, explained in *Variety* that "this has created great resentment from designers that I have been given this opportunity" because Local 892 typically has a higher unemployment rate than 705.[24]

Such conditions exacerbated the already infamous competitiveness that characterized costume departments. Even in the more secure days of the studio system, anecdotes about designers concerned that assistants would replace them feature within film histories. Howard Greer famously remarked in his autobiography that he hired Edith Head because she posed no threat to him.[25] The freelance market only intensified these feelings, as designers competed with peers and supervisors for work. Thus, building the kind of solidarity necessary for collective action became increasingly difficult. As the costumer and designer Stephanie A. Schoelzel explained: "As long as we continue to allow ourselves to be separated and isolated by the different business structures that hire us, as long as we are further separated and sometime pitted against one another, by the different unions and locals that have jurisdiction over our various work venues, we will continue to be kept on the lowest end of the pay scale."[26]

The subject of merging Locals 705 and 892 as a response to such difficulties has been broached numerous times in the locals' history. The most recent discussions took place in the late 2010s, when (then) executive director of the CDG, Rachel Stanley, told *Variety* she had spent three years trying to merge the unions in a bid to strengthen their position when it came to collective bargaining. However, according to Stanley, "they were unable to overcome the conflicts between their contracts."[27] The conflict is typically that designers are "on call," whereas those belonging to Local 705 are paid the union negotiated hourly rate. In addition, those in Local 705 are kept on staff during production whereas the design team's role (theoretically) ends once shooting starts.[28] Consequently, there remains a strong feeling, at least at an administrative level, that respecting this division is important, and this is reflected in the protocols for putting a crew together (as detailed earlier in this chapter).

Jurisdictional conflicts continue to plague the unions even as opportunities to design increase alongside the explosion of original content and streaming. According to the costume designer Ann Roth, "The rapid increase in design opportunities floods the industry with young, hungry people that may happily take the outdated scale rate, and not argue, feeling grateful for the chance to design."[29] Thus, although seismic shifts that have occurred within the industry on an economic, technological, and cultural scale have fundamentally changed the entertainment industry, for the costume unions, history seems to repeat itself. The same challenges remain—namely, building solidarity among their members and across locals in order to gain the respect they deserve.

(In)Visibility and Costume Labor

Despite the significant workforce required to bring characters to life through costume, these workers' labor is typically rendered invisible. Just as Kate Fortmueller argues in relation to acting in chapter 10 on the Screen Actors Guild–American Federation of Television and Radio Artists (SAG-AFTRA), often the invisibility of costume workers is explained away as a consequence of contemporary narrative film. In order to preserve the suspension of disbelief, costumes must appear not as costumes but as clothes that have been selected by the character in their fictional but recognizable world. A character must be credited with their image, not a design team. If costume is too visible, it is often taken as a failing of the designer; as Landis claims, "It's the character the public should remember, not the clothes."[30] While such an explanation might work for narrative film, it does not help explain costume workers' lack of recognition in factual programming, nor can it be reconciled with the fact that fashion designers regularly receive publicity and credit when they supply pieces for a production.

As Salvador Perez's comments at the opening of this chapter suggest, many have attributed this lack of recognition to the gendered nature of the work. This is not simply the fact that women constitute 85 percent of union members in the CDG and 80 percent of Local 705, but rather the labor undertaken by both the design and the wardrobe team is coded as feminine. For the costume department, the knowledge of fabrics, sewing, beading, pattern cutting, and dressmaking has long been associated with women's domestic labor. For designers, there is an assumption that their role, at least for contemporary productions, involves mainly "shopping," which is typically viewed as a feminine leisure activity and in opposition to "work." This erases not only the labor of the design team but also that of the costumers, dyers, and fitters in the costume department, who transform off-the-rack items to meet the requirements of the scene.

Moreover, both departments undertake other kinds of feminine labor in the form of affective care work that goes unrecognized. Stories of difficult stars refusing to wear particular colors or demanding certain kinds of patterns (e.g., Joan Crawford's shoulder pads) are well documented within the trade press, and the ability to manage volatile personalities while completing tasks set by the designer is a necessary part of the job.[31] This kind of diplomacy and the soft skills required for such time-consuming emotional labor are viewed as an extension of the role, and one that is particularly well suited to the "natural" maternal, nurturing state of women. The detrimental effect this kind of additional free labor has on the gender pay gap of women is widely acknowledged within academic scholarship, and therefore it is unsurprising that pay inequity has been a long-standing issue for both unions.[32] In a recent podcast conversation, then president of Local 705 Nickolaus Brown suggests that the reason costume remains one of the lowest-paid departments has to do with not only the significant number of women and LGBTQ+ members in the wardrobe department but also the large number of immigrant workers in manufacture.[33]

The acknowledgment of racial discrimination is relatively recent in the union's history, which has not always advocated for BIPOC members. As Nielsen observes, "[Al]though Local 705 of the Motion Picture Costumers Union (MPCU) had women and many ethnic groups represented in the costume manufacturing departments, Black Americans were not among these workers."[34] It was not until the 1960s that the first Black wardrobe men and women were hired, and even then, their treatment within the industry and by other union members was incredibly poor. Ted Ellsworth (the first president for Local 705) recalls an occasion in which a very skilled Black seamstress, Grace January, was placed at Paramount but quit within a week because "they would either not give her any work at all or just give her dirty work to do."[35]

By the late 1960s, Local 705 was among the more ethnically diverse craft unions, with 20 percent of its 900 members identifying as non-white. This, according to Eithne Quinn, could be attributed to the union's representation of skilled costume house workers but, more significantly, the high numbers of minoritized workers in laundry and janitorial roles.[36] Racism within the creative industries in general, and within costume departments in particular, has recently been the subject of much discussion by the unions. In 2019, Local 705 was the subject of media attention when the racist outburst of Heather Patton, a union member, went viral.[37] Several fellow union members called for Patton's expulsion and were disappointed with the local's slow and bureaucratic response, though she was eventually removed. Following the murder of George Floyd in 2020 and the related Black Lives Matter protests, both Local 705 and Local 892 established diversity committees to amplify the voices of BIPOC practitioners and address concerns regarding systemic racism within the industry.

While the public visibility of such pledges to address inequalities and amplify marginalized voices remains an important part of anti-racist efforts within the industry, there are concerns from union members that these gestures are not enough. Three of the cochairs of Local 705's committee stepped down in protest, questioning the sincerity of the union when it comes to addressing racial injustice.[38] Similarly, Imani Akbar, a Local 892 Diversity Committee member, has observed a loss of momentum with regard to diversity initiatives, recently claiming, "If [the CDG had] the fervent energy that they have with pay equity for inclusion, that would help."[39] Thus, these internal difficulties, when it comes to recognizing and correcting injustices, hamper the larger project of addressing inequalities and invisibility with the aim of creating a more just and equal workplace.

Visibility and the Media

Making visible the labor of costume work to both the public and the industry itself was seen as a necessary step in gaining the financial and social recognition the profession deserves. Consequently, both the CDG and the MPCU regularly publish their own media content, which serves not only as a method of communicating relevant union news but also as a tool for educating both the industry and the public about the skills and labor costume work requires. Like most unions, Locals 892 and 705 generate regular newsletters for members. Ellsworth decided to create a newsletter (*The Costumer*) in 1941 for the benefit of those serving in World War II. The newsletters communicate relevant union business, events, and minutes of general meetings but also include longer letters, think pieces, and articles that help communicate the core values held by the organizations and contribute to the construction of a professional identity. While these longer pieces tend to express the views of the leadership within the organization, they nevertheless reveal an insight into the kinds of issues and concerns that plague the profession.

The CDG expanded its print media more recently and in 2005 began to publish a quarterly magazine, the *Costume Designer*. The magazine, accessible via the guild's website, contributes to the larger goal of gaining visibility and recognition for those the guild represents. The inaugural issue sets out its agenda in the "President's Letter": "Our political strategy is education. Educate the industry, the press and the public about costume design and our status, prestige and salaries will be secure."[40] To these ends, the spring 2006 issue reports the hiring of a new publicist for the CDG, Lisa Taback. Taback began as a publicist for Miramax in the 1990s and has since become one of the most sought after awards strategists, joining Netflix after the streaming site acquired her independent consulting firm in 2018. Taback's appointment by the CDG was an attempt to meet three interrelated objectives: to "raise the profile of Costume Designers in the public eye, to educate our industry to the contribution of Costume Designers as storytellers first and to combat the misconception of 'fashion in film.'"[41] Part of Taback's remit was to work with the various subcommittees of the CDG dedicated, first, to increasing opportunities for members (e.g., a reality committee was established to convince television producers that a designer was necessary for reality TV shows) and, second, to setting up outward-facing events culminating that year in the recognition of costume design at the Scottsdale Film Festival. The festival was attended by Deborah Nadoolman Landis (then the CDG president) and Michael Wilkinson and claims to be one of the first festivals in the world to honor costume designers.

Award ceremonies in general form part of a larger strategy designed to gain public visibility and recognition for costumers' and designers' labor. The MPCU set up the annual Costumers' Ball in 1948, which not only served as an opportunity to celebrate exceptional costume (the ball included the Adam and Eve Awards, designed to recognize members) but, importantly, functioned as a fundraising event for the costumers' welfare fund. The Costume Designers Guild Awards, however, did not begin until 1998.[42] There were concerns among the awards' creators that such an occasion may exacerbate the feelings of competition and rivalry that had long plagued the industry. On balance, however, it was decided that the awards would not only serve as a necessary step toward increasing public and industry awareness of costume design but also create a sense of solidarity among designers that would strengthen the collective power of the union.[43] Moreover, the awards have increasingly become politicized spaces in which designers give voice to their concerns within the industry. The 2021 CDG Awards amplified the concurrent campaigns for pay equity, and the awards' official Twitter account posted testimonies of support from above-the-line and below-the-line staff alike.

Media visibility is crucial in achieving the central aims of both the guild and the costumers union: it offers an opportunity to build solidarity and boost morale by honoring the important work that costume departments do; it provides an opportunity to "educate" the general public about the skill such work requires; perhaps most important, it provides a public platform from which to speak back to an industry that has hitherto failed to acknowledge its importance.

Unprecedented Times: Labor Crises of the COVID-19 Pandemic and Beyond

The COVID-19 pandemic galvanized union members and is regularly cited by below-the-line practitioners as a wake-up call that brought into sharp focus the fact that their working conditions were completely unsustainable.[44] For some, it was the forced downtime that had exposed their neglected personal lives; for others, it was the reality of their precarious economic situation. The pandemic also bolstered a sense of camaraderie between all IATSE unions but particularly so for Locals 705 and 892. Mutual aid groups were organized to help retired members and members living with disabilities, who were the most vulnerable.

Locals 892 and 705 were particularly active as part of the initiative and teamed up, as their skills were required for making masks for local health care professionals and the public. A COVID-specific response initiative, IATSE C.A.R.E.S (Coronavirus Active Response and Engagement Service), was set up to coordinate volunteers across all the locals. Members not only made masks during the break in production, using their supplies for jobs they no longer had, but also designed bespoke patterns for different kinds of face coverings and created tutorials to be distributed to the public. As such, those "feminine" skills so often overlooked and undervalued in their day-to-day lives were of crucial importance during a global public health emergency.

The increased focus on sustainable and safe working conditions and the sense of community the pandemic brought prompted a "Hollywood labor rebellion."[45] As production slowly returned amid the ongoing health crisis, in October 2021, the largest potential strike in Hollywood's history was narrowly averted, as IATSE and the AMPTP reached an agreement regarding working conditions for below-the-line workers. The dispute was mainly over long hours, inadequate rest periods, and the need for a living wage for the lowest-paid workers but also included various demands related to equality, diversity, and inclusion. Members of Locals 705 and 892 voted overwhelmingly to strike and, with the other eleven locals, took to their social media channels to share their support. Moreover, many practitioners shared their stories of unsafe working conditions, discrimination, and microaggressions in the mainstream press. Reiko Porter, a costumer, told *Variety* how she narrowly survived a car accident after falling asleep at the wheel following seven months of nonstop work.[46] Another costumer, Brittny Chapman, was featured in an article in the *Los Angeles Times* in which she detailed her experiences of being followed around luxury stores while shopping for productions and being routinely stopped by security as she attempted to enter film sets.[47] The visibility of such stories put pressure on producers to address such issues during contract negotiations.

Although a deal was reached in late October, there remained concerns that the new agreement did little to tackle the most serious issues that disproportionately affect those working in wardrobe. Trade presses reported that many members of IATSE were bitterly disappointed with the agreement.[48] Locals 705 and 892 both voted overwhelmingly against the deal. The leadership of Local 892 encouraged members to vote for ratification, whereas Nickolaus Brown, at that time president of Local 705, has gone on record to note his disappointment with the deal. In a podcast recorded following news that a deal had been struck but before its ratification, Brown explained that his main reservation about the proposal was that it did little to improve the day-to-day working lives of costumers. Significantly, for Brown, this had to do with the rest periods, which failed to acknowledge that costumers are some of the first crew members on set and the last to leave. The contract promises a minimum ten-hour break between wrap and call (as opposed to eight hours as it had been). However, costumers arrive on set earlier than call time to prepare, and they only leave once actors have had makeup removed, showered, and returned costumes, which the costumers then have to organize for wrap and write up for laundry.[49] This oversight, Brown argues, comes from a fundamental lack of knowledge from those above the line of the kinds of work costumers do and the time it takes to do it. Indeed, this may account for the diversity in opinion between the leadership of Locals 705 and 892, as the contract of the costume designer ends before shooting begins. However, in the winter issue of the *Costume Designer* following the vote, Salvador Perez acknowledges the results of the vote (for both 705 and 892) reveals that those working in costume are perhaps more affected than those in other departments by the issues on the table.[50] Indeed, the social media channels for both 892 and 705 in the run-up to the negotiations shared a common position on the problems with Hollywood's toxic work environment and communicated the strength of feeling among members.

The public displays of compassion and kindness shown in the early days of the pandemic exposed the uncaring realities of the industry and arguably strengthened resolve as negotiations took place between IATSE and the AMPTP.

When production resumed, many members were disappointed to find that the industry had not made any fundamental changes to the working environment despite claims that the health and safety of crew members were of utmost importance. In an interview with *Variety* ahead of the negotiations, the costume designer Mandi Line (who had been central to mask-making initiatives during lockdowns) encapsulated the feeling among many union members as she stated: "The pandemic across all industries brought out the need to find mental stability. We all felt what sitting with our fragile human selves looked like. Then to take those slowed down fragile minds and bodies right back to the normal we have all known—we are breaking. The pandemic has reminded us we have a voice. If we don't say what we need we will keep breaking."[51] The additional, uncompensated care work the pandemic required fell disproportionately to women across the globe, and this was replicated within the mutual aid groups set up within IATSE. Those unions with majority women members (such as Locals 705 and 892) felt the burden of additional unpaid labor while their livelihoods were under threat. Thus, although the pandemic may have galvanized workers, the agreement reached between the producers and IATSE made no attempt to provide reparations for the invisible, feminine care work those in costume performed both on and off set.

Conclusion

The 2021 negotiations engendered unprecedented levels of collaboration among the craft and technical unions and drew attention to the pervasive nature of Hollywood's toxic work environment. However, a paradigm shift in which design and wardrobe teams are recognized as creative workers would require a level of public and professional visibility that is yet to be fully realized. Despite efforts by both unions, but particularly the CDG, to educate the industry and the public, gains in this area have been at best piecemeal.

The difficulties in building long-lasting solidarity within and across both unions remains a challenge due to the precarious nature of the work, despite changes in production and an increase in demand from streaming services. The various strategies employed by the unions to gain recognition are themselves limited by the culture in which they operate. Neoliberal production cultures, in which individuals are regularly required to go above and beyond to make a living, can never be truly challenged by organizations that also rely on the invisible, unpaid labor of rank-and-file members. Despite initiatives designed to redress past and present inequalities, such work still requires the invisible, unacknowledged labor of those most marginalized. Thus, the union has a complicated relationship when it comes to invisible, uncompensated labor. On the one hand, the union's main purpose is to gain those in costume the respect, credibility, and financial compensation they deserve; to do this, however, requires more unpaid, emotionally intensive labor on behalf of its members.

The official union material circulated to members regularly calls on the "good-will" of members to give their time and energy for the collective good of the union. Members are regularly invited to join the numerous committees established to deal with central concerns of the unions, including equality and diversity committees and those associated with care work. As such, these demands on time and labor may (inadvertently) impede efforts to increase visibility and create a culture change on set when these efforts are not acknowledged or compensated off set.

The histories of the CDG and the MPCU demonstrate how patterns of discrimination built into the early days of filmmaking in Hollywood continue to shape the cultures of production for those working in costume. The gendered and racialized dynamics of the labor continue to disadvantage those working in this below-the-line area of the entertainment industry, which remains one of the more diverse areas of film and television production. Understanding the idiosyncrasies of the unions can do more than better illuminate the context within which costume labor takes place; more important, it can increase the visibility of those who so often are left out of media histories. As scholars, archivists, and audiences, we have an opportunity to contribute to this alternative future by recognizing the contribution of those working in costume. By recovering and amplifying those voices seldom recorded, a more nuanced understanding of the precise nature of these injustices is possible. It is also necessary if one wishes to imagine an alternative future in which labor is recognized and valued.

Notes

1   Johnson's career as a costume designer for feature films began in 2005 with *Hard Candy*. While she has never explicitly named the film in which this error happened, it is important to note that it is a relatively recent incident.
2   Salvador Perez in Jazz Tangcay, "Costume Designers Discuss Pay Inequality: 'This Is about Feeling Devalued,'" *Variety*, February 6, 2020, https://variety.com/2020/artisans/awards/costume-designers-pay-equity-1203487872/.
3   Whitney Friedlander, "Women in Art Director, Costume Groups Are Still Fighting for Equality," *Variety*, November 1, 2016, https://variety.com/2016/biz/news/art-director-costumes-groups-gender-inequality-1201905400/.
4   Elizabeth Nielsen, "Handmaidens of the Glamour Culture: Costumers in the Hollywood Studio System," in *Fabrications: Costume and the Female Body*, ed. Jane Gaines and Charlotte Herzog (Routledge, 1990), 175.
5   Rachel Stanley in Todd Longwell, "Costume Designers Fight Gender Bias and Pay Inequality," *Variety*, August 21, 2018, https://variety.com/2018/artisans/news/the-handmaids-tale-1202911250-1202911250/.
6   Deborah Nadoolman Landis, *Hollywood Sketchbook: A Century of Costume Illustration* (Harper Design, 2012), 61.
7   Landis, 60.
8   David Chierichetti, *Hollywood Costume Design* (Macmillan, 1976), 7.
9   Chierichetti, 10.
10 Landis, *Hollywood Sketchbook*, 22.

11 Tino Balio, *Grand Design: Hollywood as a Modern Business Enterprise, 1930–1939* (University of California Press, 1985), 92.

12 Nielsen, "Handmaidens of the Glamour Culture," 176.

13 Nielsen, 179.

14 See Membership Classifications, MPC IATSE Local 705, accessed May 16, 2024, https://www.motionpicturecostumers.org/classifications/.

15 Hugh Lovell and Tasile Carter, *Collective Bargaining in the Motion Picture Industry: A Struggle for Stability* (Institute of Industrial Relations, University of California, Berkeley, 1955), 30–32.

16 These departmental divisions continue to structure union membership in Local 705, which includes the categories of finished, custom-made, and costume house employees and now also live television costumers.

17 David Chierichetti, "Sheila O'Brien," *Film Fan Monthly*, October 1978, 24.

18 Anon, "Scrapbook," *Costume Designer*, Summer 2015, 34.

19 Chierichetti, "Sheila O'Brien," 24.

20 Prudence Black and Karen de Perthuis, "Postwar Hollywood, 1947–1967," in *Costume, Makeup and Hair*, ed. Adrienne L. McLean (Rutgers University Press, 2016), 98.

21 Becky Sue Epstein, "Art Directors in East-West Dispute," *The Hollywood Reporter*, July 25, 1979, 24.

22 "Duties of a Costume Supervisor," *The Costumer*, August 2014, 4.

23 Anna Wyckoff, "Spotlight on Assistant Costume Designers," *The Costume Designer*, Spring 2014, 22–24.

24 Anon, "Temperamental Mates," *Variety*, November 23, 1997, https://variety.com /1997/film/news/tempermental-mates-1116675438/.

25 David Chierichetti, *The Life and Times of Hollywood's Celebrated Costume Designer, Edith Head* (HarperCollins, 2003), 11.

26 Stephanie Schoelzer, "Costumers, Costume Designers and the Union," accessed May 16, 2024, http://www.stephstuff.com/costumer/costumeunions.html.

27 Stanley in Longwell, "Costume Designers Fight Gender Bias and Pay Inequality."

28 Many costume designers dispute this, and many stay on set throughout but are not adequately compensated.

29 Tangcay, "Costume Designers Discuss Pay Inequality."

30 Deborah Landis, "President's Letter," *Costume Designer*, Spring 2006, 6.

31 Chierichetti, "Sheila O'Brien," 23.

32 See the work of Arlie Hochschild, especially *The Managed Heart: Commercialization of Human Feeling* (University of California Press, 1983).

33 Nickolaus Brown, "Hollywood on the Record: What's REALLY Happening on Set? with Shay'La Banks and Nickolaus Brown," *Optimize Yourself*, hosted by Zack Arnold, October 28, 2021, https://podcasts.apple.com/gb/podcast/ep168-hollywood -on-the-record-whats-really-happening/id1276450332?i=1000540003741.

34 Nielsen, "Handmaidens of the Glamour Culture," 168.

35 Nielsen, 168.

36 Eithne Quinn, *A Piece of the Action: Race and Labor in Post–Civil Rights Hollywood* (University Press, 2019), 93–124.

37 Dana Harris-Bridson and Zack Sharf, "After Heather Patton's Racist Rant Goes Viral, a Fellow Costumer Seeks Her Union Expulsion," *IndieWire*, September 26, 2019, https://www.indiewire.com/2019/09/racist-rant-costume-designer-heather -patton-union-expulsion-1202176886/?fbclid=IwAR3mO_8jakN_RrXW9bA8AE Hgjn2ijIKz9NERXxGXySoNX8qjgn_SpW6N-6c.

38 Anousha Skoui, "A Hollywood Union Tried to Promote Diversity. Then Things Got Complicated," *Los Angeles Times*, February 15, 2022, https://www.latimes.com/entertainment-arts/business/story/2022-02-15/diversity-drive-motion-picture-costumers-iatse.

39 Fawnia Soo Hoo, "The Real Reason Costume Designers Are Paid Less Than Their Peers," *Fashionista*, May 5, 2022, https://fashionista.com/2022/05/costume-designers-pay-equity-wage-gap.

40 Deborah Landis, "President's Letter," *Costume Designer*, Fall 2005, 9.

41 This misconception refers to the assumption that fashion designers create the look of productions, and the role of the designer is that of "creative shopper."

42 An earlier attempt at a charity ball designed to honor best dressed stars was launched in 1966 but ended promptly in 1967.

43 Deborah Landis, "President's Letter," *Costume Designer*, Winter 2006 7.

44 Gary Baum and Katie Kilkenny, "Inside the Hollywood Labor Rebellion: 'We Have Awoken a Sleeping Giant,'" *The Hollywood Reporter*, December 17, 2021, https://www.hollywoodreporter.com/business/business-news/hollywood-workers-2021-labor-rebellion-1235062315/.

45 Baum and Kilkenny.

46 Jazz Tangcay and Dan Doperalski, "Portraits of IATSE: Medical Scares and Car Crashes—Why Members Voted Yes on Strike Authorization," *Variety*, October 8, 2021, https://variety.com/2021/artisans/news/iatse-medical-scares-car-crashes-members-voted-yes-on-strike-authorization-1235083837/.

47 Skoui, "Hollywood Union Tried to Promote Diversity."

48 Gene Maddaus, "IATSE Contract Ratification Decided by Razor-Thin Vote Margins in Two Guilds," *Variety*, November 15, 2021, https://variety.com/2021/film/news/iatse-contract-vote-razor-thin-margins-1235112711/.

49 Brown, "Hollywood on the Record."

50 Salvador Perez, "President's Letter," *Costume Designer*, Winter 2021, 13.

51 Mandi Line in Tangcay and Doperalski, "Portraits of IATSE."

8

Animation

• •

Hollywood Outliers, Industry Firebrands

DAWN M. FRATINI

Since the formation of the American film industry, animation workers have been regarded by the Hollywood studios as industry outliers. This status has frequently put animators and their unions at a disadvantage when dealing with challenges such as technological shifts and runaway production. Recently, however, their perceived position on the fringe of Hollywood may have finally worked in their favor. While strikes by the Writers Guild of America (WGA) and the Screen Actors Guild–American Federation of Television and Radio Artists (SAG-AFTRA) made headlines during 2023's "hot labor summer," the Animation Guild (TAG), International Alliance of Theatrical Stage Employees (IATSE, or the IA) Local 839, was able to quietly rack up historic victories. TAG's winning streak began when the animators emerged victorious from their 2022 negotiations with a strong contract that recalibrated their agreement to address the realities of streaming media and remote production. From there, they put their plans for expansion into overdrive, enlarging their jurisdiction by unionizing workers in New York, Texas, and Puerto Rico. They also incorporated previously exempt production and remote workers at Walt Disney Animation Studios. During the IATSE summer 2023 convention, IATSE's executive board rewarded TAG's efforts by granting them national jurisdiction. This status paves the way for them to seek nationwide standards of pay, benefits, and conditions and to combat runaway production on the national level. These historic wins set standards not only for the animation sector but also for similarly situated visual effects and video game industry workers who have only just begun to unionize.

Animation's peripheral relationship to the live-action film industry can be traced back to the origins of American commercial film production around the turn of the twentieth century on the East Coast. Studios specializing in animation were separate from those producing live action and used very different production methods. When live-action filmmaking migrated to Southern California in the 1910s and shifted to feature-length production, established animation studios such as Bray, Barré, Pat Sullivan, Van Beuren, and Paul Terry remained on the East Coast and continued to produce shorts. This meant that animated cartoons became subordinate to live-action feature films as part of a "full program" and that these animation producers and studio personnel were not part of the early Hollywood community or its social and professional organizations. Animation has remained in a subordinate position relative to live-action Hollywood ever since.

The unionization of American animators began relatively late in contrast to most other groups within the motion picture industry: 1937 in New York and 1941 in Hollywood. The history of American animation unions can be divided into three periods, with the 2022 contract marking the beginning of a fourth. These periods roughly parallel eras in Hollywood history, though changes in live-action Hollywood often caused countervailing reactions in the animation industry, which, for example, was forced to move earlier and more thoroughly from theatrical to television production. The first of these eras, from the mid-1920s to 1951, roughly corresponds with the classical Hollywood studio era, when animated shorts were produced primarily to accompany live-action features. It comprises early organizing attempts in the late 1920s and early 1930s, the unionization of the Fleischer Studios in 1937, and the organization of Hollywood animators under the Conference of Studio Unions (CSU) in the early 1940s. This affiliation put them in opposition to IATSE in the so-called War for Hollywood, the backlash of which marked them as targets during the House Un-American Activities Committee (HUAC) "witch hunts."

The second era is marked by a shift away from theatrical short animation toward television animation with its much lower budgets and faster turnaround times. This period lasted from 1951, when the animators affiliated with IATSE, to approximately 1994 when the industry shifted to computer animation. This was a period of struggles for residuals and against runaway production, and of a prolonged weakening of animation unions. This course reversed, however, with the "renaissance" in animation of the early 1990s.

The third era begins with the surprise success of Pixar's computer-animated *Toy Story* in 1995 and is characterized by radical shifts in production and exhibition technologies. During this era, traditional 2D cel animation was discontinued in favor of 3D computer animation production, causing sweeping changes in workflow, job classifications, and pipelines of production, distribution, and exhibition, the ramifications of which the union has struggled with ever since.

The success of TAG's recent contract negotiations, ratified in July 2022, signaled a new era in which streaming services and remote work have become part of the new normal, and long-standing pay gaps and poor working conditions are finally being addressed. While globalized production presents continual challenges for TAG, its new national status lays the groundwork for future strategies to protect jobs and standardize wages and conditions in a global workforce.

Early Attempts at Organizing Animators

In 1925, Bill Nolan, an animation pioneer working at Pat Sullivan's studio, formed the first animators' cooperative, the Associated Animators, though according to animation historian and TAG president emeritus Tom Sito, it "never really got off the ground."[1] Sullivan's studio, which produced the *Felix the Cat* cartoons, was, like all the earliest American animation studios, on the East Coast. It was not until late 1923, when Walt and Roy Disney established the Disney Brothers Cartoon Studio, that animation came to California. Disney was, at the time, a quaint company with only about a hundred employees by 1931.[2] Other Hollywood-based animation studios followed, including those of Leon Schlesinger, Charles Mintz, Walter Lantz, Ub Iwerks, and Hugh Harman and Rudolf Ising. None of these animation producers were members of the studio trade organization, the Association of Motion Picture Producers (AMPP), which left them outside of the Hollywood studios' inner circle. However, as most of them contracted with a major studio for distribution, they could not be said to be wholly independent either. Schlesinger provided shorts for Warner Bros., Lantz for Universal, and Iwerks and Harman and Ising for MGM. Disney shorts were distributed first by United Artists and later by RKO.

The AMPP studios, to which the animation industry was beholden, were still managing to avoid unionization of most creative categories into the early 1930s. Los Angeles in general remained staunchly anti-union, and it was in that environment in 1932 that animators from the Ub Iwerks Studio began clandestine meetings as the Animators' Society, inviting artists from other studios to join them. Myron "Grim" Natwick, designer of Betty Boop and later of Snow White, was elected their first president. The society met for years, striving toward but not attaining union status because, according to Sito, "supervisors would find out about the meetings from snitches and threaten their artists with dismissal."[3]

Back in New York, Van Beuren Studios animators Hicks Lokey, Bill Littlejohn, Frank Amon, and John McManus attempted to start their own society, but when word got back to their hot-tempered boss Burt Gillette, Lokey and Amon were promptly fired.[4] Shortly thereafter, in late 1934, the Animated Motion Picture Workers Union (AMPWU), an offshoot of the Artists Union, began organizing efforts at Van Beuren. The Artists Union had ties to the Communist Party, although many of the animators apparently did not know this. When Gillette somehow learned that inker Sadie Bodin, AMPWU recording secretary, had discussed unionizing with her co-workers, she too was fired. In response, she and her husband formed the first picket line outside an American animation studio.

In the spring of 1935, the struggling Artists Union began to disintegrate. However, its Commercial Artists division, which was the parent to the AMPWU, was granted an AFL charter and became the Commercial Artists and Designers Union (CADU) in late 1936.[5] It would be CADU that would eventually succeed in unionizing New York animators.

Meanwhile in Hollywood, IATSE had managed to gain control of nearly all the below-the-line workers by the mid-1930s. However, rumors of ties to the Chicago syndicate and backdoor deals with the AMPP fueled an anti-IATSE sentiment among many in Hollywood's workforce. In April 1937, the Painters Local 644 stepped in to offer an alternative to those trades not yet organized by or affiliated with IATSE in the form of the revived Federated Motion Picture Crafts (FMPC).[6] Although the FMPC was ultimately undermined by IATSE and the AMPP, Herbert Sorrell of the Painters emerged as a working-class hero and rising star in Hollywood's labor scene. The stage was set to unionize the animators at last under the guidance of CADU in New York and Sorrell in Hollywood.

Unionizing Animation: CADU and the SCG

The Fleischer Studio, home to *Koko the Clown*, *Betty Boop*, and *Popeye*, in the heart of midtown Manhattan, was founded and operated by brothers Max and Dave Fleischer. According to Max's son Richard, the brothers believed their "studio was one big happy family of almost 250 employees."[7] In early 1937, when a delegation brought a list of complaints to Max, he did nothing, assuming these employees to be only a small faction. One month later, over 100 Fleischer employees had joined CADU, most of them from the lower-tier positions: in-betweeners, inkers, and painters. Max met with the union reps, but, considering their demands for a closed shop and double pay for overtime to be outrageous, he refused to recognize the union.

On May 7, 1937, the pro-union Fleischer employees went on strike, picketing the studio singing, "I'm Popeye the Union Man." When nonstriking animators and cameramen returned from dinner to find the entrance blocked, a fight broke out. That was the first skirmish in a protracted and dramatic strike that dragged on until October. Before it was over, longshoremen had joined the picket lines, and Mayor Fiorello La Guardia tried to intervene.[8] In September, the National Labor Relations Board (NLRB) ruled in favor of the union, but the Fleischers appealed.[9] It was not until their distributor Paramount exerted pressure that the Fleischers gave in and signed the union contract. According to Sito, "Eyewitnesses to the talks said Max looked ill, like he was suffering from nervous exhaustion or ulcers." This was the first artists' contract ever signed with an American animation studio. It included a 20 percent raise, a forty-hour week, one week of paid vacation, holidays, sick leave, and screen credits. The Fleischers won a small victory in avoiding a closed shop, agreeing to 60 percent union employees and 40 percent nonunion.[10]

They carried on that way for a time, but the Fleischers were not done fighting back. Following Walt Disney's smash hit *Snow White and the Seven Dwarfs*, the Fleischers convinced Paramount that if they relocated to Florida, tax incentives and lower labor costs would enable them to complete their own feature film, *Gulliver's Travels*. With the studio itself as collateral, Paramount issued them a loan to cover relocation, a new state-of-the-art facility, and completion of *Gulliver*.[11]

The Fleischers were determined that this move would enable them to oust the union, which, after affiliating with the Congress of Industrial Organizations (CIO), had become the United American Artists (UAA). In their negotiations with the UAA, the Fleischers demanded an NLRB election be held after the relocation to Miami. Since the strike, the studio atmosphere had grown hostile to former strikers, most of whom opted to quit and remain in New York. In contrast, company loyalists were offered perks and subsidies to make the move. Thus, once in Miami, the union was easily voted out of the studio.[12] But it was not the big win the Fleischers had imagined.

The Fleischers had grossly miscalculated the costs of operating in Florida. In addition to the exorbitant costs of the new facility itself, all their supplies had to be shipped from New York, and film returned there for processing. They also found they had to offer huge salaries to lure artists away from New York and California to finish the film on time.[13] On top of this, *Gulliver's Travels*, released in December 1939, was not the international smash-hit *Snow White* had been. As war spread across Europe and Asia, American film exports were curtailed, which proved calamitous for both Fleischer and Disney, because they relied on foreign sales in addition to domestic box office to recuperate the high production costs of feature-length animation.[14]

The Fleischers' second feature, *Mr. Bug Goes to Town*, had the further misfortune to premiere on December 5, 1941, two days before the bombing of Pearl Harbor. Paramount had also commissioned a series of *Superman* shorts to be produced in the Fleischers' patented and expensive Rotoscope technique. The *Superman* shorts cost approximately $50,000 each (in contrast to their *Popeye* shorts, which averaged $16,000), further draining the studios' reserves. In 1942, Paramount called in their loan and took ownership of the studio. In a bitter twist, Paramount moved the studio back to New York, renamed it Famous Studios, and immediately signed a union contract with the Screen Cartoonists Guild.[15] Ultimately, the Fleischers' dogged determination to dodge the union put them on a path to a financial disaster that cost them their company.

On the heels of the short-lived success of CADU at Fleischer in 1937, the Screen Cartoonists Guild (SCG), which had evolved from the Artists' Society, began asserting itself as an unaffiliated local union seeking bargaining recognition with Hollywood's cartoon studios. They got off to a flying start in 1938 by filing a complaint with the NLRB against Schlesinger with none other than Carey McWilliams, the prominent California author, activist, and lawyer, representing them. Complaints against Metro and Lantz were filed soon after.[16] These actions were stalled, however, by a backlog at the NLRB.

In October 1939, the SCG voted to affiliate with the International Brotherhood of Painters, Paperhangers and Decorators, thereby aligning themselves not only with Sorrell and Painters Local 644 but with the anti-IATSE, "progressive" movement as well. SCG Local 852 received its charter in January 1940.[17] With Sorrell's guidance, things began to take a turn. By November, SCG president Bill Littlejohn had negotiated a closed-shop contract at MGM.[18] They were next certified as the bargaining agent at Screen Gems in February 1941 and at George Pal Productions that March.[19]

Leon Schlesinger, whose studio produced Warner's *Looney Tunes*, defiantly closed his studio "on account of strike" rather than agree to the SCG's contract.[20] Sorrell later testified that he instructed the SCG to increase the base salaries of the lowest-paid brackets $1,300 each day the studio remained closed. "Give me that!" Schlesinger said, finally, grudgingly signing the contract and adding, "Now, what about Disney?"[21] By 1941, Walt Disney Productions was by far the biggest animation studio in Hollywood with approximately a thousand employees—five times as many as at Schlesinger's studio. According to Sito, "The entire cartoon industry understood that the real decision of whether animation artists could ever function as a union labor force would be made at Disney's."[22]

IATSE had made attempts to organize Disney when *Snow White* was nearing completion. At that time, top animator and Goofy creator Art Babbitt was so alarmed at the prospect of being under IATSE leader Willie Bioff's control that he went to Disney attorney and vice president Gunther Lessing. Lessing advised Babbitt to form an alternative, in-house organization, and Babbitt, somewhat naively, did not realize that this would constitute a company-dominated union rather than an independent craft union.[23]

Babbitt formed the Federation of Screen Cartoonists in January 1938 and was elected president. The federation received NLRB certification in July 1939.[24] Babbitt tried to live up to his position, but it soon became clear that Disney management never intended to bargain with the federation. It existed merely to dissuade other, legitimate unions from encroaching. Thereafter the federation fell dormant.[25]

In November 1940, the SCG, riding the momentum of their success at MGM, began holding meetings of Disney animators at the home of layout artist Dave Hilberman. By early December, Sorrell and Littlejohn, armed with cards from a majority of Disney artists, sought recognition from management but were turned away. Disney management countered with a request for an NLRB election to verify employees' allegiances. Walt implored Babbitt to rekindle the federation, promising a closed shop to block the SCG's intervention. Babbitt instead defected to the SCG team.[26] On January 14, 1941, the SCG filed an "unfair practices" complaint with the NLRB, citing the federation as a "company union" designed to interfere with legitimate unionization of Disney employees. This was followed by a threat from the AFL to "place the Disney company's products on unfair lists throughout the United States and Canada."[27]

Unionization efforts came at a time when Disney was struggling financially. *Pinocchio* and *Fantasia*, both released in 1941, had been expensive to produce and failed to turn substantial profits with the loss of the European box office. Between 1941 and 1942, the studio lost $1 million.[28] Walt gathered his staff to deliver what he thought was a heartfelt speech pleading for increased productivity to save the studio and less time spent trying to unionize. Many remembered it as patronizing and even insulting. It galvanized the SCG, which held its own meeting shortly thereafter, electing Babbitt as chairman of its new Disney Unit and Hilberman as secretary.

On April 30, the NLRB ruled in favor of the SCG, agreeing that Disney's federation was indeed a "company union." In May, while Disney appealed, the cash-strapped studio laid off workers. Of the twenty animators let go, seventeen were SCG members. Outraged, the SCG voted to strike unless Disney met with their committee. Instead, Disney retorted by firing Babbitt. On May 28 at 6:00 A.M., 300 furious employees arrived to picket the Disney studio.[29] The strike was on.

The Disney strikers settled in for a long haul, setting up camp across the street complete with food service and fundraising events (figure 8.1). The division between the pro-union strikers and the anti-union nonstrikers did not *necessarily* have anything to do with prestige or title. Many of Disney's top, highly paid animators crossed the picket line to work and remain loyal to Walt and the studio, but others not only supported the strike but aided in the organizing efforts. As had occurred at Fleischer four years earlier, the bitterness between those who struck and those who crossed the picket line grew more vitriolic as the weeks passed.[30] The strikers hung vice president Lessing in effigy and paraded ugly caricatures of Walt. The Society of Motion Picture Film Editors joined the picket line on June 3, and Schlesinger animators arrived every Wednesday. Frank Tashlin, head of Columbia's new Screen Gems, would stop by on his way to work to staff up by hiring picketers. On June 13, the AFL boycott of Disney products went into effect, and by the end of June, the *New York Times* front page declared, "One thing has been destroyed—the camaraderie which for years distinguished the Disney plant from other Hollywood film factories."[31]

The story of the great Disney Studios strike has been recounted in multiple histories.[32] It is usually depicted as a battle between liberal, somewhat naive Babbitt and stubborn, paternalistic Walt Disney. While this Brutus-and-Caesar clash of personalities is irresistible to Disney enthusiasts and critics alike, they

FIGURE 8.1 Strike benefit flyer. (Courtesy of Oviatt Library Special Collections, California State University, Northridge.)

were not the only larger-than-life personalities involved. Labor historian Laurie Pintar defines Sorrell's persona in terms of masculinity and militancy, which, she argues, "was viewed as a source of empowerment for American working-class men in their labor struggles."[33] Hilberman would later recall, "I winced because he . . . said things like we ought to 'squeeze [Disney's] balls 'til he screams.'"[34] Babbitt, on the other hand, was known as a swinging bachelor who, Ward Kimball recalled, "liked to have a cause."[35] By all accounts, he and Walt did not personally like each other from the start. Many said, in hindsight, that it was Lessing's bad advice that steered Walt and Roy wrong, by creating not one but several company unions and refusing to negotiate with the SCG. Lessing, too, was a big personality whom animator Jack Kinney called "a terribly egotistical guy" known for constantly bragging he had once represented Pancho Villa.[36]

Then there was IATSE's Willie Bioff. Despite having been indicted for tax evasion in January 1940 and extradited to Chicago to serve a pandering sentence, Bioff was still holding on to his control in Hollywood in early 1941. IA president George Browne painted him a labor hero and political victim, but just days before the Disney strike commenced, both men were indicted on extortion charges.[37] Nonetheless, as Mike Nielsen put it, in the short time between the indictment and his trial, "Bioff dealt his last hand at the producers' labor relations gaming table": he tried to muscle in on Disney.[38]

It is unclear exactly how Bioff got involved. Bioff and Browne maintained a "sweetheart deal" with the AMPP: in return for payment, they kept wages down and maintained a no-strike policy.[39] Walt Disney Productions, however, was not then a member of the AMPP. On the contrary, during the summer of 1941, Walt was attending meetings of a group soon to be known as the Society of Independent Motion Picture Producers. The society's express purpose was to push back against the oligopolistic stranglehold on film distribution of the Motion Picture Producers and Distributors of America (MPPDA)—the East Coast affiliate of the AMPP.[40] Lessing claimed that it was the SCG that got Bioff involved when it asked IA projectionists to boycott Disney films.[41] If such a request was made, Sorrell apparently knew nothing of it. He later claimed he had had Bioff surveilled and thus discovered that Roy Disney had paid him a visit.[42] However it came about, Bioff was suddenly in the middle of things.

On June 30, Disney sent cars to transport SCG leaders to the Roosevelt Hotel for a meeting. As they drove off, Hilberman realized they were headed instead to Bioff's ranch and demanded to be let out. The others continued to the ranch, where Roy, Lessing, and Bioff offered a closed shop, 50 percent retroactive pay for the strike time, two weeks' paid vacation, and wage increases across the board. The catch was, of course, that they disassociate from Sorrell and the Painters and affiliate instead with IATSE.[43] The SCG representatives declined.

In response, Walt Disney took out an ad in *Daily Variety* appealing, "To My Employees on Strike," repeating Bioff's frequent accusation that Sorrell was a communist agitator. The SCG responded with an ad of its own the next day: "The door is open for negotiations except at Willie Bioff's ranch."[44] Bioff's next move was to broker a closed-shop contract between Disney and all of the other AFL unions that had been supporting the strike—the Teamsters, the IBEW, the Plasterers, and the IA sound men, lab workers, utility workers, projectionists, and cameramen. Although these accounted for fewer than a hundred of the strikers, the headlines gave the impression that the SCG was losing support.[45] That marked the end of Bioff's involvement not only in the Disney matter but in Hollywood labor in general. Both he and Browne were convicted of extortion in November.

The Disney strike, in the meantime, remained at a stalemate through late July when U.S. Conciliation Service commissioner Stanley White was called in to mediate. According to Sorrell, White finally advised him to reach out to the Giannini brothers, who owned the Bank of America—and Disney's debts.[46] That proved to be the turning point. On July 28, Commissioner White and Commissioner James Dewey met with Sorrell, SCG leaders, and Disney management and successfully outlined a deal.[47] Part of the fallout of this was that the Bank of America became much more closely involved in Disney studio operations. They immediately demanded cost-cutting measures, including further layoffs, the details of which were to be part of the strike settlement.[48]

In early August, Walt and a small entourage of Disney artists departed for a goodwill tour of South America, leaving Roy to deal with the layoffs. Roy submitted to the SCG a list of 256 employees to be let go, of which 207 were former strikers. The SCG was not pleased. With tensions mounting again, Roy closed the studio and flew to Washington, DC, to meet with the Conciliation Service and plead for a speedy ruling on the matter. Roy made two more trips to Washington before a ruling was finally issued that set specific ratios of strikers to nonstrikers to be laid off. This settlement marked the end of the strike at last. Work resumed at the Disney studio on September 16, 1941.[49] Walt himself returned on October 4 and was, unsurprisingly, unhappy with the results, but there was no changing it. The studio went forward as a union shop evermore. As had been the case in the aftermath of the Fleischer strike, the studio atmosphere was forever changed. It was the end of the era of the "family-style" studio and the beginning of animation as a serious business.

Many of the personal divisions caused by the feud were never healed or forgiven, and many former strikers left Disney when it became clear they would be ostracized.[50] It seems, in the end, it was not the union that Walt Disney could not forgive, but the challenge to his personal authority over his own company. Six years after the end of the strike, with the entirety of the U.S. involvement in World War II transpiring in between, Walt Disney would testify before HUAC still harboring bitterness and looking to settle scores.

The War for Hollywood and the Terrytoons Strike

On the East Coast, the UAA had been disintegrating since the Federal Arts Project had ended, but it collapsed entirely when the United States entered World War II. In 1943, SCG Local 852 sent Pepe Ruiz, an assistant animator at MGM, to New York to organize SCG Local 1461 there. Gordon Whittier and Johnny Gentilella of Paul Terry's Terrytoons became the local's first president and vice president, respectively, and Ruiz stayed on as business manager. Ruiz, who had been instrumental in organizing Local 852, was friendly with Herb Sorrell, whom he unabashedly admired, naming him "the Father of the organized screen cartoonists in the country."[51] Corresponding by letter and telegram over several years, Ruiz would repeatedly call on Sorrell for advice and offer his support in return as Local 1461 faced the longest strike in American animation history at the same time that Sorrell fought against IATSE domination in the War for Hollywood.

In November 1941, on the very day that *Variety* reported Willie Bioff had been convicted of extortion under the gleeful headline "Bye, Bye Bioff," the trades also reported that Sorrell had been elected president of the newly formed Conference of Studio Unions, another lateral grouping of Hollywood's progressive, demo-cratic unions, like the FMPC before it.[52] Among its initial member unions was SCG Local 852.[53] Although IATSE's new president, Richard F. Walsh, was prom-ising a new era of autonomy for IA locals, distrust of IATSE and the AMPP remained high. The entry of the United States into World War II put Hollywood's labor issues temporarily on hold, but a jurisdictional dispute between the CSU and IATSE in October of 1944 set in motion the chain of events that led to violent picket line skirmishes a year later. The animators were not directly involved in this conflict between IATSE and the CSU because, although they were affiliated with the CSU, their representation was undisputed, and they had nothing to do with the AMPP. They negotiated with the Animated Film Producers Association (AFPA), which Schlesinger had established in 1942.[54] Some Local 852 members nonetheless picketed in support of the CSU until the situation became too vola-tile.[55] On the East Coast, Ruiz roused Local 1461 to pass a resolution in support of the CSU strikers and made sure their support was announced in the press.[56]

Paul Terry had been working in animation since 1915. In contrast to Disney, he had no artistic aspirations for his cartoons and was widely reputed to pinch every penny. When he got wind of Local 1461's efforts to unionize his employ-ees, he promptly fired both Whittier and Gentilella, in violation of the Wagner Act. The NLRB forced Terry to rehire them, and he reluctantly signed a union contract in 1944. However, by the time it was up for renewal in June 1945, World War II was ending, and the Truman administration was ushering in a pro-business era. Taking advantage of the changing tide, Terry repeatedly delayed his contract negotiations.[57]

In January 1946, when renegotiating the Famous Studios contract, Local 1461 demanded and won wage parity with animators on the West Coast.[58] When it was once again time to negotiate the annual Terrytoons contract, Ruiz was ada-mant that Terry match this also. In a brief period of calm between skirmishes in Hollywood, Sorrell personally called Terry, threatening him with "the full weight of the Brotherhood of Painters" should he fail to agree to the animation wage standards.[59] Ruiz was dazzled by this, but Terry was not cowed, and his employees had already lost heart. When a strike vote was called, only thirty of Terry's sixty-five employees voted, and they voted twenty to ten against striking.[60] Terrytoons went on with no union contract.

In July, after winning a 25 percent wage increase for all CSU members, Sor-rell intervened once more in the Terrytoons struggle, this time enlisting the help of the AMPP's labor negotiator emeritus, Pat Casey.[61] The pressure from Casey, along with negotiating assistance from John Scotti of the New York Sign, Picto-rial, and Display Union, finally gained some ground for SCG Local 1461.[62] Terry granted them a closed shop on July 15, 1946, but he denied them overtime, vaca-tion, and seniority and, worst of all, wage parity. Ruiz worried that if he capitu-lated to Terry, he would be unable to maintain bicoastal wage and benefit standards with other New York studios.[63]

Ruiz was, however, able to secure a 25 percent increase for cartoonists at Famous to match the 25 percent the CSU had won for Hollywood cartoonists.[64] With things looking up, SCG Local 1461 sent half of their monthly dues to the CSU's strike fund, so reverently did Ruiz and his local believe in Sorrell and his cause.[65] Unfortunately, things began spiraling downward for Sorrell and the CSU thereafter. In March 1947, Sorrell was badly beaten and left by the side of the road.[66] Then the IBEW ordered their Hollywood members back to work, irreparably undercutting the CSU's united front. The Story Analysts broke ranks next, disaffiliating with the Painters to become IA Local 854.

Meanwhile, Local 1461 had allowed Terry to stall negotiations for nearly two years. By May 1947, the Terrytoons employees were making 30 percent less than their peers. Ruiz saw no alternative but to order a walkout of Terry's thirty-eight union employees and to request NLRB support.[67] The NLRB ordered the strikers back to work pending negotiations but, taking a cue from the AMPP's successful tactics against the CSU, Terry locked them out.[68] Unable to turn to the embattled CSU, Ruiz sought help from the Painters International and the AFL to no avail. Writing to Sorrell in July, Ruiz entertained the idea of abandoning the Painters and affiliating with the CIO.[69] Sorrell advised Ruiz against that, saying, "I won't always be in trouble."[70] Ruiz, ever loyal, stuck with Sorrell and the Painters, but unfortunately for Ruiz, Sorrell was wrong: as far as Hollywood was concerned, he was in trouble ever after.

The Disney studio had had no labor troubles after unionizing six years earlier, but when Walt Disney testified before HUAC on October 24, 1947, it was clear he was still nursing grudges. He named former SCG secretary David Hilberman as "the real brains" behind the 1941 strike and someone whom he believed to be a communist, along with William Pomerance and Maurice Howard, the former and current business managers of Local 852.[71] In the intervening years, Hilberman had formed the highly regarded United Productions of America (UPA) with other former Disney animators and then gone on to launch Tempo with Pomerance in New York, which produced animated television commercials. Disney's testimony not only affected the few he named but eventually drew the scrutiny of animators with whom Hilberman and Pomerance had affiliated on both coasts.

Disney also testified at length about Sorrell, complaining about his tough-guy tactics. He noted Sorrell had told him that he was not a communist but had used their money in the past. "If he isn't a communist," Disney quipped, "he sure should be one." The tide had turned against Sorrell. Four days later his own union, Painters Local 644, voted to allow members to cross the picket lines to return to work. As one of the biggest locals in the CSU, this marked the beginning of its end.[72] Likewise, on November 15, in New Rochelle, several of Terry's key animators crossed their own picket line and returned to work, breaking the Terrytoons strike, which officially concluded on December 19. The strike had lasted eight months and remains the longest in animation history. It won Local 1461 nothing at all.[73]

The Cartoonists Untethered

The CSU continued for a few more years but with dwindling ranks. The Painters International pressured Local 644 to oust Sorrell, but they defiantly re-elected him.[74] This put both SCG locals, which were closely associated with Sorrell, in a tough spot. In June 1950, Littlejohn, Local 852's president, wrote to Ruiz that there was talk among members of leaving the Painters to affiliate with IATSE. Further, the Red Scare in Hollywood was beginning to divide Local 852 cartoonists as resentment against left-leaning members grew. Littlejohn wrote to Ruiz, "The Disney guys don't like me because I am the Herb Sorrell influence in the union which is supposed to be another way of saying I am a commy [sic] too."[75]

Both SCG locals believed it was in their best interest to disaffiliate with the Painters' International, which had lost its own Hollywood local to IATSE and was trying to sacrifice Sorrell in a shady deal to win it back.[76] But there were many members on both coasts who would rather go independent than affiliate with their long-term nemesis IATSE, and affiliating with the communist-backed CIO was out of the question. In October 1948, SCG Local 1461 joined with ten other New York locals in a failed attempt to form an East Coast alliance like the CSU.[77] The following year Ruiz met with the independent National Association of Broadcast Employees and Technicians and advised Sorrell and Littlejohn that affiliating with them would set the cartoonists up to work in television, but neither responded.[78] Although Ruiz and Littlejohn were longtime friends, Ruiz was so frustrated by October 1950 that he wrote, "With all sincerity I can tell you now that I'm reaching the point where I don't give a shit about you fellows."[79]

In their next contract negotiations, Local 852 attempted to lay the groundwork for disaffiliating from the Painters. They submitted a proposed basic contract to the AFPA with the stipulation that it would be valid between the producers and Local 852 "or its successor." The producers refused this stipulation, meaning that should Local 852 cease to exist, so would their contract.[80] Representation of the cartoonists would then be up for grabs, opening the door for the IA to call for an election that they could very well win, since their staunchly anti-communist position had begun to look like shelter from the HUAC storm.

In a move of startling irony, United Productions of America (UPA), the industry rebel formed in 1945 by leftist, ex-Disney animators, joined the AFPA, putting UPA management on the same side of the bargaining table with Warner Bros., MGM, Walter Lantz, and, of course, Walt Disney Productions. UPA cofounders Hilberman and Zack Schwartz had sold out to their partner Steve Bosustow in 1946 and decamped to New York. It was some time before HUAC's Hollywood investigations caught up with them there. UPA, on the other hand, was in the thick of things and gaining a reputation as the studio formed by and employing "a bunch of Reds."[81] According to UPA writer Bill Scott, Bosustow feared losing his studio and so "joined the Producers' Association to show he was anti-communist."[82]

In December 1950, SCG Local 852 voted to disaffiliate from the Painters, thereby becoming an independent union, but this turned out to be a temporary solution.[83] When HUAC resumed its Hollywood investigations in 1951, they interviewed former Schlesinger background artists Eugene and Bernyce Fleury. Although their testimony revealed almost nothing new, it was subsequently used to target UPA animators Phil Eastman, John Hubley, Bill Melendez, and others.[84] In October UPA fired Eastman and Scott, who was not a communist but believed he was fired so that it would not appear Eastman was being blacklisted.[85]

It was in this atmosphere that Roy Brewer and the IA made their play to affiliate the cartoonists. In January 1952, the majority of SCG members voted in favor of joining IATSE and re-formed as the Motion Picture Screen Cartoonists (MPSC), Local 839.[86] There were, however, enough members opting to remain independent so that SCG Local 852 carried on well into the 1970s with contracts at smaller, independent animation houses. This created the unusual situation of two local Hollywood animation unions coexisting for more than a decade.

UPA-employed members voted to remain independent, but because UPA had joined the AFPA two years earlier and the other AFPA studios were bargaining with the MPSC Local 839, the UPA crew was given no choice but to join that union. Once UPA was under IATSE jurisdiction, the IA compiled a list of UPA employees with communist connections and turned it over to Columbia Pictures, UPA's distributor.[87] The named employees were given a choice: write a letter of confession and contrition or leave the studio. If UPA did not comply, Columbia would cease to distribute its cartoons. Melendez, Jules Engel, Fred Grable, Bill Hurtz, Paul Julian, and Herbert Klynn wrote letters and managed to keep their jobs, but Hubley and Myer Schaffer, who had been members of the Communist Party, refused and resigned.[88]

Following the lead of its West Coast sibling, SCG Local 1461 of New York also affiliated with IATSE becoming MPSC Local 841, with Ruiz remaining its business agent.[89] No one knows exactly why, but suddenly, without argument, Paul Terry signed a union contract with the new IA local that was identical to the 1947 SCG contract for which Ruiz had fought so long and hard. Perhaps Terry had concluded that it would not be worth fighting the IA. Terry was nothing if not a shrewd businessman; when he retired a few years later, he sold his studio and invested in Disney stock.[90]

The Shift to Television Animation

The Red Scare was not the only dramatic challenge to Hollywood in the early 1950s. Movie theater attendance was in a precipitous decline; by 1956 it was nearly half of its 1946 high. Television shouldered the blame for this change as it was becoming the dominant entertainment medium in the United States. The

Paramount Decrees which forced the major studios to divest their theater chains, led to shifts in exhibition that included a sharp decrease in the demand for theatrical short animation, which was simply too expensive. According to Sito, between 1947 and 1961, the cost of a cartoon produced in Hollywood was between $50,000 and $90,000. By 1961, studios were demanding that budgets be slashed to $6,500, and, one by one, they closed their in-house animation units: MGM in 1957, Warner Bros. in 1963, and Paramount's Famous in 1967. Of course, the Walt Disney Studios continued to produce theatrical, feature-length animation, but the box office disappointment of the very expensive *Sleeping Beauty* in 1959 necessitated a devastating round of layoffs, reducing the animation staff from 500 to 75 employees.[91]

In the early 1950s, few animated programs were produced specifically for television, with exceptions such as Jay Ward's *Crusader Rabbit* (1950–1951) and the interactive *Winky Dink and You* (1953–1957). There was, however, a demand for animated commercials, and new, independent studios specializing in these sprung up on both coasts, competing for artists.[92] Many blacklisted animators found they could work more easily in this field because commercials did not have on-screen credits. In the second half of the decade, more animated series began to appear produced by independent studios that specialized in extremely low-budget television animation. Whereas a theatrical short had typically taken six to eight weeks to produce, animated television series demanded sixteen thirty-minute shows in six to eight months.[93] That schedule required the use of simplified and limited animation more akin to the UPA modernist style than the naturalism of the Disney style in the prewar years. UPA itself moved into television with the *Gerald McBoing Boing* show in 1956.[94]

When MGM closed its animation unit in 1957, William Hanna and Joseph Barbera immediately launched a studio of their own, Hanna-Barbera, to produce television animation. Their first series, *Ruff and Ready*, debuted in December of that year. With their streamlined production and emphasis on quantity over quality, Hanna-Barbera grew to dominate television animation throughout the 1960s and 1970s. Though Hanna-Barbera did have a contract with MPSC Local 839, the company found ways to circumvent the standard contract to economize. Hanna-Barbera offered animators "$10 for every foot over the eighty-foot-a-week quota," so that, while it did not pay overtime, artists worked longer of their own accord to obtain the bonus.[95] Concurrently, Jay Ward partnered with Bill Scott to produce *Rocky and His Friends*, featuring Bullwinkle Moose. Jay Ward Productions contracted with the independent SCG Local 852. Nonetheless, both Jay Ward and Hanna-Barbera used foreign labor for ink and paint work—animation's version of "runaway production"—to keep their costs down.[96]

By the late 1960s, the field of animation in the United States had been completely upended. Eighty percent of employment was in television, and because the work was seasonal, the average length of employment was approximately twenty-eight weeks per year in contrast to the fifty weeks worked by Disney feature animators. While the average IA member employed in live action worked 1,448 hours per year, 1,309 was the average in animation.[97] To make ends meet, artists might freelance doing commercials, industrial shorts, or television specials from November through April. Such was the established norm for animation workers in the 1960s through 1970s, an era commonly referred to as the "lost generation," during which very few new animators entered the industry.[98]

In part as a solution to the seasonal nature of television work, Local 839 put residuals at the top of its negotiating agenda in 1969. Live-action writers, actors, and directors had already won residuals for television rebroadcasts, as had voice artists and musicians working in animation. Local 839 argued that residuals would "bring animation artists up to parity with everyone else in the entertainment industry."[99] Residuals, though, would apply only to the top-tier creatives (i.e., animators and animation writers), not to inkers and painters.

The independent SCG and its business agent Larry Kilty had already unsuccessfully sought residuals for commercial animation in 1955.[100] Kilty was a controversial figure. He had been expelled from Local 839 in 1953 and joined the SCG, but when it was revealed that he was secretly attempting to reunify the two unions under IATSE, Kilty left the SCG before Littlejohn could pursue punishment. He then rejoined MPSC Local 839 and became its business agent. In 1969, Kilty was still pursuing reunification of the two unions and had conceived a plan for an "Animation Basic Local" that would include camera and editing personnel. To him the issue of residuals was an annoying distraction.[101]

While the MPSC president Lou Appet approached SCG leadership to join forces to negotiate for residuals and a runaway production clause, Kilty and his supporters held informal meetings with painters, most of whom, thanks to the industry's glass ceiling, were women. According to Sito, "They argued convincingly that there was no need to risk their steady employment to strike so that male animators could make even more money." The AFPA was able to exploit the resultant disunity. By July, with negotiations at a standstill, Local 839 sought permission from IATSE to strike against the AFPA, but many below-the-line workers declared they would not support a strike.[102]

At the same time, the independent SCG, still deeply distrustful of the IA, not only declined to support Local 839 in seeking residuals but merged with Teamsters Local 986, which promptly secured contracts with ten independent film companies.[103] Finally, IATSE president Walsh visited the negotiations between Local 839 and the AFPA and forged an agreement securing nothing but a few token salary increases—no residuals, no runaway clause, no Animation Basic Local. The membership was so upset that it rejected the contract offer, prompting Walsh to threaten the "unruly" local with disciplinary action. The subject of residuals would not be brought up again until 1994. The fiasco of the 1969–1970 contract negotiations left the union weakened and divided between the above-the-line animators and writers and the below-the-line inkers and painters.

The cartoonists began the next decade with $9 million in television production on the slate for 1970, but by 1979 that number had shrunk and the industry had become more reliant than ever on global labor.[104] The MPSC estimated that 75 percent of work was being sent overseas. Lou Scheimer, president of Filmation Studios, the only major producer of Saturday morning cartoons to keep all production in the United States, told the *Los Angeles Times* that some network contracts *required* programs be produced overseas to save costs.[105] Producers estimated a studio could "cut total production costs nearly 50% by having the work done in Korea, Spain, Taiwan, Australia and other countries."[106]

In the contract negotiations of 1979, a runaway clause was at the top of the agenda, and Local 839's membership approved a strike if necessary. It was the ink and paint jobs, still performed primarily by women, that were being sent overseas. Business agent Bud Hester cited a shift in the demographics of the union's female members as contributing to a renewed activist spirit: "Nine-tenths of our women are self-supporting. Before, most of them were married, and they accepted the five or six months of employment and then collected their unemployment checks. Now we have a lot more women who need a steady pay-check coming in."[107]

The walkout was timed to coincide with the animated television industry's late summer production peak, targeting only Hanna-Barbera, Ruby-Spears, and DePatie-Freleng Enterprises, which together produced the bulk of children's network programming. The strategy worked. Local 839 got its runaway clause, which stipulated that producers could not send work overseas unless every local union member was already employed.[108] This was an important, but, as it would turn out, short-lived victory.

When the Local 839 contract came up for negotiation again in 1982, the producers, who by then had joined the major Hollywood studios in the Alliance of Motion Picture and Television Producers (AMPTP), demanded the removal of the runaway clause. Local 839 stood its ground and called for another strike, but this time, rather than targeting a few key studios, the entire membership walked out. Unfortunately for Local 839, having learned from 1979, the producers had stockpiled material in advance so they could meet the fall schedule deadline, and since IATSE president Walter Diehl had not approved the strike, he gave other IA locals permission to cross Local 839's picket lines.

As the strike dragged on, old divisions within the union were reawakened: because the inkers and painters had not supported the animators in 1969, the animators were not enthusiastic about supporting them in 1982. Animators began doing scab work at home. Then a Disney lawyer found a loophole in the union contract that allowed members to resign from the union, relinquishing voting rights but retaining the right to be protected by union rules and to receive health and pension benefits, which instigated mass union resignations at Disney and Don Bluth Productions. From its high of 2,079 in 1979, membership in Local 839 plummeted to 866. After ten weeks, the strike effort imploded. Local 839 had to sign a humiliating contract: no runaway clause, seniority clauses compromised, and amnesty for all artists who had done scab work.

The union was so weakened that DIC, a French animation company, was able to set up in Los Angeles in 1983 as a nonunion shop with the bulk of production being done cheaply overseas.[109] In 1984, Don Bluth refused to renew his union contract and in 1989 moved his entire Sullivan Bluth Studios to Ireland, taking advantage of tax incentives there.[110] In 1985, Walt Disney, under the management of Michael Eisner, moved its meager animation staff of 125 off the Burbank lot to an industrial building in Glendale and sold two series, *The Gummi Bears* (NBC) and *Wuzzles* (CBS), to be animated completely overseas.[111] Filmation, champion of union labor, began slipping into the red in 1987 and was forced to send work abroad before selling out completely to a Swiss company in 1988.[112]

In perhaps the most degrading blow, Local 839 was omitted from the IATSE Studio Basic Agreement of 1985. By 1988, Local 841 in New York had become so small that it had to merge with the IA Cameramen, Local 644, before disappearing altogether.[113]

The 1990s Animation Boom, Followed by a Bust

Suddenly, in 1990, after decades of struggle, the animation industry experienced a renaissance sparked by the success of Disney's animated feature *The Little Mermaid* and Fox Television's *The Simpsons*, both premiering in 1989. In response, Warner Bros., Twentieth Century-Fox, and the newly launched DreamWorks SKG started feature animation divisions. Three independently produced animated series on the Nickelodeon network, *Doug*, *Rugrats*, and *Ren & Stimpy*, were so successful that, in 1992, Nickelodeon also launched its own animation studio. Suddenly animation was hot, and the studios could not get enough qualified people.[114] Unfortunately, this increased demand did not mean more members for Local 839 because new independent production companies such as Klasky-Csupo, Spümcø, and Film Roman were nonunion shops, as was Pixar, the rising star of computer animation in Northern California.

Because the staffs of Fox Television's *The Simpsons*, *King of the Hill* (both animated by Film Roman), and *Family Guy* (Fuzzy Door) were not represented by MPSC Local 839, the WGA was able to unionize their writers in 1998. Historically, at union animation studios, writers were members of the animators' union because theatrical animated shorts and features were drawn out on storyboards rather than scripted. In television animation, scripted writing became more common to facilitate the tight turnaround times.[115] Had these production companies been union shops, their writers would have been members of Local 839, but because they were not, the writers were up for grabs. This uncomfortable situation also drew attention to the fact that WGA writers were higher paid than animation writers belonging to Local 839, a serious problem that was still unresolved as of 2023.[116]

Meanwhile, the success of feature animation underscored another unhappy fact: the animators were the only artists not earning residuals. According to Sito, "A chorus singer in New York on the *Beauty and the Beast* soundtrack got a bonus check from Disney of $175,000, the artist who drew the characters got a one-time unofficial bonus of around $5,000." In 1994, Local 839 began laying the groundwork for a lawsuit to sue for residuals, but key Disney animators backed down. With so many animators working nonunion in television, Local 839 did not have the solidarity or strength to push the issue further.

Inevitably, the boom that expanded the industry too far and too fast went bust. By 1999, the *Los Angeles Times* reported that the days of large salaries for animators were ending: "Chastened by pricey box-office disappointments, runaway costs and competing animated movies . . . profit-starved studios are cutting back on the number of films they release, trimming fat production deals and scrutinizing costs."[117] Local 839 was further weakened by the shift to computer-based animation precipitated by the success of nonunion Pixar's *Toy Story* in 1995. The major studios (such as Disney and DreamWorks) were union shops, but they partnered with independent computer animation studios such as Pixar and Pacific Data Images, which were not.

In 2001, the Academy Awards debuted the new Best Animated Feature category, and while this seemed to signal that the field of animation was at last getting Hollywood recognition, this was also the year Sito dubbed "The Year from Hell." In March, Disney announced plans to lay off 4,000 employees and scale back feature animation.[118] Artists with decades of experience were told they must transition to computer animation or be replaced. Local 839 lost 1,000 union jobs between 1998 and 2001 as members migrated to lower-paying, nonunion positions. By 2003, one-third of Local 839's members had lost their jobs, and there were five suicides among them.[119] Perhaps to reframe its relevance and scope, Local 839 changed its name from the Motion Picture Screen Cartoonists to The Animation Guild in 2002.[120]

The volatility of this period was apparent as Paramount, Fox, and Warner Bros. closed their feature animation units and, in March 2002, Disney announced more layoffs. From a high of 2,200 animation employees in 1998, Disney's staff dropped to 600 by January 2004. The company closed its Florida animation studio and announced its partnership with Pixar would end in 2005. Subsequently, Disney's stock fell as Pixar's rose. This was but one factor signaling a new era for the animation industry. Another was the proliferation of series animation, which came to be seen as a reliable source of relatively inexpensive programming for cable networks, and later for streaming services. One industry analyst in 2007 told the *Los Angeles Times*: "It's convenient filler material and it's replayable for generations into the future."[121]

Stabilization in this sector of the industry enabled TAG to make dramatic progress in unionizing previously nonunion companies, including Nickelodeon in 2002 and DPS Film Roman in 2004.[122] TAG's membership bounced back from 1,600 in 2004 to 2,400 in 2008, to 4,500 in 2019, and to approximately 6,000 in 2022.[123] The union was at last experiencing steady growth, but after over three decades of struggle, it had a lot of ground to make up in its contracts. They still included neither residuals nor parity for their writers, nor protections against runaway production.

Animation's New Deal and New National Status

Because the animation industry had been dealing with remote, global production since the 1960s, practices and pipelines were already in place that enabled production to continue when the COVID-19 pandemic shut down live-action filming in 2020–2021.[124] This put TAG in an unusually strong position when its contract came up for renewal in July 2021. Although its negotiations were postponed because IA Master Agreement negotiations continued into the fall, the delay gave TAG valuable time to mobilize. Members took to social media, rallying support under the hashtag #NewDeal4Animation, while the executive board launched the Tactical Action Group (TAG-TAG) focused on member outreach to record and address members' concerns and to foster a sense of unity and determination.

Writers' pay was high on the negotiating agenda. Going into negotiations, the weekly minimum pay for animation writers was $2,064, while WGA rates ranged from $4,063 to $5,185.[125] Another priority was the substantial pay gap between color designers and character and background designers. Teri Hendrich Cusumano, chair of the Color Design Committee, argued this reflected an age-old gender bias as color designers, the digital descendants of inkers and painters, tended to be women.[126]

Perhaps the most urgent issue on the table involved a 2009 addendum to the basic contract, Sideletter N, which addressed "new media," namely, "productions made for distribution via the internet."[127] In the early days of the internet, Sideletter N originally allowed for "freely negotiable terms and conditions," that could mean much longer hours and lower pay than for television series work. In 2015 and 2018, Sideletter N was adjusted, but streaming services such as Netflix and Amazon Prime were still able to pay far less than the industry standard for original animated series.

After six months of negotiation, from November 29, 2021, to May 27, 2022, TAG got its new deal. Although it did not win everything it had wanted, the new contract corrected outdated categorizations, and structures were realigned to address the complexities of the contemporary industry. Among TAG's victories was a general 3 percent wage increase, the establishment of a minimum wage for high-budget streaming content, and an additional 4 to 12 percent wage increase for color designers. Significantly, for the first time, animation writers were granted their own job classification and framework for a standardized means of advancement. While these measures did not immediately remove wage disparities for animation writers and color designers, they were strong first steps and laid the groundwork for future improvements. Other highlights from the contract included the creation of the Labor-Management Cooperative Committee and of "a pathway to union-covered remote work outside of L.A. County." Perhaps the most dramatic success came in the form of an 87 percent ratification vote from a turnout *three times* that of the preceding ratification vote (figure 8.2).[128]

This was only the prelude to TAG's recent historic achievements. Under the current leadership of President Janet Moreno King, business manager Steve Kaplan, and organizers Ben Speight and Allison Smartt, TAG has expanded its reach to workers outside the Los Angeles area and to categories of workers not previously represented. In January of 2022, workers at Titmouse Animation in New York voted to join TAG, followed by the crew of *Tooning Out the News* in September. In April 2023, Powerhouse Animation joined TAG from deep in the heart of the right-to-work state of Texas, followed in July by the workers at Gladius Studios in San Juan, Puerto Rico.[129]

Their efforts were rewarded at IATSE's midsummer 2023 meeting when the general executive board voted unanimously to grant Local 839 national jurisdiction over animation workers. As Kaplan reported: "President Loeb remarked that he sees TAG has made a commitment and dedicated the necessary resources to our growth, which has made us one of the most aggressive organizing Locals in the IATSE. As such we deserve the national jurisdiction."[130] TAG's new status may not change much for current members, but it secures their reach and industry status and paves the way for a national standard for animation work and wages—the very goal that Pepe Ruiz struggled for in the 1940s and 1950s.[131]

TAG has also expanded its jurisdiction by unionizing the previously excluded categories of production and remote workers. Production workers had been considered "management," and therefore exempt, but by early 2023 TAG had unionized this group of workers on the shows *Rick and Morty*, *Solar Opposites*, *The Simpsons*, *Family Guy*, and *American Dad!* and at Titmouse, Shadowland, and Nickelodeon studios. TAG was met with resistance at Walt Disney Animation, which requested a determination by the NLRB.[132] This stalled the matter for 267 days, but the NLRB ultimately authorized a vote, which was carried by 93 percent.[133] One month later, a group of ten Disney Animation Studios employees working remotely across six states followed suit, filing for an NLRB election of their own, marking yet another historic first.[134]

During this same period of growth for TAG, IATSE made bold moves to unionize VFX and video game workers, recognizing parallels and overlaps between these two crafts and animation.[135] TAG organizer Ben Speight has been instrumental in the VFX effort, which won its first victories in August 2023 when VFX workers at Marvel and Walt Disney Pictures voted to unionize.[136]

FIGURE 8.2 Animation Guild "Union Strong" graphic from *Keyframe*, Spring 2022. (Courtesy of The Animation Guild.)

The Gameworkers union got underway the following month with a unanimous vote of the workers at Workinman Interactive of New York.[137] These fledgling unions will be looking to TAG as a model and inspiration.

Conclusion

We can learn several things from the history of these animators' unions. For producers there is a cautionary tale. Disney's infamous 1941 animators strike has perhaps given the studio a reputation for being unfriendly to labor, but in the eighty-plus years since Disney Animation became a closed shop, there has been relatively little labor-related unrest there. Clearly, unionization did not put it out of business nor even hamper it in the long run. On the other hand, those that tried to escape unionization by relocating, such as the Fleischer Studios and Sullivan Bluth Studios, eventually shuttered.

For union members, TAG demonstrates that tenacity pays off in the long game. TAG has certainly had its lean decades when demise seemed inevitable, but in 2023 it was nearly 6,000 strong and was ushering in a new era of solidarity and expansion as it pushed for meaningful changes to adapt to the complexities of the twenty-first century globalized workforce. The animators' successes are carving out a path for their fellow artists in the visual effects and gaming sectors to follow.

Notes

1 Tom Sito, *Drawing the Line: The Untold Story of the Animation Unions from Bosko to Bart Simpson* (University Press of Kentucky, 2006), loc. 921, Kindle.

2 Charles Solomon, *Enchanted Drawings: The History of Animation* (Random House, 1994), 68–69.

3 Sito, *Drawing the Line*, loc. 921–936, 1280.

4 Harvey Raphael Deneroff, "Popeye the Union Man: A Historical Study of the Fleischer Strike" (PhD diss., University of Southern California, 1985), 88–90.

5 Gerald M. Monroe, "The Artists Union of New York" (PhD diss., New York University, 1971), 187–188.

6 Ida Jeter, "The Collapse of the Federated Motion Picture Crafts: A Case Study of Class Collaboration in the Motion Picture Industry," *Journal of the University Film Association* 31, no. 2 (Spring 1979): 41.

7 Richard Fleischer, *Out of the Inkwell: Max Fleischer and the Animation Revolution* (University Press of Kentucky, 2005), loc. 723–724, Kindle.

8 See "Pickets Swarm at Midtown Shops," *New York Times*, August 1, 1937, 1–2; and "LaGuardia Offers Aid," *Motion Picture Herald*, July 3, 1937, 14.

9 "A. F. L. Film Union Named: Labor Board Rules It Is Agency for Fleischer Employees," *New York Times*, September 13, 1937, 2.

10 Sito, *Drawing the Line*, loc. 1162–1168.

11 See Jerry Fairbanks and Robert Carlisle, prods., "The Fleischer Studios in Florida," *Popular Science*, Episode 5 (Paramount Pictures, 1938), 6:33.

12 Deneroff, "Popeye the Union Man," 288–289, 230–231.

13 Sito, *Drawing the Line*, loc. 1168–1194.

14 Solomon, *Enchanted Drawings*, 66–67, 82–83.

15 Sito, *Drawing the Line*, loc. 1197–1214.

16 "Schlesinger Named in Labor Complaint," *Motion Picture Daily*, January 2, 1938, 2.

17 "NLRB Rules Studios Must Deal with Cartoon Union," *Boxoffice*, January 20 1940, 32.

18 "Independent Guild for Fox White Collars," *Boxoffice*, November 2, 1940, 23.

19 "The Screen Cartoonists Guild Won Another Victory . . . ," *Motion Picture Herald*, February 15, 1941, 48; "Averting a Threatened Strike, George Pal Productions," *Boxoffice*, March 1, 1941, 87.

20 "Schlesinger Closes Studio," *The Exhibitor*, May 21, 1941, 8.

21 Testimony of Herbert K. Sorrell and George Bodle, *Jurisdictional Disputes in the Motion Picture Industry,* Hearings Before a Special Subcommittee on Education and Labor, House of Representatives, Eighth Congress, Second Session, Volume 3, February 25, 26, 27, March 1, 2, 3, 4, 5, 9, 10, 11, 12, 16, and 17, 1948, printed for the use of the Committee on Education and Labor, 1912, https://archive.org/details /jurisdictionaldio3unit.

22 Sito, *Drawing the Line*, loc. 1304–1305.

23 Neal Gabler, *Walt Disney: The Triumph of the American Imagination* (Alfred A. Knopf, 2006), 584–591.

24 Michael Barrier, *Hollywood Cartoons* (Oxford University Press, 1999), 283.

25 Jake S. Friedman, "Picket Lines in Paradise," *American History*, June 2017, 45.

26 Gabler, *Walt Disney*, 585–587.

27 "File Labor Charge against Disney," *Boxoffice*, February 8, 1941, 37.

28 Douglas Gomery, "Disney Business History: A Reinterpretation," in *Disney Discourse: Producing the Magic Kingdom*, ed. Eric Smoodin (Routledge, 1994), 74.

29 Barrier, *Hollywood Cartoons*, 285–286; "Screen Cartoon Guild Votes Strike at Disney's Tomorrow," *Los Angeles Times* (hereafter *LAT*), May 27, 1941, 1.

30 Jake S. Friedman, *Disney Revolt: The Great Labor War of Animation's Golden Age* (Chicago Review Press, 2022), 188–213.

31 Thomas Brady, "Whimsy on Strike," *New York Times*, June 29, 1941, 1.

32 In addition to Sito, *Drawing the Line*; Gabler, *Walt Disney*; Barrier, *Hollywood Cartoons*; Mike Nielsen and Gene Mailes, *Hollywood's Other Blacklist: Union Struggles in the Studio System* (London: BFI, 1995); and Friedman, *Disney Revolt*. See also *American Experience*, season 28, episodes 1–2, "Walt Disney," directed by Sarah Colt, aired September 13 and 14, 2015, on PBS.

33 Laurie Pintar, "Herbert K. Sorrell as the Grade-B Hero: Militancy and Masculinity in the Studios," *Labor History* 37, no. 3 (June 1, 1996): 395.

34 Marc Eliot, *Walt Disney: Hollywood's Dark Prince* (Birch Lane, 1993), loc. 2489–2490, Kindle.

35 Noell Wolfgram Evans, "Popeye Pickets and Other Exploits in Animation Unions." *Written By* 12, no. 5 (2008): 60.

36 Jack Kinney, *Walt Disney and Other Assorted Characters* (Harmony Books, 1988), 138; Eliot, loc. 1157.

37 "Bioff Gives Himself Up: Union Leader Accused of Extortion Released on Surety of $25,000," *LAT*, May 25, 1941, 1.

38 Nielsen and Mailes, *Hollywood's Other Blacklist*, 67.

39 George H. Dunne, *Hollywood Labor Dispute: A Study in Immorality* (Conference Publishing, 1950), 2–4.

40 J. A. Aberdeen, *Hollywood Renegades: The Society of Independent Motion Picture Producers* (Cobblestone Entertainment, 2000), 81.

41 "Pickets at Disney's Call 'Em 'Goons,'" *Daily News*, July 10, 1941, 5.

42 Testimony of Herbert K. Sorrell, *Jurisdictional Disputes In the Motion Picture Industry*, 1908.

43 Gabler, *Walt Disney*, 604; *Jurisdiction Disputes*, 1908–1909.

44 "Dear Walt," *Daily Variety*, July 3, 1941.

45 "Nine Unions End Strike at Disney's," *LAT*, July 9, 1941, 10.

46 Herbert Knott Sorrell, *You Don't Choose Your Friends: The Memoirs of Herbert Knott Sorrell*, interviewed by Elizabeth I. Dixon, UCLA Oral History Project, 1963, 70–71.

47 "Disney Studio Strike Ends; Unionists Back to Jobs Today," *LAT*, July 29, 1941, A3.

48 Among other measures, they cut off the studio's food service and put a moratorium on feature films not already in production. See Gabler, *Walt Disney*, 613–614.

49 "Disney Peace Seen," *The Exhibitor*, September 17, 1941, 17.

50 Friedman, *Disney Revolt*, 235–236; Sito, *Drawing the Line*, loc. 1657–1674.

51 Letter from Pepe Ruiz to Herb Sorrell, April 11, 1945, Motion Picture Screen Cartoonists Guild, Local 839 Collection, 1937–1951, Cal State University Northridge, Oviatt Library Special Collections (hereafter MPSC Collection), Box 1, Folder 5.

52 Arthur Ungar, "Bye, Bye Bioff," *Variety*, November 12, 1941, 3; "Studio Unions Conference Elects Temporary Officers," *Film Daily*, November 12, 1941, 7.

53 John Cogley, "Report on Blacklisting," Fund for the Republic, 1956, 53.

54 "Animated Producers to Meet Tomorrow," *Film Daily*, March 17, 1943, 2.

55 Sito, Drawing the Line, loc. 1838–1839.

56 Letter from Shirley Knoring, Recording Secretary, Local 1461 to Herb Sorrell, President, Conference of Studio Unions and attached Resolution (April 11, 1945), MPSC Collection, Box 1, Folder 5.

57 Sito, *Drawing the Line*, loc. 2293–2320.

58 "Par Cartoonists Agree to Union Contract, Up to Coast Wages," *Variety*, January 30, 1946, 13.

59 Letter from Herb Sorrell to Pepe Ruiz, February 7, 1946, MPSC Collection, Box 1, Folder 6.

60 "Cartoonists Vote against Strike," *Motion Picture Daily*, March 1, 1946, 7.

61 Letter from Pepe Ruiz to Herb Sorrell, July 12, 1946, MPSC Collection, Box 1, Folder 6; Telegram from Pepe Ruiz to Herb Sorrell, July 15, 1946, MPSC Collection, Box 1, Folder 6.

62 Letter from Pepe Ruiz to Herb Sorrell, May 9, 1946, MPSC Collection, Box 1, Folder 6.

63 Letter from Pepe Ruiz to Herb Sorrell, July 20, 1946, MPSC Collection, Box 1, Folder 6.

64 "25% Wage Increases to N.Y. Cartoonists," *Motion Picture Daily*, February 4, 1947, 11.

65 Telegram from Pepe Ruiz to Herb Sorrell, January 15, 1947, MPSC Collection, Box 1, Folder 7.

66 Telegram from Julie to Pepe Ruiz, March 3, 1947, MPSC Collection, Box 1, Folder 7.

67 "Break Off Wage Talk in 'Lab' Controversy," *Boxoffice*, May 24, 1947, 45.

68 Letter from Pepe Ruiz to Herb Sorrell, April 13, 1947, MPSC Collection, Box 1, Folder 8; "Green Will Call Meeting to End Hollywood Strike," *Motion Picture Daily*, April 26, 1947, 16.

69 Letter from Pepe Ruiz to Herb Sorrell, July 13, 1947, MPSC Collection, Box 1, Folder 8.

70 Letter from Herb Sorrell to Pepe Ruiz, July 16, 1947, MPSC Collection, Box 1, Folder 8.

71 Testimony of Walter E. Disney, Hearings Regarding Communist Infiltration of the Motion Picture Industry Before the Committee on Un-American Activities House of Representatives, Eighth Congress, First Session, October 20, 21, 22, 23, 24, 27, 28, 29 and 30, 1947, printed for the use of the Un-American Activities Committee, 282–285, https://archive.org/details/hearingsregardin1947aunit.

72 "CSU Strike Nears Fadeout as Studio Painters Local Votes Return to Work," *Variety*, October 29, 1947, 6.

73 Sito, *Drawing the Line*, loc. 2359–2366.

74 Sorrell, *You Don't Choose Your Friends*, 222–224.

75 Letter from Bill Littlejohn to Pepe Ruiz, June 14, 1950, MPSC Collection, Box 1, Folder 9.

76 Letter from Pepe Ruiz to Herb Sorrell, December 13, 1950, MPSC Collection, Box 1, Folder 11.

77 "11 Eastern Unions in a United Front," *Variety*, October 6, 1948, 6.

78 Letter from Pepe Ruiz to Herb Sorrell, January 27, 1949, MPSC Collection, Box 1, Folder 9.

79 Letter from Pepe Ruiz to Bill Littlejohn, October 20, 1950, MPSC Collection, Box 1, Folder 9.

80 Letters from Bill Littlejohn to Pepe Ruiz, October 30 and November 2, 1950, MPSC Collection, Box 1, Folder 11.

81 Adam Abraham, *When Magoo Flew: The Rise and Fall of Animation Studio UPA* (Wesleyan University Press, 2012), 124–126.

82 Karl Cohen, "Blacklisted Animators," in *Animation: Art and Industry*, ed. Maureen Furniss (Indiana University Press, 2012), 166.

83 Letter from Bill Littlejohn to Pepe Ruiz, December 6, 1950, MPSC Collection, Box 1, Folder 11.

84 Karl Cohen, "Toontown's Reds: HUAC's Investigation of Alleged Communists in the Animation Industry," *Film History* 5, no. 2 (June 1993): 192–193.

85 Keith Scott, *The Moose That Roared: The Story of Jay Ward, Bill Scott, a Flying Squirrel, and a Talking Moose* (St. Martin's Griffin: 2001), 41–42.

86 "News in Brief," *Motion Picture Daily*, January 25, 1952, 3. Bill Scott, the writer fired from UPA, became the independent SCG's first post-schism president, and Bill Melendez, its business agent.

87 Cohen, "Blacklisted Animators," 165–166.

88 Abraham, *When Magoo Flew*, 129–131. Hubley was unofficially blacklisted and forced to use a front for a few years, but he went on to win three Oscars, two Annecy Awards, one Annie, and one Jury Prize at Cannes for his short films, coproduced by his wife, Faith.

89 "'IA' Now Dominates Cartoonist Field," *Film Daily*, April 30, 1952, 1.

90 Evans, "Popeye Pickets," 63.

91 Sito, *Drawing the Line*, loc. 2414–2415, 2479–2485.

92 Dave Glickman, "Hollywood Boom: Video Spurs Employment," *Broadcasting*, October 15, 1951, 73.

93 Sito, *Drawing the Line*, loc. 2505–2533.

94 Maureen Furniss, *A New History of Animation* (Thames & Hudson), 2016: 218–224.

95 Sito, *Drawing the Line*, loc. 2255–2527.

96 Scott, *Moose That Roared*, 74–85.

97 Steve Hulett, "When Local 839 Fought for Residuals," The Animation Guild (blog), July 5, 2006, http://animationguildblog.blogspot.com/2006/07/when-local-839 -fought-for-residuals.html.

98 "After a Long, Lean Time, Animators Are Back in Demand," *LAT*, August 19, 1990, 1.

99 Evans, "Popeye Pickets," 63.

100 "Cartoonists List Demands in New Contract Bargaining," *Broadcasting*, June 20, 1955, 86.

101 Sito, *Drawing the Line*, loc. 2735–2738.

102 "Pictures: IA Cartoonists in Strike Posture," *Variety*, July 30, 1969, 30; Sito, *Drawing the Line*, loc. 2743–2759.

103 "At Deadline: Cartoon Strike Threat," *Broadcasting*, July 21, 1969, 9.

104 "Cartoonists as Exception to Product Slump," *Variety*, March 11, 1970, 36.

105 Tim Waters, "800 Film Cartoonists Threaten Strike: Walkout Planned Monday over Work Being Sent Overseas," *LAT*, August 11, 1979, A20.

106 Tim Waters and Harry Bernstein, "Cartoonists May Be Ordered Back: Unionist Expected to End Walkout by 1,200 Cartoonist Strike," *LAT*, August 15, 1979, E1.

107 Waters, "800 Film Cartoonists Threaten Strike."

108 Evans, "Popeye Pickets," 64.

109 Daniel Akst, "DIC Enterprises Emerges as Animation Industry Giant Studio City Firm Changing Saturday Mornings," *LAT*, May 28, 1985, 2.

110 Jack Mathews. "The Old Magic Is Back: Irish Heat," *LAT*, November 12, 1989, 6.

111 Ellen Farley, "Disney Animators Fear for Future," *LAT*, February 7, 1985, 1.

112 James Bates, "Animation in Red Ink Cartoon Factory Filmation Is under Orders to Cut Costs, and a Plan to Shift Some of Its Production Overseas Has Alienated Workers," *LAT* (Valley Edition), August 25, 1987, 9A.

113 Tom Sito, "Guild History: The '50s through the '90s," The Animation Guild, accessed May 16, 2024, https://animationguild.org/about-the-guild/the50s-the90s/.

114 Charles Solomon, "After a Long Lean Time, Animators Are Back in Demand," *LAT*, August 19, 1990, F94.

115 Lorenza Munoz, "Action Continues on Animated Programs; Most Shows Don't Fall under WGA Contracts, a Boon to Nickelodeon and Cartoon Network," *LAT*, December 17, 2007, C1.

116 Ryan Faughnder, "No Picketing for Pixar? Why a Writers' Strike Won't Hobble Animation Studios," *LAT*, April 27, 2017, https://www.latimes.com/business /hollywood/la-fi-ct-writers-strike-animation-20170426-story.html.

117 Claudia Eller and James Bates, "Animators' Days of Drawing Big Salaries Are Ending," *LAT*, June 24, 1999, 1.

118 Claudia Eller and James Bates, "Company Town: Disney Plans Big Cuts in Feature Animation; Entertainment," *LAT*, April 24, 2001, C1.

119 Tom Sito, "The Year from Hell: State of the Industry: 2001: Hard Times in Toon Town," *Millimeter* 29, no. 12 (December 2001): 18, 20; Sito, *Drawing the Line*, loc. 3910–3912.

120 Staff and Wire Service, "Briefcase: Valley Edition," *Daily News*, August 10, 2002, B3.

121 Munoz, "Action Continues on Animated Programs."

122 Evans, "Popeye Pickets," 64; Sarah Baisley, "DPS Film Roman Joins Animation Union Merriment," *Animation World Network*, December 14, 2004, https://www .awn.com/news/dps-film-roman-joins-animation-union-merriment.

123 George Lynell, "Out of the Picture: Toontown Darkens for L.A.'s Animation Artists, as Computers and an Overseas Workforce Overtake Their Future," *LAT*, March 21, 2004, E1; Bob Strauss, "Animation Jobs Are Booming in Southern California. Here's What It Takes to Get Them," *San Gabriel Valley Tribune*, January 25, 2019.

124 Aaron Simpson, "For the Animation Industry, the Coronavirus Crisis Has Created a Big Opportunity," *Cartoon Brew*, May 1, 2020, https://www.cartoonbrew.com /ideas-commentary/for-the-animation-industry-the-coronavirus-crisis-has-created -a-big-opportunity-189911.html.

125 Gene Maddaus, "Animation Writers Hope to Close Pay Gap with Their Live-Action Counterparts," *Variety*, November 23, 2021, https://variety.com/2021/film /news/animation-writers-animation-guild-labor-negotiations-1235118230/.

126 Gene Maddaus, "New Animation Contract Narrows Gender Gap," *Variety*, July 5, 2022, https://variety.com/2022/tv/news/animation-guild-new-contract-ratified -1235309449/.

127 "What You Need to Know about Sideletter N," The Animation Guild (blog), accessed May 17, 2024, https://animationguild.org/sideletter-n/.

128 "New Deal 4 Animation," The Amination Guild, accessed March 22, 2023, https://animationguild.org/ratify22/.

129 Jamie Lang, "Workers at Texas' Powerhouse Animation Become First Group from a Right-to-Work State to Join the Animation Guild," *Cartoon Brew*, April 25, 2023, https://www.cartoonbrew.com/artist-rights/powerhouse-animation-studios-tag -union-vote-228190.html; Amid Amidi, "Animation Workers at Puerto Rico's Gladius Studios Vote to Unionize with Animation Guild," *Cartoon Brew*, July 18, 2023, https://www.cartoonbrew.com/artist-rights/animation-workers-at-puerto -ricos-gladius-studios-vote-to-unionize-with-animation-guild-230687.html.

130 Steve Kaplan, "From the Business Representative, Steve Kaplan," *The Pegboard* 52, no. 8 (August 2023): 6–7.

131 Paula Spence, "Our Union: Going National!," *The Pegboard* 52, no. 8 (August 2023): 3.

132 Katie Kilkenny, "Behind the Animation Guild's Push to Organize Production Workers," *THR*, June 16, 2022, https://www.hollywoodreporter.com/business /business-news/animation-union-pushes-production-workers-strategy-labor-katie

-kilkenny-1235164936/; Jamie Lang, "Walt Disney Animation Studios Production Workers, Artists Hold Solidarity March as Studio Refuses to Recognize Bargaining Unit," *Cartoon Brew*, April 4, 2023, https://www.cartoonbrew.com/artist-rights /walt-disney-animation-studios-production-workers-march-227572.html. The production workers category includes production managers, supervisors, coordinators, assistants, and writers' assistants.

133 Michael Zee, "Walt Disney Animation Studios Production Workers Vote to Unionize with IATSE," *Variety*, November 1, 2023, https://variety.com/2023/film /news/walt-disney-animation-studios-production-workers-vote-to-unionize-iatse -1235776929/

134 "Historic Unionization Effort: Animation Workers at Walt Disney Animation Studios' Traveling Lab Organize to Secure Remote Work Inclusion," press release, November 29, 2023, https://twitter.com/iatse/status/1729951943252951289?s=61&t =1iSlHTxmW9wloFP2s4gWTg.

135 "Growing Our Union Further—Animation, VFX and Gameworkers Win a Seat at the Table," IATSE, February 6, 2023, http://iatse.net/growing-our-union-further/.

136 Jazz Tangcay, "Disney and Marvel VFX Unionization Likely to Spur More: This Is about 'Respect for the Work We Do,'" *Variety*, October 3, 2023, https://variety.com /2023/artisans/news/marvel-disney-vfx-artists-unionize-iatse-1235733825/

137 "Workinman Interactive Workers Unanimously Unionize in Historic Labor Board Vote," IATSE, September 27, 2023, https://iatse.net/workinman-interactive-workers -unanimously-unionize-in-historic-labor-board-vote/.

Part II

The Guilds

• •

Hollywood's Creative Class

KATE FORTMUELLER

> They've tricked us into thinking we can't
> do it without them. The truth is they
> can't do anything of value without us.
> —Charlie Kaufman, Writers Guild of
> America Awards, 2023

Upon receiving the 2023 Screen Laurel Award from the Writers Guild of America (WGA) for his work advancing the literature of film, Charlie Kaufman took a moment to reflect on the value of creative labor and the fundamental tensions of the film industry. On the one side, there are the writers, directors, and actors (not to mention all the crew members) who are responsible for the creative vision and the actual work that attracts audiences. On the other, there are the agents, producers, studios, and networks responsible for shouldering the financial risks of getting a project off the ground and, ultimately, to audiences. Film and television needs artists, but it also needs money, and tensions typically arise when film financing becomes more important than film art (or even old-fashioned entertainment).

Two months after Kaufman's rousing call to attention, the WGA went on strike. Studios, networks, and streaming services, collectively represented by the Alliance of Motion Picture and Television Producers (AMPTP), offered marginal increases on residuals and refused to discuss changes to writers' rooms and the future of artificial intelligence in writing. As they had done at the start of past negotiations that resulted in strikes, they lamented soaring production costs. The actions of the other two above-the-line unions reflected their relative positions in the WGA's fight. The Directors Guild of America (DGA) entered negotiations and quickly struck a deal, while the Screen Actors Guild–American Federation of Television and Radio Artists (SAG-AFTRA) overwhelmingly authorized a strike and walked out of negotiations on July 14, marking the beginning of the first dual strike since 1960 and fundamentally reshaping how we are to understand the above-the-line unions and their work.

The myriad images of celebrity actors, directors, and writers walking picket lines in front of the studio gates reflect the popular conception of these so-called above-the-line professions. But the keen eye might notice there are far more picketers behind them who are not well known or famous. The WGA, SAG-AFTRA, and the DGA represent familiar, critically lauded writers, directors, and stars, but they also represent journeyman actors, background performers, unit production managers, and assistant directors, and are joined by "pre-WGA" aspirants. Many in the guilds are not as famous or as rich as the public assumes, but instead work sporadically and often not enough to qualify for health benefits through the union, which was stressed on the unions' social media sites and used as talking points in reporting during the 2023 strikes.[1] Some writers, actors, and directors have the leverage to negotiate favorable terms; however, as Miranda Banks writes in chapter 9, "In a book called *Hollywood Unions*, writers and readers alike must weigh the opportunities and the struggles of being a member of a unionized labor force."

Unions can offer bargaining benefits to their members that they could not achieve on their own, but the decision to unionize antagonizes employers. Historically, given the close relationships between studio heads, producers, directors, writers, and stars, this tension has been one of the core dilemmas of the prestigious above-the-line unions since their formation in the 1930s. The WGA, SAG, and the DGA were formed as a response to Depression-era cuts only when writers, actors, and directors realized that their creative importance, individuality, and fame were all irrelevant to studios that chose to see them as bloated budget lines. Every time studios (and now networks and streamers) lament the high cost of production, the above-the-line unions realize the protection offered by their unions. But often those lessons get lost amid internal conflicts stemming from the professional diversity within these glamorous unions. In addition to wage and residual increases, the guilds have focused more on ephemeral values such as professionalism and prestige over the kinds of quality-of-work-life negotiations that are the focus of the International Alliance of Theatrical Stage Employees (IATSE) locals.

Elite members of the WGA, SAG-AFTRA, and the DGA bring visibility to their unions as they win accolades at union award shows, through photo ops such as that of Tom Hanks speaking at a rally for SAG's commercial strike in 2000, or through features such as the one in *The Nation* in 2023 with Fran Drescher, the SAG-AFTRA president and former star of *The Nanny*. Although the most famous members are the most visible, these members often benefit the least from union negotiations. Terms negotiated by the unions represent minimums for members, which means the elite members do not benefit from the salary and pension negotiations as much as they do the work conditions, health benefits, and residuals. Above-the-line unions, which set hours, overtime, minimum rates, credit, and residuals, primarily benefit the middle class of Hollywood workers who cannot rely on the strength of their names as leverage for back-end participation.

There are many bargaining affinities between the WGA, SAG-AFTRA, and the DGA, even if the unions have not always stood in solidarity. In 2023 the unions made history when they all stood in solidarity with the striking writers and actors either on the picket lines or, in the case of IATSE and the Teamsters, by helping shut down productions by promising not to cross active picket lines. The above-the-line unions have practiced pattern bargaining, which means that successful bargaining for one union sets a precedent for terms that the other unions can expect during their negotiations. Thus, this kind of solidarity is mutually beneficial even if it is rare.

The above-the-line unions are linked even more so by professional and cultural similarities, as well as claims to prestige. This is different than the IATSE below-the-line locals, which have shared organizational histories and numerous jurisdictional battles that have led to their current structure and division of locals. Each chapter in this part of the book illuminates the histories as well as the professional and cultural specificity of the above-the-line unions. This introduction focuses on their commonalities, conflicts, and the key challenges that sometimes unite the WGA, SAG-AFTRA, and the DGA in strikes and other times puts them at odds.

Professionalism

Writing, acting, and directing are all passion careers in a highly competitive industry. Unions offer career-specific workshops and networking events to members, and film programs around the country offer a variety of classes and degree tracks that provide young people opportunities to hone their vision and skill. But to achieve success in one of these fields, young aspirants are told that they need to be dedicated, passionate, and sometimes to "do whatever it takes." Historically, gumption has not been a characteristic of professionalism.

Definitions of professionalism can be indicated by external factors (such as a union card), or as a set of behaviors that are an intersection of career and identity. As such, professionalism might be achieved by tangible benchmarks, such as degrees, licenses, or accreditations (teachers), or by adopting common languages and standards (engineers). It also might include aspects of self-identity, as in the case of doctors and lawyers, for whom professionalism might be tied to "cognitive exclusiveness," or privileged possession of specialized knowledge.[2] Professionalism has also been defined as a perspective, or the ability to see "the relative importance of one's work and its ethical and social aspects."[3] In the postindustrial climate, Kathi Weeks posits that dedication to work is now a characteristic of professionalism that is common across many career sectors.

Although some of the aspects of Hollywood professionalism now resemble those in other professions, the nature of film and television work as an artistic pursuit, in which some directors and actors feel it is necessary to sacrifice relationships, health, ethics, and money to achieve their creative vision, aligns Hollywood's professionalism with other creative pursuits. The fact that this is a potentially lucrative industry with many collaborators raises the stakes and intensity of decision-making. Union membership, as I write in chapter 10, is often an important indicator of Hollywood professional *status*, but professional behavior operates on a sliding scale depending on where a writer, actor, director, or crew member falls within the Hollywood hierarchy. Powerful above-the-line creatives are supposed to be passionate advocates for their vision, but those who work in a below-the-line capacity as background performers or assistant directors are supposed to facilitate the creative vision of others. The unions help define these hierarchies, but they have not taken a leadership role as organizations that define ethical behaviors.

In Hollywood, film and television are commercial products made by creative people who are interested to some degree in making art. There are several ways these objectives can collide; whether it is when a writer refuses a note from the network, or an actor takes too much time preparing and misses a call time, creative people are often emotional about their work. Actors such as Christian Bale and Tom Cruise have famously crossed the line by screaming at colleagues about professionalism on set, in both cases, with no professional consequences. Writing about the twenty-first-century understanding of the term, Kathi Weeks explains, "To act like a professional—to be professional in one's work—calls for subjective investment in and identification with work, but also a kind of affective distancing from it."[4] Hollywood careers demand investment in and identification with the creative work, rather than detachment. As a result, there is often more of an industry-wide tolerance of aggressive, eccentric, and otherwise inappropriate behavior from some of the biggest names (which can give permission to less prominent individuals to do the same) in the business as they continue to strive for greatness.

The history of Hollywood is filled with stories of directors pushing their actors to achieve realism in their performances. While some examples, such as James Cameron fitting *Titanic* stars in period underwear, seem eccentric, other demands, such as Cameron revolutionizing underwater cinematography and motion capture techniques and asking his actors to learn to act underwater, demonstrate how this kind of commitment to the craft is at times valorized. However, there have historically been directors, including Bernardo Bertolucci, Alfred Hitchcock, and Stanley Kubrick, who were known for pushing their stars to the physical and emotional brink. While there has been some re-evaluation of these directors' tactics, their films continue to populate screening lists in film classes and lists of the greatest films of all time, underscoring a particular set of professional values. SAG-AFTRA has implemented reporting procedures for harassment complaints (see chapter 10), but generally the unions have sought no role in curbing such behavior.

Prestige

As the introduction to this book explains, studios and the Academy of Motion Picture Arts and Sciences (AMPAS) actively tried to prevent writers, actors, and directors from unionizing in the silent era. Unlike the crew members whose work was invisible to the audience, writers, actors, and directors possessed well-known names and sometimes familiar faces. It is easy to imagine how studios in the 1930s, which sought to control the public images of their stars, felt about the prospect of their movie stars on the picket lines. Fortunately for studios, they did not face an above-the-line strike until 1952 (by the Screen Writers Guild prior to its name change); the next above-the-line strike was in 1960.

Each union cultivates a different type of prestige, which is a kind of respect and renown that comes from creating beloved or critically well-regarded films and television shows. Creators of respected films and television shows will often be given more bandwidth on future projects and a platform to weigh in on a wider range of issues. David Simon, a former journalist and the creator of HBO's *The Wire* (one of the prime scholarly and critical examples of "prestige TV"), has been lauded for his work as a television writer but also has been shown respect as an astute critic of contemporary American politics and Hollywood as an industry by journalists who seek him out for commentary. Prestige might also be associated with impeccable taste or glamour, which are often (especially historically) seen as innate qualities of Hollywood stars. For example, Audrey Hepburn lent her fresh face and on-screen glamour to Givenchy, the French luxury fashion and perfume house.

For the writers and directors, their unions have been essential to help foster the prestige of their professions above others in the media industries. In her book *Writing for Hire*, the lawyer Catherine Fisk shows how screenwriters distinguished themselves from advertising copywriters and developed prestige by assigning authorial credit to screenwriters (even if they do not retain ownership rights).[5] Similarly, as Virginia Wright Wexman explains, for the DGA, credit has also "help[ed] to create the perception of the directors as artists."[6] Yet, as Maya

Montañez Smukler explains in chapter 11, "The elevation of the director has been necessitated by elitism that fosters exclusion." While this process is important for elevating directors' roles, by definition, it means that the contributions of others on set are often devalued. Regardless of how these workers have cultivated distinction, their unions have been essential for translating this prestige into tangible contract benefits and financial terms. Unions do not make actors, writers, and directors famous, but they do provide their members access to jobs in films and television series with broader distribution and higher production and marketing budgets.

Prestige is not the same as power. Writers, actors, and directors create and breathe life into film and television series, but they very rarely retain ownership rights over their works. In the media industries, power comes from the money to finance a project and the ability to retain ownership over intellectual property that can continue to generate long-term profit. Individual directors, writers, or stars (Francis Ford Coppola, Mel Gibson, and Kevin Costner excepted) rarely have the capital to finance, market, and distribute a feature film, which means they predominantly cede power and ownership to producers, studios, and distributors with enough capital to get the film on-screen (and preferably in theaters).

While studios and networks retain legal rights over films and television shows, the WGA, SAG-AFTRA, and the DGA have been able to negotiate residuals—a hard-fought bargaining right that guarantees payment for reuse of their creative work—on behalf of their members. Residuals are calculated based on where a film or television episode initially played (theater, broadcast network, cable network, etc.) and where it replayed (broadcast network, cable network, premium cable network, streaming service, etc.). This formula has ensured that Hollywood unions not only constantly renegotiate the existing residual formulas but also must bargain for new residual terms with the arrival of every new distribution method.

Above-the-line unions posed their first meaningful challenge to new forms of distribution in 1960, when the writers and actors went on strike over residuals for films on television. Studios refused to negotiate terms with the unions for the profitable films on television throughout the 1950s, but, as Jennifer Porst points out, by 1960, the studios had a change of heart and were willing to negotiate residuals for pre- and post-1948 films because the arrival of color television would diminish the value of black-and-white films.[7] This was the tale of two strikes: writers held out for 153 days (5 days longer than their 2023 walkout), whereas actors negotiated a deal at the 43-day mark (unlike in the more contentious fight of 2023).

Each subsequent strike of the twentieth century would continue to center on residuals as the above-the-line unions continually sought to share in studio and network profits. Although the actors' and writers' strikes overlapped in 1960, these groups were not working closely with each other or other unions as a united front to negotiate residuals. These prestigious unions, each with its influential members, have struggled to manage members' big personalities and internal factions. The interests of above-the-line unions often aligned, but when it came time to negotiate, solidarity has evaded them for most of their history.

Union Conflicts and Solidarity

Above-the-line unions have struggled to represent their members due to intra-union conflicts created by factions, as well as interunion conflicts that stem from conflicts of interest and lackluster support during negotiations and strikes. In the above-the-line unions, intra-union issues are often culturally specific to each union. As I write about in chapter 10 on SAG-AFTRA, several internal conflicts have plagued this now-merged union, including the wide variety of performers in the union and the cultural distinctions between film and television that long kept the performers' unions separate. Like SAG-AFTRA, the DGA also represents a diverse group of members, and some current members, such as the unit production managers, have not always been part of the union. The below-the-line members have struggled to have their needs prioritized next to those of their director-bosses.

The history of SAG-AFTRA is fraught with interunion (and later intra-union) disputes. SAG's and later AFTRA's relationships to other creative unions and guilds in Hollywood and New York were instrumental in both the development and the continued power of performers' unions. Union solidarity was not an immediate given, and there can be strategic advantages to working with, or in some cases against, other unions. For example, SAG achieved recognition over time, first by gaining IATSE's blessing, which helped the guild negotiate its first contract with the Association of Motion Picture Producers (AMPP). However, SAG retained its jurisdiction over screen actors by working with and against other unions. It was only later, after the 1980 strike, that both SAG and AFTRA began to see many of the benefits of working together. Although the Hollywood unions have long histories, their origins were messy and their dominance not inevitable. After World War II, with the guilds more entrenched, the unions were positioned to benefit from strike solidarity and an understanding that all demands and gains are relational.

The above-the-line unions must constantly negotiate their relationships to each other, something that happens not only during periods of strikes and labor actions but also daily as some of the most famous members navigate the profession as hyphenates, such as writer-directors and actor-directors. For writers who also work as "showrunners," their position as both workers (writers) and management (showrunners have supervisory roles as producers) has posed conflicts of interest since long before the term came into use in 1995.[8] The threat of writer-producers performing writing duties during a strike has historically been a concern for the WGA. As Miranda Banks explains about the 1960 strike, "There was much anxiety about whether hyphenates would go out on strike, or, if they did not, whether they would sabotage the strike by writing during the walkout."[9] Writer-producers who stand with striking writers by refusing to "scab" or perform writing duties during a strike are often vocal about their position and identity as writers. However, hyphenates have long been seen as workers who can help ease labor tensions. During the 1988 WGA strike, Hollywood attorneys invited eight hyphenates to meet and strategize an approach to resolve the strike—a meeting that I can write about because four of the hyphenates immediately reported this to WGA leadership.[10]

The creation of the term *showrunner* has only made this internal tension between writer and producer more fraught. In 2023, studios, networks, and streamers and the DGA called back showrunners from the picket lines to perform their supervisory duties, which include the long-fought-over "a through h functions."[11] These functions have been the subject of lawsuits and National Labor Relations Board (NLRB) disputes since 1973 and include the following duties performed on set:

(a) Cutting for time;
(b) Bridging material necessitated by cutting for time;
(c) Changes in technical or stage directions;
(d) Assignment of lines to other existing characters occasioned by cast changes;
(e) Changes necessary to obtain continuity acceptance or legal clearance;
(f) Casual minor adjustments in dialogue or narration made prior or during the period of principal photography;
(g) Such changes in the course of production as are made necessary by unforeseen contingencies (e.g., the elements, accidents to performers, etc.);
(h) Instructions, directions, or suggestions, whether oral or written, made to writer regarding story or screenplay.[12]

At the core of these disputes is the nature of these tasks and whether they constitute writing.

The 2023 strike revived past challenges for Hollywood above-the-line workers and tested the limits of union allegiances. Since many of the divisions between unions stem from administrative distinctions and attempts to leverage power, it can be easy to think about these as getting in the way of the art. As an activist, organizer, WGA member, and DGA member during the 2023 strike, Boots Riley wrote about the challenges of putting aside his art for workers' greater good: "You'd think that when I was told that I shouldn't promote my show, having been an organizer, it'd have been an easy choice with no second thoughts. But it wasn't, it was a really hard thing to process. Hard partly because I'm an artist who has become a little narcissistic as I've had to think that whatever art I'm doing is the most important thing in the world—just to push through the many obstacles and get it done."[13] As Riley explains, for artists, thinking like a worker is no easy task. However, what the history of organized creative labor tells us is that sacrifice and solidarity are how artists can make a living from their work.

The actual work of writers, actors, and directors has little in common, but as workers within the Hollywood production system, these individuals collaborate closely and share a sense of authorial control over the creation of film and television shows they make. As a result, they are often negotiating and fighting for the same conditions that make film and television jobs a sustainable career: residuals, health care, pensions, and working conditions conducive to creative work. This combination of professional differences, despite similar labor concerns, has meant the unions can find points of solidarity, even if that is occasionally short-lived.

Notes

1 For example, see Danielle Broadway, "Hollywood Stars Stand by Actors Not 'Swimming in Money,'" *Reuters*, June 29, 2023, https://www.reuters.com/lifestyle /hollywood-stars-stand-by-actors-not-swimming-money-2023-06-29/.
2 M. S. Larson, *The Rise of Professionalism* (University of California Press, 1977), 15.
3 John Weckert and Richard Lucas, "On the Need for Professionalism in the ICT Industry," in *Professionalism in the Information and Communication Technology Industry*, ed. John Weckert and Richard Lucas (ANU Press, 2013), 6.
4 Kathi Weeks, *The Problem with Work: Feminism, Marxism, Antiwork Politics, and Postwork Imaginaries* (Duke University Press, 2011), 74.
5 Catherine Fisk, *Writing for Hire: Unions, Hollywood, and Madison Avenue* (Harvard University Press, 2016).
6 Virginia Wright Wexman, *Hollywood's Artists: The Directors Guild of America and the Construction of Authorship* (Columbia University Press, 2020), 66.
7 Jennifer Porst, *Broadcasting Hollywood: The Struggle over Feature Films on Early TV* (Rutgers University Press, 2021), 169.
8 Miranda Banks, *The Writers: A History of American Screenwriters and Their Guild* (Rutgers University Press, 2015), 197.
9 Banks, 145.
10 "Pressure Put on Writer-Producers to Help End Strike," *Variety*, July 13, 1988, 7.
11 Lesley Goldberg and Katie Kilkenny, "Studios Demand Showrunners Work during Writers Strike," *The Hollywood Reporter*, May 5, 2023, https://www .hollywoodreporter.com/tv/tv-news/disney-demands-showrunners-work-during -writers-strike-wga-1235480879/.
12 Goldberg and Kilkenny, "Studios Demand Showrunners Work."
13 Boots Riley, "'Sorry to Bother You' Director Boots Riley on WGA Strike, Struggle, Solidarity, Sacrifice & AI—Guest Column," *Deadline*, May 17, 2023, https:// deadline.com/2023/05/wga-strike-boots-riley-guest-column-1235367232/.

9

Writers

• •

Scripting the Narrative
of Hollywood Labor

MIRANDA BANKS

QUESTION Why do you think writers have been at the forefront of labor issues in
   Hollywood?
NORMAN LEAR (*All in the Family, Maude, The Jeffersons, One Day at a Time*) Maybe
   because they are paid to think.[1]

If I ask you, what does Hollywood labor look like, the image of the hustle and
bustle of a production might come to mind. Whether or not you have ever been
on a Hollywood set, most people can easily call to mind, from films or television
series about Hollywood, a vision of all the busyness just before the director calls,
"Action!": actors muttering their lines while makeup folks double-check that
there is no sheen on actors' noses from hours under the lights; electricians and
gaffers adjusting those aforementioned lights; camera operators making sure they
have the focus correct and the frame adjusted for the start of the next take; prop
people moving a judge's gavel or a cowboy's lasso into position in just the right
way for the camera; costumers checking a hem or the tilt of a hat; and then the
assistant director calling, "Rolling." Or perhaps you might think of front-office
executives and their assistants on the phone or at lunch meetings making
deals with talent agents. But rarely when we conjure up the image of labor in

Hollywood do we think of a solitary person sitting in a home office or at a kitchen table clicking away on a computer for hours on end. Sometimes Hollywood writers work at a studio and will have pitch meetings. If they work on a television series, they will likely spend hours together in a writers' room, and if they produce their episode, they might spend time on set. But a lot of the work a writer does is quiet, isolated, dull, and unglamorous. Though it takes some physical toll (think hunched shoulders, spectacled eyes, carpal tunnel syndrome), much of the labor of writing is mentally exhausting, requires long hours, and demands detailed work of the mind.

Historically, the labor of screenwriting—especially film writing—has always been an outlier to the communal, cooperative vision of the collaborative art of Hollywood production. Even when writers have worked on a studio lot, their best ideas sometimes happen away from the desk. Anyone who has ever written knows that sometimes it is in the moments of pause, rest, or contemplation, or in the midst of the mundane, that great ideas coalesce. Many writers I have interviewed say that their greatest ideas—or their solutions to a narrative conundrum—have come to them while they were making dinner, walking around the block, or driving to work. The same can be said, in fact, for the work of a costume designer, a cinematographer, or an editor. The work happens at work, but it also might stew in one's mind. This does not mean that writing, like other media work, is not physically demanding or laborious, but a writer's craft demands focus and creative vision—and sometimes those might not happen on the studio lot, which can frustrate studio executives.

Jack L. Warner, the president of Warner Bros., was particularly tetchy when it came to his perception of writers' labor on the studio lot. In 1937, he sent the following memo to "All Writers":

> Certain writers have become very lax in the hours they keep at the Studio, coming in late in the morning and leaving early in the afternoon. . . .
>
> Is it not asking too much for a writer to be at his desk sometime between 9:00 A.M. and 9:45 A.M.; even the elite in any other business come to work earlier than that. Therefore, I must insist that more regular hours be kept in the future by those of you who have been coming in late and leaving early.[2]

Now, when so many people work freelance or eke out a living in a gig economy, our notion of what labor looks like in the United States has changed. These days, only an elite group of film and television writers on contract have a designated, personal office on the studio lot. Most writers do their work off-site. during COVID-19, studio executives learned that remote work gave employees the flexibility that some of them see as desirable in a job.[3] Office staff and equipment are reduced, and production funds are no longer needed to feed hungry writers at lunchtime.

If writers are no longer on studio lots en masse, then the misunderstood labor they produce has little chance of being better respected by studio executives, completed during traditional work hours, and geographically situated within the studio. While the Hollywood writer is sometimes absent (i.e., working on their next project or the next episode) during production, their creative alchemy—the script—holds the kernel of so much of what we as audiences love about cinema and media: character and story. They are both vital and central—and yet positioned outside the lens of what we so often imagine the making of film and media means. This essential and yet often invisible positioning is just one reason that the Writers Guild has been at the center of more labor disputes than any other union or guild.

In its ninety-year history as a trade union, the Writers Guild has served as a dominant voice in Hollywood, fighting for the rights of creative workers. The Screen Writers Guild, originally founded as a social group of Hollywood writers in 1921, was reinvented as a labor union in 1933 during the Great Depression and, with the addition of television writers most notably, became the Writers Guild of America (WGA) in 1954. Generation by generation, writers and their union have fought to stay afloat amid evolving screen technologies, production methods, distribution models, and shifts in the industry's economy. As a union, the WGA has initiated action in pursuit of collective rights more frequently than any other professional group in Hollywood.

The WGA is the bargaining agent for writers working for American signatory studios and production companies represented by the Alliance of Motion Picture and Television Producers (AMPTP). The Writers Guild represents writers in film, television, and streaming series, as well as some news, prime-time animation, and video game writers. For the writers working under its protection, the guild convenes and mobilizes members, addresses their concerns, negotiates and enforces contracts, lobbies on behalf of its members, represents screenwriters to the outside world, and preserves the craft of screenwriting. While it does not represent all writers who work in these areas—not all production companies are signatories—the guild also has networks of writers who regularly convene and connect about labor issues within other key sectors, such as animation, nonfiction, independent film, reality TV, podcast series, and video games.

In 1954, the merger of the Screen Writers Guild, the Television Writers Association, and the Radio Writers Guild—previously represented by separate organizations—led to the creation of the current jurisdictional umbrella organization, the WGA. The organization consists of two branches: the Writers Guild of America, East (WGA East; headquartered in New York, originally focused primarily on live television, radio, and news writers, and affiliated with the American Federation of Labor–Congress of Industrial Organizations [AFL-CIO] since 1989), and the Writers Guild of America West (WGA West; headquartered in Los Angeles, representing Hollywood's film and scripted television writers). While the numbers are always in flux, as of 2024, the WGA

East has approximately 4,700 members and the WGA West 11,000 full members. Both branches of the WGA combined are significantly smaller enterprises than its fellow bargaining organizations the Directors Guild of America (DGA; approximately 18,000 members), Screen Actors Guild–American Federation of Television and Radio Artist (SAG-AFTRA; approximately 160,000 members), and International Alliance of Theatrical Stage Employees (IATSE; approximately 168,000 members).

While the Writers Guild has gone on strike more than any other Hollywood labor group, it has also battled internally (between its East and West branches) and with other professional associations within Hollywood (namely, the Association of Talent Agents between 2019 and 2021). Over the course of Hollywood's history, writers and their guild have negotiated with the studios to hold onto their professional rights in the face of rapidly evolving industry economics and shifts in media platforms.

This chapter identifies a few key labor concerns of Hollywood writers, tracking the Writers Guild by examining seven concepts that exemplify what is collectively at stake for writers and for their union: authorship, contracts, labor, jurisdiction, character, representation, and technology.[4] Because writers have been at the forefront of more labor disputes in the industry, one could see them as the first to address—the advanced guard, per se—in battles over the rights of creative professionals in Hollywood. Every battle has had its challenges, naysayers, and costs. At times, this has made the Writers Guild the enfant terrible; at other moments, it has paved the way for transformative changes that have helped more than just its own membership.

Seven Concepts to Understand the Writers Guild

Authorship

Soon after the passage of the Copyright Act of 1909, Hollywood lawyers rewrote individual employment contracts to ensure that studios would hold corporate authorship for all work they produced. When writers have been on long-term contract, the contract language often asserted that the literary material a writer composed, submitted, or produced while contracted by a studio "shall automatically become the property of the producer who, for this purpose, *shall be deemed the author* thereof" (italics added).[5] While some writers still work under long-term contracts, most others make a living by having a production company buy a script, at which point the copyright transfers to that company. Even though they still receive credit, they are no longer authors of their work: the script is the property of the legal author. Since media companies began adopting this language over a century ago, it has placed ever more control of copyright in producers' hands.

But the clause as written takes this one step further: studios are legally defined not just as the owners but also as the authors of a writer's work. Writers do not hold private intellectual property rights.[6] Instead, what they have had since is a "written by" credit. And credit was critical to the future success of a writer: good credits meant better pay. If a film is successful, then a writer (and their agent) is in a better position to negotiate future contracts or compensation for subsequent screenplays.[7] Credit determinations have always been critical to verifying a writer's reputation, clout, and pay. The notion of being an author, in some ways, does not make sense in media production, as the script is only a blueprint of what will ultimately become something else: a filmed piece of work.[8] There is a disconnect between authorship and ownership in relation to copyright law; even with these clauses that have long positioned a studio as the author of a work, historically and still today within American law, legal authorship is not as meaningful (legally and often financially) as copyright ownership.[9]

As an article in the *New York Times* described in 1916, the circumstances for the writers of films were markedly worse than for other writing professions: "conditions in the motion picture industry are more unsatisfactory than in any other field in which an author is active. The author is practically at the mercy of irresponsible and diabolical producers."[10] The article listed complaints by screenwriters that were long and varied, including accounts of underpayment, outrageous delays in returning scripts, producers butchering scripts, plagiarism of stories, and ambiguous contracts. While these were frustrations, they alone were not cause for actionable change by writers as a community of laborers. The Great Depression would change this.

Contracts

Although altercations between studios and employees had been common early in the history of the American film industry, a revolution in the industry's employment structure began in the 1930s. As discussed in part I of this book, IATSE's successful stand against the studio heads and competing unions during the Depression catalyzed the above-the-line creative talent to organize across the studios. Writers recognized that although individual contracts and salaries were manageable, protection by a union contract was more secure.

Hollywood had two advantages at the end of the 1920s that softened its fall: first, the coming of the sound in 1927 and, second, the desire of some Americans to use a portion of their rapidly dwindling funds on escapist entertainment.[11] The coming of sound energized Hollywood and audiences alike: audiences craved this new medium that now included talking, singing, sound effects, and music—all of which Hollywood saw could help amplify character and story. Dudley Nichols, who wrote the screenplays for *Bringing Up Baby*, *Stagecoach*, and *Scarlet Street*, celebrated the expansiveness of cinema and the creative opportunities of cinematic storytelling: "In spite of its complicated mechanics, the motion picture is, in the present writer's opinion, the most flexible and exciting story telling medium in the world. Its possibilities are enthralling. It is a continual challenge to the writer. With talk has come *character*, the one phase of human existence that never palls in interest. When people talk they reveal themselves.

And once you have character, and its endless diversity and interest, you will never run out of 'stories.' Character itself is the best of all stories."[12]

Projectionists and theaters suffered the impact of the Great Depression quite quickly, but the studios themselves were able to weather the first years before the economic decline hit their bottom lines. When the financial downturn began to have serious effects on studios, Hollywood's top executives turned to their nonunionized contract employees, claiming studio bankruptcy if employees did not take drastic pay cuts. While some creative workers had their doubts about studios' read of their own financials, writers, actors, and directors agreed to retrench to save Hollywood.[13]

In light of the realization that the moguls were cutting nonunionized workers' salaries while not cutting their own, writers determined they needed a labor association to help hold a unified line in negotiations with their employers to protect their economic and creative rights. In 1933, the Screen Writers Guild and the Screen Actors Guild formed as trade unions and drafted their first Minimum Basic Agreement (MBA) for the studios to sign; the Directors Guild followed in 1936. But it took writers the better part of a decade of difficult battling with studio heads for jurisdiction and for the sides to agree to the terms of the first MBA. By 1940, the writers were virtually the only above-the-line employees at the studios working without the protection of a contract or bargaining rights.

After eight years of struggles and negotiations with the studios, the Screen Writers Guild finally agreed on a first contract for its members in December 1941—just weeks after the Japanese attack on Pearl Harbor.[14] It was the attack that pushed the studios to agree to the guild's terms; with the United States' entry into the war, Hollywood needed its writers to help churn out pictures that would support the war effort. The guild signed its first contract, the Producer–Screen Writers Guild Inc. Minimum Basic Agreement of 1942, with the eight major studios—MGM, Paramount, Warner Bros., Columbia, RKO, Twentieth Century-Fox, Universal, and Loew's Inc.—that controlled 95 percent of first-run exhibitions in the United States. Three independent producers also signed: Republic Pictures, Hal E. Roach Studios, and Samuel Goldwyn.

The Writers Guild's MBA determines the basic labor rights, benefits, and protections that must be met at a minimum in a contract that any individual writer makes with a signatory studio. Modified during cyclical negotiations, the MBA is the cornerstone of any agreement between signatory companies who hire professional writers for film and television. The writers' first contract defined guild control over the determination of screen credits, with an arbitration committee to handle any disputes, a minimum wage of $125 per week for all writers, and a mandatory termination notice for independent writers after eight weeks of employment (otherwise they would be considered contracted employees). These first three terms have been foundational for the guild ever since: the guild determines screen credits and adjudicates these credits if there is an arbitration, and the guild ensures minimum fees for all writers signing a contract with a signatory company.

One interesting addition to this long-term contract articulated that a studio owned rights to writers' work for the length of the contract—not just for cinema but for any emerging media on the radar of executives or their lawyers at the time. Though the first commercial television sets became popular only in the late 1940s, studios began putting clauses into writers' contracts about a decade earlier, as the first television systems were being developed and tested in the 1920s. The screenwriter Devery Freeman (*Ziegfeld Follies*, *The Loretta Young Show*) recalled:

> This was a time when . . . studios took the philosophy that when they hired a
> writer, they were buying his ideas, they owned them forever in perpetuity. . . .
> My first contract . . . you would see that they would throw in everything but
> the kitchen sink in terms of the future. The future that they didn't know
> about. They were tying up television rights. . . . Now television didn't exist. It
> certainly didn't exist as theater [laughs]. Perhaps a picture was being sent
> experimentally, but television didn't exist. It was just a remote long-range
> billion to one shot theatrically to most of our way of thinking, yet, just on the
> off chance, it was put into contracts.[15]

As television became a significant source of competition for audiences' eyes, ears, and wallets in the 1950s, Hollywood studios—and the creative labor unions—shifted gears to ensure that this new upstart medium would serve as a source of increased income and opportunity.

The hard-fought battle for a contract had stirred long-standing enmity. Writers were not just creatives; rather, they were creative labor. And their fight for unionization, as well as some of the scripts they wrote that expressed sympathy for progressive ideals, put them in the line of fire from conservative politicians and studio moguls.

Labor

In a book called *Hollywood Unions*, writers and readers alike must weigh the opportunities and the struggles of being a member of a unionized labor force. Much was gained by screenwriters unionizing. But as World War II ended and the Cold War began, Washington politicians placed the film industry at the center of a campaign to rid American cultural institutions of any hint of communism—and labor leaders across different industries were some of the first to be singled out for interrogation. In May 1947, key members of the House Un-American Activities Committee (HUAC) came to—and for—Hollywood. The top of their list of so-called subversives? Members of the Screen Writers Guild. HUAC's chairman, J. Parnell Thomas (Republican of New Jersey), told the press during their visit: "Ninety percent of Communist infiltration in Hollywood is to be found among screenwriters."[16] Then ten individuals—eight of them writers—were brought to Washington to be tried. They were thereafter known as the Hollywood Ten. John Howard Lawson, the cofounder and first president of the Screen Writers Guild, was the first person called to the stand. Though Lawson attempted to make a speech, Thomas interrupted him with two questions: "Are you a member of the Screen Writers Guild?" and "Are you now or have you ever been a member of the Communist Party of the United States?" The juxtaposition of the questions was designed to imply that membership in the Writers Guild was just as sinister as membership in the Communist Party.

In its history, the WGA has called a strike seven times when negotiations with the studios have stalled: in 1960, 1973, 1981, 1985, 1988, 2007–2008, and 2023. This is in part the result of the nature of writers as much as it is about the design of the union's membership. Although writers have not consistently mobilized for social justice or workers' rights, the Writers Guild has always been the most politicized among its fellow organizations. Many chalk up this reputation to writers' eccentric personalities. But perhaps the most clear and obvious reason that writers are better equipped to drum up support in Hollywood is that every guild member performs the same labor: putting words on paper. The other three Hollywood unions—the DGA, SAG-AFTRA, and IATSE—service vastly larger constituencies with needs so diverse that a united front proves tricky when it comes time to negotiate with the monolithic Alliance of Motion Picture and Television Producers (AMPTP).

Jurisdiction

One might assume that the geographic and industrial boundaries of "Hollywood" have remained fixed—and yet, which media and which media workers are included have changed over time. What needs to be located in Los Angeles for something to be considered a Hollywood film: the production company or the production? What about if Los Angeles was where the deal was signed, the script was written, or where primary production or postproduction occurred? What if a film or television series was shot entirely in other states or countries but was funded by a production studio based in Los Angeles? What about video games, podcasts, web series, and reality TV that are made by people who work in Hollywood—is it then Hollywood content? These questions speak to jurisdictional concerns that have been present for Hollywood creative guilds since the coming of television but have increased in import as the diversity of entertainment media has grown and writers working in nonunionized media desire union representation.

By expanding the jurisdictional reach of a trade union especially into new areas of employment that are profitable and growing, a union in turn grows its membership, professional clout, and financial coffers. In the early 1950s, television was a burgeoning industry and one where writers generally had more creative control than in cinema, even while they were peddling the wares of sponsors. Three other trade associations were vying with the Screen Writers Guild for the right to represent these writers: the Radio Writers Guild, the Dramatists Guild (representing playwrights), and the newly formed Television Writers Association. While each guild made its case for jurisdiction, television writers themselves were not convinced that any of these organizations understood and would be responsive to the specificities of their labor practices. If television writers were add-ons to a union designed for another medium's writer, could they truly help them in their campaign for better pay and solid benefits?[17]

In 1952, a total of 375 writers were contracted to television shows; of those individuals, the Screen Writers Guild represented approximately 70 percent—mostly because they had also written screenplays for theatrical films.[18] After a series of battles and negotiations, the Screen Writers Guild successfully lobbied the National Labor Relations Board (NLRB) and the television writers themselves to control the trade agreements. In 1954, the Screen Writers Guild officially changed its name to acknowledge the diversity of its membership: the WGA, with branches in both the East and the West. Choosing this broader title was a prescient decision, allowing the guild to make a clearer argument for the expansiveness of its jurisdictional reach into other areas of media—as it has done with its online media contracts.

Currently, the WGA has caucuses and working groups to promote the status of writers within a number of areas of media and entertainment, even if they do not have jurisdictional rights to represent, support, and promote those writers in their contract negotiations: animation, independent film, reality TV, scripted podcasts, and video games.[19] While individual production companies working in these media and platforms have decided to unionize, these are either areas where the union has failed to make headway in unionizing (reality TV) or where it has not yet gained traction as a labor union for this community of workers (video game writers).

Character

Landing a job as a unionized Hollywood writer is extremely difficult; making a lifelong career of it is even tougher. While not all of the work has gone to white, cisgender, able-bodied, thirty- to fifty-five-year-old straight men with college degrees, such men have been the perennial beneficiaries of an industry that has long favored those with connections to those already inside. However, since the 1990s, the composition of Hollywood writers has ebbed and flowed, but in general has become more racially and ethnically diverse. There are also more women-identifying writers, more LGBTQ writers, and broadly more writing jobs available.

The number of scripted television series has grown exponentially, especially during the 2010s; this growth has been accompanied by a marginal increase in the number of women-identifying writers and Black writers, as well as a slower increase in the number of writers of color and LGBTQ-identifying writers. Data-driven studies have helped advocates impress upon executives and industry leadership the built-in inequities of power and opportunity and the potential to create meaningful change. I have found this to be its own process of data shaming: using data to impress upon companies to make changes if only for the fact that when the data are reported, social media and individuals will be called out, or shamed, for their dismal inequities or glaring lack of diversity.

Data on the demographics of Hollywood writers—questions like who is hired (as well as rehired and/or promoted) or their professional success—are only as good as the research questions scholars and industry leaders conducting studies have previously asked. While combing through information is possible, many historical datasets are limited by past assumptions or omissions. Key limitations revolve around medium specificity, intersectionality, and asking for the unknown. Regarding medium specificity, while studies of on-screen representation are conducted on film and television, many studies that explore representation behind the screen focus on jobs in television rather than film, and on fiction rather than any other genre or type.

Many of these behind-the-scenes studies cover more television, in part because the number of people employed in making television is significantly higher. However, of the television series covered, the studies usually focus on prime-time network series (or heavily promoted scripted streaming shows). The overall rate of turnover of television employees is slower than in film (television series that run longer than one season can provide longer-term employment).[20] Because of this, the number of active WGA members included in many of these television reports offers a larger sample size. As well, because these datasets often cover only prime-time scripted series (or their streaming equivalent), the data fail to track who is working in children's programming, daytime television, and news—areas where women have had more access to writing jobs.[21]

In 1974, at the height of the women's movement in the United States, the WGA Women's Committee commissioned the first major statistical survey of writers' genders within American television. The impact of the study was in the conversations it engendered within the leadership of the guild but also, and more importantly, within the leadership at television studios and on series. Women started getting more freelance scripts bought and ultimately more jobs. Awards season was impacted by these cultural shifts: that same year the Academy of Television awarded writing Emmys to Treva Silverman for *The Mary Tyler Moore Show*, Joanna Lee for *The Waltons*, and Fay Kanin for the made-for-television film *Tell Me Where It Hurts*. Variety specials and series starring women fared well, two of them in the writing categories, with the special *Lily* winning as well as *The Carol Burnett Show*. The most awarded show of the night was *The Autobiography of Miss Jane Pittman*, a groundbreaking television movie adaptation that told the story of a Black woman born into slavery who survives harrowing racism and violence and lives long enough to participate in the civil rights movement of the 1960s.[22]

While the Writers Guild was the first Hollywood union to examine gender disparity, the study looked only at prime-time television writers. A key problem with much of the resulting data is that they fail to identify writers' identities intersectionally: in particular, those of Black women and women of color. Details about the numbers of Black women and women of color working within the industry were rarely distinguished from those about white women or from Black men and men of color—both groups that were better represented in the industry than Black women or women of color. Although the number of Black women and women of color working as writers in prime time has often been negligible or zero, the power of a zero would have been significant to detail.

The work of the WGA's Women's Committee was a major influence on female actors who soon conducted their own survey on employment, as well as on female directors who did the same for the Directors Guild Women's Steering Committee, an organization that went on to sue Hollywood for hiring discrimination based on gender.[23] But the battles were hard-fought—and just because a writer was a part of the guild did not mean they were necessarily well employed. For example, in 1983, of the 100 African American writers surveyed by the Black Writers Committee of the WGA, only 8 were working on a full-time basis.[24] The data on film and television today show that numbers have generally improved, but the challenges are still great. Studies by the Women's Media Center at UC San Diego, the Ralph J. Bunche Center at UCLA's Hollywood Diversity Report and the Annenberg Inclusion Initiative at the University of Southern California's Annenberg School for Communication have some small power to inform, persuade, convince, or shame the media industries to address their efforts (or lack thereof) to diversify its employee pools.[25]

The politics of who is counted—and who decides what is worthy of counting—is a critical issue for theories on employment, media, and identity.[26] Every new set of reports engenders conversations within the industry, and in the ensuing years slight upticks—and some downslides—have occurred.[27] While there are more writers of color working in the industry than in decades past, in particular in television, of far deeper concern is the extraordinary income gap between white and minority writers, not for entry-level work but for midcareer writers. The gap has much to do with the kind of television being made in 2023: many series are only eight to twelve episodes long, writers rarely have access to set because of changes ushered in by compliance rules instituted during the COVID-19 pandemic, and the residuals for most series decreased dramatically in this digital and streaming era. A writing job in the current TV landscape pays out significantly less than average shows during the lucrative decades of the three-network era (think of the difference between audience numbers and residuals on a series from the 1980s versus today). So, while there is more diversity in the room, the job itself is rarely as lucrative as it once was.

Representation

It might sound trite to hear that representation matters in more ways than one in Hollywood, but the axiom is true. As many media scholars have examined and as was touched on in the previous section, representation of women, of people of color, of people with different abilities, of people of different ages, and of people from different countries and different backgrounds matters both on-screen and behind the scenes. But in Hollywood there is a second meaning to representation: the talent agent or agency that advocates for a particular creative worker in contract negotiations. In the history of Hollywood, the work of talent agents and agencies has stayed in the background. The talent agent has been fodder for insider jokes and is most frequently noted outside Hollywood as those unknown names of folks thanked during awards ceremonies. Agents represent talent—generally taking a 10 percent commission on their clients' salaries. While some writers also have talent managers, who are focused on advising their clients on their career goals, I focus here on the agent because it is their role to negotiate their client's wages and contracts, a role that connects them more explicitly to the role of the WGA.

The film industry is a fascinating ecosystem, where casual meetings can be as important as formal interviews or pitches, and where job contracts are regularly negotiated. In both situations, having the support and advice of an agent can be critical. As Tom Kemper writes in his history of agents: "Hollywood is a business world embedded within a social network (and vice versa)."[28] The power that agents wield is not just in the emotional labor—or soft skills of reading a room and the art of persuasion. They know what people are making and what studios are willing to pay for that labor. In this moment of increased visibility around inequities for Black, Latinx, Indigenous, and Asian American voices, the power an agent has to ensure their client's deal is commensurate with that of people at the same level cannot be overstated. A talent agent, especially for female clients or for clients of color, can fail to—or fight to—ensure that their client receives equitable pay.

The focus of attention around labor and Hollywood has long been on studios and talent—not on relationships between talent and their representatives. But in April 2019, 7,000 American film and television writers fired their agents during television's all-important staffing season. As someone who has studied the WGA and tracked labor negotiations, I considered not only the length of this dispute significant, lasting almost two years, but also the nature of it as one that was not between signatory companies and unionized employees. This was a *firing* of agents by the writers they represent.

The Artists' Manager Basic Agreement, established in 1976, had never been updated, and the trusted relationship between agents and writers was fraying in the face of transformative changes in talent agencies' business model. After months of failed negotiations to update the document and address the changing role of talent agencies in the making of film and media, the association of talent agents and the WGA hit an impasse. Creative talent took aim not at their employers but rather at their employees, believing that their support team had become their competition for fair wages and compensation. David Simon, the showrunner for *The Wire* and *Treme*, minced no words in his takedown of what he saw as profiteering by agencies: "If you can only leverage profit for yourself, but not for me, what the f-ck do I need you for? Why are you on this ride at all? At the point that he can only achieve benefit for himself and not for his client, what the f-ck good is an agent?"[29] That so many writers were willing to step away from these relationships to ensure their rights as clients shows that while Hollywood might be a social network built on interpersonal relationships, writers as a union were determined not to put personal relationships in the way of their professional and financial rights.

Several issues led to the mass firings, but I want to point to the two most significant and compelling of these to better see important trends and changes in how labor and creative production are changing as the financialization of Hollywood has become the industry's inevitable reality. As Andrew deWaard deftly tracks in his article "Financialized Hollywood," in the 2010s talent agencies started looking beyond legacy talent and envisioning new clientele, and their new parent owners—private equity firms—were eager to increase revenue streams.[30] Film and television were not enough. Talent agencies went from being in the business of representing clients to representing content. This happened in two key ways: packaging fees and agencies building producing arms. Agents have had a long-standing practice of bundling talent around a piece of intellectual property. But, in fact, what was once a package is increasingly just a writer and a script. And, for that, the agencies were taking fees directly from the studios. Thus, for a typical series that went to air, agencies might be seeing between $30,000 and $100,000 in fees per episode—and that fee would be theirs for the entire run of the series. While a showrunner might appreciate that they would not have to pay at 10 percent, instead other writers on the same series found that their own agents were at times making more money than they were for a particular series. With 87 percent of all series aired in 2016 and 2017 being packaged by agencies, and 79 percent of those being packaged by just three agencies, the production arms of agencies were gobbling up a bigger piece of the financial pie for the entire life of a television series' run.[31] This money did not feed back into creative labor.

As well, some agencies were starting to produce series, turning a writer's agent into a writer's producer—and the money to be made here was what the Hollywood producer Gavin Polone called "the golden goose."[32] The problem with this was an agent's divided loyalties. The WGA called this move going from a "service for their varied client list into a vertically integrated cartel."[33] It took two years, but the writers ended up with a rare win over private equity—but this was one battle in the war of the financialization of Hollywood. The writers' win here ensured not just divestment from production but also that agencies would sign what the WGA initially had called a code of conduct agreement.[34] The terminology here is not lost on anyone in Hollywood. Agents, long considered aggressive players in Hollywood, were being put in their place by the writers' agreement. The agencies agreed to end packaging by 2022 and reduce their stake in their production arms to no more than 20 percent. The Writers Guild stood its ground in ways that ultimately benefited other creative talent guilds, which could stand in support without firing their agents.[35]

If Hollywood is a business world embedded within a social network, and vice versa, then relationships are everything. As collaborative labor that often demands the shared participation of over 200 skilled workers—and that is just on a single set—the nature of these business relationships and of talent's trust in their intermediaries is vital.

Technology

As studio and network ownership has changed, corporate leaders have found different ways to use new technology to change audience habits. Industry leadership's harnessing of technology has not just an impact on availability of jobs but also compensation and working conditions. It is not just technology that shapes labor, but how studios, networks, and tech companies wield technology that matters.

Studios and networks tell stories, but first and foremost, they are in the audience-generating business. The technology of cinema created new jobs, new roles, and new millionaires. But the finances have always been volatile—it is a fickle business. The first Hollywood studio heads mostly came to production after being in exhibition. Many started their careers in entertainment running vaudeville houses or movie theaters. They knew what audiences wanted, and they made their decisions based on those experiences. Because of this, they knew high turnover of films and a focus on stars and genre films would bring in steady audiences. The late 1960s were a tumultuous time in which Hollywood saw significant drops in profits—the new technology, television, was stealing their audience. In the face of economic crises for film, businesses wholly unrelated to film swooped into Hollywood to purchase studios and add a little prestige to their profits. In 1966, the Gulf + Western manufacturing conglomerate purchased Paramount Studios; in 1967, the insurance and investment company TransAmerica bought United Artists; in 1969, the parking and property management company Kinney National purchased Warner Bros., and the real estate mogul Kirk Kerkorian bought MGM. With leadership of studios in flux, new executives like Robert Evans at Paramount and John Calley at Warner Bros. turned to young writers and directors to make less expensive films. Although the work of media makers did not fundamentally change, executives were open to new ideas and edgier material, and so producers, writers, directors, and actors started making films that pushed the boundaries of what had been seen before in Hollywood, some of which ended up becoming among the most celebrated films in American film history.[36]

Once a generation, technological changes in film and media transform not just the economics of the industry but also the nature of work. When this happens, systems of compensation for that type of work often need to be renegotiated. This happened for writers with the coming of sound, with the advent of the television rerun, again with VHS, and then with the DVD. For example, in 1960, writers (and actors) went on strike because films and television shows, which had generally been shown immediately, were now getting re-aired on television multiple, often dozens, of times. Television stations had hundreds of hours to fill each week, and old films and television series made for great content. Writers went on strike to demand that they get paid for these re-airings and reruns. Out of this negotiation, writers began getting royalties, and ultimately, residuals for the reuse of their work.

Then, when the Writers Guild went on strike in 2007, a central concern was residuals, but this time for on-demand digital views. While the studios argued that streaming whole series was simply a promotional opportunity, not a new platform, writers knew that streaming was the wave of the future. Just a month after the 2007–2008 strike ended, the first major streamer, Hulu, was launched as a joint endeavor between legacy media NBC Universal and tech companies AOL, MSN, Myspace, and Yahoo. Again, the industry began to transform.

Streaming media, and the tech companies like Netflix, Apple, and Amazon that entered Hollywood using new platforms, privilege technology and brought with them a data-driven understanding of audiences that they refused to share with talent. These streamers changed the landscape of film and media production and distribution, such that payment models needed to be restructured for writers (and all Hollywood workers)—especially those beginning their careers or in the middle class—to receive fair compensation for their labor.

Streamers prefer to save money by ordering shorter series seasons and staffing smaller writing rooms, which contributed to a rise in the number of series between 2009–2023 (what has been called Peak TV). Writing jobs during this time multiplied to meet the demand, but the pay scale for these series often was well below that of the networks, and with small pickups of episodes, the work was of far shorter duration than in past eras (making 6 episodes rather than 13, or in earlier decades as many as 26 or 34). As well, with the rise of artificial intelligence (AI), another new technology, writers pushed back on studios interested in turning to machines to spin out story ideas.

Leading up to the 2023 walkouts, residuals, which had long been a part of writers' pay structures, were diminishing. Companies such as Netflix preferred a series of payouts rather than residuals, and much to the dismay of Hollywood talent, this meant they were not given regular access to audience data throughout the life of their programs. This worked to the financial advantage of a few A-list writers for a while, but even top talent lamented that the lack of transparency with respect to audience data made it difficult to judge the success of their work. For most television and streaming writers, these changes to production and financing meant a deep squeeze on their salaries. It was for these reasons and others that representatives of the Writers Guild and SAG-AFTRA walked out of negotiations in the spring and summer of 2023, respectively.

The writers reached a deal on a new contract just five days shy of their longest strike ever and made significant gains with respect to salary, success-based incentives, minimum staffing requirements, residuals, and AI, with the actors remaining on strike well into the fall. The writers' and actors' contracts reflected the sacrifices made during the long strikes and industry shutdown. Although the Writers Guild was able to achieve protections for its profession, the many gains were made against the backdrop of an industry in a state of perpetual change in a particularly volatile financial and technological moment.

Conclusion

Unions still matter in Hollywood, and not only for those whose work is made under studio lights. The labor of writing matters not just to writers or to audiences who crave good stories but to all of the writers' collaborators in the construction of great Hollywood stories. Collaboration across Hollywood is critical to the success of a film or series but also to the health of the industry. Whether they are seen as the provocateurs or the front lines of the labor movement in Hollywood, writers have been central characters in the story of labor activism within the industry, and the narrative is one that well deserves our attentive viewing.

Notes

1   Norman Lear, interview with the author, August 20, 2013.
2   Screen Writers Guild Records, 1921–1954, Writers Guild Foundation Archive, Shavelson-Webb Library, Los Angeles.
3   Ryan Faughnder and Anousha Sakoui, "How Will Hollywood Get Back to Full Speed? After the Pandemic, Some Things May Never Return to Normal," *Los Angeles Times*, April 14, 2021, https://www.latimes.com/entertainment-arts/business/story/2021-04-14/how-will-hollywood-production-get-back-to-full-speed.
4   For much more detail on this topic, see Miranda Banks, *The Writers: A History of American Screenwriters and Their Guild* (Rutgers University Press, 2015).
5   This appears in multiple places, including Section 11 of the Academy Code and Section 10 of the Screen Playwrights Code. It is mentioned, as well, in the NLRB assessment "In the Matter of Metro-Goldwyn-Mayer Studios and Motion Picture Producers Assn., et al., and Screen Writers Guild Inc., June 4, 1938, 22–25; and in *Decisions and Orders of the National Labor Relations Board* 7 (May 1, 1938–June 30, 1938): 690.
6   Catherine L. Fisk, "The Role of Private Intellectual Property Rights in Markets for Labor and Ideas: Screen Credit and the Writers Guild of America, 1938–2000," *Berkeley Journal of Employment and Labor Law* 32 (2011): 257, UC Irvine School of Law Research Paper No. 2011–17.
7   The possessory credit is not legally concomitant with copyright. As the legal scholar Catherine Fisk lays clear in her work on the possessory credit, neither

writers nor directors can lay claim to authorship; rarely, in fact, do producers even hold the copyright under their own names. As Fisk explains: "Because of copyright's work for hire doctrine, legal authorship of a motion picture is not factual authorship and is often a legal fiction in every sense of the term.... Courts play virtually no role in this all-important area of 'law.'" Catherine Fisk, *Writing for Hire: Unions, Hollywood, and Madison Avenue* (Harvard University Press, 2016), 218. Because of this, neither the WGA nor the Directors Guild has applied intellectual property law—or any civil proceedings for that matter—in their disputes over this credit.

8   While auteur theory—and the celebrity that surrounds it—has become a common framing of work in Hollywood, surprisingly authorship, as such, does not have such a critical role in Hollywood. In part, that is what has made the concept of auteurship so compelling in Hollywood, as it often is focused on identifying a singular visionary behind a collaborative work.

9   Jessica Litman, keynote address, "Working with Intellectual Property: Legal Histories of Innovation, Labor, and Creativity," Stanford Program in Law, Science, and Technology, and Program in History and Philosophy of Science, Stanford University, April 23, 2021. See also Jessica Litman, "Breakfast with Batman: The Public Interest in the Advertising Age," *Yale Law Journal* 108 (1999): 1735, Available at https://digitalcommons.law.yale.edu/ylj/vol108/iss7/14.

10   "Committee Urges a Writers' Union," *New York Times*, July 16, 1916, 17.

11   In the span of just two years, film attendance in the United States jumped from 60 million in 1927 to 110 million in 1929. See "Introduction of Sound Created a Box Office Bonanza, but Problems as Well," IATSE, accessed June 23, 2021, https://www.iatse.net/timeline.

12   Dudley Nichols, "Conversation Piece," *Screen Guilds Magazine* 2, no. 1 (March 1935): 5.

13   I cover this in much more detail in Banks, *The Writers*, 27–32.

14   Banks, 44–65.

15   Devery Freeman, interview by the Writers Guild Oral History Project, April 4, 1978, Writers Guild Foundation, Los Angeles, 4–5.

16   Nancy Lynn Schwartz, *The Hollywood Writers' Wars* (McGraw-Hill, 1982), 257.

17   "New Television Writers Union Opens Offices," *Los Angeles Times*, August 26, 1952; press clippings, Writers Guild Foundation, Shavelson-Webb Library, Los Angeles, CA.

18   "Writers Call Strike against TV-Alliance: Seek 100G Fund," *Daily Variety*, August 6, 1952; "TV Strike Spurned by Radio Writers: Guild Calls Action of Authors League Illegal and Declares It Will Not Support Tie-Up," *New York Times*, August 18, 1952.

19   Both the WGA East and the WGA West have caucuses or alliances in a number of areas. For reference, see the following websites as examples: https://www.wgaeast .org/wgaaudio/; https://www.wgaeast.org/caucuses/; and https://www.wga.org/the -guild/going-guild/caucuses.

20   As Maya Montañez Smukler writes: "Between 1949 and 1979, according to the Committee's findings, 7,332 feature films were made and released by major distributors. Fourteen—0.19%—were directed by women." Maya Montañez Smukler, "Liberating Hollywood: Thirty Years of Women Directors," *CSW Update*, UCLA Center for the Study of Women, 2011.

21   For much more detail on this, see Miranda Banks, "Unequal Opportunities: Gender Inequities and Precarious Diversity in the 1970s US Television Industry," *Feminist Media Histories* 4, no. 4 (2018): 109–129.

22   The miniseries, which is based on the novel by Earnest Gaines, preceded *Roots* by three years.

23 See Maya Montañez Smukler, *Liberating Hollywood: Women Directors and the Feminist Reform of 1970s American Cinema* (Rutgers University Press, 2019).

24 Calvin Kelly, interviewed by Charles Sullivan, Black Writers Committee, WGA-W Newsletter, December 1983.

25 Among the most recent studies from these centers are "WMC Investigation 2021: Gender and Non-acting Oscar Nominations," 2021, https://womensmediacenter .com/reports/wmc-investigation-2021-gender-and-non-acting-oscar-nominations -full-report; Darnell Hunt and Ana-Christina Ramón, "Hollywood Diversity Report 2021," https://socialsciences.ucla.edu/wp-content/uploads/2021/04/UCLA -Hollywood-Diversity-Report-2021-Film-4-22-2021.pdf 2021; and "Inclusion in the Director's Chair," https://assets.uscannenberg.org/docs/aii-inclusion-directors -chair-20200102.pdf 2021, from the Annenberg Inclusion Initiative at USC's Annenberg School for Communication.

26 Elsewhere I have used alternate datasets to help enrich my reading of the employ- ment landscape. U.S. Commission on Civil Rights, "Window Dressing on the Set: Women and Minorities in Television," A Report of the United States Commission on Civil Rights, Washington, D.C., August 1977. Wherever possible, in my years of studying the Writers Guild, I have tried to make quantitative data come alive through qualitative interviews with historically marginalized groups. Miriam Posner and Lauren F. Klein, eds., "Data as Media," special issue, *Feminist Media Histories* 3, no. 3 (2017); Catherine D'Ignazio and Lauren F. Klein, *Data Feminism* (MIT Press, 2020).

27 For example, see William T. Bielby and Denise D. Bielby, *The 1987 Hollywood Writers' Report: A Survey of Ethnic, Gender and Age Employment Factors* (Writers Guild of America, West, 1987).

28 Tom Kemper, *Hidden Talent: The Emergence of Hollywood Agents* (University of California Press, 2009).

29 David Simon, "'But I'm Not a Lawyer, I'm an Agent,'" *Audacity of Despair*, March 18, 2019, https://davidsimon.com/but-im-not-a-lawyer-im-an-agent/.

30 See Andrew deWaard, "Financialized Hollywood: Institutional Investment, Venture Capital, and Private Equity in the Film and Television Industry," *JCMS: Journal of Cinema and Media Studies* 59, no. 4 (2020): 54–84.

31 Jonathan Handel, "Television Packaging Deals: All the Confusing Questions Answered," *The Hollywood Reporter*, April 3, 2019, https://www.hollywoodreporter .com/news/general-news/what-exactly-are-packaging-fees-a-writers-agents-explainer -1198974/.

32 Gavin Polone, "Here's the Long-Shot Way Hollywood Writers Can Win the War on Agents," *The Hollywood Reporter*, March 26, 2019, https://www.hollywoodreporter .com/news/general-news/gavin-polone-heres-how-hollywood-writers-can-win-war -agents-1197093/.

33 David Robb, "WGA Report Calls Big Agencies a 'Cartel' as Talks Resume with ATA," *Deadline*, March 12, 2019, https://deadline.com/2019/03/wga-report-talent -agencies-cartel-talks-resume-today-1202574058/.

34 The WGA East and the WGA West crafted the WGA Code of Conduct agreement to standardize and regulate the relationship between writers and agencies. This is now called a franchise agreement in the final document; see https://www.wgaeast .org/wp-content/uploads/sites/4/2020/10/wga_code_of_conduct_4-13-19.pdf.

35 It is worth noting that SAG-AFTRA expressed immediate support of the WGA, putting out a press release at the end of March after the WGA voted, whereas the DGA, true to its typically more pro-studio, pro-business approach, waited until

January 2021 to express support. David Robb, "SAG-AFTRA Stands with WGA In Its 'Struggle' with Talent Agents," *Deadline*, March 31, 2019, https://deadline.com /2019/03/sag-aftra-wga-ata-talent-agents-writers-guild-of-america-1202586006/; David Robb, "DGA Sides with Writers Guild in Its Dispute with WME over Endeavor Content," *Deadline*, January 12, 2021, https://deadline.com/2021/01/dga -sides-with-writers-guild-in-its-dispute-with-wme-over-endeavor-content -1234672501/.

36 Thomas Schatz, "The Studio System and Conglomerate Hollywood," in *The Contemporary Hollywood Film Industry*, ed. Paul McDonald and Janet Wasko (Wiley-Blackwell, 2008), 18–19.

10

Actors

• •

Balancing the Needs of Extras, Actors, and Stars

KATE FORTMUELLER

"When did you get your SAG card?" This question, a staple on the red carpet of the Screen Actors Guild (SAG) Awards, was directed at Ty Burrell, who quipped, "*Law & Order* got me my SAG card." He then explained, "I would do one every other year and nobody noticed I was playing different characters."[1] Interviews at the SAG Awards and social media campaigns that focus on union cards perpetuate this understanding of the role unions play in professionalization and personal success, in this case in the transition from work playing unidentifiable roles to SAG Award–winning actor. Obtaining a union card is a transformational moment in which actors gain professional status, but symbolically, it unites the fragmented collection of 160,000 on-screen workers as members of the Screen Actors Guild–American Federation of Television and Radio Artists (SAG-AFTRA).

On screen and in marketing materials, actors are the most visible media workers: stars market the movies; character actors enrich the plot or add comic relief; and extras populate the background, enhancing the realism of the mise-en-scène. Union members are young and old and represent many different races, ethnicities, and gender identities. Industrially, actors are a prominent labor group, since screen talent accounts for about half of Hollywood union members. U.S. screen actors—as well as a range of other screen performers, including broadcast hosts, dancers, and voice actors—are all represented by SAG-AFTRA.

One of the challenges to understanding SAG-AFTRA is figuring out how to characterize the work of different types of performers and the union's varied membership. In the first book about SAG's history, David Prindle focused on the union's political ideology to relate SAG to broader American political histories. However, strict attention to decision-making at the top neglects the voices of the rank and file that constitute the bulk of membership. Archival documents of internal conversations and trade publications that showcase disagreements, along with oral histories, interviews, and some luck in unearthing letters or transcripts in the archives, supplement official union histories and create a fuller picture of actors and their union.

Throughout the separate and joint histories of the Screen Actors Guild and the American Federation of Television and Radio Artists (AFTRA), the rules for who could join the union have changed. Actors' jurisdictional disputes began in the early twentieth century when Actors Equity Association (AEA) tried unsuccessfully to expand its geographic and industrial reach beyond New York theater into Hollywood. Equity's failure reveals the distinct elements of film performance labor culture and foregrounds the difficulties associated with unions trying to expand their membership into new media.

After World War II, many actors engaged in a series of interunion struggles when they began to rethink the jurisdictional boundaries of the existing stage, screen, and radio unions. The extras left SAG to start their own union, while other actors considered the potential benefits of merging all the stage and screen performers' unions. The unions were unable to reach an agreement to merge in 1952, primarily because SAG blocked the merger. Yet even though the screen unions, SAG and AFTRA, retained their distinctions as the film and television union, respectively, they bargained together into the twenty-first century. The unions eventually voted to merge in 2012 when television contracts became more essential for working actors.[2] Although SAG's ability to retain its autonomy demonstrated its strength in the 1950s, the two unions' "Stronger Together" position in 2012 was indicative of fundamental changes in the media industries that have made distinctions between film and television more permeable in terms of both method of distribution and cultural importance.

Through a great deal of conflict and, eventually, collaboration, SAG, AFTRA, and later SAG-AFTRA have been essential voices that have shaped the development of screen acting as a profession and practices of Hollywood production. Union histories are often peppered with worker and management disputes, but what makes actors' unions unique among those in Hollywood is their long history of internal conflicts and contested jurisdictions. No other media union has as much disparity between its most elite members and the average union card holder. Although SAG and later SAG-AFTRA have benefited from the power of their stars, the diversity of interests also creates challenges for performers' unions to support all members.

SAG's Rocky Beginnings

From the earliest days of Hollywood filmmaking, union organizers sought to represent screen performers. The primary challenge was finding common grievances and working conditions that would unite not just the featured players but also those in supporting and background roles. Given the differences in work, job security, and experiences of workplace abuses, organizers were unsuccessful at uniting extras and working actors. Ultimately, it was not until industry-wide austerity measures fueled by the Great Depression that stars, contract actors, freelance actors, day players, and extras were able to unite around a common threat, leading to the formation of SAG and the negotiation of its first Minimum Basic Agreement (MBA) in 1934.

The Actors Equity Association, founded in 1913 and recognized by 1919, represented stage actors and did not initially take film acting seriously as an art or the industry as a viable threat to the theater. By 1920, the union felt it necessary to send its executive secretary, Frank Gillmore, to Los Angeles to organize screen actors under the professional norms and guidance of the theater. Extras were momentarily organized as the Motion Picture Players Union (MPPU) after the International Workers of the World (IWW) and an array of organizers all failed to forge new extras unions at the time Gillmore arrived. Yet AEA still focused its sights on extras and subsumed the existing MPPU, believing that those who suffered some of the most visible labor injustices needed to organize first.

The abuses extras faced seemed to happen at every stage of the profession: casting, on-set, and payment. To get cast on a Hollywood film, extras had three options: use a personal connection, traverse the city and wait at studio gates, or visit one of the employment bureaus downtown to inquire about work. One such extra who attempted all three approaches to finding background work was Leo Rosencrans. In letters to his family in Ohio, Rosencrans documented his various unsuccessful attempts to find work in 1916, which ultimately led him to quit the movie business after two weeks and return to Ohio.[3] Once hired, extras might be offered additional money to perform dangerous stunts. After finishing a day's work, extras also found themselves returning to casting bureaus to exchange vouchers for cash—after paying a hefty fee to the casting bureau. For extras, the abuses were not simply isolated or individual events; they were a result of a corrupt system with no oversight.

For those who did manage to find a modicum of success as extras, there was costly upkeep involved in making themselves attractive hires. Dress extras, or those who maintained high-end wardrobes for their roles, often booked more roles. For example, Bess Flowers, who began working as an extra in 1923, appeared in 350 films over the course of her long career as background.[4] Although Flowers found notoriety among film buffs, her success was based on her extensive wardrobe, which reduced studio costuming costs.

Like many other groups, AEA failed to organize extras and actors. The journalist Morton Thompson summed up his position in four words: "Equity wasn't daring enough."[5] The labor historians Louis Perry and Richard Perry gave a nuanced interpretation of AEA's failure: first, silent screen actors felt they had been demeaned by theater actors. Second, the conditions of screen acting were more dissimilar to theater than AEA understood. Third, film actors, unlike theater actors in the 1910s, could not rely on sympathetic strikes from other unions to help shut down productions given that unions had little presence in the industry at the time. Finally, Hollywood actors were willing to accept low wages and poor working conditions based solely on the possibility of future success.[6] In essence, organizers failed to grasp not only the working conditions on set but also the cultural conditions that led many actors to accept risks and low or no pay.

In the 1920s, the studios, through efforts by Will H. Hays (head of the Motion Picture Producers and Distributors of America [MPPDA]), managed to appease actors and stave off unionization. When Frank Gillmore tried to meet with Hays in 1924, he was dismissed by Hays, who claimed that actors were partners, rather than workers, in the filmmaking process.[7] In reality, actors were workers under restrictive contracts, but labeling them as "partners" collaborating with the studios suggested they had power within a system that was designed to exploit them.

In 1925 and 1927, respectively, the major studios collaborated to found Central Casting and the Academy of Motion Picture Arts and Sciences (AMPAS) to address labor problems of the different classes of performers. Central Casting dealt with extras' day-to-day problems. The agency was explicitly tasked with consolidating extras casting into a single office to distribute work fairly and efficiently. This resolved some casting problems, but over several decades the organization still faced accusations of favoritism from extras who felt like work continued to be inconsistent while others continued to receive preferential treatment.

The AMPAS bylaws charged the Conciliation Committee with the "promotion of harmonious and equitable relations within the production industry," which often translated into payment disputes.[8] In lieu of unions, the Conciliation Committee adjudicated member conflicts. After two years, the committee had heard twenty-five disputes (with many more resolved by other committees or dismissed); 44 percent of the complaints were filed by actors—more than any other branch.[9] Although AMPAS repeatedly claimed that the standard contract and resolution procedure usually favored the complainant, it found itself defending the organization against allegations of discrimination in its own newsletter.

The piecemeal resolutions and "harmonious relations" sought by the Academy were no match for the Depression, which threatened a wage cut for all actors (including stars). This also coincided with changes such as the passage of the National Industrial Recovery Act (NIRA), which improved the political and cultural climate for unions such that union organizing became easier—even in the notoriously "open shop" city of Los Angeles. After decades of unionization attempts, actors finally began to organize.

Actors and other top talent gathered in their professional groups—the Masquers Club, the Dominos, and the Hollywood Cricket Club—during meals and away from their workplaces to talk about unionization. What emerged from these conversations was the Screen Actors Guild, which was incorporated as a legal entity in June 1933.[10] The union had a tiered membership, with extras making up the lowest and a nonvoting group. Organizing was the first hurdle for screen actors, but they also had to achieve recognition from the producers and the well-established International Alliance of Theatrical Stage Employees (IATSE, the focus of Part I).

Producers and IATSE refused to recognize SAG until the actors threatened to strike alongside IATSE's rival union, the Federated Motion Picture Crafts (FMPC). Out of fear that the actors would help provide the FMPC too much leverage, IATSE changed course and helped SAG to ratify its agreement with the producers.[11] Although SAG never actually went on strike in 1937, this demonstrated the effectiveness of cross-union collaboration.

The basic terms of SAG's first contract in 1937, as David Prindle points out, established key elements of SAG contracts for subsequent decades, such as terms for workdays and improved working conditions for all actors and extras.[12] However, the emphasis in the contract was on establishing scale, or minimum rates for day players and weeklong contract work that some actors could use for a basis of negotiation. SAG initially represented all screen performers, including extras. From the outset, this created internal conflict, a situation that would only increase as the film industry transformed into the media industries.

With few successful actors who had experienced the hardship and exploitation of extra labor firsthand, it was difficult to convey these conditions and the importance of changing them to the broader membership of working actors. As Leo Rosten's study of working actors would later indicate, only 1.9 percent (less than one in fifty actors surveyed) experienced work as an extra.[13] From the perspective of the SAG Board of Directors during founding conversations, it was clear that the guild was "founded for actors only," meaning extras were marginalized from the very beginning.[14] This understanding of SAG's history, as a union that included extras but was formed for working actors, helps to clarify why and how SAG identified with white-collar professional standards and ideals rather than blue-collar concerns about the number of workdays in a year. Questions of jurisdiction and whether SAG could effectively represent its diverse membership would be central to intra-union *and* interunion conversations that would lead to changes to SAG's structure, but not its white-collar labor identity, in subsequent decades.

From Radio to Television: The Origins of AFRA and AFTRA

The American Federation of Radio Artists (AFRA), like SAG, was born in the Depression during a wave of organizing after the NIRA passed in 1933. There are several key similarities between the founding of SAG and the founding of AFRA. Despite jurisdictional claims, AEA was unable to organize both film and radio actors. Much like SAG, AFRA also negotiated its first collective bargaining agreement in 1937. Despite some parallels in their histories, key differences between film and broadcast technologies led to divisions between the unions.

One of the major differences between AFRA and SAG was that the broadcast union had a wider array of members across the United States. AFRA members were performers, but also news broadcasters with different responsibilities and workplace practices. As Rita Morley Harvey points out, "[AFRA cofounders] conceived . . . of a federation of autonomous locals, one in each center, whose executive secretary (chief administrator and negotiator) would bargain for contracts tailored to the area's staff and freelance artists."[15] By combining workers who voiced fiction and nonfiction in different regional hubs, AFRA was more decentralized than SAG and even AEA, both of which had strong regional identities.

From the perspective of performers, the nature of radio as a live medium shaped how contracts were conceived. Radio relied on a combination of live broadcasts and recordings, just as television would later. Screen actors sometimes performed multiple takes to achieve a single great performance, but radio actors often had to repeat a performance multiple times or stay in the studio in the event of a problem with a recording. The unique characteristics of broadcast performance meant that AFRA developed a system for residuals, or payment for reuse of materials, well in advance of SAG. Only two years after AFRA formed, members of the Associated Actors and Artists of Americas (AAAA; also known as 4As), an organization formed in 1919 beneath the American Federation of Labor as an umbrella for performers unions, began discussions about television broadcast jurisdiction. Throughout those conversations, AFRA relied on its experience with radio to argue that redistribution of media should be an important component of any new television contract.

Every performer's union would eventually weigh in on the question of who should bargain for television actors. In addition to AEA, AFRA, and SAG, the Chorus Equity Association (CEA), the American Guild of Musical Artists (AGMA), and the American Guild of Variety Artists (AGVA) debated whether television should fall under the jurisdiction of the stage, broadcast, or film union. As SAG's executive secretary Kenneth Thomson explained in some of the earliest jurisdictional conversations: "If television broadcasts are centered around legitimate theatre, unquestionably Equity would be in the best position to give service to the artists. If, on the other hand, television should center in the motion picture field, there is no doubt that the Guild would be better equipped to perform necessary duties. If, as is more likely, television remains primarily a radio problem, then the rights of the membership of AFRA must be considered very carefully."[16]

When discussion about television jurisdiction was reinvigorated after World War II, the unions had two proposals on the table: merging all unions or forming a separate bargaining unit for television that would eventually be subsumed by AFRA. Claiming jurisdiction over television was important organizationally, but this contentious issue alienated some of the members who were simply concerned about their own opportunities to work. Writing to Equity leadership only a few months after the merger failed in 1949, Alan Hewitt, an outspoken actor and pro-merger advocate, explained, "I didn't care about Equity's claim to TV, or anybody else's claim. What would be best for me when I started to work in TV? [...] It is good and worthy of respect or loyalty or affection only so long as it protects my working conditions and continues to try to improve them."[17] Hewitt's comments are straightforward in the assertion that the role of a union is to negotiate the best contract possible for workers, but perhaps implicit in these comments is a sense of exasperation with jurisdictional disputes that simply delayed television contract negotiations as unions continued their infighting.

With each union claiming that performance work on television mirrored its own working conditions, rather than granting jurisdiction to a single union, the 4As formed the Television Authority (TvA) in 1950 to bargain for TV actors. The TvA resolved some issues, but SAG continued to fight over filmed television jurisdiction. Eventually, the unions took their conflict to the National Labor Relations Board (NLRB), which ruled in favor of SAG to maintain its jurisdiction over filmed television. The TvA was a blip in the history of screen performers, but one that ultimately led to AFRA's triumph. Two years after its founding, TvA merged with AFRA to form the American Federation of Television and Radio Artists and consolidated to better negotiate with broadcast networks that represented both radio and television.

AFRA's transition to AFTRA was closely tied to the specificity of radio (and later television) as having production processes and conventions that differed from both film and theater. Thus, one way to add to the histories of media technologies can be to consider how workers understood differences between technologies and the significance of technological changes. In the case of organizing performers in broadcast media, radio and television's abilities to replay and recycle performances were of paramount importance.

Extras Take Center Stage

As the actors unions turned their attention to television, the extras found themselves feeling more marginalized within the concerns of the unions. When

SAG was founded, extras were included as nonvoting junior members, but by 1940, only a few years after signing their first Minimum Basic Agreement, the SAG Board of Directors enlisted the executive staff and the legal department to develop a plan to sever extras from the union. Concurrently, extras, including Harry Mayo, the chairman of SAG's Extras Advisory Committee, began to organize their own union: the Screen Players Union (SPU).

In a move to gain autonomy, Mayo filed a complaint against SAG with the American Federation of Labor (AFL) on May 13, 1941, arguing that SAG failed to sufficiently represent extras, and therefore extras should be able to represent themselves.[18] One of his primary complaints was that SAG negotiated rate increases for speaking roles but not for background.[19] By the time the AFL put jurisdiction of extras to a vote in December 1944, 76 percent of extras voted overwhelmingly in favor of representation by SPU.[20] But like many previous extras unions, SPU was short-lived. Although the NLRB granted SPU the right to bargain for extras, the 4As claimed that SPU did not provide effective or democratic representation and instead recognized a new union called the Screen Extras Guild (SEG).[21]

SEG took over in 1945, but this certainly did not resolve or even address all the problems. This body of inconsistently employed Hollywood workers still had many grievances with their union and the services of Central Casting. While the union engaged in internal debates over what constituted its biggest problem and what it should negotiate for, SEG was also notoriously inaccessible or unhelpful for people of color. Charlene Regester explains that "for African-Americans, being employed in white Hollywood meant being employed as an extra," but this did not mean that Black extras were welcomed into the union in large numbers.[22] At the same time, as the actor Frances Williams noted, "The Screen Extras Guild had black members who were almost never hired."[23] What Williams observed was a function of Hollywood filmmaking reflecting the racism of the era, but also union policies that restricted Black members. Thus, while unions ushered in some important professional standards, they also affirmed Hollywood's systemic whiteness.

The idea that an extras union was best suited to resolve the problems of background actors seemed sound, but as the history shows, it has always been difficult to sustain a union of extras. Part of this might be attributed to the fact that many see these positions as temporary and prefer not to professionally identify as background. But some of the problems SEG experienced may have stemmed from the arrival of television (which required fewer background actors) and the shift in bargaining priorities toward residuals.

SAG and AFTRA Strike!

For their first two decades, SAG and AFTRA leadership and membership focused on establishing key contract terms about rates and set working conditions. But in the 1950s the performers' unions prioritized residuals, which benefit those who work consistently rather than the more conventionally blue-collar focus on workdays. Actors have gone on strike against the companies that constitute the Alliance of Motion Picture and Television Producers (AMPTP) three times (1960, 1980, and 2023), and central to each bargaining slate has been a groundbreaking plan for residuals.

Although radio and television performers commonly received residuals, when the unions began to raise the issues of residuals for *film*, they were attempting to establish a new mode of compensation with a new agreement and standardized rates. During the 1960 contract negotiations, SAG negotiators requested residual payments for all televised films from 1960 forward, along with a lump sum credit to the pension fund for films made between 1948 and the date of the new contract, and a 5 percent contribution (based on earnings) to the SAG pension, health, and welfare program.[24] When studios refused on the logic that actors should not be paid twice for one job, 83 percent of SAG members voted to strike.

The SAG, AFTRA, WGA, and DGA contracts all expire at different times but in relatively rapid succession; thus, a long-running strike could easily bleed into the next set of negotiations (as it did in 1960 and 2023). In 1960—after a thirty-three-day standoff—SAG reached a compromise: residuals would be paid on films from 1960 forward, with an additional $2.5 million paid toward their pension and health care fund. Even though the strike did not turn Hollywood upside down—the studios only had to pause production on eight projects—it successfully established a more robust residual payment structure and laid the groundwork for one of the most important financial changes for actors, writers, and directors in the history of Hollywood.[25]

While actors were successful in making their case for residuals, extras were not.[26] After an unsuccessful attempt to negotiate residuals in 1966, extras became increasingly critical of their leadership. The failure to align extras with the broader priorities of Hollywood's unions and guilds contributed to SEG's long deterioration that began in the 1960s with independent filmmakers turning to use nonunion extras, the elimination of background work due to runaway production, and the rise of television production in the United States.

The prioritization of residuals was significant in an industry where unions could never seem to find a means to help actors make a consistent living and offset the sporadic pay of project-based employment; residuals from legacy films provided a partial solution. Actors already received residuals for kinescope, a type of recorded replay, of East Coast broadcasts on the West Coast, but the 1960 strike marked the first SAG victory for residuals. However, the agreement had limitations: it was a contract only with the film studios, and only for select films that were rebroadcast on television, thus encompassing only one method of replay.

In the late 1960s and early 1970s, SEG's organizational troubles contributed to extras leaving in droves. In 1968, SEG attempted to raise its membership fees to alleviate some of its budgetary troubles, but this did little to improve the union's bargaining position or provide improved services for extras, which frustrated membership even more.[27] A few years later, in 1972, 500 members dropped out of SEG, which diminished membership fees and signaled that the union no longer effectively served its base. Behind closed doors the union was plagued by infighting and power struggles over expenses and how best to support extras, signaling the beginning of a twenty-year decline that would eventually result in extras rejoining SAG in 1992.

As SEG struggled, SAG and AFTRA grappled with prime-time reruns and the arrival of VHS in the 1980 negotiations. SAG and AFTRA decided to draw a hard line with VHS and other supplemental market agreements, refusing to believe the studios' line that these technologies would not generate significant profits for the industry. Negotiations stalled, and on July 21, 1980, SAG and AFTRA walked out. One of the complicating factors in the strike was that the unions were negotiating jointly, but the issues on the table did not affect them equally. For example, the issue of prime-time reruns was more significant for AFTRA, which represented series performers, than for SAG. To bargain successfully, the negotiators had to make sure that improvements in one area, such as supplemental markets, did not come at the expense of other contract terms. As the strike stretched on into September, *Variety* reported that the main sticking points for SAG and AFTRA were related to specifics about *when* (after how many airings or units sold) residuals would kick in for pay TV, videodiscs, and videocassettes.[28]

By the end of September, the negotiating team reached what it considered reasonable new minimums and residuals, but this resolution was met by vocal dissenters. Over the next month SAG leadership battled with members critical of the plan led by spokesman Michael Swan, as well as Ed Asner, Bob Ferro, Brit Lind, Jack Lindine, Thomas Logan, and Bruce Stidham. On October 10, 1980, the SAG board and the anti-ratification group paid for dueling open letters in *Variety* to summarize their respective positions. The open letter supporting the agreement emphasized the substantial (over 30 percent) gains in minimums and residuals, a dental plan, a new affirmative action program that would encourage more diverse hiring, and wider application of California child actor laws to wherever minors worked.[29] The oppositional stance hinged solely on the terms for pay TV, videocassettes, and videodiscs.[30] The different positions on the contract terms reflected the interests of two key union groups. The union achieved terms that would benefit a wide range of membership, but the opposition focused on improving residuals for working actors.

Of particular concern for those who opposed ratifying the agreement was the fact that producers had unlimited airings of a film on pay TV for ten days before triggering profit for actors. The pro-ratification group dismissed the concern that this would be a weak foundation for pay TV, stating, "We are confident that it can and will be improved in future negotiations."[31] Both sides relied on speculation to make their case: the anti-ratification group relied on SAG members to agree with their speculation about the future of technology, and the negotiating committee asked members to trust them. Despite the controversy among a minority of actors, the gains and the desire to return to work all contributed to 83.4 percent of SAG ratifying the new contract.[32] The final contract was almost a full percentage point higher than the producers' initial offer, with actors receiving 4.5 percent of the producers' gross after the sale of 100,000 units (videocassettes and videodiscs).[33] This percentage increase was hard-fought and represented incremental victories over the course of the strike.

The introduction of television and VHS meant that studios had new revenue streams for their old films. When Netflix introduced streaming in 2007, it would appear to be another new form of distribution, but the changes wrought by streaming services, which soon became studios, were fundamental in terms of financing, contracts, and distribution. Union contracts with the streaming services-cum-media producers (Apple, Amazon, and Netflix) differed from those with the legacy studios, but their contracts followed the same logic of other new technologies, like television and VHS. Since streaming was new, these services' future profits were uncertain, and therefore the earliest contracts were minimal. In this case, residuals were based on licensing agreements for existing shows and for streamers' original programs they were minimal because streamers' cost-plus financing model paid more money upfront. For actors this had broad implications for earnings. Star contracts were reconfigured so that actors received more money before the film or show was released to the streaming platform, giving them little to no success-based revenue, even if their film or show continued to be successful.

By the time the TV/Theatrical contract came up for renegotiation in 2023, cable was losing 15,000 subscribers per day, and streaming had almost fully replaced cable as the primary television distributor in the United States.[34] Actors needed to make up ground during their negotiations and find a way to participate in streaming's profits. As was the case in 1960, SAG-AFTRA walked out of negotiations and joined the WGA on strike. Although residuals and some form of success-based payment for streaming media were central to this round of negotiations, SAG-AFTRA also negotiated for rate increases, protections against artificial intelligence, and changes to audition practices. When SAG-AFTRA finally reached an agreement—after the longest strike in the unions' history—the response leading up to ratification was mixed. One hundred percent of the SAG-AFTRA board and nearly 98 percent of the union authorized the strike, but the agreement was ratified by 86 percent of the board, and as the details of the contract trickled out to voting members, many (as discussed in further depth in the coda to this book) voiced strong criticisms of the artificial intelligence provisions.

SAG and AFTRA have long been stratified unions, and their management and negotiating teams have been tasked with representing a wide array of members with varied incomes and levels of fame. Thus, it should come as no surprise that in the wake of actors' strikes, there has historically been a vocal minority that wants to reject contracts following strikes. For example, 83 percent of the SAG board and 90 percent of the AFTRA board supported the agreement following the 1980 strike. A vocal minority took out advertisements explaining their position in *Backstage*, but the majority of the membership still ratified the contract (83.4 percent). Even when actors' contracts represent record gains, it is possible that they might still fall short of the desired terms or outcomes.

The SAG-AFTRA Merger

Performers' union mergers have a long and controversial history beginning with the first proposal to merge all of these unions in 1939. All mergers have logistical challenges, including consolidating administration, acquiring new debt, and merging retirement plans, but these are administrative hurdles. The broader philosophical pros and cons are what have historically weighed on a membership's decision. Those in favor of merging say that a large union, which can cause a more significant work stoppage during a strike, wields more power at the bargaining table. Those against a merger claim that a smaller union can assume more homogeneity among membership demands and be more focused on the rank-and-file membership during contract renegotiations. These differences in positions broadly characterize the membership factions and union priorities for the sixty-year period in which a merger of screen performance unions was under discussion.

Performers' unions first entertained the idea of a merger to resolve the dispute over television jurisdiction. Although SAG and its consistent ally SEG were successful in stopping the merger in 1949, the subject of merger persisted over subsequent decades. Actors such as Alan Hewitt continued to write to their unions and speak in favor of merger wherever he thought he might find a sympathetic audience, which was primarily in the AFTRA ranks.

A significant part of the internal debates and institutional histories of SAG and later AFTRA can be characterized as jurisdictional disputes. As the introduction to part I of this book shows, some below-the-line jurisdictional disputes ended in violence. Rather than confrontations on the picket lines, SAG and AFTRA fought over contracts through salty correspondence and in-person meetings over professional identities, who the unions should serve, and what advantages could be gained by expanding union membership. Although a larger union could draw more dues from the populous membership base, actors opposing the merger pointed out that an expanded union might fail to meet the needs of middle-class members in different performance or media sectors. As distinctions between media forms began to erode in the twenty-first century, this argument became less compelling to members who found themselves paying dues to multiple unions. Further, these interunion disputes seemed, at least to some, to undermine negotiating positions.

The idea of a merger was revived in earnest after the 1980 strike. By 1981, most screen actors felt there were significant benefits to a merger and approved a three-phase plan for unification. Phase 1 was to jointly negotiate contracts, phase 2 to combine union governance, and phase 3 was the final merger. After implementing this plan, the process stalled for over three decades. In 2003, union leadership tried to progress to phase 2 of the merger plan, but SAG and AFTRA membership campaigned to keep the unions separate. Central to understanding the conflict between the unions were the realities that these unions had different levels of prestige, different membership requirements (AFTRA's bar was lower), and an emphasis on different mediums (film vs. television). For SAG members who were adamantly against the merger, these factors contributed to a perception that AFTRA would be a burden to the storied screen actors' union.

Ultimately, the growing cultural importance of television helped make the merger more palatable to many SAG members in 2012. Television and commercials had long been the greatest source of work for actors, but contracts on television series were split between AFTRA and SAG. In 2009, only 37 percent of NBC, CBS, ABC, Fox, and the CW programs were under AFTRA contracts, but by 2010, the percentage of AFTRA shows had ballooned to 54 percent. During this same period, television was also becoming more widely accepted as a venue for quality writing and performances. Thus, the trend toward AFTRA's dominance over television contracts and the increased cultural value of television indicated that SAG ultimately needed AFTRA as a bargaining partner and that it would not constitute a lowering of the union's prestige.

In the first half of the twentieth century, union members favored more professionally homogeneous unions divided by medium. As the media industries began to generate increased profit through reproduction and new modes of distribution, and television became more culturally respected, the original place of production mattered less for union members. SAG-AFTRA now represents 160,000 members in negotiations against media conglomerates, but even as cultural distinctions between media have eroded, the variable levels of prestige among the diverse membership have not.

Actors' Grievances: Blue-Collar Problems and White-Collar Solutions

Throughout their respective histories, SAG and AFTRA have represented thousands of members with diverse skill sets, aspirations, and careers. One thing, however, has remained consistent: negotiations benefit the minority of members who work consistently. Although unions need to represent all members on professional issues, SAG and AFTRA are unique because of the high percentage of members who work infrequently and fail to meet the threshold to qualify for health benefits, making it hard to address their workplace issues. In the case of SAG and AFTRA, this has often meant that the unions support a minority, rather than a majority, of their members.

Although job placement is often one of the primary concerns of blue-collar unions, the thousands of actors who are primarily concerned with finding sufficient work do not have recourse to their union, which cannot intervene in the hiring process. Instead, SAG, AFTRA, and SAG-AFTRA evolved to focus on white-collar demands, such as residuals, which offer the most benefit to those who work sporadically but consistently. White-collar unions provide the advantages of collective bargaining but none of the employment security of blue-collar unions.

Acting is a fiercely competitive profession, with thousands of people—union and nonunion—vying for limited positions. Casting, from leading role to background actor, is based largely on appearances, which can include physicality, race, ethnicity, and gender presentation. For many women (especially those over thirty), BIPOC, queer, and differently abled actors, opportunities are restricted by the stories being told and the choices being made about casting. Legal scholar Russell Robinson has written about how Hollywood casting practices, which often specify race and gender in casting breakdowns, are protected under the First Amendment and Title VII. As Robinson writes, "The casting process . . . lies at the nexus of two quite different doctrinal regimes: (1) a First Amendment rule protecting artistic freedom, and (2) employment regulation banning hiring decisions based on impermissible factors. When viewed through the lens of artistic freedom, casting announcements parroting the script's sex and race preferences may strike us as reasonable and unoffensive. But when we place them in the context of employment discrimination law, we can see the highly anomalous nature of casting."[35]

Acting is a form of highly visible and creative work that presents unique challenges to increasing diversity and creating tangible gains in hiring. Filmmakers are protected when they specify race, gender, and age range in casting breakdowns. Thus unions, which may want to help a wider range of women and BIPOC people to find work, do not have recourse that would allow them to fight for inclusive hiring practices. Instead, unions must find ways to encourage a wider array of on-screen stories that would create more advantageous casting possibilities for underrepresented groups.

Diversity committees within SAG and AFTRA designed initiatives to influence culture and create demand to diversify stories. In 1972, SAG and AFTRA performers formed national women's committees to address women's employment struggles in the industry and ethnic minority committees to address injustices faced by people of color. These committees were part of a movement in the above-the-line unions. However, as Miranda Banks and Maya Montañez Smukler show in their respective work on the WGA's and the DGA's women's committees, these histories reveal more cultural roadblocks than transformative changes to decision-making and hiring.[36] Given that unions have few options to affect hiring, they struggled to implement policies and instead were left trying to change cultural practices.

SAG and AFTRA are unable to directly affect hiring practices, which has made it difficult for the unions to serve most of their members. Actors can also be limited by their perceived skill level and abilities and may need to hone their craft before they are ready for their close-up. Contemporary unions offer an array of workshops to help members develop professional skills, but much of the additional training comes from classes and workshops that actors pay for out of pocket. This has been a source of frustration for all underemployed members, but it also means that the union is unable to fully contribute to diversity efforts in Hollywood. Rather than negotiating for more opportunities for underrepresented members, SAG-AFTRA must resort to toothless cultural initiatives, which creates challenges for advocates of more inclusive hiring practices in media.

Actors in the Wake of #MeToo

Actors struggled through myriad workplace abuses as early as the 1910s and 1920s related to job availability, hours, compensation, and the sexual exploitation of aspiring actresses, which would later be known as "casting couch" scandals, in which directors and producers took advantage of aspiring stars.[37] Many of these sex scandals captured the national imaginary and would come to expose Hollywood's pervasive labor problems in the 1920s amid growing societal concerns about women's virtue. In an industry with uncertain career paths, where women gained employment based on looks, the issue of morality, rather than wages and working conditions, was what jolted the studios into short-lived action. Despite attempts to rationalize the casting process through Central Casting and the many efforts of female stars to dispel the idea that women were cast as a quid pro quo for sleeping with powerful producers and directors, pernicious rumors have persisted.

Rather than framing casting couch scandals in terms of rape, assault, or harassment, industry organizations, including SAG, historically addressed these as problems of "morality." Implicit in many of the casting couch stories is an assumption that fame-seeking women court advances from powerful producers. In a 1975 *Variety* article titled "'Casting Couch': Fiction or Fact?," SAG announced the intention to "investigate methods by which its members can air and get solved their 'morality' complaints."[38] In this context, *morality* is a euphemistic term, which suggests a range of behaviors and minimizes the power dynamics that are implicit in the casting couch. However, as the article makes plain, actors were unclear about how to raise and address these problems related to morality, whatever they might be.

As allegations against actors such as Noel Clarke and Kip Pardue indicate, women have been harassed and assaulted by union peers, and the problem cannot be reduced to casting couch power abuses. For much of their early histories, SAG and, to some extent, AFTRA prioritized on-set working conditions. They protected against abuses on set in relation to overtime or dangerous stunts, but the union did not address on- or off-set harassment and sexual assault within this context of worker protections. Some of this is likely due to a lack of social awareness and a permissive climate around harassment in the workplace, but that does not change the fact that the existence of harassment in Hollywood was an open secret for decades. Many condemned it as an abuse of power, but unions and studios did not take action to stop the behavior of well-known predators.

In the wake of allegations beginning in 2017 against producer Harvey Weinstein and other industry players who abused their positions of power to harass and assault women—many, but not all, of whom were actors—some pointed to SAG-AFTRA as being part of the problem rather than the solution. Writing for *The Jacobian*, the actor Morgan Spector explains that even though SAG-AFTRA has a "zero tolerance" policy for harassment, the process of reporting placed a great deal of pressure on individual actors, and the union offered little workplace support or advocacy.[39] SAG-AFTRA is against sexual harassment and assault, but as was the case with the minority and women's committees in the 1970s, the efforts of the performers' unions were inadequate to the task of supporting the safety of women in Hollywood.

SAG-AFTRA responded with additional policies and its new Four Pillars of Change Initiative to help its members in early 2018. The four categories identified general goals, such as "expand our capacity to intervene rapidly and forcefully to protect our members," and enumerated specific resources, such as establishing a trauma hotline, increasing educational efforts, and developing new resources.[40] SAG-AFTRA expanded its efforts to protect members, but these still were not wholly integrated into contracts and on-set safety measures. In the year following these new procedures, SAG-AFTRA was enmeshed in numerous cases, including Sarah Scott's allegations against Kip Pardue. Pardue was found guilty, but Scott came out publicly against SAG-AFTRA's reporting procedures and policies, stating that the guild guidelines are "not protective measures with penalties and fines attached."[41]

To minimize physical risks to performers, SAG-AFTRA began working with Intimacy Directors International in 2019 to create safer and more professional sets. Intimacy coordinators, as Inge Sørensen writes, "discuss and plan the practical, physical and psychological preparations for and the performance of these scenes [involving nudity and sex] with the actors, crew, the Director and the Producer, as well as negotiate and supervise their filming."[42] As Sørensen points out, intimacy coordinators work to ensure performers' safety, mitigate risks to production companies by keeping projects on budget and schedule, and provide evidence that studios and unions are making an effort to change in post-#MeToo and post-Weinstein Hollywood.[43] These efforts are commendable, but it is notable that SAG-AFTRA enlisted help from outside the union. As safety concerns have shifted, unions have increasingly outsourced support and care labor, thus expanding the number of, in this case, nonunionized people working on set.

Sexual harassment and assault have long been concerns for women auditioning and working on set. The position of the union has been to denounce harassment and assault, but changes to contracts and more concrete inclusion of these terms into negotiations have been slow to arrive at the bargaining table. In previous eras, internal debates over union priorities were often based on job hierarchies, with some members bristling at the union addressing any issues around race and gender. The #MeToo allegations were an important crisis point for the union, which made these long-running issues more urgent in the minds of all members, even if they might disproportionately affect women.

Safety in COVID Times

As the coronavirus spread worldwide in early 2020, SAG-AFTRA was vocal about issuing "do not work" orders. Actors were both at the forefront of the closures and particularly vulnerable on set. At least publicly, the shutdown seemed to start when actors Tom Hanks and Rita Wilson announced that they had tested positive for COVID-19 while shooting *Elvis* in Australia. In subsequent weeks, sets shut down around the world, and union productions were slow to resume, even after guidelines were in place and shooting was allowed to restart, largely out of concern for actors' safety. Actors need to be on set and in close physical proximity to other actors, as well as crew members such as makeup artists, hairstylists, costumers, and directors. At a time when everyone was supposed to be physically distancing, actors were especially vulnerable.

By the end of the summer, few productions had successfully resumed; those that did were able to do so through complicated logistics, frequent COVID testing, and creative filming practices. Tyler Perry set up a production bubble at his notoriously anti-union studio, while other films and television shows used the zoning system, which meant actors encountered fewer people on set. *The Bold and the Beautiful* experimented with using mannequins for body doubles in intimate scenes, to keep actors physically distant without disrupting the story. While many of these productions were able to commence filming safely, shooting for *The Batman* shut down three days into production when the film's star, Robert Pattinson, tested positive for COVID-19. The risk of COVID-19 introduced challenges to the production process, but ultimately on-set work resumed more quickly than theatrical exhibition.

Production pauses affected the ability of all actors to work, but theatrical closures had a particular impact on an elite few. The result of the prolonged pandemic was that film studios began to release big-budget films day-and-date, simultaneously in theaters and streaming, or directly to their streaming platforms. These decisions had a dramatic impact on stars' incomes as they were bought out of back-end deals tied to the theatrical box office. As a result of these new distribution strategies, Scarlett Johansson's representatives filed a breach of contact complaint against Disney, which released *Black Widow* day-and-date in more than 4,000 theaters and on Disney+. Disney settled this complaint out of court, giving Johansson an individual victory. Johansson's brief battle against Disney did not involve her union but instead her highly paid team of lawyers and agents working on her behalf to establish a precedent for other top-earning talent.

During the pandemic closures, SAG-AFTRA returned to its original focus: negotiating working conditions to keep actors safe on set. With respect to earnings, however, there was little the union could do to alleviate financial pressures for their members. Successful stars turned to their teams to recuperate lost bonuses, and regularly working actors supplemented their incomes with residual checks, but those who relied on regular and consistent work as they built their careers had to wait for production to resume.

Conclusion

Whether on set, at the negotiating table, or on the picket line, media making is a collaborative endeavor that shapes the final product on the screen. As the history of SAG and AFTRA shows, collaboration between workers does not always resolve smoothly. The differences between types of work, experience, and individual bargaining power have all historically created tremendous internal conflict within the unions. The dynamics of white-collar identity, despite labor precarity, alongside the emphasis on appearance in the profession create unique vulnerabilities for actors. For better or worse, these interpersonal forces within unions have shaped the contours of this competitive and precarious job that offers creative satisfaction to many and fame and stability to a select few.

Notes

1 *E! Live from the Red Carpet*, January 27, 2013.
2 I will only refer to SAG-AFTRA as a merged union for events after 2012.
3 Kate Fortmueller, *Below the Stars: How the Labor of Working Actors and Extras Shapes Media Production* (University of Texas Press, 2021), 22–26; Charlie Keil, "Leo Rosencrans, Movie-Struck Boy: A (Half-)Year in the Life of a Hollywood Extra," *Film History* 26, no. 2 (2014): 31–51.
4 For more on Bess Flowers, see Beverly Linet and Margorie Rosen, "Huff-Buffs and the Ephemera Mystique," *New York Magazine,* August 16, 1971, 60–61; Scott Feinberg, "20 Feet from Movie Stardom: The Overlooked Story of Hollywood's Greatest Extra," *The Hollywood Reporter* (hereafter *THR*), February 20, 2014, https://www.hollywoodreporter.com/race/20-feet-movie-stardom-overlooked

-682162; Will Straw, "Scales of Presence: Bess Flowers and the Hollywood Extra," *Screen* 52, no. 1 (Spring 2011): 121–127.

5 Morton Thompson, "Hollywood Is a Union Town," *The Nation* 146:14, April 2, 1938, 381.

6 Louis Perry and Richard Perry, *A History of the Los Angeles Labor Movement, 1911–1941* (University of California Press, 1963), 342.

7 Sean P. Holmes, *Weavers of Dreams, Unite! Actors' Unionism in Early Twentieth-Century America* (University of Illinois Press, 2013), 157–158.

8 Academy of Motion Picture Arts and Sciences, Constitution and Bylaws, 1927, 14–15, AMPAS Reference Collection, Margaret Herrick Library, Academy of Motion Picture Arts and Sciences (hereafter AMPAS), https://digitalcollections .oscars.org/digital/collection/p15759coll4/id/4288/rec/1.

9 Percentage calculated from "Bulletin no. 21, June 3, 1929," 10–11, AMPAS Reference Collection, Margaret Herrick Library, AMPAS, http://catalog.oscars.org/vwebv /holdingsInfo?bibId=69418.

10 For further explanation of this process, see David Prindle, *The Politics of Glamour: Ideology and Democracy in the Screen Actors Guild* (University of Wisconsin Press, 1988), 22.

11 Ida Jeter, "The Collapse of the Federation of Motion Picture Crafts: A Case Study in Class Collaboration," *Journal of the University Film Association* 31, no. 2 (1979): 42; Prindle, *Politics of Glamour,* 26–28.

12 David Prindle, *Politics of Glamour,* 32.

13 Leo Rosten, *Hollywood: The Movie Colony* (Harcourt, Brace, 1941), 336.

14 Untitled Board of Directors Memo, February 19, 1940, Stephan Vaughn Collection, Box 3, Wisconsin Center for Film and Theater Research, Madison, WI.

15 Rita Morley Harvey, *Those Wonderful Terrible Years: George Heller and the American Federation of Television and Radio Artists* (Southern Illinois University Press, 1996), 23.

16 Kenneth Thomson to Frank Gillmore, June 29, 1938, Folder 31: Associated Actors and Artistes of America Records, New York University, Tamiment Library and Robert F. Wagner Labor Archives, New York, NY.

17 Alan Hewitt, "Letter to Equity, December 3, 1949," Alan Hewitt Papers, Box 1, New York Public Library for the Performing Arts, New York, NY.

18 Anthony Slide, *Hollywood Unknowns: A History of Extras, Bit Players, and Stand-Ins* (University Press of Mississippi, 2012), 209.

19 "Guild Defends Its Effort for Screen Extras," *Los Angeles Times* (hereafter *LAT*), April 4, 1944.

20 "Film Extras Vote to Break from Screen Actors' Guild: Defeated Union Pans Fight for Bargaining Power," *LAT,* December 18, 1944.

21 "AAAA Backs Film Extras' Guild in Row with Screen Players Union," *New York Times,* May 18, 1945.

22 Charlene Regester, "African American Extras in Hollywood during the 1920s and 1930s," *Film History* 9, no. 1 (March 1997) : 96.

23 Anna Christian, *Meet It, Greet It, and Defeat It: The Biography of Frances E. Williams* (Milligan, 1999), 160, quoted in Gerald Horne, *Class Struggle in Hollywood, 1930–1950: Moguls, Mobsters, Stars, Reds, and Trade Unionists* (University of Texas Press, 2001), 52.

24 For further details, see Howard Kennedy, "SAG, Studios Recess Talks over Week End," *LAT,* March 19, 1960; "SAG Package Plan Weighed by Producers," *LAT,* March 21, 1960.

25 Penelope Houston, "After the Strike," *Sight and Sound* 26, no. 3 (1960): 108.

26 Vance King, "SEG Pitches TV Reuse Payment for Blurbs," *THR*, November 14, 1966.

27 "Screen Extras Guild Finances Need Fixing," *Variety*, May 29, 1968, 14.

28 Will Tusher, "SAG-AFTRA Return to the Bargaining Table after Mulling Producers' 'Message,'" *Variety*, September 3, 1980, 1.

29 "We Urge a Yes Vote on the SAG Contract Referendum," *Variety*, October 10, 1980, 12; see also Howard Osofsky and Jan Schneiderman, "The California Gold Rush: SAG's 1980 Strike Revisited," *Journal of Arts Management and Law* 12, no. 2 (Summer 1982): 14.

30 "To the SAG and AFTRA Membership," *Variety*, October 10, 1980, 13.

31 "We Urge a Yes Vote on the SAG Contract Referendum," *Variety*, October 10, 1980, 12.

32 Dave Kaufman, "SAG Overwhelmingly OK's New Pact," *Variety*, October 24, 1980, 1.

33 Will Tusher, "Strike's Impact Spreads; Prune Prod. Payrolls," *Variety*, August 6, 1980, 1, 92.

34 Luke Bouma, "2023 the Year Cable TV Died? It Is Starting to Look That Way," *Cord Cutters News*, October 22, 2023, https://cordcuttersnews.com/2023-the-year-cable-tv-died-it-is-starting-to-look-that-way/#:~:text=Rapid%20Decline%20In%20Cable%20TV,every%20single%20day%20in%202023.

35 Russell K. Robinson, "Casting and Caste-ing: Reconciling Artistic Freedom and Antidiscrimination Norms," *California Law Review* 95, no. 1 (2007): 2.

36 Miranda Banks, "Unequal Opportunities—Gender Inequities and Precarious Diversity," *Feminist Media Histories* 4, no. 4 (Fall 2018), 109–129; Maya Montañez Smukler, "Thirty Years of Women Directors," UCLA CSW Update Newsletter, January 1, 2011.

37 For detailed discussion of these scandals, see Denise McKenna, "The City that Made the Pictures Move: Gender, Labor and Los Angeles, 1908–1917" (PhD diss., New York University, 2008).

38 "'Casting Couch': Fiction or Fact?," *Variety*, May 21, 1975, 32.

39 Morgan Spector, "Harvey Weinstein's Crimes and SAG's Failure," *The Jacobian*, October 17, 2017, https://www.jacobinmag.com/2017/10/harvey-weinstein-union-sag-aftra-hollywood.

40 Gabrielle Carteris and David White, "Ensuring Safe and Equitable Workplaces," SAG-AFTRA, accessed May 18, 2024, https://www.sagaftra.org/files/call_to_action_final.pdf.

41 Dave McNary, "Matthew Modine, Rosanna Arquette Allege Gabrielle Carteris Mishandled SAG-AFTRA's Sexual Harassment Protections," *Variety*, August 1, 2019, https://variety.com/2019/film/news/sag-aftra-gabrielle-carteris-criticized-sexual-harassment-protections-1203287493/.

42 Inge Sørensen, "Sex and Safety on Set: Intimacy Coordinators in Television Drama and Film in the VOD and Post-Weinstein Era," *Feminist Media Studies* 22, no. 6 (2021): 5.

43 Sørensen, "Sex and Safety," 12.

11

Directors

• •

Power, Prestige, and the
Politics of Authorship

MAYA MONTAÑEZ SMUKLER

The Directors Guild of America (DGA) was founded by all men who were each successful in their craft, and the business of making motion pictures has for generations enforced the white, patriarchal hierarchy that structures media production, emphasized by the organization's mandate: "one director to a picture."[1] The elevation of the director has been necessitated by elitism that fosters exclusion: talent may be nurtured by hard work and practice, but greatness is one of a kind. Despite this origin story and its mandate, the DGA, in fact, represents the directorial team—assistant directors, unit production managers, associate directors, stage managers, and production associates—working in film, television, digital content, and new media production. Established in 1936, the DGA (originally the Screen Directors Guild) was founded by a group of feature film directors to protect their artistic rights and economic security; in doing so, the guild established the director as the pinnacle of creative and financial negotiating power. As the guild's membership has expanded, in tandem with the changing means of production, distribution, and exhibition, every new generation challenges this mandate in different ways as it continues to guide the organization's bargaining priorities and public image.

Directors themselves have debated their role as the single author, or as a member of a collaborative team. Dorothy Arzner, who worked as an editor and scenario writer during the silent era before she started directing during the transition to sound and into the classic studio period, told *Silver Screen* magazine in 1931 that "directing is compromise.... Ideally the director is like the conductor of an orchestra and all the players work in perfect harmony."[2] Alejandro González Iñárritu, a contemporary filmmaker, describes how he and the cinematographer Rodrigo Prieto have, over the years, "developed a communication level that is not only effective and very productive, but also very profound. We skip all those things that you normally have to go through when you start collaborating with someone. We just go straight to the DNA."[3] Other directors have felt more protective, and even territorial, in asserting their authority over the filmmaking process. "The creation of art is not a democratic process," proclaimed Steven Spielberg during the controversial debate over the colorization of black-and-white films that took place in the late 1980s. "The public has no right to vote on the artistic choices that go into filmmaking. The public has the right to accept or reject the result, but not to participate in the action."[4]

This chapter examines how the DGA has asserted the value of artistic excellence in the business of making and selling mass media through the job of the director—specifically the feature film director—as a mix of craftsmanship and celebrity, an expert of often mythical status. Over the course of its history, the guild has grappled with and adjusted to a changing media industry, from the ascendancy of television in the 1950s to the convergence of film, television, and digital media platforms starting, most prominently, around twenty years ago. In navigating its power and influence within a broader cultural context, the DGA has been forced in times of great social and political upheaval—during the Hollywood blacklist and the civil rights and feminist movements—to examine its values as an organization representing a large and complex membership that is diverse in its professional experiences and personal identities.

The director's position in film culture has often served as the arbiter of artistic taste and aesthetic standards. Virginia Wright Wexman's *Hollywood's Artists: The Directors Guild of America and the Construction of Authorship*, the first book-length study of the Directors Guild, examines the role of the film director as an individual artist who functions and thrives within a community of peers "working in concert with larger trends both within the film industry and in the popular imagination, [and] the DGA's efforts have helped overcome traditional biases against the idea of mainstream cinema as an art form and of Hollywood directors as artists."[5] Building on Wright Wexman's argument, this chapter considers the guild's role in negotiating the often incongruous partnership between creative and labor rights by sustaining the elevated and powerful status of the director within a membership that also represents below-the-line crew.

Over the course of film history, all kinds of critics, from the mainstream press to academic journals, and, more recently, self-assigned reviewers on social media platforms, have contributed to the lionization (through flops and successes) of directors. Audience tastes measured by box office numbers or sales of books, toys, and apparel across ancillary markets can contribute to a director's hiring fate, profit margins, and trendsetting influence. Film canons built and maintained by historians, cinema studies courses, and film society lists establish standards for what constitutes a "classic," "the best," and "the greatest," keeping individual directors and their bodies of work relevant, in conversation and discoverable, until perhaps a generational tide turns. The DGA is frequently historicized, often by the guild itself, as one of the industry's most powerful labor organizations. Central to that power is the guild's priority in shaping and selling creative authorship, efforts that often overshadow the below-the-line crew whose invaluable work in supporting the director does not translate as easily to celebrity status.

Creative Struggles: The Establishment of the Screen Directors Guild

Before the DGA was officially established in 1936, directors made efforts to organize in different ways. Formed in 1915, the Motion Picture Directors Association (MPDA) was described as "part gentleman's club, part think tank and part quiet lobbying organization" with a robust membership between 100 to 200 men.[6] A few women were admitted to the MPDA as "honorary members," including Lois Weber in 1916.[7] In 1927, directors, writers, and performers joined the anti-union Academy of Motion Picture Arts and Sciences (AMPAS), buying into the pitch about prestige over an interest in the employment rights that a union would provide. However, in the 1930s, Hollywood successfully unionized: the Screen Actors Guild and the Screen Writers Guild were formed in 1933. In the same period, directors sensed that their creative authority would be threatened as the transition to sound centralized production under the authority of studio executives.

In 1935, future DGA members began to meet clandestinely, and the group incorporated in January 1936. Although descriptions of the DGA's formation vary slightly across sources, the following summary is consistent with most accounts. The *Motion Picture Herald* reported that forty of the highest-paid and most well-known directors had resigned from AMPAS to form the DGA. The group listed many grievances, but of primary concern "was a desire to protect themselves against producers who recently had been minimizing the power of the directors."[8] Additional concerns included "more time to study a script before shooting... halting the practice of giving a director a script only one or two days before shooting is to start; elimination of second units, only one director on a picture; abolish the practice of keeping directors out of cutting rooms. Allow directors to follow their pictures through to the final editing."[9] The directors had met secretly with officers from the Screen Actors Guild and the Screen Writers Guild, and a corporate charter was obtained under the name Screen Directors, Inc.

On January 16, 1936, the DGA held its first membership meeting at the Hollywood Athletic Club, with 40 directors in attendance; less than a week later another membership meeting was called, with 125 directors present, 75 of whom had already signed up.[10] The temporary officers list included King Vidor, president; Lewis Milestone, first vice president; Frank Tuttle, second vice president; William K. Howard, secretary; and John Ford, treasurer. The board of directors consisted of Frank Borzage, Clarence Brown, John Cromwell, Howard Hawks, Wesley Ruggles, Rouben Mamoulian, William Wellman, Gregory La Cava, Edward Sutherland, and H. Bruce Humberstone.

In 1937, the DGA expanded its membership to include the directors' crew, admitting assistant directors and unit production mangers, and substantially increasing the guild's membership from 90 to 550.[11] Producers balked at this decision. Darryl F. Zanuck drew attention to the hierarchy within the guild by making a distinction in how "directors perform a service which is fundamentally creative. . . . On the other hand, the unit manager and the assistant director represent the business and managerial side of production." This distinction placed the two groups at odds. Zanuck further contended that adding these below-the-line positions as members would give the directors "greater numerical strength" during contract negotiations.[12] Wright Wexman reasons that the guild's leadership, as represented by the most successful and best-paid directors, must have understood that including lower-ranking members of the director's crew would give the group more validity as a labor organization advocating for equitable pay, fair working conditions, and their creative rights. In turn, the impact of a strike would be more detrimental if it involved large numbers of employees who handled the logistical details of production.[13] Members of the directorial team would receive protection from the guild, as outlined in its contract with the producers. Under the Basic Agreement, minimum pay would be established, and positions for first and second assistant directors would be provided for on every feature and short film, therefore ensuring job opportunities for those who were guild members; any disputes with producers would be settled under the terms of the contract. Furthermore, assistant directors considered their job to include creative responsibilities that supported and contributed to the work of directors; representing those two positions within the same guild would provide continuity and conducive circumstances for collaboration.[14]

Unsurprisingly, negotiations with producers were difficult, and it was not until 1939 that the DGA had a signed agreement with the studios. The course of events entailed hearings before the National Labor Relations Board (NLRB) in 1938. Frank Capra, who had not yet assumed a formal leadership role in the nascent guild beyond his membership, was then president of the Academy and led a heroic intervention in the battle to negotiate with the producer Joseph

Schenck. The new contract established minimum salaries for assistant directors, including those who were freelance. The producers fought, and won, to prevent the unit production managers from joining the directors for fear that their membership block would add to the guild's power.[15] Unit production managers then formed a separate union, the Unit Production Managers Guild, before eventually merging with the DGA in 1964.

The DGA's first contract made clear the director's authority in all areas of a film's production, establishing how "'directing' or 'direction,' is unique and all embracing." The contract detailed the ways "he," the director, would work closely with all creative units on a film's production, including "story, acting, dialogue, movements, music, song, dance, camera, photography, sound recording, scenery, costumes, props, make up, etc. The director's task is to contribute creatively to all these elements and to guide, mold and integrate them into one cohesive dramatic and aesthetic whole."[16]

In its formative years the DGA fought for the creative rights of an entitled class within the filmmaking community. The press enjoyed calling out the wealth and privilege of the new guild leaders. The author of one *Hollywood Reporter* column seemed almost incredulous when writing that the organization would be made up of "studio workers from the $100,000 a year brackets down to the daylaborers," and how it was such a surprise that "the industry's most individualistic group" had finally organized.[17] Several of the early guild leaders were producers themselves, and several had negotiated independent contracts during an era of studio control. For example, writer-director-producer Capra's negotiating prowess was legendary because he could bridge the schisms between director and producer. This blend of industry stature, collective confidence drawn from individual bravado, and solidarity between directors and below-the-line fellow members would give the guild unique strength and complexity.

Heroic Legacies: Patriotism and the Loyalty Oath

Hollywood's participation in World War II is defined by great displays of community and patriotism. Directors' participation, most famously by the "Five Came Back" (Frank Capra, John Ford, John Huston, George Stevens, and William Wyler), as Mark Harris calls them in his book, who served in the military and made training and propaganda pieces for the United States armed services, fostered an image of artists driven by politically enlightened goals.[18] To question this group's loyalty to the United States was unimaginable, as, according to Capra: "It would be impossible for me to ever be dis-loyal [*sic*] to America. It would also be impossible for me to ever be anything but violently anti-Communist."[19] The image of industry patriotism, however, was challenged by the actions of the House Un-American Activities Committee (HUAC), which, starting in 1947, began to attack Hollywood in its investigation and accusations of communist influence and sympathy.

Among HUAC's industry targets was a group that became known as the "Unfriendly Nineteen," which included the directors Herbert Biberman, Edward Dmytryk, Lewis Milestone, Irving Pichel, and Robert Rossen. Biberman and Dmytryk became part of the Hollywood Ten and were cited for contempt of Congress, and each served a prison term. An ideological showdown erupted, drawing party lines between the conservative Cecil B. DeMille and liberal Joseph L. Mankiewicz, who was guild president at the time. Membership debates regarding a mandated loyalty oath further polarized guild leadership. The specter of blacklisting had descended on the film and television community, revealing political and ideological fissures among high-ranking DGA membership; their conflicts and dilemmas echoed those taking place in Hollywood and nationwide.

The issue, which has often been referred to as a guild "civil war," came to a head when DeMille proposed that members take a mandatory loyalty oath, disavow communism, and provide information on the political beliefs of all the actors and technicians they employed as a condition for being allowed to work in Hollywood. The results would then be sent to prospective employers, with the clear implication that failure to sign would ensure employment rejection. Mankiewicz, who had voluntarily signed the oath and, by many accounts including his own, did not appear to oppose taking the oath in principle, took issue with making it mandatory. Further, he did not approve of making public the results of each member's oath-taking decision. While Mankiewicz was out of the country, DeMille orchestrated, through questionable tactics and without Mankiewicz's knowledge, the machinations of an impeachment by securing a vote of 547 to 14 that the loyalty oath would be a requirement for membership in the DGA.[20] Upon his return, Mankiewicz insisted on a public meeting of all the members to debate and decide the issue. That meeting was held on October 22, 1950, in the Crystal Room of the Beverly Hills Hotel in front of 500 members (with only 240 senior members eligible to vote).[21] The vote was cast in support of Mankiewicz.

Scholars have interrogated the meeting and the events leading up to it across a wide range of sources; most scrutinized are the accounts by directors who were witnesses and sometimes active participants.[22] One salient point for historians and historical subjects alike is that memories are unreliable over time, and what emerges are compelling myths surrounding real events. The DGA's official telling of the events as published in the *DGA Quarterly* in 2011, on the guild's seventy-fifth anniversary, told the story as a thriller, with the tagline: "Could ideology destroy fraternity?" In the end, the guild and the core of its fraternal brotherhood were salvaged, and the organization moved forward with a semblance of cohesion. Both protagonists maintained their high level of respectability in the guild and in the industry. Mankiewicz won the award for Outstanding Directorial Achievement for *All About Eve* at the 1950 DGA awards. (The film also swept the Academy Awards, winning an Oscar for Best Picture and Best Director.) In 1953, the guild bestowed its first lifetime achievement award on DeMille.

This period is often historicized by framing the guild conflict as a power struggle around political ideology and freedom of expression waged between two high-profile directors and underlined by acts of individual male heroism. Instead, what emerges is a far less easy story of hero versus villain or conservative versus liberal. The headline-grabbing showdown between DeMille and Mankiewicz appeared to have a minor political impact in stemming the tide of anti-communist fear and paranoia that was rampant in Hollywood. For these directors, freedom of political expression mingled with a shared sense of patriotism, and their identity as working commercial artists within a professional ecosystem manifested in complex interpersonal relationships and debate. If the purpose of the DGA was to ensure its members' potential to work and thrive professionally, the HUAC hearings and loyalty oaths threatened the guild's unity. This historical episode points to how generational attitudes in DGA leadership shape the culture of the guild as it handles large social, political, and industry-specific issues that demand a public-facing stance that might be tangled up in a romanticized notion of organizational identity and the very real, day-to-day needs of its members.

Television Boom and the Demand for Creative Rights

Concurrent with the cultural threat of HUAC, the expansion of the media industry to include television presented a larger strategic challenge for the future of directorial work and the DGA. The rising popularity of television also coincided with the issuing of the Paramount Decrees in 1948 that began to dismantle the motion picture studios' system of vertical integration of production, distribution, and the ownership of movie theaters. As a result, the number of produced feature films began to drop, but the studios expanded to invest in television productions to fulfill broadcasts' demand. This created new job opportunities for directors and their teams and boosted membership numbers for the guild. Technological advancements introduced by the expansion of commercial television opened up creative possibilities within the medium, as much as this innovation and marketplace growth began to infringe on directors' creative rights.

The television director and the feature film director have frequently been placed at creative odds with each other. The writer-producer (what would later be called a "showrunner") develops a television series, and the television director, who works on discrete episodes, is often historicized as having little power to influence the overall style and structure of a series. Compared with the mythology of the feature film director as the single author of a movie, the television director is a day player. The DGA argued for the status of the television director in its push to represent those professionals in the medium's ascendency during the late 1940s. As early as 1947, the DGA began preparations to include television directors and assistant directors within its membership ranks, arguing that the two mediums—motion pictures and broadcasting—were similar in their use of camera and editing techniques.[23]

In 1950, the DGA announced that it would take action to establish jurisdiction over directors working in live and taped television. This led to a protracted struggle between the DGA and the Radio and Television Directors Guild (RTDG), which, founded in 1947 as the Radio Directors Guild with its headquarters in New York City, represented many directors working in the field. The RTDG considered the DGA's move the start of a "national war," emphasizing what it perceived as cultural distinction and craft hierarchy between West Coast film and East Coast television in how "TV men will choose a truly democratic union in which they can have a share in their destiny rather than a second-class citizenship in a screen union dominated by big-time Hollywood directors."[24] After several years of conflict, in 1959 the RTDG merged its 856 members with the DGA's 734 directors and 478 assistant directors, bringing the latter's total to 2,068 members.[25]

The addition of television directors and assistant directors would gradually account for most jobs held by guild members. In 1957, half of the jobs held by DGA members were in television; within a year, that number would rise to 60 percent; by 1959, close to 70 percent of guild members were working in the broadcast medium.[26] The recognition of the television director transformed the guild not only financially through membership dues but also in its executive leadership. The organization's presidents, most noticeably starting with Delbert Mann in 1967, worked regularly, and with great financial and creative success, in both film and television.

Assistant and associate director membership increased with the RTDG and DGA merger in 1960, and again in 1963 when the assistant directors of International Alliance of Theatrical Stage Employees (IASTE) Local 161 joined the DGA; in 1964, below-the-line membership expanded again to include the Unit Production Mangers Union.[27] Previously, there had been some debate about whether the assistant directors should join the directors, but by the 1960s all parties agreed that they fit better with the DGA than in a trade union.[28] These employment gains contributed to the DGA's revenue through membership dues; as the guild prospered, it was able to add member benefits such as a pension plan and residuals that, in turn, reinforced the organization's prestige and status within the industry, within its community of members, and for those aspiring to work in the profession and have their labor rights represented by such an organization.[29]

These years of membership growth and guild prosperity fostered a push for more creative rights to be enforced under the guild's purview and ultimately covered in its Basic Agreement. Internal committee building was a common and normalized approach within DGA culture as a way for members and leadership to generate discussion and debate that would inform the process of contract negotiation. Starting around 1960, Elliot Silverstein, a prolific television director, led the drive for what would be known initially as the DGA's Bill of Creative Rights. Infuriated by his experiences working in television with editors who refused to allow the director to oversee postproduction, Silverstein mobilized support among his colleagues to advocate for inclusion within the guild's contract that the director (in both film and television) be present and consulted during postproduction and ultimately assembling what would become the "director's cut."

Vital to Silverstein's advocacy of creative rights was the rule that one director was hired and responsible on a project, a rule he considered so "sacred... you'd have to wrestle me to the ground." This rule, which was ratified in the 1978 contract, would protect a director from a studio, production company, or network assigning multiple directors in order to, as Silverstein warned, "speed up production." For Silverstein, the fear was that production companies and networks would "become the uber-Directors. They would have the vision; you would be simply an engineer, [a] traffic cop... without this one Director to a film, we'd very quickly become the Writers Guild, with four or five Directors on a film."[30] There have been exceptions to this one-director rule when members of a team could prove they had a history of working together. Pairs of siblings have been the most common example (e.g., Ethan and Joel Coen, Albert and Allen Hughes, Lana and Lilly Wachowski), Daniel Kwan and Daniel Scheinert, referred to as "the Daniels," make up a recent creative team. There have also been well-known disputes regarding the sole director credit. Robert Rodriguez, in production on *Sin City*, resigned from the DGA in 2005 when the guild denied giving a shared directing credit to Rodriguez and Frank Miller, the author of the comic on which the film was based.[31]

Over many years of often difficult negotiations, the demands in the original Bill of Creative Rights have been made part of the Basic Agreement's Article 7: Director's Minimum Conditions—Preparation, Production and Post-Production. The principles of creative rights emerged in the 1960s, as they were intended to inform employment practices during all phases of production. They likewise shaped future debates over a director's control of a work in which the copyright was owned by a separate business entity once the work was completed and distributed to a mass market.

During the 1980s, as the media industry entered an era of deregulation and conglomeration, the DGA entered a battle of moral rights regarding the colorization of primarily classic black-and-white Hollywood films for broadcast and home video distribution. The media mogul Ted Turner, who in 1986 bought the MGM library with approximately 3,600 titles, viewed colorization in monetary terms. "Movies were made to be profitable," explained Turner. "They were not made as art, they were made to make money, and any moviemaker who did make movies for art's sake is out of business... they say colorizing is vandalism. It's not vandalism because we are not tearing anything up. We're just making an improved version."[32] The DGA and its members disagreed, arguing that colorization altered the original version so much that it desecrated the work and the director's intention. The common analogy was to compare classic films with classic paintings to demonstrate how motion pictures required and deserved legal protection as objects of valuable cultural heritage in the face of profit. "If one doesn't feel that culture and art are more important than commerce," argued Francis Ford Coppola, "then anyone can buy a Picasso painting and cut it in half because they figure they can sell it as two."[33]

In its effort to stop colorization, the DGA based its argument on moral rights as informed by the international Berne Convention that upholds an artist's right to prevent any change to their work that is misrepresentative or degrading.[34] Over some years, high-profile filmmakers testified before Congress, while the guild submitted, unsuccessfully, a complaint with the U.S. Copyright Office in an attempt to block the filing of copyrights for newly colored films on the grounds that they were knockoffs. Joining the DGA's fight against colorization were the American Film Institute, the American Federation of Television and Radio Artists (AFTRA), the American Society of Cinematographers (ASC), the Screen Actors Guild (SAG), and the Writers Guild of America (WGA). The colorization of feature films posed a creative rights matter for the DGA that was tied to the marketplace. Gary R. Edgerton argues that while the DGA and individual film directors framed the fight as a moral issue infringing on the director's artistic right, the guild, along with SAG and the WGA, were attempting a strategy to negotiate with the Motion Picture Association of America over increasing profits from cable television and the home video market. The film studios, the National Association of Broadcasters, the Video Software Dealers of America, and the Association of Independent Television Stations presented a powerful front that the guild could not surpass.[35] Ultimately, after some years of battle and debate, U.S. copyright law, which did not recognize artists' moral rights, defined a film director's role as a "work for hire." The DGA had failed in its efforts to establish the sought-after legislation.

The advancement of creative rights, as defined and advocated for by the DGA in the guild's efforts to influence an industry code of conduct, continuously evolves to meet shifting business models and technological innovation—even if that evolution has often been prompted by a battle. Today these kinds of debates around the growth of technology and its use to enhance media productions center on generative AI and the way those tools threaten job stability and creative authorship. Consumer opinion and demand have shaped the guild's priorities in that creative rights are not solely about a director's freedom of artistic expression, but because directors' work does function in a marketplace, audiences' tastes and cultural trends must be taken into consideration. Most artists must work for a living, and directors are no exception.

Creative Rights without Civil Rights

The negotiations, initiated during the 1960s, around the expansion and strengthening of working directors' creative rights brought questions of accountability to the forefront. What responsibility did the DGA have in advocating for the hiring of its members who faced obstacles of gender and racial bias that prevented them from getting hired in the first place? What role did the guild play in perpetuating the values of prejudice and discrimination that defined the entertainment industry? One such criticism was that the DGA's experience roster required too much work experience to qualify for guild membership.

Established in 1962, the experience roster created obstacles for those with less experience to meet the membership requirements for assistant positions. DGA members, and those working toward membership eligibility, felt the guild had a duty to provide training for those entering the field at the assistant director level and to create opportunities for women, who at the time were mostly white, and for men of color to break into the profession. Long-standing institutionalized systems of industry discrimination had prevented these individuals' access. In a 2005 interview, Abby Singer, an assistant director, unit production manager, and member of the DGA since 1949, who was white, recalled the rampant racism he witnessed by some white crews. While working on the *Doris Day Show* (1968–1973, CBS), Singer supervised the grip and gaffer staff. When white male crew members refused to work with Black and Latino co-workers, Singer responded, "Fellas there's the front door." As Singer recalled, "That was bad but it was much worse with women. The crews hated to take orders from women as Assistant Directors. Hated it. You can't believe the trouble."

In the 1950s, the television boom created more jobs, and the guild allowed members' children to join, sometimes without adequate qualifications. "There were no women at the first time," remembered Singer. "Prior to that, the sons of members became assistant directors and some guys had three and four sons. Some had none. They had daughters, daughters were kaput, no way. That didn't happen until about the 1970s when affirmative action came in."[36] In 1966, the DGA admitted its first African American man to the assistant training program, Charles Washburn, and its first woman, Daisy Gerber, both of whom would have long and productive careers as assistant directors in film and television.[37]

Activists began organizing, specifically within the professional guilds, during the 1970s, targeting racist and sexist employment practices within the entertainment industry. The Writers Guild Women's Committee was founded in 1971, followed by the Writers Guild Black Writers Committee in 1976.[38] The Screen Actors Guild founded its Women's Committee and Ethnic Minority Committee in 1972.[39] (SAG's and the WGA's activism is discussed in chapters 9 and 10.) These groups conducted the first statistical surveys documenting the low employment numbers of women and people of color in the guilds' respective crafts; the results were circulated in the trade papers, generating much debate about the industry's culture of exclusivity.

The Women's Steering Committee (WSC) was founded at the Directors Guild in 1979 by six women members—Susan Bay, Nell Cox, Joelle Dobrow, Dolores Ferraro, Victoria Hochberg, and Lynne Littman—each highly qualified and with a number of industry awards to their names, but unable to secure work directing film or television.[40] The group questioned how, as members of one of the most powerful guilds in Hollywood, they were at such a professional disadvantage, and what responsibility the DGA, as their labor representatives, had in advocating for employment equity. With the support of Michael Franklin, the guild's national executive secretary at the time, the group established the WSC and conducted statistical research on the employment status of women directors. What they discovered was that between 1949 and 1979 the major distribution companies released 7,332 films, of which seven women directed 14, or 0.19 percent. In television, twenty-two women directed 115 of approximately 65,500 hours of prime-time dramatic broadcasting. Of that 115, an estimated 35 hours were directed by Ida Lupino; of the eighteen women who directed episodic programs, six were also the producer and/or star of the series (e.g., Lucille Ball, Penny Marshall, Mary Tyler Moore, and Meta Rosenberg). WSC members debated internally as to whether the DGA, whose membership and executive leadership were dominated by white men, would be their best advocate in taking the statistics public.

The WSC was soon joined by the Ethnic Minorities Committee (EMC), established in 1980, whose organizing members were Ivan Dixon, Wendell Franklin, Reuben Watt, and William Crain. Some members of the EMC had tried unsuccessfully to organize within the guild years prior but were told that civil rights and racial justice advocacy were not a function that the DGA served. Support among the board of directors for these committees was not enthusiastic. The board did not want to get involved in an industry-wide civil rights battle, but the WSC found an advocate in Franklin, and with what it called the "Co-ed Committee": the directors Gil Cates, Jack Haley, Boris Sagal, and Jay Sandrich. In June 1980, the WSC, endorsed by the board, held a meeting with leading producers, showrunners, and network and studio executives in which Cates and Franklin presented the numerical evidence that demonstrated the low number of women hired to direct film and television. They recommended a voluntary affirmative action–type solution of hiring a certain number of women directors per season.

The response to the DGA meeting with industry representatives was mixed and mostly generated an apathetic response from producers and executives. Following the meeting, Franklin attempted to communicate and work with those industry personnel to participate in the DGA's affirmative action program, devised by the WSC. The response continued to be tepid until the guild, which had invested considerable public-facing efforts and resources, filed discrimination complaints with the Equal Employment Opportunity Commission (EEOC). In 1983, the DGA filed a class action lawsuit with the U.S. District Court for the Central District of California against Warner Bros. and Columbia Pictures for employment discrimination against its women and minority members, directors, and assistant directors, in violation of Title VII of the Civil

Rights Act of 1964. In 1985, Judge Pamela Rymer ruled against the guild and in favor of Columbia and Warner Bros. Judge Rymer's decision was determined by multiple issues. First, the DGA presented a conflict of interest as an organization with a predominantly white male membership; therefore, it might be implicated in the discrimination of the plaintiffs. Second, the lawyers representing the DGA, Taylor, Roth & Hunt, also represented the guild during its contract negotiations, thus presenting another conflict of interest.

The defense's argument and the judge's decision reinforced concerns that the WSC had wrestled with from the start: that the guild was part of the problem. There could be no mistaking that the DGA, since its inception, was dominated by white men who were the most successful in the profession and that the guild's culture of exclusivity was a part of and perpetuated Hollywood's culture of exclusivity. Since the WSC's first wave of activism in the 1970s, members have continued to call out DGA leadership for contributing to longstanding patterns of discrimination in the entertainment industry. Filmmaker Jamaa Fanaka, one of the founding members of the DGA's African American Steering Committee in 1993, filed several anti–racial discrimination suits against multiple film studios, television networks, and the Directors Guild itself during the 1990s, where he referenced the arguments made in the 1983 case.[41]

In 2015, the American Civil Liberties Union submitted a letter to the EEOC requesting that the commission initiate charges against motion picture studios, networks, and the DGA for discriminatory hiring practices against women directors.[42] The letter cited extensive research—reaching back to the 1970s—and interviews with contemporary directors and members of the Directors Guild explaining how the guild circulates a small list of eligible women directors to potential employers that excludes a larger, more comprehensive representation of qualified potential hires.

Over time, the DGA has reframed the guilty verdict by focusing the attention on the organization's newfound commitment to diversity. Thus, it has avoided drawing attention to the guild's implication in the court's decision or the WSC's initial struggle to gather support.[43] The expansion of "diversity" committees began in the 1990s with the African American Steering Committee, the Asian American Committee, the Eastern Diversity Steering Committee (representing African American, Asian, Native American, Latino, and Arab–Middle Eastern Guild members located on the East Coast), and the Latino Committee. To date, the DGA has elected two women presidents (both white): Martha Coolidge, elected in 2002, and Lesli Linka Glatter, in 2021. In 2013, Paris Barclay was elected the guild's first Black and openly gay president. In more recent years, the Directors Guild has posted on its website answers to many of the questions posed by its members. Many questions center on the DGA's complicity in the media industry's culture of exclusion, to which the guild responded as follows: it is not responsible for hiring directors and their teams; its membership is a reflection of employers' hiring practices; through the guild's different approaches (collection and publishing of statistical research, diversity provisions in the Basic Agreement, networking opportunities), it strives "to convince employers to take ownership of the issue [of gender and racial bias]."[44]

Representation has always been a juggling act for the Directors Guild. The guild must mediate within its membership ranks as a labor organization that represents above-the-line and below-the-line crews. Within those categories are members who are employed regularly and will collect residuals and contribute to their pensions, and those who struggle due to workplace discrimination based on gender, race, and seniority. On top of that, the guild strives to maintain the mythology of the individual director—the visionary, the leader, and the hero—as part of a creative community. The guild must balance its goals of producing both art and commerce to meet the demands of a constantly changing media industry.

The Twenty-First-Century Director and the Guild

At the time of this writing, the media industry has experienced a historic period of strikes and contract negotiations (which is discussed in the Coda). On May 10, 2023, the Directors Guild began to negotiate its contract, which was set to expire on June 30, 2023, with the Alliance of Motion Picture and Television Producers (AMPTP). Historically, the Directors Guild negotiates its contract with the producers ahead of the writers and actors. The DGA's president Lesli Linka Glatter, writing a guest column for *Variety* a day before the talks with the AMPTP commenced, promised guild membership a fierce negotiation. "We're going to fight," stated Linka Glatter, "no matter what it takes—for a strong contract that treats our members fairly and allows us to share in the success of an evolving entertainment industry."[45]

The DGA's tentative deal was announced on June 3 and ratified on June 23. The new contract included a general wage increase of more than 13 percent over three years; gains for television directors, including additional paid postproduction days on high-budget subscription video on demand (SVOD) and pay TV series; and additional contributions to the pension and health plan for directors, assistant directors, and unit production managers. New to the contract was a Parental Leave Fund. Impacting directors' creative rights were the inclusion of a "soft" preparation time before preproduction starts, and an increase in the director's cut period. Gains for the directorial team included a pay increase for associate directors and stage managers for work on holidays and a seventh workday, and residuals for directorial team members. Resonating with the writers' and actors' negotiations was a new structure for global SVOD residuals based on foreign subscribers and, like the writers' agreement, a clear statement that generative AI does not constitute a person, which means that DGA duties must be assigned to a person, and studio executives must meet with the DGA twice a year to discuss intended uses for AI. The contract reinforced a commitment to diversity, including that CBS, ABC, NBC, Sony, Warner Bros., Paramount, and Netflix will all guarantee that participants in their television director diversity programs will direct at least one episode, an agreement whose legacy is rooted in the reform efforts initiated by the DGA Women's Steering Committee in the late 1970s and early 1980s.[46]

While the negotiations proceeded without delay and the new contract was approved by a vote of 87 percent—6,728 members voted out of 16,321 eligible voters (41 percent)—during the ratification process and the months following, public debates surfaced among DGA and WGA membership, and from many who belong to both guilds.[47] Gary Scott Thompson and Larry Charles, both director-producer-writers of film and television, were vocal on the social media platform X about their choice to vote no against the contract because they felt the negotiations undermined the members of the Writers Guild who, at the time, were on strike. "Directors are selling out the rest of the #DGA membership to gain more power in episodic TV at the expense of the #WGA and #Showrunners," accused Thompson.[48] Charles positioned himself in the middle, acknowledging with gratitude the gains he would receive from the contract. "I'm *really* proud to be a director. . . . I've been very lucky," he admitted. "But I was a writer first. . . . I consider myself both a writer and a director."[49] Conceding that, because the contract was sure to be ratified, his no vote would be only symbolic, Charles voiced his privilege as a director to support the writers. During this period, the guild posted a series of short campaign videos on its website featuring all kinds of members—directors, including some who were writer hyphenates, and below-the-line crew, assistant directors, unit production managers, and stage mangers—urging others to vote yes on the new contract.

In October, days after the WGA ratified its new contract ending the guild's 148-day strike, the DGA emailed its membership expressing disappointment in the "recent news articles and social media posts misrepresenting the extraordinary gains [the guild] made" in its contract negotiations. The email, which was shared by the press, reiterated the gains made in the contract and took the opportunity to voice support for the writers and actors, as well as IATSE and the Teamsters, who would be negotiating their respective contracts in 2024. The email reinforced a common theme of how the guild builds strength by working together within its ranks and across the industry: "We achieved these hard-fought gains because of our unity and resolve and the more than a year and a half of research and preparation that preceded the start of our formal negotiations, as well as the support we received from our sister Guilds and Unions."[50]

The range of viewpoints expressed from members across the DGA, the WGA, and some members of SAG-AFTRA made salient not only the inherent tensions within guild "unity" but also criticisms about the Directors Guild's perceived power. Some felt the DGA had used the WGA strike to its advantage, and at the expense of the writers, in negotiating with producers. Many were clear that each guild represents a unique membership that demands labor protections specific to the respective crafts. And still some conveyed solidarity and speculated that the AMPTP negotiated with the DGA to undercut the writers and the actors.[51]

In early June, as the DGA negotiated its tentative agreement, the extraordinary prospect of all three guilds striking at the same time seemed possible. However, the chances of such a moment were always unlikely: while the WGA and SAG have a strong strike history, the DGA has gone on strike only once, in 1987, for a few minutes on the West Coast and three hours in New York. Gil Cates, an award-winning director and producer of film and television who served as the president of the guild two times and held multiple leadership roles, including as a member of six negotiating committees, contextualized what he described as the Directors Guild's exceptional ability to avoid striking because of its acumen for understanding the economic maneuvers of the film and television business and for holding the most fundamental role in the production of a motion picture:

> The guild had never struck before and for good reason because we really understand management better than all the other guilds. We're responsible to management for delivering these movies. Someone at Universal says, "OK, I'm going to greenlight a 120-million-dollar movie . . ." and who do they go to to make it? They go to the director to make that movie. I mean, there are other people involved—producer, writer, actors, etcetera., but essentially, it's the director that controls the making of that movie. So, we know them and they know us. And it's no surprise that we haven't struck. We're a smart guild, we know what their business is and we can work it out.[52]

The different ways in which the DGA's 1987 strike has been historicized by the guild, the press, and individual members of the guild's negotiating team resonate with many of the insights and reactions to the 2023 contract talks and the directors' stature, power, and sense of entitlement within the terrain of industry labor organizations and contract negotiations. At the time, in 1987, the press reported that the negotiations had stalled with the AMPTP over the payment of residuals to directors for films sold to pay-per-view cable television.[53] (This is a legacy issue that continues to dominate today's negotiations with regard to streaming services.) The DGA's official history describes the decision to strike in similar terms as a dispute over "pressure from the major studios to roll back minimum residual compensation and other minimum terms and conditions."[54] Cates, who had recently been elected for his third term as guild president just as the 1987 contract negotiations were about to commence, told a variation on the story during his Directors Guild Visual History interview conducted in 2002 that, as expected, positioned the DGA at an apex of strength and confidence: this negotiation was not a struggle for respect but a process in which the guild would assert its well-established position of power.

According to Cates, one of the contentious issues during the negotiations had to do with the producers' presentation credits on a film. At the time, there was no existing agreement on the limitation of those credits; the guild wanted to restrict the presentation credits to include only studios that were making many films each year; the producers agreed. However, on the night before the negotiations were settled, the producers pushed to add the prominent television producer Aaron Spelling to the list of presenting credits. The guild was not opposed to Spelling in particular but rather was enraged because of the last-minute addition after the two sides had agreed on the presenting credit terms. "Everybody around the table voted to strike, the [unit production managers] the [assistant directors]," remembered Cates, "because they saw it as a diminution of the director's persona that somehow at this last minute to come in and try to sneak that in, who the hell are these guys? . . . [The move to strike] signaled: don't f-ck around with the DGA . . . Of course, with the Writers Guild, they go out on strike every year, it seems to be, like, why not?" For Cates, the DGA did not strike for an economic issue but for reasons of "conscience" and issues that were "right for directors." In this interview the esteemed director-producer-negotiator who had been a tremendous force in the guild's leadership ranks for decades, as a representative for the guild, expressed an expected boldness and bravado regarding how the DGA saw itself as a group not to "f-ck around with" and superior to the writers who, as implied by Cates's comment, were perpetually ill-equipped to negotiate successfully and instead resorted to strikes to resolve contract disputes.

The Directors Guild, with its distinctive membership of above-the-line and below-the-line employees, finds itself committed to a unique and evolving challenge. Juxtaposed with the discourse that took place during the 2023 contract negotiations, Cates's perspective and tone, albeit in the candid setting of a long-form interview years later, reveal an arrogance that has since entered a sustained period of generational transformation. The proliferation and power—creative and financial—of the director-writer-producer within emerging content platforms have made membership and alliances across guilds more complex, at times more contentious, and often even more collaborative.

What remains for audiences, production entities, marketing campaigns, and film studies courses, and for directors themselves, is an expectation of the swagger identified with a singular artist who informs and controls creative power. Steven Spielberg, using his prerogative and platform as one of Hollywood's most successful filmmakers, spoke on behalf of audiences in 2019 as he fueled a debate about the theatrical exhibition of feature films versus SVOD. "I hope all of us really continue to believe that the greatest contributions we can make as filmmakers is to give audiences the motion picture theatrical experience," said the veteran filmmaker. That year, fellow directors Joel and Ethan Coen's *The Ballad of Buster Scruggs* and Alfonso Cuarón's *Roma*, each produced by Netflix and given limited theatrical runs, were nominated for Academy Awards, with Cuarón winning the Oscar for Best Director and Best Cinematography and *Roma* for Best Foreign Language Film. Spielberg, at the time, was critical of how films produced by streaming services could qualify for Academy Awards eligibility through a limited "token" theatrical release. "[I]n fact, once you commit to a television format, you're a TV movie," he said, making a hierarchical distinction between big and small screens.[55]

Several more top-tier directors have made films for Netflix (and other SVOD companies), including Noah Baumbach, Jane Campion, Guillermo del Toro, David Fincher, Spike Lee, and Martin Scorsese. Many have been nominated for Academy Awards, including Campion, who won an Oscar for Best Director in 2022 for her film *The Power of the Dog* and *Guillermo del Toro's Pinocchio*, which won Best Animated Feature Film in 2023, both Netflix films. Not long after, Spielberg's Amblin Partners signed a production deal with Netflix.[56] In these high-profile examples—and there are as many or more early career filmmakers debuting films on streaming platforms—innovations in media production and distribution technology and business models have contributed to directors' celebrity status and critical reception.[57] As the twenty-first-century director continues to evolve across a fragmented and ever-expanding media industry, the Directors Guild will be tested as the organization navigates the constant blurred line between art, entertainment, commerce, and innovation. The guild holds a responsibility to protect and advocate for the employment rights of a membership that represents and reinforces the hierarchical labor structure at the center of media production and is embedded in the cultural imagination of the consumer market in which it thrives.

Notes

1 *Directors Guild of America: Creative Rights Handbook, 2023–2026*, https://www.dga .org/Contracts/Creative-Rights; Ted Elrick, "Singularity of Vision: The Origin of the One Director to a Film Policy," *DGA Quarterly*, May 2004, https://www.dga .org/Craft/DGAQ/All-Articles/0405-May-2004/Singularity-of-Vision.aspx.
2 Dora Albert, "She Thanks Her Lucky Stars," *Silver Screen*, February 1931, 61.
3 Alejandro González Iñárritu, "Iñárritu on Method," *American Cinematographer* 92, no. 1 (January 2011): 38.
4 David A. Honicky, "Film Labelling as a Cure for Colorization (and Other Alterations): A Band-Aid for a Hatchet Job," *Cardozo Arts & Entertainment Law Journal* 12, no. 2 (1994): 424.
5 Virginia Wright Wexman, *Hollywood's Artists: The Directors Guild of America and the Construction of Authorship* (Columbia University Press, 2020), 36.
6 Steve Pond, "Before the Guild," *DGA Quarterly*, Winter 2011, https://www.dga.org /Craft/DGAQ/All-Articles/1004-Winter-2010-11/Features-Before-the-Guild.aspx.
7 Karen Ward Mahar, *Women Filmmakers in Early Hollywood* (John Hopkins University Press, 2006), 181.
8 "Directors Join Movement for 'One Big Union' in Hollywood," *Motion Picture Herald*, January 25, 1936, 27.
9 "Directors Form Guild" and "Directors' Reasons for Guild," *The Hollywood Reporter* (hereafter *THR*), January 17, 1936, 1–2.
10 David Robb, "Directors Guild Born Out of Fear 50 Years Ago," *Variety*, October 29, 1985, 1. Also see "A Guild for Directors," *New York Times*, January 26, 1936, X5; Steve Pond, "A Guild Is Born," *DGA Quarterly*, Winter 2006, https://www.dga.org /Craft/DGAQ/All-Articles/0604-Winter2006-07/Features-A-Guild-is-Born.aspx.

11 Wright Wexman, *Hollywood's Artists*, 18.

12 Robb, "Directors Guild Born Out of Fear," 83, 90; "Producers and Directors Clash over Labor Setup; Zanuck Calls Them 'Creative Artists'; Tells Why," *Variety*, August 25, 1937, 7, 29.

13 Wright Wexman, *Hollywood's Artists*, 18.

14 "NLRB Reveals SDG Demands," *THR*, September 16, 1938, 1, 4; "What's 'Creative Ability' of Unit Men, Ask Prod'rs," *THR*, September 8, 1938, 3.

15 Robb, "Directors Guild Born Out of Fear," 83, 90–91.

16 DGA Constitution, Directors Guild of America Files, Box 14, Oviatt Library, Special Collections, California State University, Northridge, cited in Wright Wexman, *Hollywood Artists*, 21fn43.

17 "Directors Form Guild," *THR*, January 17, 1936, 1–2.

18 Mark Harris, *Five Came Back: A Story of Hollywood and the Second World War* (Penguin Publishing Group, 2015).

19 Letter from Frank Capra to John Ford, December 19, 1951, in John Ford Papers, Lilly Library, Indiana University Bloomington, Box 3, Folder 6, cited in Wright Wexman, *Hollywood's Artists*, 93n42.

20 James Ulmer, "A Guild Divided," *DGA Quarterly*, Spring 2011, https://www.dga.org/craft/dgaq/all-articles/1101-spring-2011/feature-loyalty-oath.aspx.

21 "Mankiewicz in Overwhelming Victory over DeMille-Rogell Director Faction," *Variety*, October 25, 1950, 5, 16. For more press coverage of the meeting, see Thomas, F. Brady, "Hollywood Divided by Loyalty Pledge Issue," *New York Times*, October 22, 1950, X5; Thomas F. Brady, "Hollywood Turmoil," *New York Times*, October 29, 1950, 101; "Manky Urges Signing of Oath," *Variety*, November 1, 1950, 15.

22 For histories of the DGA loyalty oath debate, see Kevin Brianton, *Hollywood Divided: The 1950 Screen Directors Guild Meeting and the Impact of the Blacklist* (University Press of Kentucky, 2016); Victor S. Navasky, *Naming Names* (Penguin Books, 1980); Wright Wexman, *Hollywood's Artists*.

23 "Screen Directors Guild East Making Strong Pitch to Include Televisioners," *Variety*, June 18, 1947, 5, 20.

24 "RTDG Board," *Broadcasting*, September 4, 1950, 72.

25 "2,068 Directors under One Guild," *Variety*, December 9, 1959, 5.

26 Robb, "Directors Guild Born Out of Fear," 151.

27 "Big Union for Directors," *THR*, September 18, 1959, 9; "N.Y. Assistants Move into Directors Guild," *Variety*, January 8, 1964, 24; "Unit Mangers Guild in Meld with Directors, *Variety*, August 14, 1963, 28; "Asks Recognition of Unit Managers Status," *Variety*, May 6, 1964, 13.

28 "Eastern Asst. Directors Negotiating," *Variety*, November 13, 1963, 7.

29 Robb, "Directors Guild Born Out of Fear," 96.

30 Elliot Silverstein, interviewed by Robert Markowitz, Visual History, Directors Guild of America, May 17, 2002, https://www.dga.org/Craft/VisualHistory/Interviews/Elliot-Silverstein.aspx.

31 Dave McNary, "Double Vision Hits DGA: Co-helming Rule Jeopardizes Par's Mission to 'Mars,'" *Weekly Variety*, April 12–18, 2004, 5.

32 Greg Dawson, "Into the '90s: Ted Turner," *American Film*, January 1989, 39.

33 Susan Linfield, "The Color of Money," *American Film*, January 1987, 52.

34 Honicky, "Film Labelling as a Cure for Colorization," 409–430.

35 Gary R. Edgerton, "'The Germans Wore Gray, You Wore Blue': Frank Capra, *Casablanca*, and the Colorization Controversy of the 1980s," *Journal of Popular Film and Television* 27, no. 4 (2000): 27, https://doi.org/10.1080/01956050009602812.

36 Abby Singer, interviewed by Herb Adelman, Visual History, Directors Guild of America, May 15, 2005, https://www.dga.org/Craft/VisualHistory/Interviews/Abby-Singer.aspx.

37 John L. Scott, "Tradition Finally Broken in Director's Guild Program," *Los Angeles Times*, November 28, 1966. Also see Wayne Warga, "A 95-Pound Inspiration for Film Beginners," *Los Angeles Times*, May 19, 1968, D14; "Charles Washburn: Charlie Star Trek," *DGA Quarterly*, Summer 2011, https://www.dga.org/Craft/DGAQ/All-Articles/1102-Summer-2011/On-the-Job-With-Charles-Wasburn.aspx; "Daisy Gerber: Paving the Way," *DGA Quarterly*, Summer 2011, https://www.dga.org/craft/dgaq/all-articles/1102-summer-2011/on-the-job-with-daisy-gerber.aspx.

38 Jeanne A. Taylor, "Black Writers Committee," *WGAw News*, February 1977, 4.

39 For a history of the WGA Women's Committee, see Miranda J. Banks, "Unequal Opportunities: Gender Inequities and Precarious Diversity in the 1970s U.S. Television History," *Feminist Media Histories* 4, no. 4 (Fall 2018): 109–129; for the SAG committee, see Kate Fortmueller, "Time's Up (Again?): Transforming Hollywood's Industrial Culture," *Media Industries* 6, no. 2 (2019), https://quod.lib.umich.edu/m/mij/15031809.0006.201?view=text;rgn=main.

40 For a history of the DGA Women's Steering Committee, see Maya Montañez Smukler, *Liberating Hollywood: Women Directors and the Feminist Reform of 1970s American Cinema* (New Brunswick, NJ: Rutgers University Press, 2019).

41 For information on Fanaka and his legal efforts, see Jamaa Fanaka Papers, UCLA Library Performing Arts Special Collections, University of California, Los Angeles.

42 Melissa Goodman and Ariela Migdal, American Civil Liberties Union, letter to Anna Y. Park and Rosa Viramontes, EEOC Los Angeles District Office, May 12, 2015; Rebecca Keegan, "Female Film Directors Are on Outside Looking In, but Will ACLU Flip the Script?," *Los Angeles Times*, May 13, 2015, https://www.latimes.com/entertainment/movies/la-et-mn-aclu-gender-discrimination-hollywood-20150513-story.html.

43 Lyndon Stambler, "The Good Fight," *DGA Quarterly*, 2011, https://www.dga.org/craft/dgaq/all-articles/1103-fall-2011/history-guild-diversity-committees.aspx.

44 "DGA Diversity & Inclusion—Frequently Asked Questions," Directors Guild of America, https://www.dga.org/The-Guild/Diversity/Diversity-FAQ.aspx.

45 Lesli Linka Glatter, "DGA Is United, Prepared and Ready to Fight for Our Future," *Variety*, May 9, 2023, https://variety.com/2023/biz/news/dga-contract-negotiations-ready-to-fight-1235606628/.

46 "DGA Contract Highlights 2023–2026 Tentative Agreement," https://www.dga.org/dga/2023Negotiations/2023_DGA_BA_FLTTA_Summary_of_Agreement.pdf.

47 "DGA Membership Ratifies New Contract by Overwhelming Margin," DGA 2023 Negotiations (blog), June 23, 2023, https://www.dga.org/News/PressReleases/2023/230623_DGA_Membership_Ratifies_New_Contract_by_Overwhelming_Margin.aspx.

48 Gary Scott Thompson (@GarySThompson), "Voting NO on the #DGA contract," X, June 8, 2023, https://twitter.com/GarySThompson/status/1666832676177981441.

49 Larry Charles (@larrycharlesism), "I VOTED 'NO,'" June 7, 2023, https://twitter.com/larrycharlesism/status/1666666576677064705.

50 Elaine Low, "DGA-WGA in War of Words: 'Transparent Attempt at Face-Saving,'" *The Ankler*, October 11, 2023, https://theankler.com/p/dga-wga-in-war-of-words-transparent; also see Dominic Patten, "DGA Touts 'Extraordinary' AMPTP Contract in Email but Not All Members Agree, Calling It 'Damage Control,'"

Deadline, October 11, 2023, https://deadline.com/2023/10/directors-guild-amptp
-contract-criticism-1235570524/.

51 Lesley Goldberg, "Striking Writers Respond to DGA's Tentative Deal with Studios,
Streamers," *THR*, June 4, 2023, https://www.hollywoodreporter.com/news/general
-news/striking-writers-react-to-dga-tentative-deal-1235506889/; Dominic Patten,
Erik Pedersen, and Nellie Andreeva, "Writers React to Directors Guild–AMPTP
Contract Deal: 'WGA Takes a Stand. DGA Reaps the Rewards,'" *Deadline*, June 4,
2023, https://deadline.com/2023/06/dga-deal-reaction-striking-writers-angry
-1235408169/.

52 Gilbert Cates, interviewed by Gil Cates Jr., Visual History, Directors Guild of
America, May 21, 2002, https://www.dga.org/Craft/VisualHistory/Interviews
/Gilbert-Cates.aspx.

53 Aljean Harmetz, "Film Directors Start Strike Vote Today," *New York Times*, July 1,
1987, C17; Aljean Harmetz, "That's Hollywood: The Strike That Never Was,"
New York Times, August 9, 1987, F6.

54 "1987," Directors Guild of America, https://www.dga.org/the-guild/history.aspx
?value=1987&Decade=1980s&Year=1987.

55 Zack Sharf, "Steven Spielberg: The Greatest Contribution a Director Can Make Is
the Theatrical Experience," *IndieWire*, February 19, 2019, https://www.indiewire
.com/2019/02/steven-spielberg-theaters-over-streaming-netflix-1202045064/.

56 Brent Lang, "Steven Spielberg's Amblin Partners, Netflix Forge Film Deal in Sign
of Changing Hollywood," *Variety*, June 21, 2021, https://variety.com/2021/film
/news/steven-spielberg-netflix-amblin-deal-1235001513/.

57 Jen Yamato and Wendy Lee, "Netflix Turns to First-Time Filmmakers for an Edge
in Streaming Wars," *Los Angeles Times*, January 25, 2020, https://www.latimes.com
/entertainment-arts/business/story/2020-01-25/netflix-courts-first-time-filmmakers.

Coda

• •

Hollywood on Strike

KATE FORTMUELLER

During the summer of 2023, the Writers Guild of America (WGA) and the Screen Actors Guild–American Federation of Television and Radio Artists (SAG-AFTRA) walked out of the TV/Theatrical/Streaming negotiations with the Alliance of Motion Picture and Television Producers (AMPTP). Both strikes lasted through the fall, crushing any hope of salvaging the fall network television season and delaying planned holiday season premieres of big studio films such as *Dune: Part Two* and *Godzilla x Kong: The New Empire*. The WGA strike ended on September 27, just five days shy of its longest strike ever, while SAG-AFTRA's strike was its longest ever, finally ending on November 9. The strikes' lengths give some indication of how contentious these negotiations were.

A strike is a sacrifice of present benefits to achieve long-term gains—it is the last resort for workers' rights and contractual improvements. As this book's chapters on both the WGA and SAG-AFTRA demonstrate, since 1950, these unions are the most likely to go on strike. However, the impact of a walkout is often felt not just by union members or even those in the striking industry but also in dependent and adjacent industries. In the case of Hollywood, this means not only the salaried studio workers and marketing firms that survey audiences but also hotels, restaurants, and other businesses that depend on the constant flow of Hollywood money being spent at their establishments.[1] In the case of the 2023 strike, the impact was felt in Los Angeles and New York (the two largest

American media hubs) as well as in the states and countries that host hundreds of Hollywood productions each year.

These were the second and third strikes of Hollywood's industrially tumultuous twenty-first century, in addition to the first strike authorization vote of all the Hollywood locals in the history of the International Alliance of Theatrical Stage Employees (IATSE) in 2021 (although that strike was averted). The shift from material film cultures (relying on celluloid and tape) to a digital landscape was accompanied by newer and cheaper methods of distribution, which translated into greater profits for studios, but not for media workers. The writers were on strike in 2007–2008 over new media residuals, which just preceded the introduction of streaming on Netflix and Hulu, but the actors have not been on strike since the introduction of VHS as a new method of distribution. So, why did the unions go on strike in 2023? What drove the WGA and SAG-AFTRA to walk out of negotiations, and what did they achieve? Answering these questions and understanding the 2023 strike requires a look back at recent history, such as the consequences of new tech players entering Hollywood and the ongoing effects of the COVID-19 pandemic, but also an understanding of the Hollywood unions' histories and worker priorities covered by the scholars in this volume.

To say that a lot changed in Hollywood in the period between the WGA's 2007–2008 strike and the 2023 strike would be an understatement. The launch of streaming as a mode of delivery (first with Amazon in 2006, but more successfully with Netflix in 2007) made studio- and network-produced films and television shows as readily available (for a fee) as amateur content on YouTube, and at times broke down the distinctions between various forms of media. Over the next several years, streamers cultivated interest in their services by licensing content from a variety of sources. By 2013, however, both Netflix and Amazon were producing original series that would air exclusively on their platforms. As has historically been the case with new forms of distribution, the unions offered more agreeable terms to producers with the tacit understanding that new media forms are not initially profitable, and contracts would be renegotiated in the future. During the 2007–2008 strike, theatrical releases, broadcast, and cable were all profitable modes of media distribution, but in 2019, just as Disney and Warner Media geared up to launch their own streaming services, cable subscriptions had begun an even more significant decline, and in the spring of 2020, COVID-19 upended the theatrical business model.

Amid all the distribution turmoil that accompanied the launch of new streaming services in 2019 and 2020, writers, directors, and actors were set to renegotiate their Theatrical Film/Television Minimum Basic Agreements (MBAs). *Deadline*, the most gossipy of the industry trades, announced "TV Studios in Strike-Preparation Mode" as early as November 2019.[2] Negotiations were set to begin in the spring of 2020, but when COVID-19 swept across the globe, shuttering all

Hollywood productions, the unions lost their ability to shut down production with a strike, and all quietly negotiated their contracts.

The 2020 above-the-line negotiations wrapped up quickly, even though the WGA, SAG-AFTRA, and the Directors Guild of America (DGA) union leaders and membership were aware of the need to address the changes to the streaming landscape. However, in the intervening months between the above-the-line deals and the 2023 strike, the world was transformed by hybrid work policies and changes to the social and professional status quo due to the pandemic. Although many of the changes to *how* people worked were readily visible, what managers and producers failed to see was that pandemic closures gave employees time to rest and think about their professional futures.

Production resumed in 2020, but as several chapters in this volume explain, it almost shut down again in 2021 when members of the IATSE locals struggled to negotiate a new contract and overwhelmingly authorized a strike. Beyond a wage and residual increase, below-the-line workers were also challenging some of the fundamental practices of the media industries, mainly the long and unrelenting hours on set that have long been common practice. IATSE leadership worked with the AMPTP to avert a strike, and the union achieved a percentage raise across all contracts, and contractual guarantees about hours and workdays. Yet when members saw this agreement, many took to social media and were willing to be quoted in the industry trades about their disappointment. As one gaffer told *Variety*, "Overall, it's very disheartening."[3] This sentiment was reflected in a vote that only passed due to an Electoral College–style system that awards all of a local's votes to its majority. The 58 percent delegate approval of the contract masked the fact that in raw voting 50.4 percent of members opposed the contract. The decades-simmering disconnect between individual locals and national IATSE leadership reared its head once again.

In 2023, the WGA and SAG-AFTRA had different responses to their leadership and the contracts they achieved. WGA members were almost uniformly pleased—99 percent of members ratified the contract.[4] In contrast, SAG-AFTRA's new agreement—especially the artificial intelligence (AI) terms—was met with vocal dissent, notably from Justine Bateman but also from actors on social media and in a statement issued by Matthew Modine, a former SAG-AFTRA presidential candidate. After a month of debate among members, the agreement was approved at 78.33 percent. Although this ratification was lower than the WGA approval and SAG-AFTRA's own strike authorization vote, it was on a par with less contentious years such as 2017 (when the agreement was approved at 75.79 percent).

The 2023 strikes loomed in the background of the final writing stages of this book. Even though the strikes were impossible to ignore, it is too soon to fully grasp their ramifications for the future of the industry and for Hollywood labor more broadly. It is impossible to know the future, but in Hollywood's labor history these strikes (and near strikes) were historically unique in their ability to unite labor and transform the conversation around work conditions for below-the-line workers and remuneration for replayed content and AI protections for above-the-line workers.

Solidarity

Throughout the 2023 strike, union leaders and historians (including myself and Miranda Banks) remarked on the unprecedented solidarity across the unions.[5] As the chapters in this collection have shown, IATSE locals and above-the-line guilds have not been consistent allies, but when the WGA representatives walked out of their negotiations, two days later they walked into a rally of 1,800 Hollywood union members from the WGA, the DGA, SAG-AFTRA, IATSE, and the Teamsters at the Shrine Auditorium in Los Angeles. Writers stop writing during a strike, but if producers have stockpiled scripts, that will give them sufficient material to continue production, albeit without the possibility of rewrites. Of course, continuing television production is also contingent on whether the production is in the United States and if the showrunner aligns with the writers and walks out or stays on set as a producer and promises not to do any writer duties (although historically these have been difficult to parse). It is much easier to shut down production if IATSE and the Teamsters promise they will not cross active picket lines.

As the writers walked the picket lines, the DGA were next to step up to the negotiating table. As Maya Smukler's chapter 11 details, the DGA wrapped up its negotiations quickly, although some members, such as the writer-actor-director Paul Scheer and the writer-director Boots Riley, publicly voiced criticisms of the deal and others voiced concern that making a deal undermined the WGA strike.[6] However, as has often been the case, these were minority critiques, and ultimately the contract was ratified by 87 percent of the voting membership.

Even though the DGA settled its negotiations in June, this had no impact on SAG-AFTRA's decision to go on strike, or on the WGA's resolve to hold out for the best deal. As was clear from the WGA's and SAG-AFTRA's bargaining slates, both unions had craft-specific terms that prevented them from following a logic of pattern bargaining. As Duncan Crabtree-Ireland, the SAG-AFTRA executive director, explained of its approach, "Our bargaining strategy has never relied upon nor been dependent on the outcome or status of any other union's negotiations, nor do we subscribe to the philosophy that the terms of deals made with other unions bind us."[7] This position of union autonomy clearly guided SAG-AFTRA's bargaining strategies throughout the rest of the summer.

The 2023 strikes revealed that maintaining solidarity is an ongoing process. The above-the-line unions were negotiating for some shared issues (such as increases in wages and residuals), but others, such as regulation on mini rooms, self-tape auditions, success-based payments, and even the nuances of the AI policies were different. Unions issued solidarity statements throughout the

FIGURE C.1 Solidarity signs at the WGA strike picket outside Warner Bros., June 8, 2023. (Courtesy of SAG-AFTRA member Karina Wolfe.)

summer and walked the sidewalks in front of studios with signs thanking their union allies (figure C.1), affirming their commitments to their sister guilds, even as they had to overcome many challenges to their resolve posed from the AMPTP and members frustrated by the long summer of unemployment.

The Future of Remuneration

Writers, directors, and actors are essential creative forces behind all film and television, but they are rarely the financier. Getting something made in Hollywood requires a lot of money, and in exchange for financing production, the creatives sign over their copyright to conglomerates, studios, or networks to see their work on-screen, receive credit, and for many union members (since the 1950s) earn residuals. Residuals are a contractual condition that Hollywood workers earned by collective bargaining and striking.

Historically, residuals have been paid to artists when material is reused on a new platform (e.g., when a film goes to television, when a network episode is replayed on cable), but the WGA and SAG-AFTRA had worked out effective residual structures for media that followed a windowing model—talent received a payment when their work replayed, and certain venues were calculated to be worth more than others because they attracted more viewers and were worth more to advertisers. The streaming model levels the value of all media into a catalog of content. Both the WGA and SAG-AFTRA needed to negotiate a model for streaming that rewarded the success of their work on a medium that largely treats all media as an undifferentiated mass. Both unions negotiated improved residual rates, but more significantly they established a success-based metric that gives them another revenue stream on streaming services.

As this model is implemented in the future, it will undoubtedly influence the direction of content on streaming. This new success-based model applies only to new shows produced by streaming and does not cover reality television shows or licensed content. Journalists in the trades have commented that creatives on shows like *Stranger Things*, *Bridgerton*, and *Poker Face* would benefit from this new model, but it will be harder for shows on Amazon (which gives its streaming service to its 170 million subscribers who may have signed up for free shipping).[8] Rick Porter, a reporter for *Variety*, also speculates that the new threshold for success might influence running times, since shorter shows require less total viewing time to meet the new bonus benchmark.[9] Now that audience success matters again, it might also inspire writers to pitch shows toward a broader audience to mirror the successes of network and cable shows on streaming networks.

The Existential Threat: Artificial Intelligence

Throughout the strike, both the writers and the actors proclaimed that they were facing an "existential threat" to their profession. Although the threat facing writers and actors included the changes to pay structures of the last several decades, many focused on AI as the primary enemy of the Hollywood worker. The use of AI in Hollywood media making quickly became one of the buzzwords of the strike and a hot-button issue of the summer as articles such as "AI Poses 'Risk of Extinction' Industry Leaders Warn" appeared in newspapers around the country to discuss the threat of AI in multiple professions.[10] The language around AI evoked fears of being replaced by machines, ignoring that AI technology has aided a wide range of media-making procedures such as de-aging actors or improving render speeds.[11]

During the 2023 negotiations the AMPTP was attempting to find ways to augment the work of writers, directors, and actors with AI and therefore weaken the reliance on human labor to make media. All the unions shared concerns about AI's influence, but their concerns were craft-specific. As Hollywood unions negotiated to guarantee better protections for their members, legal cases about AI made their way through the court system. In late August, a District of Columbia federal judge ruled in the case of *Thaler v. Perlmutter* that "human authorship is an essential part of a valid copyright claim."[12] From the perspective of the members of the AMPTP seeking to extract value from generative AI, this ruling made AI-produced scripts less valuable. This case established important legal precedent, but creative figures continue to wage the battle against AI in the court system (as evidenced by a lawsuit filed by the Authors Guild).[13] However, even if the courts ruled that AI work could not be copyrighted, questions about how AI could be used to augment human work remained.

A month later, against this legal backdrop, the WGA finally reached a deal with the AMPTP over the use of AI for screenwriting. When the WGA walked out of negotiations on May 1, the AMPTP had refused to discuss contractual terms for AI. By September, the conversation around AI and writers had changed dramatically and the AMPTP met their initial demands.[14] In the new contract, writers gained control over whether and how AI can be used—this is at the writer's discretion if the company allows it. Further, AI material cannot be used as source material or to rewrite a screenwriter's work. From the perspective of the writers, this is a resounding victory, but given that AI material cannot be copyrighted, AMPTP members would undoubtedly need to be careful with AI to avoid creating IP they would not be able to control.

The possibilities and stakes for actors was always greater with respect to AI. The fear for many actors was about being replaced by AI-generated images or losing control of their image and likeness. When the actors walked out of negotiations, they announced that the AMPTP wanted to be able to scan background actors, pay them for one day of work (approximately $187), and use their images in perpetuity.[15] Whether AI technology could produce realistic replicas was almost beside the point; the idea that powerful Hollywood producers want to replace humans with digital replicas brought many of their most cliched sci-fi plots to life. Over the course of the strike, Tom Hanks also saw some of actors' worst fears come to fruition when an unauthorized image of Hanks appeared in a commercial for a dental plan without his knowledge or consent.[16] It would seem, throughout the summer and fall, that actors were justified in their concern over unchecked use of generative AI.

Whereas both directors and writers won contractual language stating that they were human, the contractual language about AI and actors is more complicated. The contract defines several new kinds of on-screen performers: employment-based digital replicas (reproductions stemming from performance within the same film), independently created digital replicas (created from a combination of images from previous performances), and generative AI "synthetic performers" (wholly digital constructions). The contract contains more granular detail about the financial terms, but informed consent is what SAG-AFTRA considers to be the contract's intervention.

The new SAG-AFTRA contract requires that producers provide clear information on the project and how digital images will be used. A clear contract that provides information about an actor's work, the job, and how their work is used might seem like a basic requirement, but it is not always a given. In fact, greater transparency that actors could use to update their list of credits and reel (a compilation of sample performance work) and ideally leverage toward future negotiations was one of the terms that voice actors were fighting for during their 2016–2017 strike.[17] However, in the case of the AI provisions, this transparency does not offer the same kind of leverage as it does for video game actors. In the case of digital replicas, producers must give performers a consent form at least forty-eight hours before their images and likenesses are captured. There is no job protection for those who fail to sign the release. Although the contract was approved, the vocal critics claim that the language of the contract is not strong enough to provide robust protections.

More broadly, some actors are concerned about the long-term impact of this contract on the industry. In international, national, and industry news outlets, Justine Bateman, a member of WGA, DGA, and SAG-AFTRA, expressed her concerns about the inclusion of "synthetic performers" in the new MBA. As Bateman explains, this allowance of AI into the contract is fundamentally different than what the DGA and WGA achieved, which is a recognition that directors and writers are human workers. Her worst-case scenario regarding use of synthetic performers demonstrates the ripple effect this practice could have on the industry: "If you don't have to shoot an actor, you don't need a set. You don't need a crew. You don't need drivers."[18] When portions of the industry go on strike, film and television production's collaborative nature becomes clear.

The uproar over the introduction of synthetic performers as a part of Hollywood production ignores the vast array of unionized below-the-line work that has already been replaced or augmented by nonunion postproduction labor. Lighting, sets, costumes, makeup, and props are all routinely "added in post," eliminating on-set work and workers. The technology companies developing tools for postproduction are incorporating AI into their software in ways that will fundamentally change many Hollywood professions.[19] In an October 2023 podcast on the topic, the designer and creative technologist Scott Eaton asserted, "Jobs will be lost. . . . And there's financial incentives for any company that's employing people to be profitable. And the more efficient employees are, probably the less employees you need."[20]

Below-the-line unions do not have prominent members, like those in SAG-AFTRA, to fight on their behalf to preserve their roles in the production process, and in case the of visual effects workers, they do not have union representation at all. If IATSE succeeds in representing more of these postproduction workers (as has been trending), issues around AI will be more and more salient across the IATSE locals' negotiations. It remains to be seen if the concessions that SAG-AFTRA felt obliged to give on the issue will have ripple effects throughout Hollywood and its unions. Whether the unions and locals can maintain solidarity while each of them fights to retain its own role in the process is still to be determined. Fighting over who is most important to a production is a worthless battle, but clearly actors are an essential piece of this codependent ecology, and their removal would undoubtedly influence how production functions.

Looking Forward

Throughout this book, the authors have illuminated historical trends and teased out recurring patterns of behavior in the histories of the Hollywood unions. The

WGA and SAG-AFTRA strikes defied many of the norms of previous Hollywood strikes, particularly in rallying support across the unions. Whether union solidarity will be precedent-setting or just a blip in a long history is difficult to say. It is likely that it will be tested as IATSE and the Teamsters head to the bargaining table in 2024.

Inevitably, Hollywood workers will continue to encounter new technologies that influence how stories are told, and the future of their work is always uncertain. However, as unions and workers look to what lies ahead for the media industries, it remains important for them to learn from historical conflicts and challenges to best confront change in the future. In the century of Hollywood unions, the industry has changed radically in many ways, while fundamental truths have remained the same. Whether Hollywood's workers labor with film or files, on sets or at computers, media production has remained a massive, collaborative endeavor that weds commerce and creativity to produce a cultural product of profound impact. As such, the people who make that product and the ways in which they are able to do their work will continue to matter.

December 2023

Notes

1 For an in-depth discussion of the number of jobs lost and how Hollywood jobs are counted, see "Finding Current Events in the Data—A Look at Strikes among Writers and Actors," *Commissioner's Corner*, Bureau of Labor Statistics, September 26, 2023, https://www.bls.gov/blog/2023/finding-current-events-in-the-data-a-look-at-strikes-among-writers-and-actors.htm.
2 Nellie Andreeva, "TV Studios in Strike Preparation Mode ahead of WGA Contract Negotiations with Overall Deals at Stake & Streamers as Wild Card," *Deadline*, November 27, 2019, https://deadline.com/2019/11/tv-studios-strike-preparation-mode-wga-contract-negotiations-netflix-streamers-overall-deals-1202795768/.
3 Gene Maddus, "IATSE Deal Could Be Rejected by Members: 'Our Leadership Let Us Down,'" *Variety*, October 17, 2021, https://variety.com/2021/film/news/iatse-deal-backlash-nothing-changed-1235091286/.
4 Bob Hopkinson, "WGA Ratifies 2023 Tentative Agreement with AMPTP," Writers Guild of America West, October 9, 2023, https://www.wga.org/news/press/wga-ratifies-2023-tentative-agreement-with-amptp.
5 Miranda Banks and Kate Fortmueller, "Unity Will Determine If the Hollywood Writers Strike is Successful," *Washington Post*, June 22, 2023, https://www.washingtonpost.com/made-by-history/2023/06/22/wga-strike-hollywood-unions-solidarity/.
6 Andreas Neuenkirchen, "WGA Strike Reacts to the DGA's 'Disappointing' New Studio Deal," *CBR*, June 5, 2023, https://www.cbr.com/wga-strike-dga-disappointing-deal-reaction/.
7 Lesley Goldberg, "Striking Writers Respond to DGA's Tentative Deal with Studios, Streamers," *The Hollywood Reporter* (hereafter *THR*), June 4, 2023, https://www.hollywoodreporter.com/news/general-news/striking-writers-react-to-dga-tentative-deal-1235506889/.

8 Katie Campione, "New WGA & SAG-AFTRA Residuals Model Explained; 'Poker Face' & 'Secret Invasion' Could Join 'Stranger Things' and 'Wednesday' In Streaming Bonus Club," *Deadline*, November 30, 2023, https://deadline.com/2023/11/streaming-model-explained-sag-aftra-wga-residuals-deal-1235642995/.

9 Rick Porter, "How the Writers Guild's New Streaming Residual Will Work," *THR*, September 27, 2023, https://www.hollywoodreporter.com/business/business-news/how-wga-streaming-residual-will-work-1235602660/.

10 Kevin Roose, "AI Poses 'Risk of Extinction' Industry Leaders Warn," *New York Times*, May 30, 2023, https://www.nytimes.com/2023/05/30/technology/ai-threat-warning.html.

11 John Kell, "How A.I. Is Reshaping the Way Movies Are Made," *Fortune*, February 14, 2023, https://fortune.com/2023/02/14/tech-forward-everyday-ai-hollywood-movies/.

12 *Thaler v. Perlmutter*, 22-1564 (BAH), (U.S. Dist. Court—D.C. 2023), 1.

13 For more on the Authors Guild lawsuit, see Alexandra Alter and Elizabeth Harris, "Franzen, Grisham and Other Prominent Authors Sue Open AI," *New York Times*, September 20, 2023, https://www.nytimes.com/2023/09/20/books/authors-openai-lawsuit-chatgpt-copyright.html.

14 For a comparison of the initial demands and final contract, see "What We Won," WGA Contract 2023, accessed May 11, 2024, https://www.wgacontract2023.org/the-campaign/what-we-won.

15 For further discussion of digital replicas for background actors, see SAG-AFTRA, SAG-AFTRA President Fran Drescher TV/Theatrical/Streaming strike press conference speech, July 15, 2023, YouTube, https://www.youtube.com/watch?v=zNS2EtQbG5I.

16 Derrick Bryson Taylor, "Tom Hanks Warns of Dental Ad Using A.I. Version of Him," *New York Times*, October 2, 2023, https://www.nytimes.com/2023/10/02/technology/tom-hanks-ai-dental-video.html.

17 For details on specific terms from the voice actor strike, see Kate Fortmueller, *Below the Stars: How the Labor of Working Actors and Extras Shapes Media Production* (University of Texas Press, 2021), 152.

18 Katie Campione, "Justine Bateman Discusses Concerns with SAG-AFTRA Deal's AI Protections, Warns Loopholes Could 'Collapse the Structure' of Hollywood," *Deadline*, November 17, 20203, https://deadline.com/2023/11/justine-bateman-sag-aftra-deal-ai-1235616848/.

19 Carolyn Giardina, "How Will Editors Use AI? The Tech's Role in Production and Post Scrutinized at IBC," *THR*, September 20, 2023, https://www.hollywoodreporter.com/movies/movie-news/artificial-intelligence-role-debated-icb-1235593802/.

20 Carolyn Giardina, "VFX Pros Debate AI's Impact on Jobs, Contracts and Creativity in 'Behind the Screen' Podcast," *THR*, October 23, 2023, https://www.hollywoodreporter.com/movies/movie-features/ai-impact-jobs-hollywood-1235623605/.

Appendix

• •

Timeline of Hollywood Strikes*

1918	IATSE studio strike (July 1–September 10) followed by secondary projectionist strike, limited success led to a one-year contract
1919	IATSE studio strike after expiration of one-year contract (September 10–26), striking workers were replaced with AFL trade union workers
1933	Sound engineers strike at Columbia (beginning July 15); became an IATSE general strike against the studios (July 22—August 8)
1935	IATSE projectionists strikes organized by George Browne and Willie Bioff
1937	FMPC strike of painters, draftsmen, makeup artists, hairdressers, and scenic artists (April 30–May 21)
1937	CADU animators strike against the Fleischer Brothers Studio in New York (May 7–October 19), union won recognition
1941	Screen Cartoonists Guild strike at Walt Disney Studios (May 29–September 21), union won recognition
1945	CSU strike against AMPP and Warner Bros. (March 12–October 24)
1946–1947	Carpenters strike (with CSU support) leading to CSU lockout (September 26–March 14), IBEW ordered Local 40 back to

*This timeline focuses on the unions covered in this collection.

	work, Story Analysis guild returned a week later, several workers and unions never returned to work
1947	Screen Cartoonists Guild Local 1461 New York strike against Terrytoons (May 16–December 19), longest in animation history, union did not prevail
1952	Screen Writers Guild television strike (August 11–November 16)
1952–1953	SAG filmed television commercials strike (December 1–February 18)
1960	WGA strike (January 16–June 12)
1960	SAG theatrical strike (March 7–April 18)
1967	AFTRA national strike (March 29–April 10)
1973	WGA strike (March–June 30)
1978–1979	SAG and AFTRA commercials strike (December 19–February 7)
1979	MPSC Local 839 strike against the Animated Film Producers Association (AFPA) for residuals (August 12–28), union wins anti–runaway production clause
1980	SAG theatrical strike (July 21–October 23)
1981	WGA strike (April 11–July 12)
1982	MPSC Local 839 strike against the AMPTP to maintain anti-runaway clause (August 6–October 16), lost anti–runaway production and seniority clauses
1985	WGA strike (March 6–20)
1987	DGA strike (three hours and five minutes on July 13)
1988	WGA strike (March 7–August 8)
2000	SAG commercials strike (May 1–October 30)
2007–2008	WGA strike (November 5, 2007–February, 12, 2008)
2016–2017	SAG-AFTRA video game strike (October 21, 2016–September 23, 2017)
2023	WGA strike (May 2–September 26)
2023	SAG-AFTRA strike (July 14–November 9)

Acknowledgments

Edited collections, no matter the subject, are a significant undertaking for the authors and editors. The process involves assembling a group of scholars willing to write the chapters, crafting a proposal, finding a publisher, writing chapters to send out for peer review, and trying to keep all the contributors on task as they juggle writing their chapters in relation to other writing projects, teaching, and personal lives. This process is complicated enough when you have unlimited time and resources available, but keeping an archivally driven collection on track during a pandemic—when most archives were closed or, at best, limiting access, made this project even more challenging.

First and foremost, we would like to thank our contributors for sticking with us through this long and challenging process. Some of you balanced the research and writing with nonacademic jobs, through significant career changes and health challenges, or with new babies. This book is about different kinds of workers and is produced by a group of scholars who have all taken different paths through their careers, and the book is richer for it.

It was important that this book contain more than images of people striking (even though the history of Hollywood unions is filled with creative and humorous signs). Strikes are moments when unions are most visible to the public, but many Hollywood workers have long careers without ever walking a picket line. We appreciate Genevieve Maxwell and Louise Hilton at the Academy of Motion Picture Arts and Sciences, Margaret Herrick Library, for helping us secure images for this collection.

Thank you to Nicole Solano and the Rutgers team for being patient with us and ushering this project through to completion. We are also appreciative of the encouraging readers who understood the value of this book both in and out of the classroom.

We brainstormed this project in March 2020, so it feels like it has been part of our lives for a long time. I (Kate) am grateful for the support of my colleagues in the School of Film, Media and Theatre at Georgia State University who made it possible for me to take a teaching leave in my first semester, allowing me to direct more attention to the final stages of the collection. Special thanks to David Lerner for supporting all my endeavors and multitasking.

I (Luci) would like to thank the faculty and staff in the Division of Cinema and Media Studies at the University of Southern California for supporting this effort on top of my work as the department's program coordinator. I also had invaluable research assistance from Erica Moulton. Eternal gratitude to my husband, Michael, and my son Wolfgang for their love and to my friends and family for always supporting me. I also have to acknowledge Jude, who came into the world and made the last part of the process a bit more challenging, but all the more rewarding. Lastly, I have to thank Kate for being the best collaborator I could ask for.

Thank you to all the creatives, union members, and union leaders who have spoken to various contributors over the course of their research. We hope that these histories illuminate the past and provide some ideas for the path forward.

Selected Bibliography

Banks, Miranda. *The Writers: A History of American Screenwriters and Their Guild*. Rutgers University Press, 2015.

Brianton, Kevin. *Hollywood Divided: The 1950 Screen Directors Guild Meeting and the Impact of the Blacklist*. University Press of Kentucky, 2016.

Caldwell, John. *Specworld: Folds, Faults, and Fractures in Embedded Creator Industries*. University of California Press, 2023.

Clark, Danae. *Negotiating Hollywood: The Cultural Politics of Actors' Labor*. University of Minnesota Press, 1995.

Clark, Shannan. *The Making of the American Creative Class*. Oxford University Press, 2021.

Curtin, Michael, and Kevin Sanson, eds. *Voices of Labor: Creativity, Craft, and Conflict in Global Hollywood*. University of California Press, 2017.

Fortmueller, Kate. *Below the Stars: How the Labor of Working Actors and Extras Shapes Media Production*. University of Texas Press, 2021.

Gray, Lois S., and Ronald L. Seeber, eds. *Under the Stars: Essays on Labor Relations in Arts and Entertainment*. Cornell University Press, 1996.

Heilman Stimson, Grace. *Rise of the Labor Movement in Los Angeles*. University of California Press, 1955.

Hill, Erin. *Never Done: A History of Women's Work in Media Production*. Rutgers University Press, 2016.

Horne, Gerald. *Class Struggle in Hollywood, 1930–1950: Moguls, Mobsters, Stars, Reds, and Trade Unionists*. University of Texas Press, 2001.

Keating, Patrick. *Hollywood Lighting: From the Silent Era to Film Noir*. Columbia University Press, 2009.

Lovell, Hugh, and Tasile Carter. *Collective Bargaining in the Motion Picture Industry: A Struggle for Stability*. Institute for Industrial Relations, University of California, Berkeley, 1955.

Maher, Karen Ward. *Women Filmmakers in Early Hollywood*. Johns Hopkins University Press, 2006.

Marzola, Luci. *Engineering Hollywood: Technology, Technicians, and the Science of Building the Studio System*. Oxford University Press, 2021.

McLean, Adrienne L. *All for Beauty: Makeup and Hairdressing in Hollywood's Studio Era*. Rutgers University Press, 2022.

Nielsen, Mike, and Gene Mailes, *Hollywood's Other Blacklist: Union Struggles in the Studio System*. British Film Institute, 1995.

Perry, Louis, and Richard Perry. *A History of the Los Angeles Labor Movement, 1911–1941*. University of California Press, 1963.

Pintar, Laurie Caroline. "Off-Screen Realities: A History of Labor Activism in Hollywood, 1933–1947." PhD diss., University of Southern California, 1995.

Prindle, David. *The Politics of Glamour: Ideology and Democracy in the Screen Actors Guild*. University of Wisconsin Press, 1988.

Porst, Jennifer. *Broadcasting Hollywood: The Struggle over Feature Films on Early TV*. Rutgers University Press, 2021.

Quinn, Eithne. *A Piece of the Action: Race and Labor in Post–Civil Rights Hollywood*. Columbia University Press, 2020.

Ross, Murray. *Stars and Strikes: Unionization of Hollywood*. Columbia University Press, 1941.

Scott, Allen J. *On Hollywood: The Place, the Industry*. Oxford University Press, 2005.

Sito, Tom. *Drawing the Line: The Untold Story of the Animation Unions from Bosko to Bart Simpson*. University Press of Kentucky, 2006.

Smukler, Maya Montañez. *Liberating Hollywood: Women Directors and the Feminist Reform of 1970s American Cinema*. Rutgers University Press, 2019.

Wright Wexman, Virginia. *Hollywood's Artists: The Directors Guild of America and the Construction of Authorship*. Columbia University Press, 2020.

Notes on Contributors

MIRANDA BANKS is an associate professor and department chair of Film, Television, and Media Studies in the School of Film and Television at Loyola Marymount University.

KATIE BIRD is a market research analyst at Screen Engine/ASI, LLC.

KATE FORTMUELLER is an associate professor of film and media history in the School of Film, Media and Theatre at Georgia State University.

DAWN M. FRATINI teaches courses on the history of animation and the Walt Disney Company at Dodge College of Film and Media Arts, Chapman University and the School of Film and Television, Loyola Marymount University.

BARBARA HALL is the archivist for the Art Directors Guild, where she manages a visual research collection and archive.

ERIN HILL is an assistant professor of media and popular culture in the Department of Communication at the University of California San Diego.

LUCI MARZOLA is the academic director and a lecturer in the Division of Cinema and Media Studies at the University of Southern California's School of Cinematic Arts.

ADRIENNE L. McLEAN is a professor of film studies at the University of Texas at Dallas.

MAYA MONTAÑEZ SMUKLER is the head of the Research and Study Center at the UCLA Film and Television Archive.

PAUL MONTICONE is an assistant professor in the Department of Radio, Television and Film at Rowan University.

HELEN WARNER is an associate professor of cultural politics, communication, and media studies at the University of East Anglia.

Index

Figures and tables are indicated with page numbers in italics.

Animators' Society, 206, 207

Appet, Lou, 219

Apple, 11, 257, 272

apprenticeships. *See* training and professional development

Arnold, John, 121

art directors/art direction workers, 136–137,
162n89, 187; affiliation of with IATSE,
155; and the Art Directors Guild, 155–158;
and directors, collaboration with, 56; in
early Hollywood, 137–138; and elevating
the craft, 151–152; growth of, midcentury,
147–151; and the League of Art Directors
and Associates, 140–145; and a new deal
for art directors (1937), 145–147;
professionalization of, 138–140; and
television's arrival, 152–154. *See also*
graphic artists/designers; illustrators;
matte artists; model makers; production
designers; scenic artists/designers; set
decorators; set designers; set dressers; set
painters; sketch artists; storyboard artists;
title artists

Art Directors Guild (ADG), 155–158, 162n89

artificial intelligence, 291; handlers for, 88;
and the 2023 strikes and agreement, 12,
234, 257–258, 272, 295, 305–306, 308–310

Artists' Manager Basic Agreement, 254

Arzner, Dorothy, 283

ASC. *See* American Society of
Cinematographers

Asian American workers in Hollywood,
89n2, 109, 254, 294. *See also* immigrant
workers in Hollywood; minority workers
in Hollywood; workers of color in
Hollywood

Asner, Ed, 271

assistant directors (ADs), 1, 243, 296, 298;
benefits for, 295; in the DGA, 52, 234,
282, 285–286; as below-the-line workers,
236; in the FMPC, 144; pay for, 46,
47–48, 53, 59, 286; second ADs, 47, 48,
52, 53; as script clerks, 45; in television,
288–289; women as, 292, 293. *See also*
IATSE Local 161

Assistant Directors Guild, 47

associate directors, 282, 289, 295

Associated Actors and Artists of America
(AAAA, or 4As), 267

Associated Animators, 206

Association of Film Craftsmen, 31

Association of Independent Television
Stations, 291

Association of Motion Picture and
Television Producers (AMPTP), 31. *See
also* Alliance of Motion Picture and
Television Producers

Association of Motion Picture Producers
(AMPP), 7, 8–9, 73, 81, 96; animation
producers outside of, 206; as antecedent
to AMPTP, 22, 31; and backlot workers
strike, 75–76; in the Browne-Bioff era,
23–27, 207, 212; and contract negotiations
and agreements, 22–23, 28, 98, 100, 145,
146, 150, 169, 239; MPPA as antecedent
to, 8; and the Terrytoons strike, 214–215

Association of Talent Agents, 246

audiotape, 127–128

auteur theory, 61, 259n8

Authors Guild, 308

Babbitt, Art, 209–211

backlot workers, 18, 68–70; and 1930s
battles, 74–79; and 1940s strikes,
together with IATSE's ascent, 79–82; and
1960s–1980s challenges, 82–86; and 1990s
consolidation and expansion, 86–87; in
the stage to screen evolution, 70–74;
what's next for, 87–89. *See also* IATSE
workers

Banks, Miranda, 13, 14, 234, 239–240,
275–276, 306

Banton, Travis, 189

Barbera, Joseph, 218

Barclay, Paris, 294

Barenna, Frank, 74

Basic Agreements. *See* Minimum Basic
Agreements; Studio Basic Agreements

basic crafts, 68–69. *See also under specific
unions, locals, and job descriptions*

Bateman, Justine, 305, 310

Bay, Susan, 292

Belasco, David, 137

below-the-line workers. *See* above-the-line
vs. below-the-line distinction; IATSE
workers; *and specific jobs*

benefits (for workers): dental, 54, 271, 309;
health care, 13, 31, 33, 52, 54, 57, 60, 115, 123,
129, 180, 181, 193, 220, 234, 235, 241, 270,
275, 295; holidays, 23, 141, 180, 208, 295;